RELIGION, ATTIRE,
AND ADORNMENT
IN NORTH AMERICA

RELIGION, ATTIRE, AND ADORNMENT IN NORTH AMERICA

EDITED BY MARIE W. DALLAM
AND BENJAMIN E. ZELLER

COLUMBIA UNIVERSITY PRESS

NEW YORK

Columbia University Press
Publishers Since 1893
New York   Chichester, West Sussex
cup.columbia.edu
Copyright © 2023 Columbia University Press
All rights reserved

Library of Congress Cataloging-in-Publication Data

Names: Dallam, Marie W., editor. | Zeller, Benjamin E., editor.
Title: Religion, attire, and adornment in North America /
   edited by Marie W. Dallam, Benjamin E. Zeller.
Description: New York : Columbia University Press, [2023] |
   Includes bibliographical references and index.
Identifiers: LCCN 2022034780 (print) | LCCN 2022034781 (ebook) |
   ISBN 9780231204446 (hardback) | ISBN 9780231204453
   (trade paperback) | ISBN 9780231555548 (ebook)
Subjects: LCSH: Clothing and dress—North America—Religious aspects.
Classification: LCC BL65.C64 R44 2023 (print) | LCC BL65.C64 (ebook) |
   DDC 204/.4—dc23/eng20221209
LC record available at https://lccn.loc.gov/2022034780
LC ebook record available at https://lccn.loc.gov/2022034781

Cover design: Julia Kushnirsky
Cover image: NightFlower/Shutterstock.com

*For our colleague and mentor
Catherine Wessinger,*

*with our gratitude for all that
you have done for us.*

CONTENTS

Introduction: Religion, Attire, and Adornment in North America 1
BENJAMIN E. ZELLER AND MARIE W. DALLAM

PART I. THEOLOGICAL ADORNMENT

1. SEVENTH-DAY ADVENTIST DRESS: "AN INDEX TO THE HEART" 23
EMILY J. BAILEY

2. CLOTHING SPIRITUAL REALITY: THE SARTORIAL STYLES OF MARY BAKER EDDY 40
JEREMY RAPPORT

3. FAITH, FASHION, AND FILM IN THE JAZZ AGE: CATHOLIC VESTMENTS ENCOUNTER THE ROARING 1920s 61
ADRIENNE NOCK AMBROSE

4. POWER BEFORE THRONES OF GOD AND MAN: WOMEN, ADORNMENT, AND PUBLIC LIFE IN WHITE AMERICAN PENTECOSTALISM 86

ANDREA SHAN JOHNSON AND LEAH PAYNE

PART II. IDENTITY ADORNMENT

5. HOLY DASHIKIS! BLACK SARTORIAL NATIONALISM AND BLACK ISRAELITE RELIGION 117

ANDRÉ E. BROOKS-KEY

6. REFINED BODIES: CLOTHING AS A VISUAL SIGNIFIER OF PIETY FOR MORMON WOMEN IN AMERICA 143

KATE DAVIS

7. THE CHRISTIAN TATTOO: MUCH MORE THAN SKIN-DEEP 165

JEROME R. KOCH AND KEVIN D. DOUGHERTY

8. "QUEENS OF THE EARTH": THE MGT UNIFORM AS A FORM OF IDENTITY CREATION AND NATION BUILDING 190

KAYLA RENÉE WHEELER

PART III. NEGOTIATED ADORNMENT

9. "YE SHALL BE NAKED IN YOUR RITES": RITUAL ATTIRE AND RITUAL NUDITY (SKYCLAD) IN NORTH AMERICAN WICCA 207

MICHELLE MUELLER

10. AMISH VOGUE: PERFORMING FASHION IN THE PLAIN WORLD 227

NAO NOMURA

11. "YOUR RELIGION IS SHOWING": NEGOTIATION AND PERSONAL EXPERIENCE IN MORMON GARMENTS 251

JESSICA FINNIGAN AND NANCY ROSS

PART IV. ACTIVIST ADORNMENT

12. DRESSED FOR GLORY: WHITE UNIFORMS IN AFRICAN AMERICAN CHURCH TRADITIONS AS VISUAL POLITICAL THEOLOGY 277

ELAINA SMITH

13. "THE HARE KRISHNA LOOK": ISKCON ADORNMENT AS RELIGIOUS ACTIVISM 295

BENJAMIN E. ZELLER

14. RELIGIOUS DRESS, THE CHURCH OF BODY MODIFICATION, AND THE FIRST AMENDMENT 320

MARIE W. DALLAM

Discussion Questions 341

Suggested Reading List 349

List of Contributors 355

Index 359

RELIGION, ATTIRE, AND ADORNMENT IN NORTH AMERICA

INTRODUCTION

RELIGION, ATTIRE, AND ADORNMENT IN NORTH AMERICA

BENJAMIN E. ZELLER AND MARIE W. DALLAM

THE YEARS 2020 AND 2021 witnessed an unusual occurrence. Scores of American evangelical Christians came out in opposition to a seemingly innocuous piece of bodily adornment, declaring their rejection on religious grounds to the wearing of said accoutrement. Reasons varied: it was anathema to cover what God created, it represented a rejection of divine providence, it was associated with secular science and liberalism, or emblematic of a violation of religious liberty. The bodily adornment? The face mask. The context? The COVID-19 pandemic, and public health measures calling for individuals to wear masks to prevent its spread prior to and after the advent and widespread availability of either treatments or vaccines against this deadly disease. While those outside the evangelical Christian community either shook their (masked) heads or scoffed at what appeared to be a bizarre rejection of a prudent personal and public health step, for many evangelicals the mask—or rather, not wearing a mask—came to represent a potent symbol of religious identity, and a physical marker of individual and group relationships with social forces such as government, science, and education. Ohio state representative Nino Vitale (Republican) made national news for his stance, linking American nationalism, evangelical Christian biblicism, and opposition to the wearing of masks. "This is the greatest nation on earth founded on Judeo-Christian Principles. One of those principles is that we are all created in the image and likeness of God. That image is seen the most by our face. I will not wear a mask," he declared.[1]

Evangelical anti-mask sentiment during the COVID-19 pandemic reveals the powerful link between religious identity, social location, and bodily adornment. Social scientists Samuel L. Perry, Andrew L. Whitehead, and Joshua B. Grubbs found that religiosity, in particular Christian nationalism, was in fact the leading predictor of whether individuals did or did not wear masks during the pandemic.[2] While anti-mask sentiment has drawn ample attention in the last couple of years, it represents a much broader set of intersections between how people adorn (or not) their bodies and their religious commitments, beliefs, practices, and identities. Liturgical clothing, ritual nudity, uniforms and monastic habits, body modification practices and taboos, and simply the rules and norms of everyday dressing and adornment all serve as examples of connection between religion and bodily adornment. This book charts those intersections, and others.

RELIGION, ATTIRE, AND ADORNMENT

The relationship between religion and dress—which includes not only clothing but adornment, modification, and undress as well—has historically received less attention than such topics as theological doctrines and religious institutions. Religious studies, emerging from Protestant church history, have tended to emphasize ideas over practices. Even when placed among other practices such as formal worship, holidays, and prayer, the act of adorning one's body has often seemed so quotidian that it has been overlooked as a subject of interest. However, the study of religion and dress actually reveals a great deal about both topics, as well as their complicated connections. It shows how people put religious ideas and values into practice in their lives, and the way that religion cannot be separated from its embodied nature as practiced by living human beings. It shows how dress is not just about pieces of cloth, and that dressing (or not) functions as an important process and practice, encoding powerful meanings for individuals and groups.

As an area of inquiry, religion and dress includes a wide range of expressions, from the orange robe that instantaneously distinguishes a religious devotee to a tattoo whose religious significance is known only to its bearer. The nun's habit may be immediately recognizable as an example of religious dress, but an Orthodox Jewish woman wearing a wig over her natural hair—a religious practice followed by many Orthodox women—may pass unnoticed. In other words, religious dress may have clear or obvious expressions, but it also takes subtle or nearly invisible forms. Furthermore, religious dress cuts across the distinctions within and between religions, often in complicated ways. One might think about the attire of religious leaders or dress codes for religious adherents, either of which are likely to include a degree of uniformity across subgroups or classes (and possibly even literal uniforms). There are also specific items of adornment that can be explored either within or across traditions, including not only clothing but headwear and footwear, hair, jewelry, and markings on the body ranging from lipstick and rouge to deliberate scars. There is modest dress, and there is forbidden dress. And there is the nexus where items of attire meet the practices of adornment, the latter defined and redefined by distinctions between sacred and profane spaces, occasions of heightened ceremonial importance, and degrees of religiosity. Further complicating religious attire are fashion and taste, and the choices made by members of religions to adorn themselves in a particular manner because of how it makes them look or feel, and not only because of religious obligations or commitments.

The essays gathered here move beyond mere description of practice to engage with questions about the relationship between religious dress, broadly conceived, and meaning making. Religion serves roles in creating identity, in drawing and crossing social boundaries, in determining controls and demonstrating resistance, and in displaying spiritual status, and all of this can be expressed in highly nuanced religious thinking and behavior. Articles of attire and acts of adornment are, for some believers, deeply expressive signs of these dynamics. As such, they can be mined for meaning. To return to the opening vignette about evangelical opposition to face masks during the COVID-19 pandemic, a careful study of the phenomenon would reveal the interconnections of ideas about the self and collective identity, control over the human body and the body politic, the relation of secular and religious institutions, obedience to divine will, fights over cultural hegemony and control, and issues of race, gender, and ethnicity. All this in less than a square foot of fabric!

RELATED LITERATURE

The study of religion and dress takes place within numerous disciplines, with the emphasis varying accordingly. Scholars in subfields of religious studies looking at material culture, as well as those focusing on the body, have sometimes examined dress; so, too, have specialists of religious traditions in which dress can play a major role, such as Judaism and Islam, and also those studying particular time periods. Going beyond the bounds of religious studies, one also finds numerous works from dress studies, fashion studies, and American studies that touch on religion as part of research focused on other aspects of dress. All of these together create an overlapping set of academic conversations within which we situate this collection of essays. It is important from the outset to recognize the existing questions scholars have asked about religion and dress, and the answers at which they have arrived.

In the past several decades, scholars in religious studies have increasingly examined the material culture of religion—including food, art, printed material, architecture, and decorative objects—to understand how material culture is used to express and ritualize human relationships to the divine, taking on complex significance to communities and individuals in the process.[3] Historian of American religion Colleen McDannell, among the first religious studies scholars involved in this research area, explains that "material culture specialists derive meanings from objects themselves by paying attention to the form, distribution, function, and changing character of the objects and their environments. They want to know how people use things and experience spaces."[4] McDannell herself focused on the everyday objects of the American Christian home, such as popular artwork, books, and kitsch. Though McDannell included dress within her formative study by considering Mormon sacred garments, the material culture turn within religious studies has rarely emphasized attire or adornment.[5] David Morgan's *The Thing About Religion: An Introduction to the Material Study of Religions* (2021) focuses on the impressive (Notre-Dame de Paris), the alluring (magic wands), and the problematic (Polynesian sacred artifacts exported as cultural icons by missionaries) as case studies. Morgan does not entirely ignore adornment, but it receives only ancillary mention in his book. "Clothing," he notes, "is an agent, a device that works *on* our bodies to change how we experience ourselves and *with* our bodies to affect those around us because we live in webs of relationships."[6] Morgan places adornment squarely within the social and cultural realms, emphasizing its role to act on a person and through a person on others.

Additionally, dress has sometimes been explored as an extension of body studies, a relatively new subfield within religious studies. Theologian Sarah Coakley's influential edited collection *Religion & the Body* (1997) primarily focuses on philosophical and theological reflections on embodiment, but Coakley pointed to central themes relevant to the study of religion and dress, such as questions of sanctification and defilement, the regulation of bodies, the ambiguity of the body, the denial and chastening of the body, and the relation of the human body to foreign objects.[7] Research on religion and the body has sometimes turned more directly to questions of dress and adornment. Scholar of the ancient Mediterranean world Kristi Upson-Saia has written of how the development of Christian ascetic dress reflected ideas of virtue, authority, and gender, and how "dress functioned as a contested symbol in the negotiation of power and identity between pagans and Christians, ascetics and laypeople, and women and men."[8] Upson-Saia's work fits into a pattern in which scholars of the ancient world have looked at the intersection of religion and dress and found issues of power, authority, and identity at the heart of sartorial practice.[9]

It is evident that attire has been explored within the contexts of some religious traditions more than others, with a particular eye toward ways that believers negotiate institutional prescriptions (and proscriptions). For instance, reflecting Rabbinic Judaism's historical emphasis on practice over belief, Jewish studies has typically paid more attention to material culture, including attire and adornment. Eric Silverman, in *A Cultural History of Jewish Dress* (2013), focused on Jewish dress in relation to concepts of identity and the body, including a thoughtful dissection of attire found specifically in the contemporary United States such as the style(s) he deems "New Jew Cool."[10] Authors in the 2013 anthology *Fashioning Jews: Clothing, Culture, and Commerce* focused on a set of interlocking sartorial practices: textual prescriptions and proscriptions of Jewish dress norms, distinctive dress practices by Jewish minorities living in diasporic contexts, the interconnections between fashion and religious dress, and questions of social and individual identity.[11] Many of the same topics interest the contributors to the present volume as well. Similarly, for decades scholars have discussed veiling practices among Muslim women, such that today one finds a vast and highly nuanced body of scholarship on this single topic coming from a wide variety of fields and disciplines. Among recent additions to this literature is scholar of gender and Islam Anna Piela's *Wearing the Niqab* (2021), which focuses on Muslim women's navigation of religious dress norms, cultural practices, and social and individual identity in two distinct cultural contexts.[12] Another notable work is anthropologist Su'ad Abdul Khabeer's *Muslim Cool: Race, Religion, and Hip Hop in the United States* (2016), which provides a refreshing shift in perspective by expanding the discussion of Muslim dress to include men. Khabeer juxtaposes trends in "urban" Muslim male attire with the "cool Muslim dandy" style, implicitly nodding toward ongoing conversations about fashion innovation among young Muslims of all genders. She also centers race and the use of fashion to negotiate race, racism, and antiracism within the American context, especially the fraught concept of Blackness within multiethnic and multicultural America.[13]

Two recent books grounded in religious studies and focused on dress are pioneering new paths for discussions of religion, attire, and adornment. Elizabeth Bucar's *Pious Fashion: How Muslim Women Dress* (2017) is based on lively ethnographic work conducted with Muslim women in Iran, Indonesia, and Turkey.[14] Bucar delves into women's dress as sites of mediation involving authority, public imagery, and individual agency in order to elucidate the complex webs of religious understanding that can be expressed through clothing. She explores the way fashion functions as a consumerist religious aesthetic and argues for recognizing personal agency even within institutional contexts. Bucar adds a global dimension beyond Khabeer's North American focus yet finds similar themes, such as negotiation of identity—in this case, less ethnic and racial identity as religious and cultural. Lynn Neal's *Religion in Vogue: Christianity and Fashion in America* (2019) is a cultural history tracing the presence of Christian imagery and symbolism in American high fashion since World War II. Neal uncovers the surprisingly influential role the fashion industry has played in the construction of religious discourse. She posits that fashion normalizes and reproduces specific visions of religion, transforming religion just as it transforms fashion.[15] The relationship between adornment and religion is therefore bidirectional in Neal's account. Neal argues that *Vogue* and other fashion magazines centered a particular model of material and aesthetic Christianity. But that vision, she explains, not only reflects but reshapes popular conceptions of what Christianity quite literally looks like. Though methodologically diverse, Bucar's and Neal's books both directly challenge perceptions that fashion is somehow at odds with religion, and they demonstrate how attention to adornment practices can push scholars of religious studies in new directions to understand religion and dress as a complicated and creative relationship and not simply a set of rules or doctrines.

Like religious studies, dress studies is vibrant and interdisciplinary, and in it one finds richly layered academic work that involves history, sociology, and anthropology, as well as very particular foci such as analysis of textiles, fashion and costume design, and aspects of business and marketing. In numerous articles that focus on the materiality of textiles, sociologist Linda B. Arthur explored the ways dress conveys social and cultural meaning. In her 1999 edited collection *Religion, Dress and the Body*, scholars from such areas as anthropology, consumer studies, and textiles and design examined religious dress primarily as expressions of power dynamics, particularly in relation to ethnicity and gender norms in the United States. Essays in Arthur's follow-up volume, *Undressing Religion: Commitment and Conversion from a Cross-Cultural Perspective* (2000), explore the same themes in cultures around the world, demonstrating that religious as well as cultural values are expressed by attire.[16] Relatedly, many fashion-centered texts have also considered religious contexts. Although it is sometimes used as a synonym for dress, *fashion* is a more specific area of inquiry because it focuses on the dynamics of popular styles of attire (and aspects of presentation that go beyond attire), which can be directly linked to both industry production and consumer audiences. There are several fine studies of fashion among the religious that often triangulate cultural context as a third major prong of analysis. The work of Emma Tarlo, an anthropologist who focuses on attire and adornment with particular interests in issues of modesty, has written several works related to religious fashion, including *Visibly Muslim: Fashion, Politics, Faith* (2010).[17] In a similar vein, cultural studies scholar Reina Lewis has written extensively on fashion and subcultural representation, including works on Muslim women that explore the juncture of fashion, shifting conceptions of modesty, and retail market forces.[18] An important point made evident by both Tarlo and Lewis is that fashion changes within religion do not necessarily parallel the forces of change in secular dress; this is because a constellation of influences that is much broader than commercial concerns may be at play.

Finally, glamour theory, associated most closely with the study of high fashion and the entertainment industry, nevertheless points to connections present in mundane as well as glamorous religious presentation. "Glamour is both a formal category and an experiential site of consumer desire, fantasy, sexuality, class, and racial identity," explains glamour theorist Judith Brown.[19] It is a dense aesthetic network infused within modernity, Brown argues, and must be traced both in terms of propagation and influence. Glamour theory points scholars to the role played by the market and marketing, celebrity, entertainment, technology, distinctions between high and low culture, and the relation of all of these to the trifecta of race, class, and gender. Each of these must be contextualized within practices of consumption and consumerism, and the specific economic contexts that shape those. Nigel Thrift therefore situates glamour theory within affect theory, which models how and why people feel particular emotions. Thrift identifies not only aesthetics but the pleasure derived from imbibing and associating with valued aesthetics, all of which are shaped by consumer-oriented market cultures.[20] While neither Brown nor Thrift analyze the religious context, the forces and relationships studied within glamour studies and affect studies are present within religious fashion as well.

In sum, there is a varied landscape of academic work that addresses the complex nexus of religion, attire, and adornment, in which religion emerges as one among many factors under consideration. But research that consistently *centers* religion in the exploration of contemporary and near-contemporary attire and adornment is a relatively new approach, and that is where the essays in this book seek to make a contribution. The authors highlight how adornment practices serve central roles in the lives of religious individuals and communities, exploring connections between dress and meaning making within religion, including aspects of self-perception, communication, and everyday action. Foremost, the authors are concerned with attire as both religious culture and religious practice, with all other considerations secondary. In other words, their questions always begin with religion. In that sense, they reverse the approach of work that originates in other fields and add a new angle to the discussions that have already begun within religious studies.

LENSES OF ANALYSIS

This book is organized by four overarching frameworks: theology, identity, negotiation, and activism. These frameworks first emerged in our previous study of another example of religious material culture: food.[21] In our 2014 edited collection exploring the relationship(s) of food and eating to religion, these four specific aspects drove themselves to the forefront of discussion. At the time, we considered them merely convenient thematic categories that readily emerged from the authors' approach to their subject matter. We found that certain essays fit together easily because they were engaging issues from a similar perspective or based on a similar set of questions. Over a longer period of reflection—especially through teaching these essays and having extended discussion with bright undergraduates in the ensuing years—we came to recognize that these are not just "themes" in the essays. Rather, theology, identity, negotiation, and activism comprise deeper lenses of analysis germane to discussions of religion and culture more broadly, because they help explain the nature of religious relationships to diverse sets of cultural practices. Like food and eating, attire and adornment are at once both objects and actions, and when undergirded by religion they become complexly layered practices that permit individuals and groups to explore ideas about humanity and its relation to the divine (theology), the relation of the self to other religious, social, and cultural actors (identity), the navigation of relationships between individuals and groups, often within religious traditions as well as outside and among those who are neither fully in nor fully out (negotiation), and the desire to enact social and cultural change both within religious groups and in broader society (activism).

Theological adornment

One way of thinking about the relationship of religion to dress and adornment is through theology. Divine instruction for humans is often thought of as being received through sacred texts and mediated by trusted, institutionally sanctioned interlocutors, and systems of belief may be regarded as static and dependable. But in fact, human understanding of divine instruction is constantly reinterpreted in relation to evolving cultural circumstances. Theological ideas can arrive anew through prophecy or visions just as they can through new readings of old texts. Theology may even be the basis of constructive activity as believers translate ideas into practices. Theological dress centers religious ideologies, and especially those religious ideologies that believers understand to connect to the divine, religious texts, and other forms of the sacred. In terms of attire and adornment, a simplistic but necessary approach to the subject asks what theology dictates about what should be worn, when, and why. But the deeper and more interesting questions challenge us to think about how adornment discloses and/or protects spiritual status; how it reveals the nuances of varying interpretations of texts and traditions; and how theological models of adornment relate to shifting cultural norms.

Four essays in the book's first section, "Theological Adornment," analyze the subject of attire and practices of adornment as refracted through theological understanding, and in doing so shed light on how believers put theology into action as well as how action speaks to deep-seated theological motivations. In "Seventh-day Adventist Dress: 'An Index to the Heart,'" Emily J. Bailey explores Seventh-day Adventist women's attire in the nineteenth century as predicated on the writings of Ellen G. White, founder and prophetess of the movement. On the front lines of the American dress reform movement, Adventist women eschewed the tight corsets and heavy skirts that were then in fashion in favor of modified dress that supported physical health, which they understood to be in accordance with God's plan. At the same time, because they anticipated an imminent return of Christ, Adventists used their attire to set themselves apart from other Americans. The result was a reformed style of Adventist dress that served as a means for preserving a unique Adventist identity in a complex and competitive American religious marketplace.

Reflecting on the same period of historical circumstances, Jeremy Rapport's essay "Clothing Spiritual Reality: The Sartorial Styles of Mary Baker Eddy" considers the unfolding situation of religious dress among Christian Scientists. Christian Science is ripe for exploration because it is a faith in which material circumstances are evidence of one's spiritual nature, and this goes far beyond the health practices for which the religion is most famously known. Using imagery from three key periods of founder Mary Baker Eddy's life, Rapport demonstrates how Eddy's clothing choices and personal appearance reflected her evolving understandings of the relationship between the material and spiritual worlds and her own changing position in those worlds.

Moving into the twentieth century, Adrienne Nock Ambrose's "Faith, Fashion, and Film in the Jazz Age: Catholic Vestments Encounter the Roaring 1920s" offers a powerful look at how a Protestant American public evolved to embrace Catholicism over the course of a century. A category of sacred garment, the Catholic vestment, serves as Ambrose's focal point to explore and demonstrate this change. She argues that two burgeoning industries in America, film and fashion, created an intertextual environment of public exposure to Catholic belief and imagery, allowing the spectacle of vestments to overshadow previous suspicions of theological difference. This led to unprecedented public expressions of Catholicism and a more widespread positive social response, which may be considered to have culminated in the celebratory 2018 Metropolitan Museum of Art exhibition *Heavenly Bodies: Fashion and the Catholic Imagination*.

The final essay in this section, Andrea Shan Johnson and Leah Payne's "Power Before Thrones of God and Man: Women, Adornment, and Public Life in White American Pentecostalism," similarly explores a century of evolving theology, demonstrated in this case as much in the media and public sphere as through overtly religious discourse. Johnson and Payne show that two distinct strains of Pentecostalism, Oneness Pentecostalism and Trinitarian Pentecostalism, have used the attire and adornment of female members to offer competing theologies about holiness, power, and authority in public life. By looking at the examples of female leaders in these traditions, particularly controversial modern figures Kim Davis and Paula White-Cain, the authors argue that the bodies of Pentecostal women are imbued with a sacramental function. As such, Pentecostal women use clothing and other external accoutrements to illustrate and enact theologies of holiness and power.

Identity adornment

The second analytical frame employed by the authors is that of *identity*. Identity helps us to understand how attire and adornment religiously demarcate people in roles and communities that may be personal as well as public. Outwardly directed attire that identifies the religious—a clerical collar, a bonnet, a modesty veil— can be easy to spot, but not necessarily easy to understand. Some types of dress are recognized and/or understood only within specific religious contexts, signifying things as varied as membership, leadership, or a particular spiritual status, and personal, individualized markers may only be fully understood by the bearer and may act as forms of communication with the divine. The ways that attire and adornment both communicate and reify religious identity tell us as much about religious practice in the modern era as it does about perception of religious people and communities.

Four essays in the second section, "Identity Adornment," highlight how attire and adornment can serve as multilayered methods of individual and/or communal religious identification. André E. Brooks-Key, in "Holy Dashikis! Black Sartorial Nationalism and Black Israelite Religion," explores the attire of Black Israelites in North America as articulations of a tension between cultural nationalism and ritual adherence. Brooks-Key posits that Black Jews/Hebrew Israelites actively use dress to take control of the Black body and reorient the meaning of Blackness as a sacred symbol. Further, he argues that Afrocentricity, cultural nationalism, and religious observance ultimately merge to create an Afro-biblical nationalist aesthetic that allows Hebrew Israelites to maintain a distinct ethno-religious identity in America.

Kate Davis, in "Refined Bodies: Clothing as a Visual Signifier of Piety for Mormon Women in America," draws on Latter-day Saint primary sources to examine the history of official discourse on appropriate clothing for the "Good Latter-day Saint Woman." Employing gender theory, Davis argues that as women cultivate their own styles within official boundaries and in alignment with community-sanctioned roles, they create and maintain a public performance of Mormon femininity that concurrently communicates the peculiar status of Mormon women. By carefully crafting an outwardly modest image, Mormon woman reaffirm this identity as set apart from the rest of the world, and the act of dressing takes on additional meaning in the performance of one's gender.

In "The Christian Tattoo: Much More Than Skin-Deep," sociologists of religion Jerome R. Koch and Kevin D. Dougherty discuss their ongoing studies of religious tattoos among college students as marks of faith. In addition to their findings about the most common words and images that appear in these tattoos, they discovered that many tattoos contain covert religious meanings that are not immediately evident upon viewing. In light of research on intrinsic and extrinsic religiosity, impression management, and emerging adult spirituality, Koch and Dougherty demonstrate that religious tattoos are a form of adornment that can communicate information about identity, affiliation, and transformation in ways that are both personal and public.

Finally, Kayla Renée Wheeler's essay " 'Queens of the Earth': The MGT Uniform as a Form of Identity Creation and Nation Building," explores the roles of the Muslim Girls Training uniform in affecting Black women's personal and religious self-conceptions. Discourse about the women's religious uniform offered a challenge to white supremacist notions of beauty, making it a uniform that women wore proudly. At the same time, Wheeler's critical examination of the adornment rules and restrictions accompanying the uniform demonstrates there were also negative impacts, making it a garment with complex layers of meaning for Black Muslim women's identity.

Negotiated adornment

Scholars of religion frequently discuss the vast fissure that lies between ideal and lived religion. That is to say, no official, codified list of beliefs and practices defining a religious tradition can ever be matched by the actual ways in which real people engage with their religion as they manage their everyday lives. In that sense, religion is always about negotiation. Newer, often younger, interpreters of norms may take a fresh approach to tradition and broaden the understandings of how attire and adornment support or express a given faith tradition. In other, more difficult situations, changes may create tensions that must be resolved through stressful and protracted processes. When material items of attire become the focus of attention, it can concretize ideological distinctions that were previously abstract or amorphous. Negotiated adornment, in other words, has the capacity to highlight deep-seated stress points within a religious tradition.

Three essays in the third section, "Negotiated Adornment," explore religious dress with particular focus on the dynamics of negotiation. Michelle Mueller, in " 'Ye Shall Be Naked in Your Rites': Ritual Attire and

Ritual Nudity (Skyclad) in North American Wicca," interprets adaptations in the Wiccan practice of "skyclad," or ritual nudity. Though once a common practice that was believed to contribute to the efficacy of magical workings, skyclad fell out of favor among late twentieth-century American Wiccans, becoming relegated to only the most significant of spiritual events and being reinterpreted both liturgically and theologically. The history of skyclad and its adaptations illustrates religious negotiations and religious meaning making of attire and adornment, including the baring of the naked body.

Having done long-term ethnographic work among Amish women, Nao Nomura offers a rare intimate portrait of this community in "Amish Vogue: Performing Fashion in the Plain World." The Amish are readily recognizable for a dress code that appears to outsiders as simple and uniform. Nomura, by exploring the subtle differences in design that allow Amish seamstresses to express creativity and individuality, challenges the scholarly consensus that fashion is absent among the Amish. She argues that Old Order Amish women are not only attuned to fashion—they also use it as a tool: by embracing and manifesting personal style and taste within the constraints of the church regulations, the women negotiate their religious identity as individuals through dress.

Mormon garments, sometimes called "sacred underwear," are a curiosity in the media. Due to the sensitive and sacred nature of garments and the historical mistreatment of them by outsiders, members of the Church of Jesus Christ of Latter-day Saints have been reluctant to answer questions about them. In " 'Your Religion Is Showing': Negotiation and Personal Experience in Mormon Garments," Jessica Finnigan and Nancy Ross make an intervention by asking such questions and exploring what the answers reveal. Based on their original, extensive survey about belief, meaning, and personal practices related to the wearing of garments, Finnigan and Ross analyze how LDS men and women of differing belief levels experience and negotiate garment wearing in their daily lives.

Activist adornment

In the final section, "Activist Adornment," three authors use the frame of *activism* in order to explore forms of religious dress that serve as tools to effect world change. Whether the attire is divinely ordained, institutionally constructed, or both, it becomes a focal point around which religious legitimacy is measured, and believers would say their work is a mandate rather than a deliberate or chosen form of activism. Within their individual contexts, the shifts these religious people seek through dress practices can be monumental in nature, striving to alter social perceptions or even consciousness itself via the adornment of bodies. In the three essays highlighting this dynamic, we see that never has the act of clothing oneself been so weighty.

Elaina Smith, in "Dressed for Glory: White Uniforms in African American Church Traditions as Visual Political Theology," explores the all-white uniforms worn in particular contexts by Protestant church women. Besides creating a unique and salient aesthetic, African American church women's practice of wearing only white is also a deeply political gesture. The visual aesthetic of the uniform declares identities that Black women are often socially denied, including roles of spiritual and communal authority. In short, the white uniform is a visual political theology that makes claims of wholeness and worthiness, and through it African American church women make declarations about themselves and prophetically interpret God's will for the world.

In "'The Hare Krishna Look:' ISKCON Adornment as Religious Activism," Benjamin E. Zeller explores Hare Krishna adornment practices as deliberate political acts. In the 1970s, the Hare Krishna movement, formally called the International Society for Krishna Consciousness (ISKCON), called for replacing most aspects of Western mainstream society with their vision of ancient Indian (Vedic) religious-cultural society. Bodily adornment functioned within the group as not only a religious practice but also a social norm and cultural expression. While early devotees adorned themselves in the "Hare Krishna look" for a variety of reasons, movement leaders increasingly used dress to position themselves within the broader culture, critiquing mainstream society and carving a niche for themselves as a source of alternative religious legitimacy. Hare Krishna bodily adornment functioned as a form of cultural activism, challenging broader norms and providing an alternate perspective as part of an agenda to spiritually transform Western society as a whole, one person at a time.

In the book's final chapter, "Religious Dress, the Church of Body Modification, and the First Amendment," Marie W. Dallam explores the history of First Amendment jurisprudence on religious dress in order to situate the specific problems faced by members of the Church of Body Modification. Regulation of dress in many American institutional settings has created standards that are largely biased in favor of Protestantism, which leads to problems for members of a church that sacralizes modifications to the physical body, such as tattoos and piercings, and which considers their display an integral part of religious practice. Forced into adversarial positions with institutions that regulate dress, these religious people necessarily become activists on behalf of an unusual cause: the embrace of unfamiliar and unconventional religious adornment.

FURTHER DIRECTIONS

Sociologist Cornelia Bohn has written that "Not all texts are textiles. But all textiles are texts or at least textual components." This is a straightforward assertion, and easy to agree with. But Bohn does not suggest that clothing is a complete system of communication, pointing out that it is more limited than spoken or written language, and must therefore be made "sociologically intelligible" by using other aspects of identity, such as religion.[22] Relatedly, Werner Enninger, a specialist on the Amish, has argued that while clothing can signify and may also communicate, to call dress a "language" stretches it far beyond its actual social, cultural, and other constraints.[23] Instead, Enninger proposes that there are links between "certain sets of clothing items and certain sets of persons," and within such nuanced configurations, actual communication via dress can occur.[24] The intricacies to which Bohn and Enninger refer are the substance of the essays gathered in this volume. Part of dress's fascinating complexity is its dual status as both an object and an action, though its significance for some individuals may also lie in the perception that it can be *only* one of these. That is why questions of religious meaning, filtered through any one of the above four frames, help us penetrate the significance of attire and adornment in particular contexts, thereby allowing us to understand the wider scope of what it seeks to communicate.

In addition to theology, identity, negotiation, and activism, readers are likely to observe additional subtextual themes woven throughout the essays in this volume. These include performativity, viewer response, uniformity, gender normativity, power and hierarchy, modest dress, forbidden dress, fossilized fashion, ritual practice, change and adaption, health and science, and commercialization and marketing. Readers are apt to think about numerous intersections between religion, dress, and adornment that did not make it into this book, and which would serve as equally instructive case studies. For instance, how is it that a specific garment, the black hat, has come to represent religious identity among the Hasidim and other Orthodox Jewish sects, and what do competing understandings of the black hat, as well as competing styles, fashions, textiles, and designs, reveal about American and transnational Judaism?[25] How do contemporary practitioners of Native American sacred traditions continue to adapt sacred clothing traditions, such as the famed "ghost shirts" that figured so prominently in the nineteenth-century Ghost Dance movement and subsequent Wounded Knee Massacre but have recently witnessed an underground resurgence among some Native American religious communities?[26] Many of the essays in this book look at peripheral movements within American religion wherein adornment practices are more striking and easier to identify and analyze. Yet the same approaches could be extended to mainline Protestants, Latinx Catholics, Reform and Conservative Jewish communities, and other traditions. Similarly, this book focuses on the American scene. Looking beyond North America, one will find not only new cases of religion, dress, and adornment, but alterative themes and interpretive lenses as well.

All of these are equally valid approaches, topics, and emphases that might readily serve as discussion points to link the essays included in this volume within new groupings, and we hope readers will discover these and others as they think about the relationships among the many subjects covered. Engagement with and critical response to these areas will serve to bolster the study of religion, attire, and adornment, and ultimately we hope that this book provides one or more starting points for scholars of religion, especially, to build field-specific conversations about dress in the years to come.

NOTES

1. Elisha Fieldstadt, "Ohio Lawmaker Refuses to Wear Mask Because He Says It Dishonors God," NBC News, last updated May 6, 2020, https://www.nbcnews.com/news/us-news/ohio-lawmaker-refuses-wear-mask-because-he-says-it-dishonors-n1201106.

2. Samuel L. Perry, Andrew L. Whitehead, and Joshua B. Grubbs, "Culture Wars and COVID-19 Conduct: Christian Nationalism, Religiosity, and Americans' Behavior During the Coronavirus Pandemic," *Journal for the Scientific Study of Religion* 59, no. 3 (September 2020): 410–11.
3. For examples, see Colleen McDannell, *Material Christianity: Religion and Popular Culture in America* (New Haven, CT: Yale University Press, 1995); Minna Opas and Anna Haapalainen, eds., *Christianity and the Limits of Materiality* (London: Bloomsbury, 2017); Leonard Norman Primiano, "Collecting Vernacular Religious Culture," *Material Religion* 12, no. 3 (2016): 381–83; Joseph Sciorra, *Built with Faith: Italian American Imagination and Catholic Material Culture in New York City* (Knoxville: University of Tennessee Press, 2015).
4. McDannell, *Material Christianity*, 2.
5. For one exception, see Anna-Karina Hemkens, "Clothing as Embodied Experience of Belief," in *Religion and Material Culture: The Matter of Belief*, ed. David Morgan (London: Routledge, 2009), 231–46, which does center the study of religion and clothing, but focuses exclusively on the Melanesian context.
6. David Morgan, *The Thing About Religion: An Introduction to the Material Study of Religions* (Chapel Hill: University of North Carolina Press, 2021), 70.
7. Sarah Coakley, "Introduction," in *Religion and the Body*, ed. Sarah Coakley (Cambridge: Cambridge University Press, 1997), 9.
8. Kristi Upson-Saia, *Early Christian Dress: Gender, Virtue and Authority* (New York: Routledge, 2011), 3.
9. See Kristi Upson-Saia, Carly Daniel-Hughes, and Alicia J. Batten, eds., *Dressing Judeans and Christians in Antiquity* (New York: Routledge, 2014). See also Aileen Ribeiro, *Dress and Morality* (London: B. T. Batsford, 1986).
10. Eric Silverman, *A Cultural History of Jewish Dress* (London: Bloomsbury, 2013), especially chapter 9.
11. Leonard J. Greenspoon, ed., *Fashioning Jews: Clothing, Culture, and Commerce* (West Lafayette, IN: Purdue University Press, 2013).
12. Anna Piela, *Wearing the Niqab: Muslim Women in the UK and the US* (London: Bloomsbury, 2021).
13. Su'ad Abdul Khabeer, *Muslim Cool: Race, Religion, and Hip Hop in the United States* (New York: New York University Press, 2016), chapters 3 and 4. Also see related conversations taking place online and in the popular press about Mipsterz and Muslim futurism—for example, on websites such as mipsterz.com and muslimfuturism.com.
14. Elizabeth Bucar, *Pious Fashion: How Muslim Women Dress* (Cambridge, MA: Harvard University Press, 2017).

15. Lynn S. Neal, *Religion in Vogue: Christianity and Fashion in America* (New York: New York University Press, 2019), 6.
16. Linda B. Arthur, ed., *Religion, Dress and the Body* (London: Berg, 1999); Arthur, ed., *Undressing Religion: Commitment and Conversion from a Cross-Cultural Perspective* (London: Berg, 2000). These two works are among the early publications in the long-running series Dress, Body, and Culture that began at Berg Publishers (and has since moved to Bloomsbury). A number of titles in this series relate to the study of religion.
17. Emma Tarlo, *Visibly Muslim: Fashion, Politics, Faith* (Oxford: Berg, 2010); see the "Suggested Reading List" at the end of the volume for several of Tarlo's other works. Recently, Tarlo has been working on an articulation of methodology for studying religious dress within anthropology; see the 2017 draft version of a forthcoming chapter, "Developing Methods for the Study of Religious Dress," Goldsmiths Research Online, last modified July 1, 2019, http://research.gold.ac.uk/id/eprint/21317/.
18. Reina Lewis, *Muslim Fashion: Contemporary Style Cultures* (Durham, NC: Duke University Press, 2015). See also Lewis's edited volume *Modest Fashion: Styling Bodies, Mediating Faith* (London: I. B. Tauris, 2013).
19. Judith Brown, *Glamour in Six Dimensions: Modernism and the Radiance of Form* (Ithaca, NY: Cornell University Press, 2018), 1.
20. Nigel Thrift, "Understanding the Material Practices of Glamour," in *The Affect Theory Reader*, ed. Melissa Gregg and Gregory J. Seigworth (Durham, NC: Duke University Press, 2010), 289–309. See also Thrift, "The Material Practices of Glamour," *Journal of Cultural Economy* 1, no. 1 (2008): 9–23.
21. Benjamin E. Zeller, Marie W. Dallam, Reid L. Neilson, and Nora L. Rubel, *Religion, Food, & Eating in North America* (New York: Columbia University Press, 2014).
22. Cornelia Bohn, "Clothing as Medium of Communication," Researchgate.net, April 2012, 5, https://www.researchgate.net/publication/328530889_Clothing_as_medium_of_Communication. Original version published as "Kleidung als Kommunikationsmedium" in Cornelia Bohn, *Inklusion, Exklusion und die Person* (Konstanz, DE: UVK Verlag, 2006).
23. Werner Enninger, "The Design Features of Clothing Codes: The Functions of Clothing Displays in Interaction," *Ars Semeiotica* 8, nos. 1–2 (1985): 81–85.
24. Enninger, "Design Features of Clothing Codes," 91.
25. Zvi Ron, "Stripes, Hats, and Fashion," *Modern Judaism* 40, no. 3 (2020): 312–26.
26. See Mary Crow Dog and Richard Erdoes, *Lakota Woman* (New York: Harper-Perennial, 1991).

Part I

THEOLOGICAL ADORNMENT

One

SEVENTH-DAY ADVENTIST DRESS

"AN INDEX TO THE HEART"

EMILY J. BAILEY

Bodies in the developing Seventh-day Adventist tradition of the nineteenth century were viewed as agents in religious practice and social change. They were God's property—loaned for a lifetime, with the expectation that they would be returned one day in the best possible condition. With this view in mind, what one ate and the clothing one wore were significant actions on the road to salvation. While early Seventh-day Adventist modifications to diet have been widely studied, it is lesser known that founder Ellen Gould Harmon White (1827–1915) and her followers also embraced and enacted their faith through clothing reforms.[1] Their challenges to late nineteenth- and early twentieth-century normative American clothing trends reveal that Adventism approached dress reforms as a means of promoting physical health, as well as in preparation for what the community believed could be an imminent return of Jesus Christ. From this perspective, the ways in which one dressed one's physical, earthly body were meant to align with ideals for the conditions of heavenly bodies that would one day be reunited with God.

FOUNDATIONS FOR ADVENTISM

Coming of age in the "burned-over district" in the 1840s, Ellen was no stranger to the residual influences of intense American religious revivalism from the Second Great Awakening.[2] Like the Puritans and other religious reformers in American history, Adventists believed that the new world was like a new Jerusalem—a promised land to which Jesus Christ would return at the end of time, which could be very soon. Revivalist populations capitalized on converting an American population ripe for social and religious change, and shared the "hope in the manifest destiny of white, Anglo-Saxon Protestant America to lead the world to its latter-day glory."[3]

There were many catalysts for religious reform during the century. Major waves of immigration, westward expansion, war, industrialism and new technologies, developing urban centers, and widespread outbreaks of diseases like cholera, scarlet fever, and typhus left citizens reeling, and immeasurably changed the American social and religious landscapes. Perplexed and in search of a sense of belonging, converts turned to new religious communities like Adventism with excitement and hope. Casting a large net, pioneering religious movements consequently found success in a competitive American religious "free market."[4] They also appealed to a lay population that had begun to feel distanced from its Protestant Christian roots across the Atlantic, as the American religious context became more unique with each passing decade. Taking advantage of the shift in the ways American religion was being approached, a new brand of charismatic preachers entered the religious scene. These nineteenth-century ministers traveled to the American frontier to preach the gospel of Christian perfectionism, gain converts, and save souls. Present since the time of the early Christian church, perfectionism hinged on a model of spiritual maturity, cultivated through baptism and the conscious avoidance of sin and vice. For some nineteenth-century religious revivalists, like those who would become White's followers, this perfectionist standpoint contended that the inhabitants of the "new Jerusalem" needed to eliminate individual and social corruptions in order for God's millennial plan to unfold.[5]

To best comprehend the Seventh-day Adventist perspective as it developed into an independent, uniquely American branch of Christian tradition, it is important to consider its revivalist underpinnings.⁶ Like many new religious movements of the time, the sect developed out of a pattern of reforms enacted at rural "camp meetings" and urban revivals. Sometimes attracting tens of thousands of participants, revivals spread innovative Christian messages, while encouraging unconventional, often embodied spiritual practices. What critics of the time called "all nonsense and noise," the wild "exercises" in which some revival participants "wrestl[ed] and pray[ed]" fell far outside the scope of mainstream Protestant behavior.⁷ Testimonies from revival meetings reveal vivid details about these physical manifestations of faith, noting that even the saying of prayers and singing of hymns could be undertaken with "much animation."⁸ Believers danced, convulsed, spoke in unknown divine languages, and went into prophetic trances. Given the agency of the physical self in this religious expression, it is not surprising that communities born from such revivalism, like Adventism, paid special attention to the ways in which the body was fed, clothed, and kept.⁹

Like the Church of Jesus Christ of Latter-day Saints, another American-born denomination, Adventism was uniquely rooted in the prophetic visions of one individual—in the case of the Adventists, those of Ellen White. As a young woman, White converted, along with her family, to Methodism at a camp meeting. After this conversion, she and her parents became familiar with the work of William Miller, a former deist and Baptist. By some accounts, Miller portended that the Second Coming, or advent, of Jesus would occur in 1843 or 1844, fulfilling prophecies based on the Old Testament book of Daniel. Miller's movement gained nearly fifty thousand practicing "Millerites by 1844, but began to unravel when Christ did not appear."¹⁰ Rather than returning to the Methodist movement, from which many of Miller's followers had been disfellowshipped because of their alternative religious views, Ellen, her future husband James, and sea captain Joseph Bates used Millerism as the foundation for a new brand of Christianity. The prophetess shared her first vision in 1844, arguing that Miller's augured event had occurred, but in heaven rather than on earth, signaling the commencement of the end times. Christ's Second Coming would occur soon, and it was time to prepare for it in soul and body.

Adopting a seventh-day Sabbath, or Saturday worship, this new community intentionally set itself apart from other Christians, who worshipped on Sunday. Adventists coexisted with the American Protestant mainline, but continued to depart from religious norms, maintaining distinct beliefs and practices based on White's prophetic visions. The desire to prime America for the coming religious reign of Christ drove members of the new community to "clean . . . up problems wherever they saw them."[11] In this quest to prepare the American promised land for Christ's return, Adventist reforms also often aligned with the broader social reforms of the time, like the movements toward temperance, suffrage, abolition, vegetarianism, and novel ways of dressing. Their spirituality was enacted through these causes and included striving for physical perfection as an embodiment of holiness. Whether or not this can be attributed to White keeping her finger on the pulse of popular trends, or was more strictly related to her prophecies, has been questioned by historians and Adventist apostates alike. What is important to consider here, however, is the points at which the Adventist Church (incorporated in 1863) converged with and strayed from mainstream culture as it vied for space and converts as a religious contender in America.

NINETEENTH-CENTURY DRESS AND DRESS REFORM

The impetus for nineteenth-century Adventist calls for dress reform was tied to a belief that one's "complete humanity" would be preserved at death, and that heaven would be populated by beings with material bodies."[12] Counter to some Christian views of the body as a sinful mortal shell to be cast off at death, this perspective instead held that it was an essential and precious salvific vehicle. Bodies needed to be fed and clothed according to God's plan so that, when Christ returned, those who achieved salvation would be prepared to join him in the flesh, and not just in spirit. This proved a challenge for some Adventist followers, as nineteenth- and early twentieth-century styles of dress became more conspicuous—and more physically restrictive—than ever, especially for women.

When White was coming of age in the early nineteenth century, women's dress dramatically shifted from a Georgian style, which favored high empire waists and loose, straight silhouettes, to one in which tight bodices required severe corseting. Newly styled bell-shaped skirts were heavy and cumbersome, with layers of crinoline petticoats, steel hoops, and fabric.[13] The harsh realities of this new prototypical dress were many, with the weight, size, and shape of women's clothing bringing scrutiny from both religious and health reformers. With dresses sometimes weighing more than ten pounds, even walking could be difficult. To mitigate the changes, articles and advice columns were devoted specifically to helping women navigate doorways and stairs and move gracefully from sitting to standing in their bulky and unwieldly outfits. Despite these dangers and inconveniences, many women strove to keep up with the fashions of the day. The motivation to adhere to the latest trends was a product of "a matrix of social, economic, and technological factors," based on models like those of the "Gibson girls."[14] Slender fashion icons, the Gibson girls embodied the height of fashion in the late Victorian and Edwardian periods, analogous to what one might find in a publication like *Vogue* today.

For White, the new fashion was problematic on several fronts. Over the course of decades, she wrote and prophesied about the negative influences of women's dress on Americans' health, behavior, culture, and even spiritual salvation. In her concern for health, she was not alone in her strong views about the physical consequences of popular dress. After the American Civil War, groups such as the New England Women's Club met to advocate for amendments to women's clothing, like the "emancipation suits" designed by female physician Dr. Mary Walker. Based on revisions to women's underclothes, Walker's design attempted to free women from the "cruel corsets, tight garters, and other underpinnings" that were proven to be injurious to their health.[15] Her altered style included a loose-fitting bodice to allow for easier movement and breathing, and pant-like drawers modeled on men's clothing. As evidenced by dress reformers' concerns, these assertions were not merely proto-feminist declarations; they were also grounded in real concerns for women's physical well-being. Male and female physicians alike fought the fashion trends of the era, noting the physical harm that they inflicted.

In 1887, an American physician tested fifty women and discovered that corsets contracted their waists by two and a half to six inches.[16] This exerted an average of more than twenty pounds of pressure on these women's ribcages and internal organs, but this figure could exceed eighty pounds for those who were especially aggressive in "training" their waist sizes.[17] To illustrate the point, J. L. Comstock, a nineteenth-century surgeon, created explicit renderings of the effects of tight corset binding on women's skeletons and internal organs. In the process of helping women to achieve the painfully thin but fashionable waists of the era, overly tightened corsets were also known to cause organ deformities, difficult pregnancies and labors, and even death. Like religious dress reformers, Comstock's concerns extended beyond this lifetime and into the hereafter. In his 1848 *Outlines of Physiology*, he lamented that "hundreds, nay thousands, of females literally kill themselves every year by this fashion in our own country: and if suicide is a crime, how will such escape in the day of final account!"[18] Fashionable modern dress was nothing short of a sinful road away from salvation.

ADVENTIST VIEWS OF DRESS REFORM

White was clearly familiar with studies like Comstock's, writing in her 1890 *Christian Temperance and Bible Hygiene* that "the suffering caused among women by unhealthful dress cannot be estimated. Many have become lifelong invalids through their compliance with the demands of fashion."[19] She believed that modern fashion was interfering with God's plan for the physical body, and noted that the harm to women's circulation, posture, breathing, and childbearing prospects caused by mainstream clothing was an "insult . . . to the Creator"—"deform[ing] that which he made perfect."[20] Fashion was instead "Satan's design," meant to "pervert every function of [the] being that life may be made miserable, and God may be dishonored in the creatures that he made."[21] Calling for what she defined as "true dress reform," White contended that the ideal clothing for women would be "suitab[le] for outdoor enjoyment" and "exercise in the open air."[22] In her personal estimation, a woman's comportment should be as simple and wholesome as the strict, bland, and meatless diet to which she encouraged her followers to subscribe. Ministers and their wives were especially charged with modeling a style of plain dress for their congregants, as any clothing "designed to attract attention to the wearer or to excite admiration" of them was to be "excluded from the modest apparel which God's Word enjoin[ed]."[23] Surviving documentation of her opinions and revelations about how to enact such reforms reveals that White's views changed through the years, but her general emphasis on modifying dress for physical and spiritual health was unwavering.

When it came to radical reforms, White began as a critic, converted to a staunch supporter, and then retreated again. Her initial claims about the secular dress reforms that she witnessed in the 1850s and early 1860s were that "God's order ha[d] been reversed, and his special directions disregarded by those who adopt[ed] the American costume," recalling a passage from Deuteronomy (22:5) in which "the woman shall not wear that which pertaineth unto a man, neither shall a man put on a woman's garment: for all that do so are an abomination unto the Lord."[24] In this, she referred to the "costume" or dress reforms of Amelia Bloomer, a somewhat inadvertent public advocate for "rational" women's dress. Active in proto-feminist circles and the reforms of the Seneca Falls Convention in 1848, Bloomer was the author of a popular feminist tract called *The Lily*. With an audience of similarly minded women, Bloomer began in the 1850s to promote a highly amended female outfit, to which she was introduced by Elizabeth "Libby" Smith Miller. A fellow supporter of women's rights, Miller wore an updated "costume," which included a short jacket and ankle-length skirt layered over loose pants. Free from binding underclothes and stiff skirts that touched the floor, women who adopted these reforms shocked mainstream America with what many perceived as their unladylike clothing, and they were often publicly scrutinized by men and conservative women, who believed that such reforms would be the undoing of traditional American society.

To appreciate the significance of these concerns, one must consider the normative view of women's roles in nineteenth-century America. By the 1870s, American Protestants "define[d] their faith in terms of family morals, civic responsibility, and . . . churchgoing"—all perceived within the feminine sphere.[25] The gender divide created by the rapid rise of industrialism in previous decades had cultivated an American culture in which women were viewed as being set apart from the corruptions of the workaday world to which men were subjected, giving them the moral upper hand. Closely tied to the spheres of domesticity and religion, middle- and upper-class women were especially looked to as models of the Christian faith.[26] The widespread success of publications about "domestic religion" by Catharine Beecher, Sara Josepha Hale, Margaret Fuller, and others bolstered the cause, painting women as the religious mainstays and moral guides of their homes and communities.[27] While this relegation of women to the domestic sphere was interpreted cursorily to imply submission and weakness, the women of White's era exerted their religious influence and authority in a way that eventually extended their power to broader social causes, like dress reform and female suffrage. This fuller picture reveals that women both created and supported, as well as confronted, the gender and religious ideals of their day. For some, women like White and Bloomer, by challenging these ideals, presented a threat not only to domestic bliss, but to social and moral order as well. While dress reform may seem somewhat insignificant to our twenty-first-century minds, at the time such actions were viewed as nothing short of a harbinger of social anarchy.

Fears about women's changing roles increased as the century progressed, and American women became more vocal and more public in their support of causes that aligned with their hopes for the future of the nation. As they engaged in marches, meetings, and public debates about temperance, abolition, and women's suffrage, questions arose about the possibility of women becoming somehow less womanly, echoing White's initial concerns about radical dress reform. In essence, these anxieties amounted to a cultural panic about non-normative female actions. Although her preliminary stance rejecting dress reform was aligned with contemporary mainstream Protestant opinion, White eventually embraced some radical changes through the agency of her prophetic visions.

White's perspective on women's dress began to shift after a spiritual vision in the early 1860s revealed quite different instructions for Adventist dress reforms. First, White suggested nothing more than that women should raise the hems of their dresses a few inches. The goal of this small reform was practical, helping women to stay modest while making their clothing last longer by preventing skirt hems from dragging on the ground. By 1868, her visions about dress reform purportedly revealed God's desire for further modifications to women's clothing. White explained that in her vision, "Our skirts are few and light, not taxing our strength with the burden of many and longer ones. Our limbs being properly clothed, we need comparatively few skirts; and these are suspended from the shoulders . . . Our dresses are fitted to sit easily, obstructing neither the circulation of the blood, nor natural, free, and full means of locomotion, but leave us to move about with ease and activity. All these things are necessary to health."[28] Where White at one time supported a more traditional, albeit simplified, view of nineteenth-century female dress, her new, divinely inspired perspective held that conventional antebellum dress was "an abomination," and she called on "every Sabbathkeeper" to "rebuke to th[e] ridiculous fashion" by embracing reform.[29]

AN APPEAL TO THE PEOPLE IN ITS BEHALF.

We are not Spiritualists. We are Christian women, believing all that the Scriptures say concerning man's creation, his fall, his sufferings and woes on account of continued transgression, of his hope of redemption thro' Christ, and of his duty to glorify God in his body and spirit which are his, in order to be saved. We do not wear the style of dress here represented to be odd,—that we may attract notice. We do not differ from the common style of woman's dress for any

FIGURE 1.1 Pamphlet, *The Dress Reform* (Battle Creek, MI: Seventh-day Adventist Publishing Association, 1868). Image courtesy of Pacific Union College Library.

For White, dress reform was rooted in the understanding that bodies needed to be fit to render service to God, so she asserted that the mainstream fashions of her time would lead to behavioral offences against the divine. She cautioned against modern styles, lamenting that "fashion rules the world; and she is a tyrannical mistress, often compelling her devotees to submit ... without reason."[30] It was "Satan, the instigator and prime mover," not God, who dictated "the ever-changing, never-satisfying decrees of fashion ... entic[ing] unwitting victims toward the 'idolatry of dress.' "[31] White taught that trying to keep up with the frenzied fashion changes of the time would ultimately "destroy ... all that is humble, meek, and lovely in character ... consum[ing] the precious hours that should be devoted to meditation, to searching the heart, to the prayerful study of God's Word. No Christian [could] conform to the demoralizing fashions of the world without imperiling [the] soul's salvation."[32]

A firm believer in frugality as an indicator of morality, White also declared that the outward appearance of her followers was "an index to the heart. When the exterior is hung with ribbons, collars, and needless things, it plainly shows that the love for all this is in the heart; unless such persons are cleansed from their corruption, they can never see God, for only the pure in heart will see him."[33] Followers of God were called to wear not just their hearts on their sleeves, but their souls as well. White contended that Christians who wished to remain in God's favor should endeavor toward two types of alternative garments: those designated in scripture, and those supported by her prophetic visions. With the former in mind, White wrote that "the apostles ... describe[d] the adornment that should be sought by Christian women," who ought to "adorn themselves in modest apparel, with shamefacedness and sobriety; not with broidered hair, or gold, or pearls, or costly array; but (which becometh women professing godliness) with good works" (she was here quoting 1 Timothy 2:9).[34] She reminded her female followers that according to the Bible, physical loveliness fades away, while "spiritual loveliness consists in harmony with Christ—the likeness of our souls to him. The grace of Christ is indeed a priceless adornment."[35] Unlike the fleeting popular fashions of the day, White alleged that a Christ-like adornment "elevates and ennobles the possessor; and it also has an influence upon others, attracting them to the Source of light and blessing."[36] Taking on the mantle of scriptural adornment, she hoped that Adventists would serve as models to their fellow citizens, with an ideal of eliminating vice in order to usher in Christ's Second Coming.

With the return of Christ believed to be close at hand, White also reflected on adornment in apocalyptic terms. As in the book of Revelation at the end of the Christian New Testament (19:14), Ellen noted that "no outward adorning can compare in value or loveliness with that 'meek and quiet spirit,' the 'fine linen, white and clean,' which all the holy ones of earth will wear."[37] This apparel would make the chosen of God "beautiful and beloved here, and . . . hereafter be their badge of admission to the palace of the King."[38] This early twentieth-century view was recorded just a few short years before White's death in 1915, but it reflected the imagery of her very first prophetic vision in 1844. In that vision, White purportedly was given a glimpse of the path to heaven, with 144,000 of God's chosen marching along it. Being led by Jesus, these people were clad in a "glorious white mantle from their shoulders to their feet."[39] Like the garb of early Christian ascetics, White's vision of heavenly clothing was genderless, homologous, and pure.[40] Similar to the teachings of eighteenth-century Shaker foundress and prophetess Ann Lee before her, White argued that this purity and cleanliness was to be imitated on earth in preparation for the eventual journey heavenward. Modeling behavior for others, earthly Adventist "dress should be cleanly," for "uncleanliness in dress is . . . defiling to the body and to the soul."[41] When believers show themselves to be "coarse and [a] spectacle unto the world" by buying into mainstream fashion, "their influence hurts t[hat] truth," distracting them and others from God.[42] To adopt a practice of simple, clean dress in this life was to move a little bit closer to God in preparation for the life to come.

It is worth noting that as far as her followers were concerned, White's convictions about women's dress had changed not because of social trends, but because of God's will. This was especially apparent when God's revelatory prescription for shortened dresses and looser clothing ended not long after it had begun. In a letter in 1897, White reflected on the widespread rejection of dress reform by American women, including those within her Adventist community, writing that in the end, "the Lord has not moved upon many of our sisters to adopt the reform dress."[43] While there is evidence of continued practice of dress reform on the part of White's female followers, she did not devote significant thought to the subject in her writing again.

WHITE'S LEGACY

This was not, however, the end of health-driven dress reforms in the Adventist movement. White's teachings lived on in the work of fellow Adventist John Harvey Kellogg. White and Kellogg maintained a long-term working relationship throughout the nineteenth century in their health-focused spiritual ministry at the Battle Creek Sanitarium in Michigan. The enterprise was founded in 1866 as the Western Health Reform Institute, but it rose to new heights a decade later when Ellen and her husband James invited recent medical school graduate J. H. Kellogg to oversee their day-to-day operations. While Kellogg ascended to fame (or by some accounts, infamy) for his unconventional approaches to diet, medicine, and wellness at Battle Creek, it is often forgotten that the roots of the institution were planted firmly in White's Adventist prophetic visions.[44]

After visiting a water cure clinic with her ailing husband in 1865, White claimed to have received a vision from God in which he called Adventists to "build a water cure and vegetarian institution, where a properly balanced course of treatments could be made available to not only Adventists, but the general public."[45] With more than fifty thousand practicing Adventists in North America, and expanding global missions, by the end of the century the venture had a firm foundation for success.[46] Although the institution was initially founded as a religious project, by the 1890s the campus counted more than eighty buildings, and Kellogg alone had treated nearly a quarter of a million patients, as only one of many physicians on staff.[47]

White relied on Kellogg and his wife Ella Eaton Kellogg to maintain her visions at Battle Creek when she began to travel, and then lived away from the site later in life. Letters between White and Kellogg suggest that the popular doctor largely deferred to White's visions and requests despite his role as director of the institution. Just as White's visions and guidance influenced Kellogg's approaches to diet and medicine at Battle Creek, they manifested in Kellogg's views about clothing and dress reform. His "gospel of good health" included insights into the importance of dressing well for one's figure, but also for one's general well-being. The best clothes for women would "imitate the lines of the natural body," while corsets were a device of the devil.[48]

IMPLICATIONS OF DRESS REFORM

Dress reform was a means for preserving a unique Adventist identity in a complex and competitive religious marketplace. Despite White's initial reservations about the "American Dress," simplicity and reform in adornment became outward hallmarks of physical and spiritual otherness and chosenness for the Adventist community. In this, White likened Adventists to the Israelites of the Old Testament, who, "as they looked upon their peculiarity of dress... were to remember that they were God's commandment-keeping people."[49] For nineteenth- and early twentieth-century Adventists, the impetus was to dress as though their earthly clothing was a symbol of their spiritual state. In all things they were to be representatives of Christ, "characterized by neatness, modesty, and purity."[50] Not concerned with moderating their comportment to mollify mainstream America, White encouraged her followers to "set a worthy example" against the normative fashion trends of her day.[51] Though the temptation to conform was strong, "the growth of the soul in grace, in purity, in comeliness is little by little—a progressive work," and Adventists were to "go forward unceasingly" to fulfill God's divine plan for spiritual and physical perfection.[52]

By the 1910s, American views about women's dress had been radically altered. With changes in clothing materials largely brought about by rationing during the World War I, the media began to favor athletic women, with lean and less shapely physiques, over the wasp-waisted Gibson girls of previous decades. Women's publications, as casters and transmitters of fashion, began to emphasize an active lifestyle, which in many ways finally brought the concerted efforts of dress reformers like Bloomer and White to fruition. The "new woman" was as likely to "read an uplifting book" as she was to "climb a tree"—something that would have been challenging if not impossible in the restrictive normative fashions of previous decades.[53]

White's writings reveal that early Adventists were at times advocates of dress reform and a unique brand of biblical feminism, but that they never fully aligned with the views of secular feminist circles because they intentionally strove to remain apart. The Adventist mission to quell Victorian views of female bodies as "inherently pathological" instead reflected recent scientific advancements in health, proto-feminist efforts, prophetic visions, and a deep desire to retain an Adventist identity that was spiritually and viscerally distinct from the American mainstream.[54] Though historically perceived as being "at odds with socially accepted values," the tradition was unusually successful at remaining comfortably outside of the Protestant mainline.[55] White and her followers likewise constructed seemingly dichotomous relationships with the physical body. On the one hand, they were intensely fixated on the promise of an imminent end time, while on the other they wished to remain "peculiarly successful in attempting to realize life-enhancing goals" through reforms in adornment.[56]

NOTES

1. Prone to visions and divine manifestations following a childhood accident, Ellen White claimed to have two significant revelations about health reforms, in 1863 and then again 1865. The first detailed the ideal of a temperate life in terms of food, drink, and labor. Clean water and fresh air were God's medicine, and meat, tobacco, drugs, caffeine, and alcohol were to be avoided.
2. This area of western and central New York was given this title because religious revivals were so common there that widespread conversions left few potential converts.
3. William G. McLoughlin, *The American Evangelicals, 1800–1900: An Anthology* (New York: Harper, 1968), 1.
4. Roger Finke and Rodney Stark, *The Churching of America, 1776–2005: Winners and Losers in Our Religious Economy* (New Brunswick, NJ: Rutgers University Press, 2005).
5. Peter Williams, *America's Religions: Traditions and Cultures* (New York: Macmillan, 1990), 180. Post-millenarian views, like those of Adventists, were popular in nineteenth-century Christian sectarian movements, and advocated that Jesus would appear after a millennium of peace and prosperity on earth. Pre-millenarian views argued the opposite—that Jesus would return to usher in the millennium.
6. Adventism was not the only religion to form on American soil in the nineteenth century; this period also saw the emergence of Joseph Smith's (1805–1844) Mormon tradition, Charles Taze Russell's (1852–1916) Jehovah's Witness movement, and Mary Baker Eddy's (1821–1910) Church of Christ, Scientist.

7. David Hempton, *Methodism: Empire of the Spirit* (New Haven, CT: Yale University Press, 2006), 56, and William Cooke, *The Methodist New Connexion Magazine and Evangelical Repository* (London: Cassell, Petter, and Galpin, Belle Sauvage Works, 1869), 36. In the early part of the nineteenth century, the mainline, or mainstream, Protestant churches were Anglican, Presbyterian, and Congregationalist. This shifted to favor Methodist and Baptist churches by the end of the century, which also faced competition from the growth of the Roman Catholic Church in America.
8. A. Lummus, "Hebron Camp-Meetings, *Zion's Herald* 1, no. 24 (1823): 94. The *Zion's Herald* (1823–8) was the first weekly American Methodist publication. It became part of the *Christian Advocate* (1826–1973) in 1828.
9. As the American Methodist community moved from sect to mainline denomination by the mid-nineteenth century, their behavior became calmer and more composed. Sectarian movements like Adventism retained more unconventional religious behavior, remaining outside of the mainline.
10. Malcolm Bull and Keith Lockhart, *Seeking a Sanctuary: Seventh-day Adventism and the American Dream*, 2nd ed. (Bloomington: Indiana University Press, 2007), 5. Similar declines can be noted in communities like the Shakers, Rappites, and Owenites.
11. Susan Williams, *Food in the United States, 1820s–1890* (Westport, CT: Greenwood Press, 2006), 207.
12. Bull and Lockhart, *Seeking a Sanctuary*, 90.
13. "History of Fashion: 1840–1900," Victoria and Albert Museum, accessed July 11, 2019, http://www.vam.ac.uk/content/articles/h/history-of-fashion-1840-1900/.
14. Nicole Tonkovich, *Domesticity with a Difference: The Nonfiction of Catherine Beecher, Sarah J. Hale, Fanny Fern and Margaret Fuller* (Jackson: University of Mississippi Press, 1997), 72.
15. Patricia A. Cunningham, *Reforming Women's Fashion, 1850–1920* (Kent, OH: Kent State University Press, 2003), 79.
16. Helene E. Roberts, "The Exquisite Slave: The Role of Clothes in the Making of the Victorian Woman," *Signs* 2, no. 3 (1977): 561.
17. Roberts, "The Exquisite Slave," 561.
18. J. L. Comstock, *Outlines of Physiology, Both Comparative and Human; in Which Are Described the Mechanical, Animal, Vital, and Sensorial Organs and Functions; Also, the Application of These Principles to Muscular Exercise, and Female Fashions and Deformities* (New York: Pratt, Woodford, and Co., 1848), 311.

19. Ellen G. White, *Christian Temperance and Bible Hygiene* (Battle Creek, MI: Good Health Publishing, 1890), 87.
20. White, 87.
21. White, 87.
22. White, 87.
23. Ellen G. White, *Child Guidance* (Washington, DC: Review and Herald Publishing Association, 1954), 422.
24. Ronald L. Numbers, *Prophetess of Health: A Study of Ellen G. White*, 3rd ed. (Grand Rapids, MI: Wm. B. Eerdmans Publishing, 2008), 457.
25. Ann Douglas, *The Feminization of American Culture* (New York: Doubleday, 1977), 7.
26. This is not to ignore working-class American women, who were held to general standards of normative fashion, but who often were not able to afford the extravagant clothing of the middle and upper classes—even though some of them helped to produce it.
27. This concept of female moral superiority was not new in nineteenth-century America. Around the time of the American Revolution, "as mother, teacher, and enforcer of virtue in courtship and marriage, woman became . . . the ideal and principal fount of Republican values in everyday life," having a significant role to play in the early American "process of Republicanization." Leslie J. Lindenauer, *Piety and Power: Gender and Religious Culture in the American Colonies, 1630–1700* (New York: Routledge, 2001), xiv.
28. *The Dress Reform* (Battle Creek, MI: Seventh-day Adventist Publishing Association, 1868).
29. Ellen G. White, "Perilous Times," in *Testimonies for the Church*, vol. 1, 4th ed. (Oakland, CA: Pacific Press, 1948), 270.
30. White, *Child Guidance*, 432.
31. White, 432–33.
32. White, 433.
33. Ellen G. White, "Wives of Ministers," in *Testimonies for the Church*, 136.
34. White, *Christian Temperance and Bible Hygiene*, 95.
35. White, 94.
36. White, 94.
37. Ellen G. White, *The Acts of the Apostles* (Mountain View, CA: Pacific Press Publishing Association, 1911), 523.
38. White, 95.
39. Ellen G. White, *Counsels for the Church* (Nampa, ID: Pacific Press Publishing Association, 1991), 34.

40. Kristi Upson-Saia, *Early Christian Dress: Gender, Virtue, and Authority* (New York: Routledge, 2011), 3.
41. Ellen G. White, *Messages to Young People* (Hagerstown, MD: Review and Herald Publishing Association, 1930), 352.
42. White, 352.
43. Ellen G. White, *Manuscript Releases*, vol. 5 (Silver Spring, MD: Ellen G. White Estate, 1990), 405.
44. White and Kellogg parted ways when Kellogg was disfellowshipped from the Adventist church in 1907 after a disagreement with White, but he remained at the Battle Creek Sanitarium through to the end of his career in the 1940s.
45. Ellen G. White, "The Health Reform," in *Testimonies for the Church*, 489.
46. "Summary of Statistics of Conferences and Missions for the Year Ending December 31, 1899," *General Conference Bulletin*, no. 3 (1899–1900): 119.
47. Mary Butler, Frances Thornton, and Garth Stoltz, *The Battle Creek Idea: Dr. John Harvey Kellogg and the Battle Creek Sanitarium* (Battle Creek, MI: Heritage Publications, 1994), 49. Battle Creek was only one of many sanitariums—so-called because of their innovative, sanitary approach to medicine—founded by Adventists. By 1878, a new health center was also built near San Francisco, California, with a half dozen others in the United States and worldwide by 1900 (Numbers, *Prophetess of Health*, 186).
48. Frances M. Steel, "Health and Beauty in Dress," in *Medical Missionary and Gospel of Health*, ed. John Harvey Kellogg (Battle Creek, MI: International Medical Missionary and Benevolent Association, 1901), 111.
49. White, "Reform in Dress," in *Testimonies for the Church*, 524.
50. White, *Child Guidance*, 413.
51. White, 429.
52. White, *Christian Temperance and Bible Hygiene*, 94.
53. Francis B. Cogan, *All-American Girl: The Ideal of Real Womanhood in Mid-Nineteenth-Century America* (Athens: University of Georgia Press, 1989), 30.
54. Anne Braude, *Radical Spirits: Spiritualism and Women's Rights in Nineteenth-Century America* (Boston: Beacon Press, 1989), 157 and 143–4.
55. Bull and Lockhart, *Seeking a Sanctuary*, 16.
56. Bull and Lockhart, 16.

Two

CLOTHING SPIRITUAL REALITY

THE SARTORIAL STYLES OF MARY BAKER EDDY

JEREMY RAPPORT

O NE OF THE most influential new religions in the United States is Christian Science. Founded by Mary Baker Eddy (1821–1910)[1] in 1879 in the context of several burgeoning mental healing and prayer movements, Christian Science took emerging ideas and practices about the self, the divine, and the relationship between the two to logical extremes in pursuit of what Eddy considered to be the single most important truth in the world: the only reality is God. By the time Eddy died in 1910, Christian Science had become the largest and most widespread new religion of the era, expanding from its origins in New Hampshire and Boston to a presence in the entire United States as well as several communities outside of North America. Eddy helped to found a newspaper—the *Christian Science Monitor*—and a seminary—the Massachusetts Metaphysical College—and trained many other Christian Science practitioners who helped to spread Christian Science and found other new religions, contributing in the long run to numerous movements associated with the modern world of alternative spirituality and the New Age movement. In addition, the textbook of the movement that Eddy wrote in an intense period of research and writing after her own personal religious experience with injury and healing, *Science and Health with Key to the Scriptures*, had become one of the best-known American alternative scriptures, providing the Christian Science movement with a textual authority that would shape the regular worship of the movement and serving as a ritual object facilitating healing and divine insight to thousands of converts and curious readers.

According to Eddy, the material world is ultimately unreal. Reality is God, the one absolutely true and good source of all that ever was, is, or will be. Understanding and living by this assertion is at the heart of the lived reality of Christian Science. The best-known facet of this central Christian Science claim is healing. Christian Science teaches that if you understand this true nature of God, reality, and the human relationship with God and reality, then you can be healed of any physical or mental ailment. Healing was a first step for Christian Science practitioners in reorienting their understanding of the human-divine relationship. Thus, these practitioners understood a specific type of material condition, in this case physical health, to indicate and reflect a spiritual reality, in this case a proper relationship with God. After all, if God was indeed all good and the only ultimate reality, then it could not be possible for humans in their true state to be ill or injured.

However, physical healing was not the only way that Eddy revealed her assumptions about the human-divine relationship. Eddy's worldview grew and adapted to her emerging religious life in many ways, and one of the most apparent, yet often overlooked, was how Eddy dressed. In this chapter, I examine how Eddy's clothing style changed to reflect her changing life position and worldview. Using publicly available pictures and descriptions of Eddy, as well archival material, I will demonstrate how Eddy's clothing choices and physical appearance reflected both her evolving understandings of the relationship between the material and spiritual worlds and her own changing position in those worlds. In addition, Eddy's practices around clothing and appearance influenced the dress and appearance of at least some Christian Science practitioners, as we will see later in this chapter.

Eddy always dressed "appropriately," that is, in a manner thought to befit a woman in her position, place, and time. Yet pictures and descriptions of Eddy over the years of the discovery and growth of Christian Science reveal that her clothing choices also reflected a sort of personal and spiritual growth process in which Eddy's clothes communicated subtler aspects of her spiritual claims. In effect, Eddy's clothing shows one important way she practiced the tenets of Christian Science. By paying attention to Eddy's sartorial choices, I show both how Eddy herself grew as a Christian Science practitioner and how paying attention to clothing can help to show how the members of one of the most influential American alternative religions understood critical aspects of the embodiment and enactment of their new religious principles. Eddy's example, in turn, helps show how even the most "spiritually" focused of American religious communities dealt with the reality of the material world.

BASIC CHRISTIAN SCIENCE THEOLOGY

One needs to understand some of Eddy's central Christian Science theological claims to clearly see the importance of her clothing choices. Eddy's attire and appearance changed noticeably over the period during which she developed the Christian Science movement. This reflected her changing socioeconomic status, but it also reflected her changing understanding of God and God's role in the material world. Therefore, one must understand how Christian Science portrays the nature of God, the nature of the world and of humans, and the relationship between God and humans in order to see how Eddy's material condition reflected parallel changes in her religious thought. Much could be said about how Eddy got to the point of the "Great Discovery," her name for the series of events that led her to her teachings on the nature of God and the human relationship with God. Yet here it is most critical to grasp the basic theology of Christian Science and how that theology understands the relationship between material and spiritual realms; only then will we benefit from further examination of Eddy's clothing and appearance.

Christian Science has a sort of inexorable theological logic to it that centers on three key points. It begins from the premise that God is the only reality in existence: an immutable, absolute truth from which all other things spring. To put it in Eddy's words, "God is love. Can we ask Him to be more? God is intelligence. Can we inform the infinite Mind of anything He does not already comprehend? Do we expect to change perfection? . . . Asking God to *be* God is a vain repetition. God is 'the same yesterday, and to-day, and forever.'" For Eddy, God knows all and sees all, and so humans cannot inform the deity of anything: "Shall we ask the divine Principle of all goodness to do His own work? His work is done, and we have only avail ourselves of God's rule in order to receive His blessing, which enables us to work out our own salvation." According to Eddy, we cannot ask God to change anything because God's work is already done. The human task, then, is to recognize and make use of the knowledge that God already is present. We must learn to see God in everything all around us: "The Divine Being must be reflected by man, else man is not the image and likeness of the patient, tender, and true, the One 'altogether lovely.'"[2] Eddy thus taught that this divine reflection will play out in an individual's actual, physical existence if the individual understands the nature of reality properly and then acts accordingly.

The second important point is Eddy's understanding of the nature of the world and the nature of humans. Eddy describes this facet of Christian Science theology in chapter 15 of *Science and Health*, "Genesis." This chapter is an exegesis on the biblical book of Genesis, in which Eddy argues that, "Spiritually followed, the book of Genesis is the history of the untrue image of God, named a sinful mortal. This deflection of being, rightly viewed, serves to suggest the proper reflection of God and the actuality of man, as given in the first chapter of Genesis."[3] Eddy therefore argued that by properly interpreting the first chapter of Genesis, humans can understand the reality of the world, our nature, and our place in the world. The story of creation as told in the book of Genesis is the story of spiritual reality. For example, beginning with Genesis 1:1—"In the beginning God created the heaven and the earth"—Eddy argues the passage signifies that the universe has "but one creator and one creation . . . [which] consists of the unfolding of spiritual ideas and their identities."[4] Continuing with Genesis 1:2—"And the earth was without form, and void; and darkness was upon the face of the deep. And the spirit of God moved upon the face of the waters"—Eddy writes that this "divine Principle and idea constitute spiritual harmony, heaven and eternity. In the universe of Truth, matter is unknown." In other words, the so-called real world is ultimately a spiritual world in which matter does not exist. For Eddy, all existence *is* this perfect spiritual and divine existence.

Finally, the relationship between God and humans is critical for the Christian Science practitioner to understand and properly enact. Because God is the only reality, ultimately all things have their existence in relationship with God. As Eddy puts it, "God, the divine Principle of man, and man in God's likeness are inseparable, harmonious, and eternal."[5] But God and humans are not the same either; rather, "God and man coexist and are eternal. God is the parent Mind, and man is God's spiritual offspring."[6] Eddy indicates that the problem is that humans have fallen into a delusion of the reality of the material world: "Material personality is not realism; it is not the reflection or likeness of Spirit, the perfect God."[7] In sum, an absolute reality that is all spiritual, love, and perfection is the ultimate reality of all creation, and when humans and the material are in a harmonious relationship with the divine reality, then the illusions of the material world disappear and a perfected existence becomes possible for humans.

Of course, Eddy's theology developed over time, as she thought about and wrote about her views and experiences of God, healing, and religious life. *Science and Health* was a long-term project, a new American scripture written and revised over many years as Eddy developed and then reencountered her ideas and practices. Just as reading a first edition of *Science and Health* reveals a different religious system from what is found in a later edition, seeing Eddy's dress and appearance in her pre- and early Christian Science periods reveals a very different person from the one who appears in later pictures, when *Science and Health* was more or less complete and when Eddy had become one the most important religious leaders in the early twentieth-century United States. In fact, Eddy's clothing and physical appearance, as well as her attitudes about the clothing and appearance of others, can serve as a proxy for her developing theological system, showing how practicing Christian Science changed the founder's life.

CLOTHING AS UNIFORM

Clothing and other types of adornment serve many purposes, from bodily protection and the maintenance of modesty to signaling status and affiliation. Clothing and adornment may do this work in formal ways, guided by the practical and symbolic needs of the organizations with which the wearer is affiliated, or, critically for the purposes of this chapter, less formal, less institutional ways, as when an individual's clothing may be read to indicate socioeconomic status. Mary Baker Eddy's clothing often acted as a type of uniform that indicated not only her social status, but also her theological assumptions; those assumptions shaped who Eddy became over the course of her life.

Many scholars have noticed the role of clothing in asserting religious identities and roles.[8] Perhaps the best-known examples in the United States are the clothing of the Catholic clergy and Catholic monastics, particularly female monastics. The sartorial style of American Catholic priests owes its distinctive look to assimilation processes over the course of the nineteenth century. As a minority religion in the century's early decades, and in states where the open expression of Catholic identity could be personally dangerous or even illegal, Catholic clerical costume was not standard for most of the first half of the nineteenth century. However, with the influx of Catholic immigrants in the second half of the nineteenth century, Catholic priests standardized their dress, largely under the direction of diocesan officials concerned with ordering a growing American Catholic Church. Priests asserted their own religious authority and signaled their submission to the church hierarchy by their manner of dress.[9] At the same time, by adopting a more standard priestly garb, clergymen were also marking a particular type of clothing as signaling a spiritual state. The priest's clothes, and in particular the clergyman's collar, became symbols of service to higher powers as well as being markers of a respected and admired profession.

A similar process occurred with Catholic nuns, with some important modifications. Over the course of the nineteenth century, as American Catholic populations grew, habits became codified and more symbolically important, with the habit itself eventually developing into a sign of the church's authority.[10] But women were subject to different sorts of clothing strictures than men were, and concern about how clothing reflected women's purity and modesty was of particular importance for Catholic nuns. As historian Sally Dwyer-McNulty notes, the work of sisters wearing standardized habits in institutions such as schools and hospitals helped to solidify the reputations of nuns and to tie the habit to the image of the nun. The habit symbolized not only their purity and their modesty, but also their hard work and their service to others. As such, people came to understand the habit, with its outer orderliness and its desexualization of its wearer, as an outer mark of a perfected and pure inner state.[11]

These religious modes of dress spoke to observers in multiple ways. Catholic dress patterns made clear the ways in which religious identities and religious messages could be communicated with clothing. They also presaged how Americans in general would come think of the symbolism and function of clothing in the late nineteenth and early twentieth centuries. As Jenna Weissman Joselit documents of the period from the 1890s to the 1930s, clothing transformed from homemade to ready-made, and in the process the meanings the general public associated with clothing also began to shift. In some ways, the ready-made clothing revolution transformed public sartorial practices, such that they more closely resembled the symbolism of clergy dress. Being able to purchase fashionable clothing made it possible for consumers to make choices about the messages their clothing sent. According to Joselit, this meant that "what one wore was a public construct, bound up with an enduring moral order."[12] Clothing had become part of an array of social messages about one's identity and inner state. In other words, clothing reflected conceptions of social order and social reality that both created and reinforced social norms.

In effect, then, we should read Eddy's clothing as a type of signaling system about who she understood herself to be and how she understood her place in the world, and in that sense, how Eddy dressed is just as revelatory about how the Christian Science theology prompted action in the world as are the much better-known Christian Science healing rituals. Eddy dressed not only to tell her followers who she was, but also to tell them *who they could be*, provided they could learn and adhere to Christian Science principles. But, of course, Eddy first had to develop Christian Science for the system to reflect her theological assumptions, and it is clear that, prior to her development of Christian Science, Eddy's clothing and appearance very much reflected a woman of her time and place.

A PORTRAIT OF ILLNESS

Eddy did not begin to develop Christian Science until she was approaching middle age, and her early life was dictated by the social and cultural expectations of women of her time and place. The few surviving pictures of Eddy's pre–Christian Science life, in combination with the even fewer reliable physical descriptions of her, suggest that, prior to her development of Christian Science, she was a conventional woman of her era, dressing and appearing in ways that would be expected given her circumstances. She was born in Bow, New Hampshire, in 1821, into a Calvinist family and brought up in that strict tradition. Eddy was the youngest of six children. Her parents ran a moderately successful farm. Her father,

Mark Baker, was apparently the more committed Calvinist of her parents, and many of the events of Eddy's early life were shaped by Baker's implementation of the patriarchal norms of the family's Calvinist tradition. For example, although his youngest daughter was considered intelligent and had demonstrated interests in poetry and literature as well as in teaching, Mark Baker feared "overeducating" her and so did not support Eddy's pursuit of education and her interests in writing.[13]

Eddy's mother, Abigail Baker (née Ambrose), was apparently less interested in Calvinist structure and had warmer, closer relationships with all her children than did Mark Baker. Historian and Eddy biographer Gillian Gill argues that Abigail Baker provided her daughter with the parental models that would ultimately shape Eddy's views of God as loving and understanding and as both father and mother, male and female.[14] It is not unreasonable to surmise that Eddy's own interest in and pursuit of religious questions may have arisen, at least in part, from the contrast between her parents' religious views and parental styles. In any case, Eddy did join the Congregationalist Trinitarian Church in 1838.[15] She was, by all appearances, doing what was expected of her.

Another important strand of influence from Eddy's early life was the prevailing attitudes and practices surrounding health and illness. The exhibition of poor health and weakness was something of a fashion for young women in antebellum America, and Eddy clearly absorbed that lesson.[16] It was also the case that ill-health and both physical and mental suffering had developed theological meaning among many nineteenth-century American Protestants. God's servants might be chosen to suffer, fulfilling their roles in God's kingdom by demonstrating to others the power of both suffering and healing. The emphasis on suffering played a role in helping nineteenth-century Americans, particularly women, create meaningful social identities by granting them at least some control over their lives.

Frailty and poor health allowed women in a Calvinist patriarchy some degree of agency in the sense of allowing them some control over how and when they interacted with the people around them and their environments. A sick person could not be expected to keep up social engagements, and if that person happened to be a woman who had little say in the nature and timing of those social engagements, then illness served to grant the suffering woman a degree of decision-making power she might not otherwise have. Certainly, many early biographers of Eddy claimed that she suffered from hysteria as child and young adult.[17] Nineteenth-century hysteria is a problematic condition from a historical perspective, and Gill does excellent work describing why this was particularly true in the case of Eddy's diagnosis.[18] But Eddy herself described other types of health problems, including digestive trouble that she attempted to treat by following a Graham diet.[19] These constant physical complaints and the accompanying need for isolation would continue throughout Eddy's young adulthood, shaping how she appeared and dressed, and strongly suggesting that, prior to her discovery of Christian Science, Eddy tried to control her life in the conventional ways available to nineteenth-century American women: by using the isolation that illness made available to her in order to avoid undesired social interactions.

Eddy married George Glover on December 10, 1843, and the couple moved to South Carolina, where Glover was working as a builder. Unfortunately, their married life was short. Glover died in late June 1844 after a brief illness, leaving Eddy a poverty-stricken, pregnant widow. The first known picture of Mary Baker Eddy, which graces the cover of Gillian Gill's biography of Eddy, was probably taken when she was a widow in her late twenties. It shows a woman who was likely depressed and in a terrible social situation. As Gill makes clear in her biography, Eddy was considered physically attractive for her time.[20] Beauty is, of course, subjective, yet it is hard to miss what the thin, almost gaunt, face, the flat, unsmiling expression, and all-black clothing suggest about the subject of the picture. Eddy was a widow in poor health, under great stress, with an infant son. Physically attractive or not, this picture of Eddy shows a woman subject to forces beyond her control, and her clothing helps to explain why that is the case. After George Glover died, Eddy was forced to return to her family in New Hampshire. A friend of her husband's helped Eddy make the journey home, but not before he and a group of her husband's friends had also raised the funds to buy Eddy proper mourning clothes.[21] Her widow's attire was literally procured for her by her late husband's male friends, suggesting the extent to which Eddy was subject to the patriarchal norms of the Calvinist society in which she grew up and the social forces well beyond her control during this period of her life.

But this early picture also suggests how Eddy thought about who she should be in her time and place. She was supposed to look unhappy; and given the social meaning of illness and suffering in nineteenth-century

America, one could even argue that she was supposed to look ill. This early picture of Eddy, then, shows a woman presenting herself according to the expectations of her culture, subject to male authority and appearing in mourning dress even when that male authority was absent. Eddy would suffer through many more years of poor physical and mental health, failed marriage, separation from her son, and poverty before her life began to turn around; and once again, her clothing and physical appearance suggest how she was experiencing and dealing with her situation. Most significantly, Eddy's clothing and appearance slowly began to reflect her chosen inner reality, rather than the social realties to which she found herself subject in the early years of her life.

A PORTRAIT OF HEALTH

As she approached middle age, Eddy remained in difficult personal circumstances. Most significantly for the development of Christian Science, she continued to suffer from intractable physical problems, including various digestive problems and an issue she referred to as a spinal ailment. But it was also in this period of her life that she finally began to solve her physical problems. Eddy had tried numerous therapies over the years, including diets, homeopathy, hydropathy, and conventional medicine, but her first real success at feeling better occurred around 1862 when she became a patient of a former clockmaker named Phineas P. Quimby. A mental healer from Portland, Maine, Quimby had developed a therapeutic system after experimenting with hypnosis for several years. In essence, Quimby taught that physical problems were the result of the patient's own thoughts, and especially their own belief that they were ill. Healing, for Quimby, centered around getting the patient to change their mind about their illness. Possibly at the urging of her second husband, Daniel Patterson, an itinerant dentist, Eddy consulted Quimby. Not only did she succeed at feeling better under Quimby's treatment, but she became a major admirer of Quimby and his work, even writing odes to him.

Pictures of Eddy from this time show a very different person than the unhappy, ill widow. In an 1864 picture, taken after Eddy had been working with Quimby for a couple of years, she is dressed in a plaid patterned dress with a stiff, white collar and a large, oval collar pin. She was in her

FIGURE 2.1 Mary Baker Eddy in 1864, after she had been a patient of Phineas Quimby's for about two years. Image courtesy of Wikimedia Commons/Creative Commons.

early forties then yet appears no older than she did in her first known picture. With a slightly plumper face and fuller hair, her appearance suggests good health. Eddy's healing work with Quimby was showing benefits, as her less formal style of dress and overall healthier appearance suggest. Influenced by Quimby's teachings, Eddy was gaining a degree of control over her life that she had not had before, so it is perhaps not surprising that when Quimby died in 1866 she was despondent, and worried that the one successful method of treatment she had ever found for her physical ailments was now gone.

It is in that context that the subsequent events of Eddy's life should be understood. In February 1866, Eddy slipped on some ice and hurt herself. While it is unclear how severe her injuries were, she certainly believed they were severe, even fearing that the injuries may have the potential to be fatal. As she convalesced, she read her Bible and prayed. According to her, after reading accounts of Jesus's healing work, she realized the entirely spiritual nature of God and of all reality, and in that realization, she was able to heal herself of her injuries. Christian Scientists now know that series of events as the "Great Discovery."

Eddy described this discovery in *Retrospection and Introspection*, her "spiritual autobiography":

> It was in Massachusetts, in 1866 . . . that I discovered the Science of divine metaphysical healing which I afterwards named Christian Science. The discovery came to pass this way. During twenty years prior to my discovery I had been trying to trace all physical effects to a mental cause; and in the latter part of 1866 I gained the scientific certainty that all causation was Mind, and every effect a mental phenomenon. My immediate recovery from the effects of an injury caused by an accident, an injury that neither medicine nor surgery could reach, was the falling apple that led me to the discovery how to be well myself, and how to make others so. Even to the homeopathic physician who attended me, and rejoiced in my recovery, I could not explain the *modus* of my relief. I could only assure him that the divine spirit had wrought the miracle—a miracle which later I found to be in perfect scientific accord with divine law. I then withdrew from society about three years—to ponder my mission, to search the Scriptures, to find the Science of Mind that should take all things of God and show them to the creature, and reveal the great curative Principle—deity.[22]

Eddy clearly understood the Great Discovery as a watershed moment. Moreover, these events prompted her to begin an extensive research and Bible-study project that would eventually result in the publication of Christian Science's great theological work, *Science and Health with Key to the Scriptures*. Eddy's life was changed, and we can see this not only in her own claims about physical healing, but in descriptions and pictures of her dress and personal appearance in photographs from the time.

Some accounts provide evidence that Eddy's attitude and self-presentation had become more confident. In a discussion of Eddy's living situation during this period, Gill writes that Eddy tended to present herself "as a woman above her circumstances, acting as if she were doing her hosts a favor by living with them. In many ways, [Eddy] was a snob, but it was this snobbery in part that gave her the courage to resist being absorbed forever into the humble social strata where she found herself in midlife."[23] George Clark, the son of the owners of a boardinghouse in Lynn, Massachusetts, where Eddy stayed during this period, described Eddy, at this point over fifty years old, as "beautiful, with the complexion of a young girl, big, brilliant, deep blue eyes, and a shower of brown curls. She habitually dressed in black, with some accent of violet and pale rose."[24]

In a photograph taken around 1870, Eddy again appears to have gained weight. She is dressed neatly, in a dark dress open at the neck, a large, white lace collar, a choker necklace, and another chain coming down the front of her dress. Her pose is relaxed and open. Whether Eddy was a "snob" or not, this updated appearance and attitude certainly suggests an emerging self-confidence that speaks to Eddy's new sense of purpose and understanding of the divine. By this time, she was fully engaged with the writing of *Science and Health*, the first edition of which would be published in 1875. She had been living by the religious tenets prompted by the Great Discovery for about four years—tenets that would insist on an already present God whose reality needed to be reflected by humans. Eddy had a religious mission, one that she believed had changed her, and that she believed could do the same for other people. We know this both because of the amazing growth and success of Christian Science in the coming years, but also because Eddy's own life was clearly materially different after she began to develop Christian Science.

FIGURE 2.2 Mary Baker Eddy around 1870, while she was in the process of writing *Science and Health*. Image courtesy of Wikimedia Commons/Creative Commons.

A PORTRAIT OF PROSPERITY

By the last stage of her life, Eddy appeared to be a very different person than the depressed, disempowered, perennially ill widow who appears in her first known picture. Clearly, her socioeconomic status had changed radically, and, for two critical reasons, we should not discount how that factored into the significance of Eddy's appearance. First, people with more economic resources and social standing can present themselves differently from those without such resources. That is a simple explanation for what we see in pictures and read in descriptions from the later stages of Eddy's life. But that simple explanation also points to the second critical reason we need to pay attention to Eddy's much improved socioeconomic status: that status was the result of Eddy's work creating Christian Science. Eddy could project the public appearance of a wealthy widow because the success of Christian Science had, in fact, made her a wealthy widow. In other words, because of Christian Science, Eddy's material reality reflected her desired self-presentation.

By this phase of her life, Christian Science had grown enough to allow Eddy a degree of financial freedom she had never experienced. Moreover, the organization had developed to a point that her constant, hands-on leadership was no longer necessary. Eddy wanted to retire to a place where she could focus on both her writing—she continued to revise *Science and Health* until the end of her life—and her religious life. After a protracted search for the best location, she settled on a small farm called Pleasant View, in Concord, New Hampshire, in 1892. This was a critical phase in Eddy's life and the development of Christian Science because it shows us how Eddy chose to construct her physical environment and personal dress once she had the means to control that environment and choose clothing she preferred. As Gill describes it, "As far as she allowed herself to be defined by her physical environment, Mrs. Eddy was in her element at Pleasant View, and she was frank in acknowledging the pleasure and comfort the place gave her."[25] Concord, with its New Hampshire familiarity, and its residents' relative lack of close experience with Christian Science, along with Eddy's financial and life station security, allowed her to, as Gill puts it, live a life of relative anonymity and normalcy while focusing on the writing and thinking she most wanted to do at this phase of her life.[26]

But the Pleasant View years also offer another critical, albeit more prosaic, piece of this puzzle. By this time, Eddy's fame and the prominence and importance of Christian Science had become clear to many people, including those who worked for Eddy at Pleasant View, and many of those people kept diaries and journals and were eager to share their memories with later Christian Scientists and historians documenting Eddy's life and the development of Christian Science. The details contained in a memoir dictated by a woman who cooked and worked in the household that Eddy established at Pleasant View are particularly insightful. Minnie Bell Weygandt was a young Christian Scientist from Fairfield, Iowa, who had moved to Boston and worked for the family of Edward P. Bates, a prominent Boston Christian Scientist. When Eddy found herself in need of help in the kitchen at Pleasant View, Bates recommend Weygandt, and she started working at Pleasant View in 1894.[27] Weygandt has much to say about the household and how Eddy ran it, and the memoir is a rich source for understanding the material elements of Eddy's life during this period, including her clothing preferences and practices.

Weygandt makes clear from the first pages of her memoir that Eddy was concerned both with her own appearance and the appearance of members of her household, especially as regards clothing. Eddy had very specific orders for the types and styles of clothing she wore as well such issues as the frequency with which laundry was to be done. Eddy also had expectations about how her household staff dressed. Minnie Weygandt described how she was advised to dress to meet Mary Baker Eddy: "Don't put on shirtwaists [a simple, button-down blouse]. They look like rags." Instead, she was told to wear a wool dress, despite the summer heat.[28] As a result, before beginning her job, Minnie's sister Mary stayed up all night making a new skirt for Minnie to wear when she met Eddy. Weygandt also tells a revealing anecdote about Eddy's coachman, August Mann. According to Weygandt, Eddy particularly liked how Mann looked: "He always sat so erect and wore his silk hat to perfection. This pleased Mrs. Eddy ... He was as neat as wax and never failed to look spick and span. Amanda [Mann's wife] said she shaved the back of his neck everyday before he took Mrs. Eddy driving."[29]

Describing Eddy's attitude about clothing and appearance, Weygandt wrote, "I do not think she ever had any patience with careless slipshod dress in anyone, and I am sure she expected that Christian Scientists would always look prepossessing and attractive."[30] The energy and precision Eddy put into the dress and grooming of those around her is revealing. Those attitudes and practices helped Eddy to create an environment in which she could focus on being the intellectual and spiritual leader of the movement she had created. This was an environment that reflected how Eddy understood the outcomes of properly understood and practiced Christian Science, which sought to project a material reality that would look neat, clean, orderly, and prosperous. The grooming and dress both of herself and those around her reflected and created the perfected world that Eddy taught would be the result of correctly understanding God, humans, and the nature of reality.

Eddy clearly cared a great deal about appearances, both personal and environmental, and she also tied these preferences and practices to Christian Science in important ways. According to Weygandt, "Christian Scientists could learn a wonderful lesson from Mrs. Eddy on order and cleanliness. She had a place for everything and everything must be in its exact place, not even a sixteenth of an inch out of its right position."[31] These precise expectations extended to clothing and laundry. Weygandt described laundry duties for the household as extensive, requiring careful work and planning and eventually the aid of people from outside the household. Eddy gave precise directions on what to wash and how, and she expected her clothing to always look clean and neat. Weygandt says, "I remember that Mrs. Eddy invariably wore black lisle stockings which Mary [Weygandt's sister, who also worked at Pleasant View] washed and stretched over a board and then ironed so that they looked like new."[32] Lisle is a type of fine, smooth cotton fabric that was used for stockings and hosiery, and Eddy's insistence on wearing it and always keeping it neat and clean not only shows her adherence to upper-class Victorian dress norms; it also suggests that Eddy's clothing preferences reflected the ideal physical states that Christian Science taught were possible.

Eddy had favorite outfits, fabrics, and colors, including lavender, white, pink, black, and gray. She preferred close, well-fitting clothes, and much of her clothing was made for her by the women in her household. Apparel that was not custom-made, such as hats, gloves, and veils, was acquired by staff members in Boston, or if Eddy's preferred style was not available there, they would send to Paris for a piece of which Eddy would approve.[33] These clothing preferences are clear in later pictorial representations of

FIGURE 2.3 Mary Baker Eddy in 1892, after Christian Science had become a successful religious movement. Image courtesy of Wikimedia Commons/Creative Commons.

Eddy from the late nineteenth and early twentieth centuries, which show a woman whose clothing is elaborate and decorative, including items such as a lustrous, dark dress with elaborate embroidery, a high neck, and a collar pin in the shape of a cross with gems overlaid on it. Approaching the end of her life and still dealing with the myriad challenges of leading a burgeoning and controversial religious movement, Eddy chose clothing that nonetheless showed a woman sure of herself and sure of the public image she wished to present. We now see Eddy as a Christian Scientist in full possession of the knowledge of the true order of reality and who, with her neat, polished, high-status clothing dressed as a person who manifested the perfection of the one true God. Eddy's Christian Science helped her to transcend the limitations and conventions of the material world and present herself in a way appropriate to the perfected states her Christian Science taught was possible.

※

Mary Baker Eddy's appearance and clothing choices from these three periods of her life—her early widowhood through to the emergence of Christian Science and eventually to the fruits of a fully developed religious system—show how this vitally important religious leader of the late nineteenth and early twentieth centuries represented herself, and by extension her religious system, to the public. Of course, much can be said about how Eddy's overall success as a religious leader might have contributed to her changing sartorial styles. But we miss a critical aspect of the developing Christian Science system if we fail to see how Eddy dealt with the material world through her clothing choices. Eddy's clothing communicated many things to those around her, but perhaps most critically they communicated how she was transformed by her religious system. Importantly, Eddy's clothing choices also help to demonstrate how her religious system made tangible the unarguable changes in the life of its founder. By paying attention to these sorts of sartorial shifts among religious leaders and practitioners, we can see in greater detail and with more authority both how religion changes people and how religion functions in individual lives. In effect, no longer must we be concerned with whether religious claims such as healing through prayer are literally true. We can instead pay attention to material phenomena like clothing to see the impact of religion on individuals' verifiable lives. That knowledge can go a long way toward better understanding both what religion is and what it does in the real world.

NOTES

1. Although her name changed several times over the course of her life, reflecting her marital status, for the sake of clarity I will use her final name, Mary Baker Eddy, throughout this chapter.
2. Mary Baker Eddy, *Science and Health with Key to the Scriptures* (Boston: Christian Science Board of Directors, 2006), 2–3. All quotes in this paragraph come from this passage.
3. Eddy, *Science and Health*, 502.

4. Eddy, 502–3. While *Science and Health* does not specify which version of the Bible is being quoted, Eddy read and used the King James Version.
5. Eddy, 336.
6. Eddy, 336.
7. Eddy, 337.
8. For examples, see Linda B. Arthur, ed., *Religion, Dress, and the Body*. (Oxford: Bloomsbury Press, 1999); Sally Dwyer-McNulty, *Common Threads: A Cultural History of Clothing in American Catholicism*. (Chapel Hill: University of North Carolina Press, 2014); Colleen McDannell, *Material Christianity: Religion and Popular Culture in America*. (New Haven, CT: Yale University Press, 1995), especially chapter seven, "Mormon Garments: Sacred Clothing and the Body."
9. Dwyer-McNulty, *Common Threads*, 16–54.
10. Dwyer-McNulty, 65.
11. Dwyer-McNulty, 78.
12. Jenna Weissman Joselit, *A Perfect Fit: Clothes, Character, and the Promise of America* (New York: Henry Holt and Company, 2001), 2.
13. Gillian Gill, *Mary Baker Eddy* (Reading, MA: Perseus Books, 1998), 34–7.
14. Gill, 26.
15. Paul Ivey, "Christian Science," in *Encyclopedia of Religion in America* (Washington, DC: CQ Press, 2010), 441.
16. As Gillian Gill explains in a lengthy endnote describing some of the larger context for Eddy's own physical problems, many biographies of prominent nineteenth-century women, including Clara Barton, Catherine Beecher, Harriet Beecher Stowe, and Florence Nightingale, among others, describe physical suffering, illness, and invalidism. See Gill, *Mary Baker Eddy*, 611n2.
17. A useful examination and discussion of the hysteria claims made about Eddy may be found in Gill, 38–48.
18. Gill, 38–48.
19. Gill, 47.
20. Gill discusses Mary Baker Eddy's supposed physical beauty in several places in her biography, especially on pages 52 and 172–73.
21. Gill, 63.
22. Mary Baker Eddy, *Retrospection and Introspection* (Boston: First Church of Christ, Scientist, 1891); Gill, *Mary Baker Eddy*, 24–25.
23. Gill, *Mary Baker Eddy*, 172. The photographs referred to here may be found in the glossy plates in the same book.
24. Gill, 173.
25. Gill, 387.

26. Gill, 387–88.
27. Minnie Bell Weygandt, "Reminiscences of Miss Minnie Bell Weygandt and of Miss Mary Ellen Weygandt," archival material from the Mary Baker Eddy Library, 1–10.
28. Weygandt, 10.
29. Weygandt, 57.
30. Weygandt, 46.
31. Weygandt, 21.
32. Weygandt, 18.
33. Weygandt, 45–68.

Three

FAITH, FASHION, AND FILM IN THE JAZZ AGE

CATHOLIC VESTMENTS ENCOUNTER THE ROARING 1920S

ADRIENNE NOCK AMBROSE

For nearly a week in 1926, Chicagoans of all faiths assembled daily to watch parades of Catholic leaders in full ecclesiastical regalia. Massive gatherings of fully vested clergy and their attendants were held at the city's largest and best-known venues. Curious Chicagoans browsed elaborate displays of the latest clerical fashions at what was then known as Municipal Pier. Not since Chicago had hosted the World's Fair in 1893, with its awe-inspiring Ferris wheel, had an occasion in the city attracted such attention. Now, just a generation after that extravaganza, an elaborate religious spectacle was drawing the masses. Chicago was the first American city to host an International Eucharistic Congress, and for Catholic leaders, the event presented a golden opportunity to display their faith to a society that seemed to crave it.

The twenty-eighth in a succession of gatherings that had begun in France in 1881, Chicago's Eucharistic Congress was a celebration of the central Catholic sacrament for which it was named. From the Greek word for "thanksgiving," Eucharist is an ancient term for the commemoration of the Last Supper, the final meal presided over by Jesus before his arrest and crucifixion. Although virtually all Christian communities commemorate this biblical event, considerable differences have arisen over the practices and interpretations associated with its celebration. Indeed, at previous Eucharistic Congresses, these differences had sometimes interfered with and even curtailed the public processions of clergy featured during the event.

In 1882, for example, officials in the French city of Avignon prohibited the principal Eucharistic procession from appearing on the city's main streets.[1] In 1904, organizers in Angoulême simply cancelled the procession, citing an infrequently enforced law prohibiting such events. Protestant resistance led to a substantially modified Eucharistic procession during London's 1908 congress. Clergy were forced to wear secular court dress rather than vestments or religious habits, and "all elements of ecclesiastical ceremonial" were to be removed. The result was an eviscerated procession, with its central feature—the Eucharistic host held aloft in a monstrance—forbidden from display.[2]

Most proximate in time to the Chicago event was the Twenty-Fifth Eucharistic Congress, held in Amsterdam in 1924. Although Dutch officials welcomed the event, they forbade religious processions on public streets. Catholic processions had a contentious history in the Netherlands, and there were laws on the books against public religious rituals.[3] The restrictive attitude seen in these previous host cities, however, was completely absent in Chicago. According to contemporary accounts, city officials cooperated fully during the five-day, city-wide celebration. One witness, an editor for the Protestant weekly the *Christian Century*, marveled at the collective effort the congress required. He admiringly described how an entire city of nearly three million "turned its streets, its hotels, its transportation, its churches, its homes, its business houses, its city administration, its stadium, its press, into a vast system of hospitality."[4]

It's not surprising that Chicago was such a hospitable location for the congress. The rapidly growing city had a large Catholic population, and Catholic politicians had become more prominent and influential in Chicago affairs.[5] Although immigration had slowed in the 1920s, the decline allowed parishes to adjust to the new demographics after decades of extraordinary growth.[6] Such circumstances aligned well with the aspirations of Chicago's most powerful Catholic leader, Cardinal George Mundelein. Mundelein was a skilled administrator with tendency toward "giantism" and "going first class," who also believed the Catholic Church could be an effective force for "Americanizing" immigrant families. As archbishop and later cardinal, he promoted policies intended to unite Chicago Catholics across ethnic lines.[7] During World War I, for example, he encouraged Catholics of all backgrounds to participate in food drives and fundraising campaigns. The cardinal's success in motivating his flock to pitch in to the war effort made a long-lasting impression on those in power, and the well-placed connections he made during the war came in handy once he turned his attention to the Eucharistic Congress. Existing relationships with city leaders ensured their cooperation with logistical challenges, and members of the mainstream press were equally well-disposed toward the cardinal and "his" congress. Three weeks before opening day, for example, *Time* magazine put the cardinal on its cover.[8] It was rare for the young American newsweekly to feature a religious leader so prominently, and the fact that Mundelein was photographed wearing multiple symbols of his ecclesiastical office made his appearance even more worthy of note. As we will see, the occasion of the Eucharistic Congress frequently prompted the sort of news coverage that was unprecedented for a religious event.

Assessments of the congress's significance have tended to focus on the impressive scale of its pageantry and the effusive reception it received, both of which signaled a new, confident phase for American Catholicism. The event has been described as a "graduation ceremony" for Catholics in the United States, the "phenomenal success" of which "confirmed the breaking out of Catholicism from the sectarian margins to the religious mainstream of American culture."[9] Cultural historian Kate Moran seconded that view, and argued that the church's transnational orientation, expressed so vividly during the congress, was a welcome postwar corrective to the nationalism that had been stoked during World War I. Moran also claimed that the hospitable response to the congress reflected a societal shift toward an "urban pluralist ethos" that rejected bigotry and prejudice in favor of mutual respect and understanding.[10]

It is hard to argue with these careful assessments, but they fall somewhat short in fully conveying the significance of the unique historical moment the congress represented. No other public display of religion in America, either before or after, has rivaled the Twenty-Eighth Eucharistic Congress in scale or reception. How was it that such a blatantly medieval public expression of Catholicism, one centered on a sacrament with a divisive denominational history and exclusionary contemporary practices, received such an enthusiastic reception? Why were objections to an aggressively Roman display of the ecclesiastical hierarchy so muted, and why was the public apparently willing to overlook what Catholic historians have subsequently described as a manifestation of unapologetic triumphalism?[11] As we'll see, a fascination with religious clothing reflected in journalistic accounts of the congress holds some clues. I argue that a burgeoning film industry created a series of "probable intertextual exposures" among contemporary observers, which in turn "may have inflected reception" of the congress.[12] As they gathered eagerly to witness the religious pageantry of the Eucharistic Congress, many spectators brought perceptions shaped by their frequent film attendance. The uniquely enthusiastic reception of the congress cannot be understood, I argue, apart from concurrent developments in film and its coverage in the press.

PUBLICITY FOR THE EUCHARISTIC CONGRESS

In addition to the support of the mainstream press in representing the congress, Mundelein had secured the skills of ambitious publicist Joseph Breen.[13] Breen's efforts resulted in extensive coverage of the congress, not only in Chicago, but across the country as well. Not surprisingly, it was the newspaper of the Chicago archdiocese, the *Catholic New World*, that set the gold standard. The paper issued a special, four-part "Eucharistic Congress Edition" on the eve of the congress's opening. Along with forty pages of copy, it featured thirty-two pages of photogravure reproductions, a process valued for the detailed color images it produced. Almost as impressive were the special sections produced by mainstream daily newspapers like the *Chicago American* and the *Herald-Examiner*. The considerable coverage by the *Chicago Tribune* before, during, and after the congress was later memorialized in a pamphlet sold as a memento.[14] Farther afield, the events of the congress were the subject of front-page headlines in cities including Key West, Florida; Washington, DC; and Elizabeth City, North Carolina.[15]

Virtually all aspects of the congress were covered in the press, but the variety of attire on display received special attention. Journalists loaded their articles with descriptions of the picturesque aspects of the event,

FIGURE 3.1 Members of the Passionist and Redemptorist religious orders march in the Twenty-Eighth Eucharistic Congress's opening day procession. Photo courtesy of the Archdiocese of Chicago's Joseph Cardinal Bernardin Archives and Records Center.

and they seemed to relish their role in educating readers on the intricacies of Catholic clerical culture. Anticipating the event, one writer described the climactic Eucharistic procession in prose typical of this coverage:

> Led by the cross-bearer who carries the Christians' standard, one representative unit will follow another in a spectacle of devotion, of splendor and glorious pageantry. Lay-confraternities with insignia and banners, religious orders of priests in cassock and surplice or in the colorful habits of their order, secular priests in brilliant vestments proceeding in majestic array under the bright sky, prelates, Bishops and Archbishops, each in their distinctive processional dress. Cardinals in red robes glittering under the rays of a June sun . . . The Eucharistic Lord carried aloft in the jeweled monstrance.[16]

In preparation for the event, newspapers in Chicago and other major American cities featured special full-color inserts showing fully vested members of the Catholic hierarchy. An official photographer had been designated to take portraits of all leading clergy involved in the planning and execution of the congress; their portraits were then supplied to the press, and members of this clerical Executive Committee were featured in special newspaper inserts.[17]

Once the congress was underway, mainstream magazines like *Time* demonstrated their facility with the specialized terminology of Roman Catholic liturgical wear, noting that among those attending mass at Soldier's Field Stadium will be "more than 500 archbishops and bishops . . . in copes and mitres and bearing croziers," accompanied by fifteen cardinals "robed in ecclesiastical red," and attended by papal knights and other dignitaries dressed in "festive cloth of gold proper for such an occasion."[18] A full-page, four-color article in the *Chicago Evening-American* was devoted to explaining "the origin and meaning of each vestment worn by the actors in the religious drama."[19] The *Herald-Examiner* featured an insert with articles headlined, "Ceremony Explained in Detail," and "Essentials of Liturgy Described," and included a detailed, full-page description of the process of vesting and the prayers to be recited by the celebrant as each garment was donned.[20] Following the mass at Soldier's Field on the specially designated "Women's Day," a *Herald-Examiner* headline proclaimed, "50,000 Watch Rites from Outside Gates: Sun-Lit Vari-Colored Dresses Banked against Black & White Nuns' Robes Make a Striking Picture."[21] The fact that much of this coverage was repackaged and sold afterward in compilations suggests that the public retained an appetite for such detail. Souvenir volumes of coverage included *A Photographic History of the Eucharistic Congress*, *XXVIII International Eucharistic Congress: A Pictorial Album*, and *The Story of the Twenty-Eighth International Eucharistic Congress*.[22]

Perhaps the most picturesque event of the week was the final climactic procession on the grounds of Saint Mary of the Lake Seminary. The seminary had only recently been completed under Cardinal Mundelein's leadership and was located in a town named for him, forty miles north of Chicago. Like a movie set, the seminary campus at Mundelein had "come into being almost in a night." Its picturesque setting, with its "fourteen hundred acres of rolling, wooded lands," "shimmering blue water," and "group of magnificent buildings, all in the purest American colonial style," created an impressive backdrop for the final day of the congress.[23]

FIGURE 3.2 Religious sisters and Catholic lay women were among the thousands who gathered at Soldier's Field for Women's Day. Photo courtesy of the Archdiocese of Chicago's Joseph Cardinal Bernardin Archives and Records Center.

Approximately five hundred thousand people reportedly traveled by car and train from Chicago "to witness the picturesque procession with Cardinal Bozano carrying the host."[24] Included in the procession were "Dominican friars in their white cassocks, Trappist and Capuchin monks in brown, Benedictines and Jesuits in black—then the resplendent, gold-draped bishops and archbishops."[25]

In their effusive descriptions of congress events, journalists did not shy away from the monarchical and medieval overtones that in another context might have been thought to conflict with American democratic and egalitarian ideals. Similarly, questions about whether such pageantry was appropriate for members of a spiritual institution inspired by Jesus of Nazareth were rarely posed, and when they were raised, were largely drowned out by hyperbolic praise. The *Literary Digest* provided a largely positive overview of the congress and a summary of its print coverage, noting only in passing that both a Baptist and Methodist paper were "moved to contrast the magnificent dramatic spectacles at Chicago with the humble associations surrounding the life of Christ on earth."[26] As we will see,

FIGURE 3.3 The entrance procession of the Eucharistic Congress's closing Mass approaches the Chapel at Saint Mary of the Lake. Photo courtesy of the Archdiocese of Chicago's Joseph Cardinal Bernardin Archives and Records Center.

the Catholic Church itself had long grappled with questions about the proper role of opulence and pageantry in Christian worship. Clearly the zeitgeist in which the congress took place was not conducive to this issue being addressed in any sustained way, however. Before turning to the larger cultural context that contributed to this disinterest, it will be useful to look more closely at the ideological differences that were in some sense buried beneath the folds of ecclesiastical garments.

DRESS, THE EUCHARIST, AND DENOMINATIONAL DIFFERENCE

Both Catholic and non-Catholic writers covering the congress acknowledged that Catholic understanding of the Eucharist differed from that of other Christian denominations. The headline from a North Carolina newspaper that proclaimed "Jesus Christ Pays His First Visit to America" was somewhat sardonically subtitled "The Roman Catholic Church Says So and Fed His Body and Blood to a Million of Its Followers in Chicago."[27] These differences had their roots in the Protestant Reformation, in which reformers rejected the Roman church's interpretation of Christ's words "this is my body" in reference to the bread and wine at the Last Supper.[28] As suggested by the North Carolina newspaper headline cited above, the Catholic understanding of Christ's presence in the Eucharist was profoundly physical in a way that the Protestant understanding simply was not. Despite variation among Protestant Christians on this issue, it is fair to say that, following the Reformation, Catholics' conviction that the bread and wine consecrated by the priest at Mass truly and fully became (transubstantiated into) the physical body and blood of Christ emerged as one of Catholicism's defining beliefs. A scholastic revival in the church, in full swing at the time of the Chicago congress, only served to reinforce this focus.

Related to the debates over how to properly understand the Eucharist, Catholics and Protestants had significantly different ideas about how their clergy should dress. Catholic understanding of the sacramental nature of ordination has influenced adherents' approach to clerical clothing. In Catholicism, the rite of ordination into clerical office conveys a fundamental change in status. For priests and higher orders, this change includes the power to perform the sacraments, which are understood as unique vehicles of divine grace. As a tangible symbol of this transformation, the bestowal of garments representative of clerical office became a central moment in the rite of ordination. Historian Dyan Elliot draws a helpful analogy when she writes that, "like the water in baptism or the material elements in other sacraments, clothing was a symbolic correlative representing the invisible grace bestowed in the course of ordination."[29] The medieval rite of ordination, still observed in the Catholic Church today as it was in the 1920s, features the laying of the garment over the shoulders of each candidate for ordination. The removal of garments was equally symbolic: a ritual divesting (literally de-vesting) conveyed a return to lay status.

Equally influential on Catholic clerical attire was the theological understanding of the Eucharist as a ritual sacrifice. Since the early Middle Ages, the offering of Christ's body and blood in the bread and wine of the Eucharist had been understood as participating directly in the sacrifice of Jesus on the cross. The Eucharist was, in fact, the only sacrament that was also a sacrifice.[30] In performing the sacrifice of the Mass, priests were understood as the successors of the Levitical priests of the Old Testament, and the "sacred vestments" described in Exodus 28 provided a template for Catholic liturgical wear. Protestant reformers, with their different understanding of both the priesthood and the Eucharist, largely rejected a sacrificial interpretation of the Lord's Supper and did not see Christian ministers as successors of Levitical priests. Thus, the priestly garments described in Exodus held no relevance for Protestant clerical dress. While the Episcopalian priesthood represented a middle way between Catholic and Protestant extremes, many Protestants rejected this compromise.

Although the specifics of clerical dress varied by denomination, Protestant clergy in the 1920s were generally advised to maintain a clean and tidy appearance, avoid "eccentric" dress, and wear black, white, or gray.[31] A 1925 *Time* magazine cover featuring a drawing of liberal Protestant pastor Harry Emerson Fosdick conforms to this ascetic aesthetic; Fosdick appears in a dark suit and tie, white dress shirt with rounded collar, and eyeglasses. He is indistinguishable in dress from the other prominent men who regularly appeared on the newsweekly's covers.[32] The garb of Protestant leaders was not uniformly austere, however. Female revivalist and Los Angelino Aimee Semple McPherson was known for a style that was influenced by the "glitz and glamour of early Hollywood culture." In the 1920s, McPherson began to incorporate elements of show business into her ministry, delivering sermons in a variety of costumes, from an ancient Middle Eastern bride to a southern belle. Her image became so ubiquitous that when she bobbed her hair in 1927, it created a media sensation.[33] Marcelino Manuel da Graça, known to followers as "Daddy Grace," also attracted attention with his distinctive style of dress, which included velvet suits, flashy jewelry, and long, painted fingernails. His evangelizing tour through southern cities in 1926 was followed closely by the press.[34]

Just as Protestant leaders were not completely immune to the appeal of sartorial splendor, resistance to lavish clerical dress could be found within the Catholic tradition as well. Early church leaders had expressed deep ambivalence about requiring special liturgical attire, and ecclesiastical legislation repeatedly banned the use of expensive materials for clerical garments. By the Middle Ages, however, the "ornate style" of liturgical vestments had become the norm, as surviving artworks and textiles attest: "from the twelfth century, ecclesiastical garb is depicted throughout Europe as made of precious silks and adorned with woven gold bands and colorful embroidery."[35] This change reflected increasing affluence in western Europe, the elevated social status of church leaders, and the emergence of a shared clerical culture. Although disagreements at all levels of the church continued over whether clerical garb should, on the one hand, aim to honor God with its majesty or, on the other, model Christ in its simplicity, Pope Pius XI evidently favored the former. During his pontificate (1921–39), "all ecclesiastical dignitaries, even the lowest, were allowed to dress in some splendor, thus participating in the splendor of the Papal Court and His Holiness's majesty."[36] Decades later, Pius's predilection for opulence was on full view at a 2018 Metropolitan Museum of Art exhibition featuring one of the pontiff's chasubles, a miter, and a pectoral cross.[37]

What was the basis for the eventual acceptance of the ornate style on the part of Catholic leaders? One answer lay in the need to prepare clergy in an era before widespread literacy or institutionalized training. As church leaders sought to train largely illiterate priests for their roles and duties, they found that an emphasis on distinctive garments with symbolic significance could be a powerful way to convey key ideas and values. Since at least the sixth century, church leaders had produced liturgical commentaries of their reflections on various aspects of the Mass. These commentaries, along with influential manuals like Gregory the Great's sixth-century *Pastoral Care*, traced the origins of ecclesiastical garments back to the priesthood of Aaron in the book of Exodus, and established allegorical interpretations for various clerical vestments. By the ninth century, vesting prayers were to be recited as the priest or bishop dressed for daily Mass, another way that clerical clothing acquired symbolic significance. Clerical virtues like justice and chastity were associated with specific garments in these widely distributed prayers.[38] Ordination rites also frequently linked each item of apparel to a distinctive virtue, and the practice of blessing liturgical vestments is attested beginning in the tenth century. An influential twelfth-century synthesis standardized liturgical practices involving clerical vestments, throughout Christian Europe and for centuries to come. Thanks in part to the wide circulation of this liturgical treatise, "clerical garb was more or less stabilized throughout Latin Christendom by the thirteenth century."[39] Not until the Second Vatican Council in the 1960s did the clothing worn by Catholic clergy undergo dramatic change.

Judging by the extensive journalistic record of the events in Chicago, the crowds that assembled for the congress in June 1926 were not overly concerned with long-standing theological debates about the Eucharist or appropriate clerical attire, simply preferring to enjoy the spectacle for its own sake. Protestant leaders and their congregations were equally willing to look past denominational differences in favor of enjoying the show. As we will see, the public was primed to appreciate the visual display by concurrent developments in Hollywood, which impacted popular perceptions of both fashion and film.

FASHION THROUGH FILM IN THE ROARING TWENTIES

By several measures, the decade in which the Eucharistic Congress made its American debut was a boom period for the U.S. film industry. Weekly domestic film attendance was between twenty and thirty million people, having nearly doubled between 1920 and 1928. During that same period, the number of theaters grew from 21,000 to 28,000; by the mid-1920s, Chicago was served by approximately 350 theaters, with an average of 900 seats in each.[40] This growth, coupled with the persistent desire of film to distinguish itself as a respectable form of entertainment, helped fuel the rise of "superspecial" (or epic) productions. In keeping with their name, superspecials established new heights in terms of production cost, film length, and ticket price.[41] With only brief interruptions, this trend continued throughout the 1920s, with particular emphasis on "epics of a more traditional kind, films with biblical or ancient-world settings."[42]

Epic films, particularly those with religious content, played an important role in industry leaders' efforts to elevate public perception of film as a form of entertainment. The five-reel *Life of Moses* (1909) is an early example of the trend toward longer, religiously themed features. Running approximately seventy-five minutes, its production budget was several times greater than what was spent on typical releases at the time. The publicity surrounding its release also broke new ground, establishing a precedent for film advertising.[43] The success of *Life of Moses* inspired later filmmakers to try their hand at religious epics.

Roughly fifteen years later, director Cecil B. DeMille impressed audiences and reviewers with *The Ten Commandments* (1925).[44] The film was one of the first to use a new two-color Technicolor process; DeMille employed it exclusively in the biblical prologue inspired by the book of Exodus (the contemporary family melodrama that followed remained in black and white). The novelty of full-color crowd scenes created a visual impact that reviewers strained to express in words. *Variety* described the opening biblical scenes as "irresistible in their assembly, breadth, color and direction,"[45] noting elsewhere that "the massive sets, kaleidoscopic scenes and bewildering costumes amazed the audience."[46] The *Sun and Globe* compared the movie, with its "scene after scene of the exodus of the Jews from Egypt," to "the crowded canvas of one of the Flemish Painters."[47] DeMille capitalized on the visual opportunities that scenes of the Exodus provided; the "white rolling sands" of central California contrasted with "vividly, picturesquely clad people" en route to freedom.[48] A prominent film historian summed up the consensus reflected in reviewers' comments by writing that "spectators were enthralled by the use of color in scenes of the exodus."[49]

The release of *Ben Hur* in 1925 was perceived in a similar vein. *Motion Picture Magazine* hailed it as a spectacle that would "widen the appeal" of film, attracting many who "aren't in the habit of going to motion pictures . . . [and giving] motion pictures a new prestige, a wider scope and a greater importance."[50] The epic scale of the production unquestionably contributed to its appeal. In addition to the well-known chariot race, reviewers praised the depiction of "the mobs surging through the Joppa Gate at Jerusalem [, which are as] memorable for the color and grandeur of the setting." The scene was shot on location in Israel, and "the old gate towers to the height of a five-story building, while under it pours a mass of seven thousand people with donkeys, camels and horses coming to pay their tithes to the Roman conquerors."[51] Extreme long shots during spectacle scenes like that at the Joppa Gate established the size and scope of the amassed crowd.[52]

Newspaper coverage of biblical epics from this period was remarkably similar in tone and emphasis to contemporary media descriptions of the Eucharistic Congress. Film critics reveled in logistical details, like the four months it took to build the circus in *Ben Hur* (1925), and the unprecedented forty-two cameras needed to film the legendary chariot race.[53] Similarly, journalists covering the Eucharistic Congress lingered on the grandeur of that event. "Chant Mass for 300,000: An Epic of Hugeness" was how one of the three outdoor Masses held at the Stadium of Soldier's Field in Grant

Park was described. Among the most impressive features was the nearly 120-foot baldachino that had been created to crown the altar. "Now turn away from the altar and face south. You look, and gasp. If sheer hugeness is . . . the commanding note of this second day of the Congress, it still is a hugeness so superbly planned that it becomes resounding poetry—an epic, as it were, of worship."[54] The shared vocabulary reflects the intertextual nature of writing about spectacle, whether cinematic or religious.[55]

In addition to religiously themed epics, medieval subjects were also a reliable source of entertaining spectacle in the 1920s. Two medieval costume dramas ranked among the most popular films between 1922 and 1927: *Robin Hood* (1922) and The *Hunchback of Notre Dame* (1923).[56] The replica of the Paris cathedral featured in the latter, constructed on a lot in California, consistently impressed reviewers. The *New York Times* noted that "if there were nothing else to see in this film, it would be worthwhile to gaze upon the faithful copy of Notre Dame."[57] Further evidence of the appeal of the Middle Ages was the extraordinary popularity of a staged pantomime entitled *The Miracle.* After a successful year on the New York stage in 1924, the production toured the United States, debuting in Chicago just four months before the Eucharistic Congress. The tale of a wayward nun and a stone Madonna that miraculously replaced her, *The Miracle* reenacted a classic medieval *exemplum* for urbane twentieth-century audiences. Judging from the effusive reviews, much of the pantomime's appeal derived from its success in invoking the reverent yet visually stunning atmosphere of Gothic worship. Wherever it traveled, the production impressed both audiences and critics:

> For a people who have lost the knack of devising their own festivals, "The Miracle" comes as a godsend, for wherever it erects the imposing Gothic arches of its cathedral interior and spreads before the eyes of today the brilliant colors of its medieval costumes and pageantry, the spirit of festival is reborn . . . As the spectacle gets under way and the vast medieval throngs pour down the aisles, brushing their many hued garments against you, and trailing their resplendent banners above your head, you are bound to have a new experience in theatre-going.[58]

Whether on stage or in the streets, spectacle clearly caught the eye of American audiences in the 1920s. The unprecedented consumption of feature films during that decade seemed to stimulate their visual appetite all the more. This was especially the case when spectacle was created, at least ostensibly, in the service of religion.

MEDIEVALISM AND MODERNITY

The persistent appeal of the Middle Ages for industrial-age Americans, so evident in the popularity of medieval films and plays, has been well documented.[59] The ideals and aesthetic associated with that lengthy historical period proved attractive to those wearied by modernity. Pattern books popularized Gothic architecture for those who wanted their homes to reflect that era's "impeccable Christian past," while historians "sought to discover in the Middle Ages an idealized and romantic version of their own puzzling world."[60] Well-known Chicago landmarks, including the Water Tower, the campus of the University of Chicago, and the neo-Gothic Chicago Temple reflect the city's attraction to a Gothic ethos.[61] Although American historians eventually outgrew the "habit of remembering the Middle Ages as a glorious epic," the tendency survived on screen and stage for decades.

Chicago's Eucharistic Congress certainly benefited from popular interest in the Middle Ages. Although most spectators were probably unaware of it, the climactic Eucharistic procession that concluded the congress had its origins in the medieval observance of the Feast of Corpus Christi. Established during the height of Eucharistic fervor, by the fourteenth century the celebration of the feast culminated in an elaborate procession.[62] Surviving sources provide detailed descriptions of clerical and lay participants, along with the vestments, banners, and flags they wore and carried. The heart of the procession was the display of the Eucharist in a monstrance, surrounded by candles, covered with a canopy, and carried by the highest-ranking ecclesiastic.

In both costume and choreography, the concluding procession of the congress, held on June 24, conformed very closely to its medieval predecessors. Visual comparisons between medieval illustrations and photographs of the congress demonstrate how faithfully the latter event followed the former ones. In part, this reflects the fact that "clerical vestiture did (and still does) exist in something of a time capsule."[63] Also preserved was the centrality of the Eucharist. At the climactic conclusion of the procession appeared "men of churchly rank, clad in the most gorgeous robes which their office permits, and all acting as an escort to the legate, who walks beneath a canopy bearing in his hands the massive silver ostensorium, a gift of the pope's, in which reposes the blessed host."[64] The legate here refers to "His Eminence, Giovanni Cardinal Bonzano, the legate of the Pope, the proxy for the very Church itself."[65]

Judging by the fashions on display at the 2018 Met exhibition *Heavenly Bodies: Fashion and the Catholic Imagination*, the medieval church has continued to remain a source of creative inspiration and widespread appeal. Although the clerical garments that the Vatican loaned for the exhibit date primarily to the eighteenth and nineteenth centuries, their iconography and construction are consistent with the style and techniques of the Middle Ages, featuring "precious silks and adorned with woven gold bands and colorful embroidery."[66] As the exhibition demonstrates, such ecclesiastical opulence inspired many of the most influential twentieth- and twenty-first-century fashion designers, including Cristobal Balenciaga, Yves Saint Laurent, and Alexander McQueen. Although the possible explanations for the enthusiastic reception to the Met exhibit are beyond the scope of this article, it is safe to say that the cultural context of late capitalism holds some clues. Inundated with representations of ornamental excess, American consumers attending the *Heavenly Bodies* exhibit seemed to be drawn to displays in which the decorative engaged with less superficial realities.[67] To consider more closely what medieval religious clothing may have conveyed to the thousands who convened at Eucharistic Congress events, it will be useful to take a look at the consumption of fashion in that era.

FASHION ON DISPLAY

The interwar period in general, and the 1920s in particular, were an era of heightened interest in clothing. Fads in clothing certainly preexisted the twenties, but that decade possessed the conditions supporting them to a degree previously unseen. "Rapid communications, cheap mass-production techniques, large-scale distribution of goods, and national advertising" all contributed to the increase in fads.[68] The emergence of "flapper culture," bobbed hair, plunging necklines, and shortened skirts proclaimed those who wore them to be fully embracing the new. College newspapers in the 1920s documented a range of fashion fads, from galoshes and yellow rain slickers to knickers and oxford bags. Not limited to the young, such trends were reflected in magazines like *Vanity Fair*, which featured ads and articles devoted to various components of fashionable dress. Readers were kept up-to-date on the latest in fabrics, color, and cut, and illustrated articles provided fashion advice specific to season and locale.[69]

Although accounts of flapper culture may suggest otherwise, the 1920s preoccupation with fashion was not restricted to women. *Vanity Fair* actually got its start in 1913 as a men's fashion magazine. By the time the magazine's popularity peaked in the following decade, its pages devoted roughly equal space to male and female attire. A 1926 advertisement proclaimed, "The mid-Victorian notion that a man must be drably clad to be correctly clothed is an obsolete as the hood skirt. Today color . . . is the keynote of smartly attired gentlemen."[70] Variety proliferated, with attention given to virtually every detail of dress. A full-page ad with six different styles of caps for men, for example, noted that "there is satisfying comfort in knowing that your headwear is the extreme exemplification of style and craftsmanship."[71] Similarly, a dress shirt company advertised six different versions of starched collars, described as "the styles of the day," suitable for "the man of affairs who wishes to appear as the well-dressed business man."[72]

Interest in fashion was reflected elsewhere in American culture in the mid-1920s. Michael Arlen's *The Green Hat* was made into a successful Broadway play in 1925, and the widely read novels of Virginia Woolf and Theodore Dreiser made frequent references to the significance of personal attire.[73] Nowhere was Americans' appetite for fashion more apparent, however, than in discourse connected with the movies. In addition to the sartorial splendor of the epics discussed above, other genres also contributed to the fashion fervor. Costume dramas *Don Juan* and *La Bohème*, both released in 1926, were praised for the lavishness of their garments. Russian romance *The Midnight Sun* (1926) was described as "beautiful beyond description . . . replete with brilliant uniforms and gorgeous settings."[74] Eager to keep pace with audiences' appreciation for fashion, director DeMille employed designer Adrian as head of costume operations for his films in 1925, and film executive Louis B. Mayer hired famous Parisian artist Erté to work on costumes for *Ben Hur* and *La Bohème*.

Also in the mid-1920s, film fan magazines began to feature fashion advice from "experts" with ties to the film industry: "During the past few years, *Photoplay Magazine* has noticed an increasing interest on the part of its readers in . . . personal adornment, and it has been making an effort through its fashion and interior decoration departments to be of service."⁷⁵ A feature with the headline "Does Your Wardrobe Reflect the Screen? Let *Photoplay* Help on Shopping Problems" encouraged readers to purchase clothing and accessories curated by the magazine's editors.⁷⁶ Just a month later, a boxed insert entitled "What They're Wearing" drew *Moving Picture Magazine* readers' attention to a photo feature in its upcoming edition in which stars posed for "fashion hints." The editors offered the following advice: "before you select your clothes for the Spring, buy the April [issue] and study the suggestions offered you by some of the best-dressed girls on the screen."⁷⁷ In its May issue, *Moving Picture Magazine* encouraged readers to host a party in which guests dressed up as their favorite stars; for inspiration, the magazine featured photos of noteworthy costumes worn by popular actors and actresses.⁷⁸

The fervor for fashion also impacted where and how clothing was displayed. A freestanding dressing room built for a fashionable film actress featured "long drawers—one apiece—for each of her heavily beaded frocks."⁷⁹ Wax figures of popular film stars wearing the latest fashions were featured in store windows.⁸⁰ In the mid-1920s, movie premieres became major events in the largest U.S. cities, coordinated by publicity firms specializing in film. These events featured "pomp, splendor, hysteria . . . lights, [and] mass intoxication," and attracted hundreds of journalists from all over the world to describe the films and the luminaries who assembled for their debut. The clothing ensembles of those who gathered were regularly a topic of comment.⁸¹ The 2018 Met Gala, at which New York's Cardinal Dolan mingled with international celebrities, could be considered a contemporary equivalent.⁸²

Fashion shows, in which the latest designs were paraded in front of an audience of potential buyers, had also become a popular pastime among sophisticated urbanites by the 1920s. Five decades later, Italian director Federico Fellini memorably combined fashion, faith, and film in an ecclesiastical fashion show featured in *Roma* (1972). European fashion designers have been making similar connections for decades, as demonstrated in the *Heavenly Bodies* exhibit. The show, the most successful in the history of the Metropolitan Museum of Art, brought together forty ecclesiastical garments and accessories on loan from the Vatican and displayed them in the context of the couture garments they inspired.⁸³ One factor contributing to the exhibit's appeal was its playfulness with boundaries, both between genders and between religion and spectacle. On the one hand, the ecclesiastical garments on display visually reinforced the observation that "the ministry is an office that, from its inception and with very few exceptions, has been gendered male."[84] On the other, the garments inspired by ecclesiastical vestments were designed almost exclusively for women to wear in secular contexts.

TRADITIONAL RELIGION IN CHANGING TIMES

The decade of the 1920s was a time of unprecedented change. "Historians have long recognized that, for better or worse, American culture was remade in the 1920s."[85] Fashion both reflected and accelerated this process. "Fashion is dress in which the key feature is rapid and continual changing of styles. Fashion, in a sense, *is* change, and in modern western societies no clothes are outside fashion."[86] Such attentiveness to fashion, and the film industry which promoted it, helped fuel America's rapidly expanding capitalist economy. Manufacturing and marketing firms profited from the increase in consumer demand generated by rapidly changing styles in clothing. Of course, the levels of consumption promoted in the pages of fan and fashion magazines ultimately proved unsustainable.[87] Meanwhile, another cultural change was underway: a decline in interest in mainline Protestantism among mainstream American youth. "Even the progressives agreed that the churches were not attracting the young. By the twenties, the young had transferred their allegiance from the churches, broad or narrow, to a different sort of God, as they invested a kind of religious devotion to their leisure pursuits, to sports, dating and song."[88]

Amid the proliferation of consumer goods on the one hand and a decline in religious observance on the other, the enthusiasm generated by the Eucharistic Congress was seen by many Americans as a reassuring sign that the nation hadn't lost its collective soul. As the *Oshkosh Northwestern* wrote, the mighty outpouring at the congress "seems to give the lie to claims often heard that religion has been losing ground in recent years, giving way to the materialistic."[89] *Time* reassured its readers that "there will be not the slightest taint of commercialism about this Congress." Sales of souvenirs were prohibited at Saint Mary of the Lake Seminary; pilgrims received an official bronze medal from Rome instead.[90] A letter from President Calvin Coolidge, delivered as a greeting to the papal legate, also expressed this sentiment. It emphasized the importance of the religious life of the nation, while suggesting that "the reason the American people are accused of undue attention to material things may be 'because in that direction we have been more successful than others.' "[91] The pageantry on display at the Twenty-Eighth Eucharistic Congress would undoubtedly be received very differently if the event were held in Chicago today.[92] But in 1926, the traditionally lavish garments in the context of Eucharistic ritual struck a chord. Betraying his clerical bias, a Dominican priest framed it this way: "the liturgical renaissance of our day is a guarantee that now, since men have the 'movie mind,' the Church will educate the heart through the eye as she did in the medieval times when books were rare."[93] The pageantry of Chicago's Eucharistic Congress found a uniquely receptive audience during a decade of excess in film and fashion, its religious spectacle appealing to Americans' collective "movie mind" in reassuring ways.

NOTES

1. Thomas M. Schwertner, O.P., *The Eucharistic Renaissance; or, The International Eucharistic Congresses* (New York: Macmillan, 1926), 96.
2. Carol A. Devlin, "The Eucharistic Procession of 1908: The Dilemma of Liberal Government," *Church History* 63, no. 3 (1994): 407–25; G. I. T. Machin, "The Liberal Government and the Eucharistic Procession of 1908," *Journal of Ecclesiastical History* 34, no. 4 (1983): 559–83.
3. Peter Jan Margry and Henk te Velde, "Contested Rituals and the Battle for Public Space: The Netherlands," in *Culture Wars: Secular-Catholic Conflict in Nineteenth-Century Europe*, ed. Christopher Clark and Wolfram Kaiser (Cambridge: Cambridge University Press, 2003), 129–51.
4. "Editorial," *Christian Century*, July 1, 1926, 827.
5. William Dever, an Irish Catholic, was mayor of Chicago from 1923 to 1927. For more on Chicago politics during this period, see John M. Allswang, *A House for All Peoples: Ethnic Politics in Chicago, 1890-1936* (Lexington: University of Kentucky Press, 1971).
6. Charles Shanabruch, *Chicago's Catholics: The Evolution of an American Identity* (South Bend, IN: University of Notre Dame Press, 1981), 166.
7. Edward R. Kantowicz, *Corporation Sole: Cardinal Mundelein and Chicago Catholicism* (Notre Dame, IN: University of Notre Dame Press, 1983).

8. "George Cardinal Mundelein: His Grace . . . His Holiness," *Time*, May 31, 1926.
9. Joseph Doherty, *Hollywood's Censor: Joseph I. Breen and the Production Code Administration* (New York: Columbia University Press, 2007), 23–24.
10. Katherine D. Moran, "The Devotion of Others: Secular American Attractions to Catholicism, 1870–1930," PhD diss., Johns Hopkins University, 2009.
11. In his classic survey, Jay P. Dolan describes the Eucharistic Congress as "Catholic triumphalism, Catholic big, at its best." Dolan, *The American Catholic Experience: A History from Colonial Times to the Present* (Notre Dame, IN: University of Notre Dame Press, 1992), 350.
12. Phrases are from William Uricchio and Roberta E. Pearson, *Reframing Culture: The Case of the Vitagraph Quality Films* (Princeton, NJ: Princeton University Press, 1993), 196.
13. Doherty, *Hollywood's Censor*.
14. *The Eucharistic Congress as Reported in the Chicago Tribune* (Chicago: Public Service Office of the Chicago Tribune, 1926).
15. "200,000 Welcome Cardinal Bonzano," *Evening Star* (Washington, DC), June 17, 1926; W. O. Saunders, "Jesus Christ Pays His First Visit to America," *The Independent* (Elizabeth City, NC), June 25, 1926; "Eucharistic Congress Ends at Chicago," *Key West Citizen*, June 25, 1926
16. Rev. Matthew A. Cummings, "The Eucharistic Procession," *New World*, June 18, 1926.
17. Giovanni E. Schiavo, *The Italians in Chicago: A Study of Americanization* (Chicago: Italian American Publishing, 1928), 185.
18. "Bouquet," *Time*, May 31, 1926, 24.
19. Marion Preece, "What Pageantry of Great Church Congress Means," *Chicago Evening American*, June 19, 1926.
20. "Congress Mass in English," *Chicago Herald Examiner*, June 21, 1926.
21. Scrapbook—Eucharistic Congress, 1926, Box # HIST/S1000/39, Archdiocese of Chicago's Joseph Cardinal Bernardin Archives and Records Center, Chicago, IL.
22. *The Story of the Twenty-Eighth International Eucharistic Congress*, compiled by Rev. C. F. Donovan (Chicago: International Eucharistic Congress Committee, 1927).
23. Paul Hutchinson, "Rome Comes to Chicago," *Christian Century*, July 8, 1926, 868.
24. "Meaning of the Eucharistic Congress," *Literary Digest*, July 17, 1926, 28.
25. "Bouquet," *Time*, May 31, 1926, 24.
26. "Meaning of the Eucharistic Congress," 26.

27. Saunders, "Jesus Christ Pays His First Visit to America," 1.
28. A version of the phrase translated in English as "this is my body" appears in Matt 26:26; Mark 14:22; Luke 22:19; 1 Cor 11:24.
29. Dyan Elliott, "Dressing and Undressing the Clergy: Rites of Ordination and Degradation," in *Medieval Fabrications: Dress, Textiles, Cloth Work, and Other Cultural Imaginings*, ed. E. Jane Burns (New York: Palgrave Macmillian, 2004), 58.
30. Jaroslav Pelikan, *The Christian Tradition: A History of the Development of Doctrine* (Chicago: University of Chicago Press, 1971), 1:168–9.
31. See the contemporary literature summarized in Leah Payne, " 'Pants Don't Make Preachers': Fashion and Gender Construction in Late-Nineteenth- and Early-Twentieth-Century American Revivalism," *Fashion Theory* 19, no. 1 (2015): 106n10.
32. *Time*, September 21, 1925.
33. In a development intriguingly concurrent with the Eucharistic Congress, McPherson mysteriously disappeared in mid-May 1926, only to resurface in dramatic fashion on June 23. See Payne, " 'Pants Don't Make Preachers.' "
34. Marie W. Dallam, *Daddy Grace: A Celebrity Preacher and His House of Prayer* (New York: NYU Press, 2007), 6, 47–51.
35. Maureen C. Miller, *Clothing the Clergy: Virtue and Power in Medieval Europe, c. 800-1200* (Ithaca, NY: Cornell University Press, 2014), 108.
36. Bernard Berthod, "From Papal Red to Cardinal Purple: Evolution and Change of Robes at the Papal Court from Innocent III to Leo X, 1216-1521," in *Robes and Honor: The Medieval World of Investiture*, ed. Stewart Gordon (New York: Palgrave Macmillan, 2001), 328.
37. Andrew Bolton, ed., *Heavenly Bodies: Fashion and the Catholic Imagination*, vol. 1, *The Vatican Collection* (New Haven, CT: Yale University Press, 2018), plates 44–47, 70, 80.
38. On medieval vesting prayers, see Miller, who notes that "the recitation of vesting prayers was a devotion enjoined upon priests that endured until the Second Vatican Council made it optional in 1965." Miller, *Clothing the Clergy*, 77–87.
39. Elliott, "Dressing and Undressing the Clergy," 56.
40. Lary May, *Screening Out the Past: The Birth of Mass Culture and the Motion Picture Industry* (Chicago: University of Chicago Press, 1980), 165. For Chicago theaters, see *Film Daily Yearbook* (New York: Wid's Films and Film Folk, 1926), 496–9.
41. The term was in regular use by 1922, but the distinction between "specials" and "superspecials" was not a precise one. See Sheldon Hall and Steve Neale,

Epics, Spectacles and Blockbusters (Detroit: Wayne State University Press, 2010), 52.
42. Hall and Neale, *Epics, Spectacles and Blockbusters*, 54.
43. Uricchio and Pearson, *Reframing Culture*, 170.
44. This 1925 silent version is not to be confused with the 1956 blockbuster of the same name, also directed by DeMille.
45. Review of *Ten Commandments*, *Variety*, December 27, 1923, 26.
46. " '10 Commandments' Picture Best of All Paramounts," *Variety*, December 6, 1923, 20.
47. Advertisement, *Variety*, January 3, 1924.
48. Edwin Schallert, "The Filming of Exodus," *Picture Play Magazine*, September 1923, 32.
49. Sumiko Higashi, *Cecil B. DeMille and American Culture: The Silent Era* (Berkeley: University of California Press, 1994), 184.
50. Agnes Smith, " 'Ben-Hur' Is Shown at Last," *Motion Picture Magazine*, March 1926, 8.
51. Ruth Waterbury, "A Modern Miracle Film," *Photoplay*, March 1926, 134.
52. Script notes specify that "the longest possible shot that can be secured" should be used for this scene. Quoted in Theodore R. Hovet Jr., "Realism and Spectacle in Ben-Hur (1880–1959)," PhD diss., Duke University, 1995, 319.
53. Waterbury, "A Modern Miracle Film," 32.
54. John O'Donnell Bennett, "The Eucharistic Congress as Reported in *Chicago Tribune*" (Chicago: Public Service Office of the Chicago Tribune, 1926), 22.
55. Although the concept of intertextuality arose in the context of literary criticism, it has broadened to include a variety of texts. See María Jesús Martínez Alfaro, "Intertextuality: Origins and Development of the Concept," *Atlantis* 18, nos. 1–2 (1996): 268–85.
56. Richard Koszarski, *An Evening's Entertainment: The Age of the Silent Feature Picture, 1915-1928* (Berkeley: University of California Press, 1990), 33, 89.
57. "The Screen: The Hideous Bell-Ringer," *New York Times*, September 3, 1923. See also "Across the Silversheet," *Motion Picture Magazine*, December 1923, 88; Review of *The Hunchback of Notre Dame*, *Photoplay Magazine*, November 1923, 74.
58. "Twenty-Five Reasons Why 'The Miracle' Is the Most Unusual Event . . ." unsigned, undated manuscript, Morris Gest Papers, Container 14.32, Harry Ransom Center, University of Texas at Austin.
59. See the sources cited in Robin Fleming, "Picturesque History and the Medieval in Nineteenth-Century America," *American Historical Review* 100, no. 4 (October 1995): 1061–94. See also Philip Gleason, "American Catholics and the

Mythic Middle Ages," in *Keeping the Faith: American Catholicism Past and Present* (Notre Dame, IN: University of Notre Dame Press, 1987).
60. Fleming, "Picturesque History," 1077.
61. On Chicago's Water Tower, see Jan M. Ziolkowski, *The Juggler of Notre Dame and the Medievalizing of Modernity*, vol. 3, *The American Middle Ages* (Cambridge: Open Book Publishers, 2018), 245–46.
62. By the early fourteenth century, a procession was "deemed the most appropriate mode of celebrating the eucharistic feast." Miri Rubin, *Corpus Christi: The Eucharist in Late Medieval Culture* (Cambridge: Cambridge University Press, 1991), 243. See also Charles Zika, "Hosts, Processions and Pilgrimages: Controlling the Sacred in Fifteenth-Century Germany," *Past and Present* 118 (1988): 38.
63. Elliott, "Dressing and Undressing the Clergy," 56.
64. Hutchinson, "Rome Comes to Chicago," 869.
65. "Bouquet," *Time*, May 31, 1926, 24. The papal legate was typically a cardinal who became the designated representative of the pope on particular missions. As such, he wore the papal mantle and other garments characteristic of the pope, but he could not display the insignia bestowed on him outside his legation territory. On guidelines for the legate's attire, see Berthod, "From Papal Red to Cardinal Purple," 319.
66. Miller, *Clothing the Clergy*.
67. Finnish religious scholar Terhi Utriainen describes "a desire for enchanted bodies" as a characteristic of present-day Western society. See her "The Post-Secular Position and Enchanted Bodies," *Scripta Instituti Donneriani Aboensis* 23 (2011): 417–32.
68. Paula S. Fass, *The Damned and the Beautiful: American Youth in the 1920s* (New York: Oxford University Press, 1977), 227.
69. "For the Well Dressed Man: Fashions for Palm Beach," *Vanity Fair*, January 1926, 74.
70. "Strong-Hewat Virgin Wool Fabrics," half-page advertisement, *Vanity Fair*, January 1926, 102.
71. "Merton Caps and Knickers to Match," advertisement for Charles S. Merton and Co., *Vanity Fair*, June 1926, 13.
72. "Follow the Arrow and You Will Follow the Style," advertisement for Cluett, Peabody, and Co., *Vanity Fair*, February 1926, 16.
73. R. S. Koppen, *Virginia Woolf: Fashion and Literary Modernity* (Edinburgh: Edinburgh University Press, 2011); William Brevda, "The Straw Hat in Dreiser's *An American Tragedy*," *Midwestern Miscellany* 42 (2014): 46–63.

74. Advertisement, *Photoplay*, February 1926, 121.
75. "Brickbats and Bouquets," *Photoplay*, January 1926, 127.
76. "Does Your Wardrobe Reflect the Screen? Let Photoplay Help on Shopping Problems," *Photoplay*, February 1926, 64–65.
77. "What They're Wearing," *Motion Picture Magazine*, March 1926, 115.
78. "Why Not Give a Movie Party?," *Motion Picture Magazine*, May 1926, 52.
79. "Studio News and Gossip—East and West," *Photoplay*, February 1926, 82.
80. "Beautiful but Dumb: Some of Peggy's New Clothes," *Photoplay*, February 1926, 70.
81. Esther Carples, "Broadway's New Sport," *Motion Picture Magazine*, May 1926, 115.
82. Jocelyn Noveck, "Inside the Met Gala: Real-Life Cardinal Gets Star Treatment," AP News, May 8, 2018, https://apnews.com/article/entertainment-ap-top-news-religion-fashion-new-york-692f8706920548f29ce96d6bd9b0e689.
83. "'Heavenly Bodies' Sets Attendance Record at Met Museum," *Hollywood Reporter*, October 11, 2018, https://www.hollywoodreporter.com/news/heavenly-bodies-sets-attendance-record-at-met-museum-1151758.
84. Payne, "'Pants Don't Make Preachers,'" 83.
85. Fass, *The Damned and the Beautiful*, 3.
86. Elizabeth Wilson, *Adorned in Dreams: Fashion and Modernity* (Berkeley: University of California Press, 1985), 3.
87. See, among others, T. H. Watkins, *The Great Depression: America in the 1930s* (New York: Bay Back Books, 2007).
88. Fass, *The Damned and the Beautiful*, 45.
89. Quoted in "Meaning of the Eucharistic Congress," *Literary Digest*, 26.
90. "Bouquet," *Time*, May 31, 1926, 22–23.
91. Quoted in "Meaning of the Eucharistic Congress," 28
92. In recent years, an International Eucharistic Congress has been held every four years. The most recent was held in 2016 in the Philippines. See "IEC: 51st International Eucharistic Congress," http://iec2016.ph/ (accessed June 18, 2019).
93. Schwertner, *The Eucharistic Renaissance*, xii.

Four

POWER BEFORE THRONES OF GOD AND MAN

WOMEN, ADORNMENT, AND PUBLIC LIFE IN WHITE AMERICAN PENTECOSTALISM

ANDREA SHAN JOHNSON AND LEAH PAYNE

IN 2015, two American women of Pentecostal background stood on the verge of becoming the darlings of the religious right. One was Paula White-Cain, a televangelist known for her flamboyant taste in clothing, personal care, and cosmetics, who in April of 2015 celebrated her third marriage, this one to musician Jonathan Cain of the band Journey. One year later, she would rise to national prominence as the pastor to the forty-fifth president of the United States, Donald J. Trump. As Trump's pastor, White-Cain rallied evangelicals around him in the wake of his 2016 electoral victory and called in "angels from Africa and South America" to support his failed 2020 run for reelection.[1] The second woman was plainly attired, bespectacled Kim Davis, clerk of Rowan County, Kentucky, who would be jailed for her continual refusal to grant licenses for same sex marriages in defiance of court orders, and who would become a global figure for the cause.

Although seemingly worlds apart in terms of their appearances, both women identify as Pentecostal, and their attire and adornment reflect distinct Pentecostal theologies about holiness, power, and authority in public life. In fact, White-Cain and Davis are inheritors of a long-standing theological tradition within Pentecostalism that links women's personal appearance to theology. This chapter explores how the bodies of white Pentecostal women are imbued with a sacramental function, their bodies and their adornment treated as outward expressions of inward holiness— or a lack thereof.[2] Pentecostal women use clothing and other external accoutrements to illustrate and enact Pentecostal theologies of holiness and power.

Pentecostalism began as an early twentieth-century form of revivalism with numerous influences, including Wesleyan-Holiness revivals, slave religion, Oberlin perfectionism, Keswick "higher life" proponents, Quakers, Mennonites, Catholics, divine healing movements, and more.[3] Growing out of the famous Azusa Street Revival in 1906, American Pentecostalism has been a notoriously fractious movement. Scholars note that race and racism, socioeconomic, political, and geographical divisions and distinctions abound in Pentecostalism.[4] There are Pentecostal offshoots based on theological controversies about everything from typical Pentecostal practice (e.g., when should one speak in tongues, and whether speaking in tongues constitutes glossolalia or xenoglossia), to adaptations of nineteenth-century Holiness movement codes for how to live a godly life. Like members of the Holiness movement before them, who believed that the Holy Spirit's inner presence should be reflected in outer modes of dress and behavior set apart from the broader American culture, Pentecostals were deeply concerned with what the Bible said they should wear, what sorts of entertainment they should consume, and what they should eat or drink.

Pentecostal theological divisions were documented in newsletters, sermons, and tracts, and they often reflected sociological distinctions like race and ethnicity, social class, or urban-rural divides. In white Pentecostal circles, the connection between the personal appearance of women and theology divides along a theological split almost as old as the Pentecostal tradition itself: the theological controversies about the godhead. This theological split, which developed after 1913, may seem minor to those outside of Pentecostal circles, but for those within it can be an issue of salvation. Essentially, Trinitarian Pentecostals view the godhead as being apparent in three distinct entities (God the Father, Jesus the Son, and the Holy Spirit), while non-Trinitarian Pentecostals (also referred to as Oneness or Apostolic Pentecostals) believe that God was manifested in the flesh through Jesus and is in the spirit through the Holy Ghost. In general, white Pentecostals who professed Trinitarian theology quickly began to adopt mid-twentieth-century mainstream fashion trends. In contrast, white Pentecostal women in Oneness traditions retained the strict modesty codes of their Holiness forebearers.

In both cases, the theological value of a woman's appearance made a powerful political and theological statement. Trinitarian women came to embrace contemporary fashion and other personal accoutrements like cosmetics, jewelry, and even plastic surgery—whether it be the calf-revealing dresses of the 1920s or thigh-high leather boots and form-fitting dresses in the early years of the twenty-first century. For these women, personal appearance became a way of displaying the favor of God. For a Pentecostal woman in public life like Paula White, her personal appearance reflects her status as an Esther figure—a consort to powerful leaders—in American public life. In contrast, Oneness women rejected popular fashion and accoutrements in favor of preserving nineteenth-century Holiness codes for modesty, including long-sleeved, floor-length dresses, makeup-free faces, and uncut hair. This outward appearance was a testimony to their inner faithfulness to the Oneness message; just as Oneness Pentecostals rejected dominant Trinitarian doctrines of God, so Oneness women rejected "worldly" norms of beauty. In addition, for Oneness women such as Kim Davis, appearance is an outward expression of an inward submission to traditional gender hierarchies, and eventually outward evidence of inner spiritual power to change the world through their controversial doctrine.

EARLY PENTECOSTAL THEOLOGY ABOUT ACCOUTREMENTS

Before there were denominational splits based on definitions of the godhead, Pentecostal concerns over women's attire developed in part due to the influence of the Holiness movement. Even after the theological split began, many Pentecostals consumed the same publications and shared common beliefs on holiness. Many of the early Pentecostal revivalists, like Maria Woodworth-Etter and Carrie Judd Montgomery, had been Holiness preachers prior to their adaptation of Pentecostal theology, and they brought their beliefs about the power of modesty for women into a movement that had been derided for its physically expressive worship style, the tendency of its members to speak in tongues, and its interracial revivals. Early Pentecostals believed that clothing had a sacramental function: it was an outward demonstration of inner sanctification.[5] While beliefs varied, the overall aim was that a holy clothed body was one that appeared "plainly attired" and in its least modified form, which happened to align with middle-class standards of modesty and respectability.[6] In the early twentieth century, that included—for women—rejecting bobbed hair (as many believed that "natural" hair for women was uncut), makeup, and elaborate jewelry, and embracing long-sleeved, full-length, loose-fitting dresses.

Discussions of such issues began to appear in early Pentecostal publications that aimed to instruct women and men on the faithful's right relationship to public life. Contributors weighed in on matters from marital relations to movie attendance to bobbed hair. In 1908, when Clara Lum and Florence Crawford moved away from the Azusa Street Revival of Los Angeles to set up a mission in Portland, Oregon, and began publishing the *Apostolic Faith* newspaper from that location, they began to discuss the issue of attire. In the paper's fourteenth edition, they addressed the teachings of the movement, citing 1 Peter 3:3–4, which emphasizes a quiet spirit rather than fancy apparel, plaited hair, or gold adornment. While they avoided offering any specific proscriptions, they did mention that one might "hold on to a little gold breastpin or ring and lose out to disobedience to God and His word." This theme was repeated in other editions of the paper, and by 1914, the list of cautions on women's apparel included admonitions against low necklines, short sleeves, invisible waistlines, and tight skirts. If appropriate garments were not available for purchase, women were admonished to make their own.[7] The editors of the *Apostolic Faith* later expanded their usual discussion of modest dress to argue against adapting any kind of uniform, such as the uniforms worn publicly by Salvation Army officers, which might draw attention.[8] Similar themes appeared in *Word and Witness*, edited by E. N. Bell, who was influential in the formation of the Trinitarian Pentecostal denomination the Assemblies of God. Bell argued that women did not have to adopt styles of dress that were too plain, and that in keeping with their natural shapes women should embrace corsets that were easy fitting rather than form-fitting to the extreme.[9]

By the mid-1920s, Pentecostal publications began to debate women's hair. The root of these discussions grew out of the debates over head coverings, as called for in 1 Corinthians 11:15: "But if a woman have long hair, it is a glory to her: for her hair is given her for a covering." Bell argued that while head coverings showed women's submission to men in biblical times, this was not common practice in contemporary society, and so women did not need to cover their head.[10] Similarly, the *Apostolic Faith* argued that head coverings were unnecessary, and cited 1 Corinthians 11:15 as both evidence that long hair was the only necessary covering and to support arguments against bobbed hair styles. In addition, they proclaimed that women should not wear clothing or other adornments that pertained to men, and that women needed to avoid jewelry, feathers, flowers, and short skirts. Immodest dress was believed to lead to a life of sin and crime and separation from God. The truly converted would be freed of a desire to dress in this manner.[11]

In this early Pentecostal perspective, modest dress served two functions. First, a modestly dressed woman would avoid leading good Christian men into sin. Christian women had an obligation to dress in a way that did not tempt men.[12] Second, a woman's modest dress would protect her from all manner of evils perpetrated by passionate and ungodly men. According to the *Apostolic Faith*, modest attire could keep women safe from street harassment.[13] Additionally, adorning oneself with a "meek and quiet spirit" in the form of modest dress, rather than flashy or immodest apparel, would mean that a woman would not only avoid leading Christian men into sin, but would attract a good husband who sees virtue on the inside rather than a sensual one who chooses a woman based on her external sex appeal.[14]

Gradually, Pentecostal newspaper editors began to write about women's dress in ways that told their readers it was about even more than a desire to free men from temptation or an indicator of personal salvation. Women's dress stood as an indicator of the status of the church at large. The editors at the *Apostolic Faith* wrote that modest attire bore witness to the story of the gospel.[15] Readers of the *Pentecostal Evangel* were warned that tolerance of modern or scanty dress indicated an unsaved heart and brought down the tone of the entire congregation.[16] However, as these authors aligned the movement with a more staid mainstream, Aimee Semple McPherson indicated a willingness to push against the same boundaries that others in the movement worked to tightly define.

TRINITARIAN PENTECOSTAL WOMEN AND PERFORMANCE OF THE GOSPEL

Sister Aimee's Pentecostal glamour

In the 1920s, few women were as famous or infamous as the twice-divorced megachurch pastor and Pentecostal star Aimee Semple McPherson. Dubbed "the prima donna of revivalism" by *Harper's Magazine* in 1927, McPherson was at the vanguard of Trinitarian Pentecostalism's innovations as the movement grew and developed. She owned and operated one of the nation's first radio stations, from which her celebrity-attracting worship services in Los Angeles, California, were broadcast nationwide. By the time she started her own denomination in 1923, the glamorous, charismatic McPherson was one of Pentecostalism's most influential voices, as well as one of America's most controversial figures.

As was the case with almost every aspect of her life, Aimee Semple McPherson's fashion choices regularly made headlines. Rather than using her clothing primarily as an external signal of austere holiness, McPherson treated her body as a tabula rasa through which to communicate her Pentecostal messages. Initially, McPherson's clothing aligned with Pentecostalism's roots in the Holiness movement and her own family roots in the Salvation Army. "She couldn't afford an expensive dress," McPherson's daughter Roberta Salter remembered from her early years, so she wore a blue and white maid's uniform and accessorized it "with a cape put on like the Red Cross nurses had."[17] As was the case for the modesty codes of the early Pentecostals, McPherson's uniform did much to promote her middle-class respectability, even as she presided over meetings wherein attendees wept, danced, spoke in tongues, and engaged in all manner of supposedly unrespectable displays. McPherson and other Pentecostal "holy rollers" were denigrated for their "wailing, hollering, and screeching," but by visually associating themselves with nursing, an acceptable profession for women that was known for cleanliness and public order, they countered this public perception.

A version of McPherson's signature pulpit outfit became the official uniform for women in the Foursquare Church, the denomination she founded, and it had theological significance as well as projecting respectability. A visual association with nursing gave Foursquare women preachers a

FIGURE 4.1 Aimee Semple McPherson, by the Gerhard Sisters Studio, ca. 1921, gelatin silver print, from the National Portrait Gallery. Image courtesy of Wikimedia/Creative Commons.

theological argument for preaching: the women who wore this uniform were visually associated with the role of a maternal nurturer who was subordinate to the "Great Physician," Jesus.[18] Unlike the Holiness attire of previous generations, this nursing uniform counterintuitively heightened the sex appeal of the wearer in the years following World War I, as nurses came to be seen as objects of soldiers' desire in the early 1920s.[19]

The nexus of the American Pentecostal movement was Los Angeles, and thus it is no surprise that Pentecostals were early adopters of the American celebrity culture that was emerging at the same time and place. The simplicity of the Holiness look, combined with Aimee Semple McPherson's early nursing-inspired uniform, was incongruous with the glamour and spectacle of 1920s Hollywood film culture. Some Pentecostals were content with this incongruity, believing that accoutrements that were out of step with what audiences saw on film bolstered the purity and power of the Pentecostal message. Holiness, argued some, was the engine—the true fire—of the Pentecostal movement. Others argued that the best way to get the Pentecostal message out to the masses was by adapting it to the times—namely, by utilizing the latest trends in popular culture. The fiery tongues of the Pentecostal movement could burn, they argued, without traditional Holiness exteriors.

McPherson and her movement were definitely in the latter camp. As images of women in film and advertising wearing shorter skirts, bobbed hair, and cosmetics started populating the American mind en masse, Pentecostal women like McPherson adapted to the times. The "tall, thin, cartoonish young woman preoccupied with dancing, drinking, and necking" shown in magazine print terrified many American Protestants. Liberals like Harry Fosdick and conservatives like Billy Sunday were unsettled by 1920s women enjoying activities—like drinking, dancing, working outside the home, or playing sports—appreciated by those with supposedly loose sexual morals.

Many Holiness and Pentecostal Protestants found 1920s clothing to be not only offensive but also sinful. McPherson, however, saw in the newfangled fashion and youth culture an opportunity for revivalist growth. "The flapper had arrived," wrote journalist Carey McWilliams, "with short skirts and bobbed hair . . . and Aimee was determined to lead the parade on a grand detour to Heaven."[20] Leading the parade, at least for McPherson and her followers, meant in part adjusting her modest uniform to the glamorous context of Hollywood culture.[21] In fact, whereas Oneness

Pentecostals remained fiercely dedicated to the nineteenth-century Holiness codes that they inherited from the Holiness movement, McPherson and her many followers let them go without resistance. "On the question of flappers," reported the *Boston Daily Globe*, "Mrs. McPherson was content to shrug her shoulders and say, 'I see beyond the cosmetics and the clothes.' "[22]

Thus, while many feared flapper fashion because of its association with worldliness and sexual impropriety, McPherson and her followers embraced many of the same cosmetics and clothes feared by their revivalist contemporaries, and in particular their Oneness counterparts. McPherson led the way with especially flamboyant and figure-flattering clothing. In place of the loose-fitting, nurse-inspired dress, by 1928 McPherson wore white formfitting dresses that were often bedazzled with sequins. "She clings to white," observed one critic of McPherson's look, "and the fabric clings to her."[23]

McPherson's attempts to strike a balance between adapting to mainstream middle American standards of beauty, utilizing her sexuality to attract audiences, and maintaining the Pentecostal heritage of modesty was frequently misunderstood by outside observers. For example, at the 1935 California Pacific International Exposition, she turned down an invitation to visit a nudist colony. In the face of this rejected overture, a disgruntled Queen Zorine, leader of the nudists who had attempted to desexualize her colony of Zoro Gardens, was reported to have said, "I did not ask her to take off her clothes. I only invited her to tea."[24]

Queen Zorine may not have realized, however, that McPherson's look was not simply an adaptation of Hollywood glamor. It also had theological meaning for McPherson's congregation and within the broader Pentecostal community. Indeed, the prominent biblical metaphor of Jesus as the bridegroom and the church as the bride was one of the most common images used in Pentecostal preaching and hymnody.[25] Pentecostal leaders including William Seymour, Gaston B. Cashwell, and G. F. Taylor regularly wrote and spoke in rapturous terms about the bride (the Pentecostal church) waiting for the return of her bridegroom (the Second Coming).[26] The white dress, the ingenue looks, and the flowers that McPherson often carried with her to the pulpit were unmistakably bridal and were clearly understood by those who saw her preach. Reporters and followers regularly commented on her "wearing the garb and manner of a bride on her honeymoon."[27] McPherson further accessorized with professional makeup and hair styling.

McPherson's shifting hair fashions became the focal point of conversation about her piety, spiritual power, and popular appeal. As was the case with their Holiness predecessors, white Pentecostals were interested in the relationship between women's hair, godliness, and worldliness. Long, undyed, uncut hair on women harkened back to biblical exhortations to women, such as Paul's claims in I Corinthians. Women who wore the latest fashion trends were accused of being "stupefied by some Satanic opiate" in the form of the "fashions of the day."[28]

In the early years of her ministry, McPherson had "high-piled, unshorn dark hair," like many women preachers in the early twentieth century, but the longer she ministered in Los Angeles, the more she began to experiment with her hair color. Whether her hair was red, platinum, or strawberry blond, McPherson's hair choices attracted national attention, and when she cut her hair into a fashionable marcelled bob in 1927, it was front-page news. It also caused a church split.[29] Pentecostal traditionalists felt that McPherson had finally stepped too far outside the traditional Holiness standards of previous generations, and as such had disqualified herself from the ministry. "Mrs. McPherson hurt her followers beyond endurance when she had her hair bobbed recently," mourned choir leader and church defector Gladwyn Nichols. Nichols and his followers were horrified, but the damage to McPherson's overall ministry was minimal; only three hundred of her estimated fifteen thousand weekly attenders felt that their glamorous pastor's personal appearance was a reason to leave.

McPherson's hair change actually reflected a shift in many Trinitarian teachings about personal appearance, worldliness, and the power of the Holy Spirit. Unlike the first generation of Trinitarian Pentecostal revivalists who adopted strict modesty codes, McPherson and her growing circle of colleagues and followers were interested in accommodating their personal aesthetics to contemporary fashion standards. Rather than viewing sartorial trend following as a mark of spiritual defect, many Trinitarian Pentecostals came to see fashion as a potential tool for visual sermonizing. "We criticize each other's dress and clothes as if the kingdom of God depended upon these things," Pentecostal preacher Charles Price argued in a 1936 bid to downplay the importance of modesty codes. Price went on to elaborate about women's modesty and its place in Christian theology and practice. "We get into the habit," he wrote, "of paying more attention to the way some woman does her hair than we do to the fact that thousands are dying around us on every hand and side without God and without salvation. Mark you, I believe in modesty in appearance, yet there are some people who seem to appoint themselves as guardians of other people's rights and liberties to such an extent that dissention is stirred up and the work of the Lord is impeded and marred."[30]

Aimee Semple McPherson's use of clothing and theology marked a change in the rapidly growing Pentecostal world. Women in the Foursquare Church imitated her bridal fashion choices, as did female celebrity preachers in the broader Trinitarian Pentecostal movement. Preachers like Rheba Crawford, Uldine Utley, and many others followed McPherson and used their good looks, on-trend clothing, and up-to-date hair to attract followers. Subsequent generations of female leaders in white Trinitarian Pentecostalism did the same, including faith healer Kathryn Kuhlman from the 1940s to the 1970s, pioneering televangelist Tammy Faye Bakker in the 1970s and 1980s, and celebrity preacher Joyce Meyer in the 1990s. These women and their imitators dressed to emphasize their femininity and reflect current fashion trends. Each woman's embrace of feminine, mainstream beautification—Kuhlman's floor-length gowns, Bakker's extensive use of cosmetics and flamboyant wigs, and Meyer's face-lift—was accepted (and in some cases celebrated) by her respective followers.

Paula White-Cain's power with prosperity

Women in twenty-first-century mainstream branches of predominantly white, Trinitarian Pentecostalism typically clothe themselves in current fashion trends, style their hair, use cosmetics and accessories, and sometimes have plastic surgery, thereby portraying ideal styles of womanliness that align with white, middle-class standards. For mainstream, non-denominational Pentecostal female leaders like Paula White-Cain, this idealized display of white femininity provides them with unspoken but nonetheless powerful theological meaning. Their external appearance can be interpreted as an expression of the prosperity gospel, or the idea that God's faithful elect will demonstrate their divine favor in the form of health and wealth.[31] As their inward souls prosper, so their outward appearance demonstrates the favor of God. Just as Aimee Semple McPherson, Rheba Crawford, Kathryn Kuhlman, Tammy Faye Bakker, and many others did in previous generations, this favored status as a woman who conforms to twenty-first-century feminine norms can be parlayed into leadership status.

The embrace of contemporary fashion as a way to display a kind of popular femininity with biblical resonance does not mean that modesty had no place in Trinitarian Pentecostal theology and practice. Historian Arlene Sánchez-Walsh has examined the behavior codes of Pentecostal Bible colleges, and her work shows that women's dress is still a site of theological and political negotiation, even in McPherson's movement.[32] Today, most Pentecostal Bible colleges regulate women's attire far more than men's, considering this regulation to be a demonstration of the entire group's moral and theological vision of the world.[33] Where their celebrity preachers are concerned, however, white Pentecostals in Trinitarian circles have a track record of elevating women whose good looks conform to mainstream standards of white, middle-class femininity and who push the movement's official standards of modesty. Whether it was curvy, petite Tammy Faye Bakker and her wide, blue eyes and high-pitched, girlish voice, or Kathryn Kuhlman's tiny frame and softly waved bob, the biggest stars have conformed to mass media versions of white femininity.

Visually, Paula White-Cain is a natural heir of McPherson, Bakker, and other Trinitarian women who treat their bodies as pliable instruments of a revivalist message, and who created a bride-of-Christ visual signal with their appearance. White-Cain has an expensive and extravagant wardrobe, professionally colored and styled blond hair, bleached white teeth, and meticulous but generously applied makeup. There are rumors that she continues to sculpt her face and body through plastic surgery. All of this, plus her telegenic smile, made her an excellent candidate to fill the shoes left by Tammy Faye Bakker and Jan Crouch in Christian broadcasting. Like those who came before her, White-Cain pushes the boundaries of modesty by wearing, say, thigh-high leather boots, or tight sweaters that draw attention to her curves. Her down-home southern accent, self-effacing humor, and on-screen warmth have made her a star.

Through her preaching—distributed to her (as of 2022) 3.4 million Facebook followers and 1 million Twitter followers—White-Cain gives her readers biblical models for interpreting her looks. Biblical women like

FIGURE 4.2 Paula White-Cain's glamourous conservatism is on display at an "Evangelicals for Trump" event in January 2020. Image credit: MPI04/MediaPunch/IPX.

Esther and Ruth are held up as models of the "decade of the woman."[34] Esther has become a figure of particular interest for White-Cain. In the fall and winter of 2016, she preached a series on the story of the Jewish woman who became an undercover advocate for her people as consort to the Persian king Ahasuerus. In this series of sermons, White-Cain preached about the "divine plan" of God and the "time, position, order, and place" in which God put Esther.[35] She told her congregation that God chose unlikely people, as in the case of Esther, to do extraordinary things. The spirit of Esther, according to White-Cain, was upon her and the faithful in her congregation. "It's your moment right now," she exhorted.[36]

As McPherson had done years earlier with the biblical model of a bride of Christ, White-Cain was preaching to her congregation and also speaking about herself. In the fall of 2016, White-Cain had become known as the "personal pastor" to Donald J. Trump following his election as president of the United States. White-Cain was a well-coiffed, meticulously dressed presence at his 2017 inauguration. In the following months, she became something of a spokesperson for Trump's "faith advisers," evangelical and Pentecostal charismatics who regularly receive White House briefings.[37] Eventually, like Esther, White-Cain claimed to be a voice—not for a persecuted ethnic minority, as was the case for Jews in exile, but for charismatic and Pentecostal Christians who *feel* minoritized in twenty-first-century America. And, like Esther, she grew to hold influence with the most powerful office in the United States as head of Trump's Faith and Opportunity Initiative in 2019.

Like Esther, White-Cain's personal appearance contributes to her success. Trump made no secret of the fact that he preferred to be around women whose personal appearance conformed to middle-class, white, Western beauty standards, and White-Cain fits this mold. On the National Day of Prayer in 2019, for example, White-Cain wore a formfitting, figure-flattering light-pink dress with pearls and professionally styled hair. White-Cain's prayer emphasized Trump's status, not as a citizen elected by a self-governing people, but as the divinely appointed ruler anointed by God. "We secure victory in the name . . . that has never failed for this nation and for my life, the name of Jesus Christ," White-Cain said. Her audience affirmed her prayers for protection over this ruler and his nation with chants of "U.S.A.! U.S.A.!"[38]

In Trump's 2020 reelection campaign, White-Cain remained supportive of the president. The week before the election, she penned an op-ed in the pages of *Christianity Today* titled "Of Course Evangelicals Should Vote for Trump," wherein she noted the policy wins Trump had guaranteed for evangelicals (his antiabortion stances, conservative Supreme Court appointments, religious freedom advocacy, pro-Israel stance, and Trumpian patriotism). When it looked like Trump had lost, she called for global spiritual reinforcements in the form of angels from South America and Africa. After Trump's defeat, White-Cain led the Center for American Values at the former president's America First Policy Institute.[39]

Echoing a common refrain in Pentecostalism, White-Cain argues that she is "not political" and that her role in the Trump administration is purely spiritual. Her role as an Esther figure in the administration is to stand up for the people of God, she argues, not any particular political platform. Yet White-Cain's own personal political opinions—which she shares widely on her various platforms—happen to overlap with many policy points that are central to Trump's white evangelical base. She has publicly celebrated conservative policy talking points on a number of occasions. For example, she regularly speaks about her opposition to abortion and her support for traditional heterosexual marriage, and she encourages women to submit to their husbands as "helpmeets." Trinitarian Pentecostal women have in the person of White-Cain a very public example of a woman who uses her dress and appearance to support the person whom some view as the divinely anointed leader of their nation.

ONENESS PENTECOSTAL WOMEN AND PRESERVATION OF THE FAITH

The development of Oneness appearance standards

Within the more conservative Oneness branches of the Pentecostal movement, clothing, hair, and the lack of cosmetics are powerful and carefully maintained signifiers of inward godliness and power. These trends are widespread among white Pentecostal groups, including people who are more isolated from the majority of Oneness adherents, such as those who practice snake handling in rural Appalachia. Maintaining such Holiness standards might seem difficult, given the styles currently sold to American women, but in recent years the world of online commerce has expanded the sartorial opportunities for such women. Along with carefully selecting items from mainstream sources, women across the country can purchase modest styles from online retailers, often those owned by other Pentecostal women. This accessibility has likely further entrenched certain modesty standards, leading to a distinct look for Oneness Pentecostal women.[40]

The visible differences between Oneness and Trinitarian Pentecostal women were not fully evident until after World War II, as pants began to appear in the average American woman's closet and as Oneness Pentecostals developed a permanent source of official publications. White Oneness Pentecostals, who had suffered through a series of splits and mergers, finally saw some denominational stability with the formation of the United Pentecostal Church International (UPCI) in 1945. Although other, smaller predominately white organizations and independent congregations still existed, the merger would create an institution large enough to maintain a church press that printed a series of official church publications that were consumed by the broader Oneness movement. As a result, regardless of which Oneness denomination or independent church a woman might belong to, the ideas on modesty to which she was exposed were likely to have come from a UPCI publication.

The church press of the 1960s reflected ideas about women's attire that mirrored those of the 1910s and 1920s, albeit with more emphasis on women avoiding apparel associated with men. For instance, a 1961 essay in the *Pentecostal Herald* entitled "What's Wrong with Wrong?" encapsulated the movement's standards from prohibitions on everything from smoking, drinking, and dancing to discussions on modest attire. Its author first narrowed in on women in shorts, slacks, and jeans as being in violation of Deuteronomy 22:5, which prohibits women wearing attire that pertains to men. It added an additional word of caution about short and tight skirts and revealing necklines, and ended with reminders from 1 Timothy 2:9. Women were also told to keep their hair long, as nature intended; short hair was associated with men and a woman with short hair was therefore seen as being in rebellion. The maintenance of long hair indicated an obedience to God's word and respect for the place that God had given women. In this early article, long hair was not explicitly linked with honoring men, as it would be in later years.[41]

By the time Elaine Lawless was conducting ethnographic work on Oneness Pentecostals in the late 1970s and early 1980s for her book *God's Peculiar People: Women's Voices and Folk Tradition in a Pentecostal Church*, she noted that clothing served to define Pentecostal women in a way that that was not unlike an ethnic identity. Among her midwestern subjects, she noted certain commonalities of dress and comportment that included plainness of color, low hemlines, long sleeves and high necklines, a lack of jewelry and makeup, and uncut hair that was often styled in somewhat dated fashions. Lawless believed that because of these styles, outsiders associated Pentecostals with the working class, but to those in the faith it indicated a willingness to abandon fashion in favor of holiness, a bond with other Oneness Pentecostal women, and a silent condemnation of the immodesty of the broader community. Lawless concluded that those outside the Pentecostal community often recognized this latter message and altered their own immodest behavior or dress as a result, for instance by covering more of their bodies, even if they were not eager to do so.[42] What Lawless found was a set of dress standards that had survived from the earliest days of the movement, when Holiness preachers and their converts set out to define the limits of modest attire.

Lawless's observations of women in the midwestern Oneness churches align with the commentary found in church publications. In 1981, Jean Urshan, the wife of United Pentecostal Church General Superintendent Nathaniel Urshan, proclaimed that the UPCI might be the only religious institution with such gender-distinct dress lines. For Urshan and others, distinctiveness of dress led to the preservation of femininity and charm and peace to the soul. Conversely, a lack of such attire would lead to disgrace and reproach. Urshan also proclaimed that these standards allowed a woman to help her husband carry out his tasks.[43] Urshan continued with these themes in later articles, proclaiming gender-distinct dress to be part of the Oneness Pentecostal heritage.[44]

While these claims betray a view of religion that is limited to particular forms of American Christianity, they also reveal that Oneness Pentecostal women had come to see themselves as set apart from other Christians in their maintenance of piety, and they felt that these standards were intended in large part to serve in support of men's roles. In 1985, San Diego pastor David F. Gray identified six lines of biblical teaching in his article "Guidelines for Christian Dress," including vanity, costliness, immodesty, gender distinction, identification with the ungodly, and typology. His discussions of vanity and costliness harkened back to the older arguments concerning 1 Tim 2:9, and his discussion of immodesty dealt with women's responsibility not to lure their brothers in the Lord into sin. His argument about modest, gender-distinctive dress was that failure to maintain it could lead women into homosexuality and result in rape, adultery, or assault. Women in pants were seen as being in rebellion against a male-dominated society. Gray also began to connect long hair to typology or symbolic meaning found in scripture. For Gray, 1 Corinthians 11 is not just a call for women to keep their head covered; rather, it sets up a typology wherein men signified Christ and women the church. Men with short hair would reveal the glory of Christ, while women should have long hair to show the subjection of the church to Christ.[45] In 1985, David K. Bernard, then a pastor in Texas who would later come to head the UPCI, would first publish *Practical Holiness: A Second Look*, a book that is still widely considered to be one of the most in-depth presentations of such views on attire. Much of his writings defining standards of Holiness dress can be traced to the early days of the movement, including acceptance of a natural form, being a good steward of resources by not purchasing costly apparel, avoiding enticing men to lust, and attracting a godlier spouse.[46]

The biggest shift in these attire and dress teachings would come in the mid-1990s, and, like the Trinitarian women, this shift would associate appearance with power. However, unlike their Trinitarian counterparts, this power was to be found not in choosing a set of garments that would gain them influence in secular corridors, but rather in maintaining long or uncut hair that would bring them power before the throne of God. Based on 1 Corinthians 11:1–16, Oneness Pentecostals had long before arrived at the conclusion that the appropriate covering for women was not a hat or scarf, but uncut hair. However, they began to emphasize verse 10, which proclaims that women have power on their heads because of the angels.[47] This concept was cemented when Ruth (Rieder) Harvey, the granddaughter of the noted early twentieth-century Pentecostal evangelist A. D. Urshan, published the book *Power Before the Throne* (1999). This work emphasizes the traditional arguments associated with long hair, such as it being an indicator of women's submission to male leadership and God's order, not just to those on earth but also to those in the spirit world. Like David Gray, Harvey believes hair is a form of typology, with men representing God and women the church and, as such, the bride of Christ, who must be covered. However, Harvey connects uncut hair with power before God, and contends that cut hair leads to a removal of God's protection, giving an example of a woman who cut her hair and whose husband then fell into adultery. Harvey provides a counterexample of a woman who, when

FIGURE 4.3 Rowan County Clerk Kim Davis's uncut and unstyled hair demonstrates her obedience to Oneness Pentecostal teachings. Morehead, Kentucky, September 2015. Image credit: AP Photo/Timothy D. Easley.

praying over her dying son, reminded God that she had not cut her hair, and claimed power from the angels for God to heal him, suggesting uncut hair might bring protection to the family. Harvey attributes this and other miracles to angels responding to a mother's uncut hair.[48]

Harvey is among the Oneness Pentecostals who use the story of Esther to associate modesty with power. For author Mary Cole, Esther's history is also the story of Vashti. Esther had her chance to appear before the throne and save her people only when Vashti refused to put her body on display for her husband's drunken guests. Vashti paid a price for this, true, but in doing so it made way for Esther and the salvation of others. Pentecostal women who say no to revealing fashions could serve as a "living testimony" to the community.[49] In *Practical Holiness*, UPCI leader David Bernard also returns to the story of Esther as a biblical example of modesty, but places the emphasis on her choice to reject an offer of cosmetics and jewelry before her night with the king.[50] For Harvey, the importance of the story of Esther is not so much her plain dress as much as her willingness to stand before the king without compromise. Women who are unwilling to compromise will find they have power because of the angels.[51]

By the 2010s, Oneness Pentecostals, influenced by David Bernard, had begun to discuss the concept of "Apostolic identity." For Bernard, Apostolic identity is defined by basic principles of Oneness theology as well as piety and Christian living.[52] Apostolic distinctiveness is reliant upon holiness, which includes inward and outward holiness and adherence to New Testament teaching on dress, among other areas.[53] While Bernard does not always tie this to particular standards of attire, such standards are nearly always implied given the context of his influential *Practical Holiness*, in which the wearing of pants, makeup, and jewelry are discouraged.[54]

For many Americans, this Apostolic identity was first visible in the third season of the reality show *Wife Swap* (2004–10), in which Oneness Pentecostal mom Kristin Hoover, the daughter of a UPCI pastor, trades places with rocker mom Tish Meeks. This move to a public performance of faith is significant, because along with maintaining strict dress standards, Oneness Pentecostals often reject ownership of television, and many do not go to the movies. In choosing to appear on this show, the Hoovers intentionally promoted aspects of their faith using a medium rejected by many inside their movement. Their choices were designed to send a message to those outside of the faith rather than within it.

While filming *Wife Swap*, the Hoover family maintained traditional dress standards for their three daughters. Discussions about the young Pentecostal women's clothes, their theology, and their sexuality occurred often in one episode, as Meeks attempted to entice the three Hoover girls to wear pants. In pre- and post-show interviews for the now defunct Apostolic zine *90&9*, Hoover said that she had felt a special call from God at the Azusa centennial celebrations the previous year, and believed that this was God using her in a previously unimaginable way.[55] Before going on the show, the Hoovers engaged in intense discussions about how they wanted to portray their faith, paying particular attention to issues associated with clothing standards. The show did not identify them clearly as Pentecostal or as associated with any Oneness organization, so viewers may have seen them only as generically Christian.[56] The Hoovers were fairly satisfied with their portrayal, and the *Atlantic Monthly* noted that the family's conservative values had been taken seriously by the show.[57]

This example aside, Oneness Pentecostal women have not typically been visible in the American media landscape. For decades, Oneness Pentecostals lagged behind their Trinitarian counterparts in developing inroads into politics. Some of the earliest political connections occurred in the 1980s, when Nathaniel Urshan worked to help the Siberian Seven, a group of Pentecostals who had sought asylum in the U.S. embassy in Moscow, gain exit visas from the Soviet Union, but very few have held significant political offices. After Bryan P. Stevenson was elected to the Missouri State Legislature in 2002, have gave an interview to the *Pentecostal Herald* in which he was able to identify only one other Oneness Pentecostal who had served in a state legislature. He expressed the view that they should be more involved in politics, not just for the sake of the role, but to further God's plan.[58] Four years later, Stevenson wrote an article proclaiming that while Christians might not win every political battle, they should show God's love and use the spheres to which God had given them access.[59] This article, which appeared about a month after the *Wife Swap* episode, signaled that Oneness Pentecostals had a growing interest in public platforms.

Kim Davis and preservation of the natural order

The message spread slowly, but in 2014, shortly after hearing a sermon on the need for Christians in the public sphere, Kim Davis decided to run as the replacement for her mother who was retiring as the clerk of Rowan County, Kentucky.[60] In 2015, Davis became a nationally recognized public figure when, in her new position, she ordered her clerks to cease issuing marriage licenses in the county so that she could avoid issuing licenses to gay couples, which, because of Davis's position, would necessarily bear her name. She cited God's authority for this action and was subsequently jailed for contempt. The office later altered the license's format so that Davis's name did not appear on it. She attracted support from conservative politicians around the country, including then presidential candidate Mike Huckabee and Senator Ted Cruz. Davis was later invited to a controversial meeting with Pope Francis and traveled to Romania to promote that country's ban on same sex marriage.[61] The incident propelled a small-town southern court clerk into the public eye. While Davis does not compare herself to Esther, she did receive fan mail that connected her to that biblical figure, who was chosen to stand before the king in defense of her people.⁶²

Despite all of the public attention, Davis maintained Oneness Pentecostal teachings on attire and attempted to avoid vanity. She never appeared to be concerned about her public image—for instance, she refused the request of an Associated Press photographer to pose for a picture—and she kept her long hair, something for which she was often publicly recognized. She also refused to have her hair further styled or to wear any makeup in television interviews.⁶³ Kim Davis's classic Oneness Pentecostal attire did not go unnoticed, and her look was replicated in a skit on *Saturday Night Live*, suggested as a costume on an LGBT website, and even turned into the stuff of lesbian jailhouse erotic fiction.⁶⁴

Although Davis herself did not overtly connect her long hair or modest attire with her stand against same sex marriage, her choice to make such a stand reflects themes associated with Oneness Pentecostal forms of modest dress, including obedience, submission, and a witness of God's redeeming power. It is clear that Davis believes God has authorized a natural order or law. When questioned about the role of God's authority over

FIGURE 4.4 The modest attire of Kim Davis, seen from the rear, is well demonstrated in this photograph from a September 2015 political event. Image credit: Pablo Alcala/Lexington Herald-Leader via AP.

the Kentucky court that had jailed her for contempt, she agreed that the court's injunction was contrary to natural law—hence her disobedience to the order.[65] The belief that God has ordained a natural order with distinct gender roles is reinforced in beliefs about proper modesty, in particular that nature intended women to have long hair and men short, the concept that fashion should not greatly alter one's natural form or appearance, and that God intended for the two genders to dress differently. These beliefs about a natural order, reinforced every time a Oneness Pentecostal opens their closet or brushes their hair, form part of a worldview in which same sex marriage is wrong because it violates a perceived natural order. Although Oneness Pentecostals are not the sole Protestants to hold this belief, in other denominations it is not reinforced on a daily basis through personal attire.

In a television interview with Megyn Kelly, Davis was asked if she knew she could have spent a year in jail. Davis responded that it had not mattered because she had vowed to serve God with her "whole heart, mind, body, and soul," and that it was a "heaven or hell issue" for her.[66] Because implementation of these modesty standards varies somewhat from congregation to congregation, Oneness Pentecostals often claim that something is or is not a "heaven or hell issue" to signify whether a particular variation of that standard would result in eternal damnation. Davis applied the phrase, which is often associated with discussions of modesty, to her choice to make a political stand on marriage, indicating that for her, these issues were part of the same discussion.

In addition, Davis sees God as the ultimate authority. When Paula Faris asked her on *Good Morning America* whether her boss was God, her constituents, or the federal government, Davis acknowledged that the constituents had elected her, but that God held the ultimate authority.[67] Following such logic, if God is the authority and God has indeed established a natural order, then it would be the duty of Christians to uphold that natural order in society. For Oneness Pentecostals, then, taking a stand against same sex marriage can become part and parcel of one's daily choice to preserve the natural order by wearing only modest and gender-appropriate apparel.

Because Davis has a complicated personal history, including four marriages to three different men, many saw her stand against same sex marriage as unbiblical as hypocritical. Davis often had to defend herself on this issue, telling Megyn Kelly that she had not judged anyone.[68] In her interview on *Good Morning America*, Davis elaborated on this point, saying that she was not a hypocrite; she admitted to her sins, but had been forgiven. It is this accusation of hypocrisy that seems to bother her the most.[69] Pentecostal women are often taught to consider modesty as a form of witness of the gospel, a silent testimony of sorts to the unsaved. Davis, who had returned to the church approximately four years prior to her arrest, clearly wanted her life to reflect such a witness. After the release of her 2018 autobiography *Under God's Authority*, she made it clear that her book was about her own redemption and her turn to God.[70] In the book, she also notes that a day after she was sent to jail, Reuters sent out a story that told her testimony and cited Acts 2:38, the verse of scripture summarizing the Oneness teaching on baptism and salvation.[71]

Teachings on Pentecostal dress have made it clear from the earliest days that modest dress can serve to bring God to the ungodly. For Davis, who adhered to fairly strict interpretations of these teachings, clothing was not enough. Despite her outward self-presentation as an inner reflection of holiness, her past failures, which she believes are forgiven, were revisited and held against her. For her, then, it is important to make sure that the redemption part of her Christian walk is broadcast more loudly, as without an understanding of redemption, she is reduced to the figure of a hypocrite selectively enforcing the Bible. It is the tension between her proclamation of redemption through her appearance and her checkered past that makes her public platform a significant one.

The Pentecostal movement has gone from the theological fringes of American religion to the center of both religious and political life in the United States, and it has done so, thanks at least in part, to the attire of women as a performance of faith. Paula White-Cain's and Kim Davis's newfound status as political figures could be interpreted as the rise of two women who were in the proverbial right place at the right time; however, their public images are instructive for students of American religion and public life. For Trinitarian Pentecostals, the aesthetic promoted among leaders accommodates contemporary expressions of the feminine. For Oneness practitioners, the visual culture celebrated among the faithful remains tied to nineteenth-century Holiness codes. For both Trinitarian and Oneness Pentecostal women, clothing and other sartorial accoutrements have deep theological value. While there are considerable differences in how the two groups view modesty, the result is that for both, women's bodies signify the values of their religious movements. Protestants are not often associated with particular forms of religious attire, but as the Pentecostals show, theological dress can be both subtle and significant.

NOTES

1. Wyatte Grantham-Phillips, "Pastor Paula White Calls on Angels from Africa and South America to Bring Trump Victory," *USA Today*, November 5, 2020, https://www.usatoday.com/story/news/nation/2020/11/05/paula-white-trumps-spiritual-adviser-african-south-american-angels/6173576002/.

2. Anthea Butler's *Women in the Church of God in Christ: Making a Sanctified World* (Chapel Hill: University of North Carolina Press, 2012) explores the relationship among clothing, personal appearance, politics, and Holiness theology for Black women in the Church of God in Christ.

3. Gastón Espinosa, *Latino Pentecostals in America: Faith and Politics in Action* (Cambridge, MA: Harvard University Press, 2014), 26; J. Brent Norris, *Oberlin: Hotbed of Abolitionism, College, Community, and the Fight for Freedom and Equality in Antebellum America* (Chapel Hill: University of North Carolina Press, 2014), 64; Joel A. Carpenter, *Revive Us Again: The Reawakening of American Fundamentalism* (New York: Oxford University Press, 1997), 81; James Robinson, *Divine Healing: The Formative Years: 1830-1890* (Eugene, OR: Wipf and Stock Publishers, 2011), i.

4. Iain MacRobert, *The Black Roots and White Racism of Early Pentecostalism in the USA* (New York: Palgrave Macmillan, 1988); Randall J. Stephens, *The Fire Spreads: Holiness and Pentecostalism in the American South* (Cambridge, MA: Harvard University Press, 2010).

5. Leah Payne, *Gender and Pentecostal Revivalism: Making a Female Ministry in the Early Twentieth Century* (New York: Palgrave Macmillan, 2015), 67.

6. "Took Her Child to See Christ, She Tells Judge," *Topeka Daily Capital*, August 13, 1915, 1.

7. "Questions Answered," *Apostolic Faith*, September 1908, 3; "Questions Answered," *Apostolic Faith*, October–December 1908, 2; "Questions Answered," *Apostolic Faith*, July 1909, 3; "Modest Apparel," *Apostolic Faith* 27 (1914): 3. The *Apostolic Faith* and most other Pentecostal publications cited herein can be found through the online digital archives of the Consortium of Pentecostal Archives, available at https://pentecostalarchives.org/collections/.

Note that in the case of *Apostolic Faith* citations, the consortium lists volume and issue numbers for some, issue numbers only for others, while for still others it includes simply month and year.

8. "Immodest Dress," *Apostolic Faith* 57 (1924): 3.
9. "The Dress Fad," *Word and Witness*, June 20, 1913, 2.
10. "Questions and Answers," *Weekly Evangel*, April 28, 1917, 9.
11. "Immodest Dress," *Apostolic Faith* 57 (1924): 3; "Immodest Dress," *Apostolic Faith* 62 (1926): 4.
12. "Concerning Women's Apparel," *Christian Evangel*, April 19, 1919, 6.
13. "The Dress Question," *Apostolic Faith* 67 (1929): 2.
14. "A Young Man's Protest Against Modern Feminine Attire," *Pentecostal Evangel*, June 24, 1922, 5; "Modern Dress Menace," *Pentecostal Evangel*, September 16, 1922, 4.
15. "The Dress Question," *Apostolic Faith* 67 (1929): 2.
16. "Is There Declension in the Pentecostal Movement?," *Pentecostal Evangel*, April 21, 1923, 2–5.
17. Kathryn Kuhlman, *I Believe in Miracles* (television program), February 15, 1973, video 236, and February 29, 1968, video 285. Records of the Kathryn Kuhlman Foundation, Billy Graham Center Archives at Wheaton College, IL.
18. Payne, *Gender and Pentecostal Revivalism*, 71.
19. Payne, 71.
20. Carey McWilliams, "Sunlight in My Soul," in *The Aspirin Age, 1919-1941*, ed. Isabel Leighton (New York: Simon and Schuster, 1949), 60.
21. Payne, *Gender and Pentecostal Revivalism*, 71.
22. "Aimee Sails South Lauding New York," *Boston Daily Globe*, March 4, 1927, 1.
23. Grover Cleveland Loud, *Evangelized America* (Freeport, NY: Books for Libraries Press, 1928), 325.
24. Richard Amero, "California Pacific International Exposition, Chapter Four: The Exposition gets Under Way—1935," San Diego History Center, accessed September 6, 2022, https://sandiegohistory.org/archives/amero/1935expo/ch4/; Jack Scheffler Innis, *San Diego Legends: The Events, People, and Places that Made History* (San Diego: Sunbelt Publications, 2004), 77–79.
25. See Revelation 21:2, 21:9, and 22:17, Matthew 25:1–13, and Mark 2:18–22; Douglas G. Jacobsen, *Thinking in the Spirit: Theologies of the Early Pentecostal Movement* (Bloomington: Indiana University Press, 2003), 102–3.
26. A. T. Lange, "The Glory that Excelleth," *Triumphs of Faith* 29, no. 11 (1909): 255; William Seymour, "Behold the Bridegroom Cometh," *Apostolic Faith* 1, no. 5 (1907): 2; George Floyd Taylor, *The Spirit and the Bride: A Scriptural Presentation*

of the Operations, Manifestations, Gifts and Fruit of the Holy Spirit in His Relation to the Bride with Special Reference to the "Latter Rain" Revival (Dunn, NC: Falcon Publishing Company, 1907); G. T. Haywood, *Baptized Into the Body* (Indianapolis, IN: Christian Outlook: Pentecostal Assemblies of the World, ca. 1925).

27. Frank Sibley, "Aimee Arrives for Big Revival," *Daily Boston Globe*, August 17, 1931, 6.
28. Thomas A. Robinson and Lanettte D. Ruff, *Out of the Mouths of Babes: Girl Evangelists in the Flapper Era* (New York: Oxford University Press, 2011), 58.
29. Payne, *Gender and Pentecostal Revivalism*, 74–75.
30. Charles Price, "Make Me a Blessing," *Golden Grain* 10, no. 11 (1936): 15.
31. See Kate Bowler, *Blessed: A History of the American Prosperity Gospel* (New York: Oxford University Press, 2013).
32. Arlene Sánchez Walsh, *Pentecostals in America* (New York: Columbia University Press, 2018), 34–51.
33. Walsh, 34–51.
34. Paula White-Cain, "Esther 2018," Paula White-Cain Ministries, accessed October 24, 2018, https://paulawhite.netviewshop.com/shopdetail/624.
35. Paula White-Cain, "Pastor Paula White-Cain Continuing on Esther," YouTube, accessed September 6, 2019, https://www.youtube.com/watch?v=iiyrZBKzno4.
36. White-Cain, "Pastor Paula White-Cain Continuing on Esther."
37. Kate Shellnutt and Sarah Eekhoff Zylstra, "Who's Who of Trump's 'Tremendous' Faith Advisors," *Christianity Today*, June 22, 2016, https://www.christianitytoday.com/ct/2016/june-web-only/whos-who-of-trumps-tremendous-faith-advisors.html.
38. Carol Kuruvilla, "Trump's Spiritual Advisor Prays to 'Stop Demonic Attacks' Against Him," *Huffington Post*, June 19, 2019, https://www.huffpost.com/entry/paula-white-trump-reelection-rally-prayer_n_5d0a5213e4b0e560b70ce30b.
39. Steve Benen, "Why in the World Would Team Trump Need a 'Policy Institute?,'" MSNBC, April 14, 2021, https://www.msnbc.com/rachel-maddow-show/why-world-would-team-trump-need-policy-institute-n1264039.
40. For examples of such websites, see "Our Story," Dainty Jewells Clothier, https://daintyjewells.com/about-us/; Skirt Society, https://theskirtsociety.com; and "About Us," Olive Drew, https://olivedrew.com/pages/about-us (all accessed August 16, 2019).
41. "What's Wrong with Wrong," *Pentecostal Herald*, September 1961, 4–5.
42. Elaine J. Lawless, *God's Peculiar People: Women's Voices and Folk Tradition in a Pentecostal Church* (Lexington: University Press of Kentucky, 1988), 36–38.

43. Jean Urshan, "The Ministry of Women," *Pentecostal Herald*, May 1981, 4–5.
44. Jean Urshan, "A Message to Wives," *Pentecostal Herald*, May 1983, 6–7.
45. David F. Gray, "Guidelines for Christian Dress," *Pentecostal Herald*, August 1985, 22–3. Carol Clemans also argued as late as 2007 that women needed to be modest to save men from lust. Clemans, "Women Beware," *Pentecostal Herald*, November 2007, 8–9.
46. David K. Bernard, *Practical Holiness: A Second Look* (Hazelwood, MO: Word Aflame Press, 2010), 155–67.
47. Cheryl Riddick. "Long Hair: Is It a Sacrifice or Is It Worship?," *Pentecostal Herald*, June 1996, 17.
48. Ruth (Rieder) Harvey, *Power Before the Throne* (n.p.: Abiding Words, 1999). Kindle Edition.
49. Mary Cole, "No!," *Pentecostal Herald*, June 1967, 16.
50. Bernard, *Practical Holiness*, 172.
51. Ruth (Rieder) Harvey, *Power Before the Throne*.
52. David K. Bernard, "Apostolic Identity," *Pentecostal Herald*, March 2010, 7.
53. David K. Bernard, "Our Apostolic Distinctiveness," *Pentecostal Herald*, July 2016, 27–29.
54. David K. Bernard, *Practical Holiness*, 155–88.
55. Steve and Kristin Hoover, "Wife Swap's Steve and Kristin Hoover—The ninetyandnine.com Interview," interview by Kent D. Curry, Ninetyandnine.com, February 12, 2007, http://web.archive.org/web/20081105084047/http://www.ninetyandnine.net/cover/20070212.html.
56. Steven and Kristin Hoover, "I Determined Not to Walk Before the Cameras Until I Had Received an Anointing," interview by Kent D. Curry, Ninetyandnine.com, February 13, 2007, http://web.archive.org/web/20100511065122/http://www.ninetyandnine.net/cover/20070219.html.
57. Michael Hirschorn, "The Case for Reality TV," *Atlantic Monthly*, May 2007, https://www.theatlantic.com/magazine/archive/2007/05/the-case-for-reality-tv/305791/.
58. "Apostolics and Politics: Involvement without Compromise," *Pentecostal Herald*, October 2003, 27–29.
59. Bryan Stevenson, "The Role of Christians in Government," *Pentecostal Herald*, March 2007, 12–14.
60. Kim Davis, John Aman, and Mat Saver, *Under God's Authority: The Kim Davis Story* (n.p.: New Revolution Publishers, 2018), 24.
61. Ed Payne and Daniel Burke, "Pope's Meeting with Kim Davis Not an Endorsement, Vatican Says," CNN, last modified October 2, 2018, https://www.cnn

.com/2015/10/02/us/kim-davis-pope/index.html; Liam Stack and Kit Gillet, "Davis Once Jailed in America, Campaigns Against Gay Marriage in Romania," *New York Times*, October 12, 2017, https://www.nytimes.com/2017/10/12/world/europe/kim-davis-romania.html.

62. Davis, Aman, and Saver, *Under God's Authority*, 101.
63. Davis, Aman, and Saver, 53, 115–16, 118.
64. Graham Gremore, "How to Get Kim Davis' Signature Look," Queerty, September 12, 2015, https://www.queerty.com/how-to-get-kim-davis-signature-look-20150912; Curtis M. Wong, "A NSFW Kim Davis-Themed Erotic Novella Is Here. Yes, Really," *Huffington Post*, last modified January 9, 2017, https://www.huffpost.com/entry/kim-davis-erotic-fiction_n_56003d44e4b08820d9197b0f.
65. Davis, Aman, and Saver, *Under God's Authority*, 81.
66. "Megyn Kelly to Kim Davis: 'Your Critics Ask, Who Are You to Judge Others?,'" *Fox News Insider*, September 23, 2015, https://www.youtube.com/watch?v=2f42KCHBgUk. The heaven-or-hell concept is also repeated in Davis's biography. Davis, Aman, and Saver, *Under God's Authority*, 12.
67. Kim Davis interview with Paula Faris, *Good Morning America*, September 22, 2015, https://archive.org/details/KGO_20150922_140000_Good_Morning_America/start/1980/end/2040.
68. "Megyn Kelly to Kim Davis: 'Your Critics Ask, Who Are You to Judge Others?'"
69. Kim Davis interview with Paula Faris.
70. "Kim Davis Releases Brand New Book 'Under God's Authority,'" *Faith and Freedom Podcast*, March 23, 2018, https://www.lc.org/faith-and-freedom-full-article/kim-davis-releases-brand-new-book-under-gods-authority.
71. Davis, Aman, and Saver, *Under God's Authority*, 137.

Part II

IDENTITY ADORNMENT

Five

HOLY DASHIKIS!

BLACK SARTORIAL NATIONALISM AND BLACK ISRAELITE RELIGION

ANDRÉ E. BROOKS-KEY

THE DASHIKI IS one of the most iconic items of clothing from the Black Power era. The colorful tunic's adoption as a symbol of Black pride during the 1960s and 1970s is well documented. The word "dashiki" comes from the Yoruba word *danshiki*, which refers to the loose-fitting pullover that originated in West Africa as a functional work tunic for men, comfortable enough to wear in the heat. The Yoruba borrowed the word from the Hausa *dan ciki*, which means "underneath." The *dan ciki* garment was commonly worn by males under large robes. Similar garments in the region date back to the twelfth and thirteenth centuries.[1]

While the dashiki is not an overtly religious garment, it has been worn by African American religious leaders such as Malcolm X and Jesse Jackson to signify reclamation of African identity among Black Americans. The dashiki has also come to serve as a symbol for the affirmation of African aesthetics of dress, and the rejection of Eurocentric norms, by countless African Americans. It has become commonplace for African American Christian churches to have designated Sundays in which congregants wear dashikis and other African clothing, particularly during February in observance of Black History Month. Notably, among African American religious groups who have adopted the dashiki, Black Israelites have a complicated history regarding this highly symbolic garment. For Black Israelites, affixing ritual tassels called *tzitzit* to the dashiki transformed the secular dashiki into what in the Hebrew language is called the *dashiki ha kadosh* (holy dashiki).

The wearing of twisted cords or tassels called *tzitzit* can be traced to two references in the Hebrew Bible, in Numbers 15:35–40 and Deuteronomy 22:12. The passage in Numbers offers a brief explanation:

> And the Lord spake unto Moses, saying, Speak unto the children of Israel, and bid them that they make them fringes in the borders of their garments throughout their generations, and that they put upon the fringe of the borders a ribband of blue: And it shall be unto you for a fringe, that ye may look upon it, and remember all the commandments of the Lord, and do them; and that ye seek not after your own heart and your own eyes, after which ye use to go a whoring: That ye may remember, and do all my commandments, and be holy unto your God. (Numbers 15:37–40, KJV)[2]

In Rabbinic Judaism, the wearing of *tzitzit* is often relegated to a ceremonial prayer shawl called a *tallit*. The *tallit* is worn during religious services, primarily by Orthodox Jewish men, and as a small undershirt-like garment called a *tallit katan* (small *tallit*) on which the twisted string tassels are often visible. Among American Jews, the size and style of prayer shawl depends largely on denominational traditions and rules developed over the past two millennia among European Jewish communities. In contemporary American Judaism, the *tallit* can inform one about the identity of its wearers in various ways. Today, both men and women wear the *tallit* in liberal streams of Judaism. The cultural anthropologist Eric Silverman states in his *A Cultural History of Jewish Dress* that, "Today, fringed wraps and scarves often transform the pews into a colorful patchwork that sews tradition to modern notions of taste, individualism, and egalitarianism."[3] For many Black Israelites, however, the wearing of *tzitzit* is not relegated solely to the *tallit*. Instead, they are worn on various types of clothing by both men and women. The wearing of *tzitzit* has become a fashion statement in and of itself, with home-based manufacturers of this item selling their wares online through platforms such as Etsy in multiple colors, as is the case for sellers of Afrocentric clothing such as the dashikis that can serve as everyday wear.

In response to the variations of styles of *tzitzit* among Black Israelites, Sholomo ben Levy, a rabbi associated with the International Israelite Board of Rabbis (IBOR), a Black Israelite organization founded in 1919, was prompted to pen an open letter entitled "Proposal for an Israelite Tzitzit," which argued for a uniform standard for this ritual item among member congregations and wider Black Israelite communities. Disseminated on the organization's website, Blackjews.org, this proposal attracted the attention of *The Forward*, a media source largely dedicated to an American Jewish audience, which responded with an article highlighting this African American religious community's attempt to codify its rituals. Why was an essay on "how to wear ritual tassels" garnering the attention of a mainstream American Jewish news outlet?

Sholomo Levy's open letter included a plea to bridge the gap between "cultural Israelites" and "Rabbinic Israelites." Their differences stem from a schism dating to the Black Power era, when segments of New York's Black Israelite community fractured along doctrinal and cultural lines over the interpretation of scriptural requirements and cultural norms.[4] According to Levy, "The Israelite Board of Rabbis advocates that we create a tzitzit for our community. The design described below fulfills all the requirements of Torah, has powerful Kabbalistic and symbolic meaning, and will provide a degree of uniformity that will define us in relation to other Jewish communities around the world such as the Ashkenazi, Sephardi, and Karaite—all of whom have distinct tzitzit."[5] Levy and the IBOR's goal was to unify the Rabbinic Israelite community around a set of common practices while making Israelites (read: Black Jews) a distinct subset of the wider Jewish world. Levy continues,

> For the Israelite community, the four corners of our garment represent the promise the God made to the prophet Isaiah: "And He will set up an ensign for the nations, and will assemble the dispersed of Israel, and gather together the scattered of Judah from the four corners of the earth." We are the people of Israel who have been dispersed. Those of us who were scattered throughout Africa millennia ago are in the process of returning to our God and reclaiming our true identity. Hence, when we look at the four corners of the tzitzit and we look in the minor we see the fulfillment of God's prophecy. The purpose of the tzitzit is to remind all Jews of the law. Those who question whether we—the descendants of slaves—have a valid

claim to the birthright and covenant must be reminded of this passage of the Torah predicting our enslavement and eventual return.[6]

Levy's intention was to make ritual practice speak to the historical circumstances of enslaved Africans in the western hemisphere, while also demarcating the norms of ritual observance among member congregations. Critical to this notion of identity is the fulfillment of biblical prophecy, which is outwardly confirmed through the wearing of *tzitzit*.

In this chapter I address the intersection between cultural nationalism and ritual observance in the dress and adornment of Black Israelites. The aesthetic choices that Black Israelites make around the wearing of religious dress and ritual items signify concerns about the reaffirmation of an African identity and its relationship to perceived notions of Jewishness/Israelite-ness. This mode of dress is reflected in the style and fabric of clothing, ranging from head coverings for men and women to the types of dress regarded as being in accordance with religious norms of modesty. A secondary concern of this chapter is analyzing the internal divisions within this religious community regarding their conceptions of biblical modes of dress as a method of defining a distinct religious identity that distinguishes itself from other African Americans and the largely Euro-American Jewish population in the United States. Finally, the chapter also charts the sartorial evolution of Black Israelites and places them in tension with the sartorial norms of the larger communities to which they belong. I argue that the concepts of Black cultural nationalism and religious observance merge to create what I will refer to as *Black sartorial nationalism*, an intentional use of dress and adornment to signify a separate ethno-religious identity. To fully understand the implications of Levy's proposal as an example of Black sartorial nationalism, I will first discuss how clothing and dress functions as method of controlling and restructuring of the Black body.

BLACK RELIGIOUS NATIONALISM, SOCIAL CONTROL, AND THE BLACK BODY

Clothing and dress have been identified as methods of disciplining the body.[7] Religious dress often performs the role of marking boundaries between the sacred and the profane. As a method of social control, some religious groups choose to freeze stylistic choices in an idealized age so as to maintain social distance from the wider (changing) society. Scholarship on the Amish, Mennonites, and Orthodox Jews argues that there is an intentional "othering" that occurs when these religious groups cement their sartorial preferences in a certain time period.[8] A similar intentional othering occurs among African American ethno-religious groups who use clothing to demarcate an identity that signifies a reclaimed or new Black identity.

Within African American ethno-religions traditions such as Black Judaism and Black Islam, groups argue that there exists a boundary between perceived slave culture and traditional or "original" African culture. But in what signifies "traditional" or "original" culture in the African Hebrew Israelites' conception of "African-Edenic"—much like the case of the Nation of Islam's "Asiatic black man"[9]—the boundary between sacred and profane is infused with notions of slave versus free. Recalling Mary Douglas's foundational work on the fear of impurity and pollution in the physical as well as social body, scholars have identified that much of the social control of ethno-religious groups was aimed at setting clear boundaries against the debilitating practices rooted in the era of enslavement.[10] For these ethno-religious groups, slavery and Western culture are pollutants that need to be expelled from the Black social body. These groups actively reformed, curtailed, and censored the traditional Black diet, dress, and behavior. As sociologist Linda B. Arthur has argued, "Dress is a means of representing culture. Both agency and control. Members of each group actively construct their own lives and use dress symbolically to express religious beliefs."[11] Black Israelites actively use dress to take control of the Black body and restructure the meaning of Blackness as a sacred symbol. In the early twentieth century, this restructuring process took the form of Black Orientalist and Ethiopianist notions of the African as a biblically rooted ethnological construction of Hamite and Semite, who represented an "Eastern/African" identity. The notion of returning to an original or authentic manner of being through language, diet, and dress was paramount in redefining African American identity away from its enslaved past.

As the collective authors of *Embodiment and Black Religion* state, "because dress . . . always mediates the presentation of bodies, it becomes both a means by which embodied identity and subjectivity are socially circumscribed or 'fixed,' as well as a vehicle for individual self-expression, aesthetic affirmation, and the construction of religious meaning."[12] Black religious nationalism has as an objective the reconstructing of a new Black identity that is distanced from the "so-called Negro"[13] identity that is associated with enslavement. Dress and adornment are one of the means through which these groups attempt to visually disrupt the images of Blackness that pervade society.

NEGOTIATING MULTIPLE SPHERES: BLACK ISRAELITES APPEARING JEWISH

An ongoing issue for Black Israelites and those throughout the Afro-Jewish diaspora is that of "appearing Jewish," meaning adorning oneself to be publicly recognizable as members of the Jewish faith. This necessarily brings into focus questions of what Western cultures recognize as "Jewish culture" (the collection of foodways, clothing, etc.), which largely mark Ashkenazi norms as distinctively Jewish within dominant white Christian society. The wearing of yarmulkes, eating eastern European "Jewish" foods, and speaking Yiddish can each be read as markers of Jewish culture in American society. Black Israelites, as well as Sephardic, Mizrachi, Asian, and other African Jewish communities, are acutely aware that these cultural referents are more European than representative of a singular Jewish identity. It is this tension between appearing Jewish to both non-Jews and Euro-American Jews that complicates Black Israelite sartorial choices.

In the United States, "appearing Jewish" has for Black Israelites traditionally meant balancing elements of African and African American culture with what can be best described as Euro-Jewish templates. This includes using African textiles such as kente cloth (Akan) in the production of *tallit*, challah covers[14] (see figure 5.1), and other ritual objects. Emphasizing the use of recognized Jewish symbols such the Star of David or the Hebrew word *chai* as jewelry allows Black Israelites to show openly and explicitly that they are Jewish rather than Christian. The overdetermining nature of African American Protestant Christianity as a cultural signpost within African American culture requires Black Israelites to dress and adorn themselves in a manner that moves between maintaining cultural ties to Blackness and the integration of Judaic symbols as markers of a non-Christian faith. For Black Israelites, African American culture is a repository of largely Christian symbols, from Sunday dinner and the soul

FIGURE 5.1 Different designs of kente cloth. Image courtesy of Wikimedia Commons/Creative Commons.

food tradition, to the gospel tradition that inflects most Black popular music, to mannerisms that represent the dominant Christian ethos. These signposts implicitly convey the message that normative Blackness is Christian. To appear as Black and Jewish thus requires a reinterpretation of Blackness and its cultural symbols. Dress is one outward expression of this nonconformity to Christian Blackness.

Conversely, there is also tension between Black Israelites and other African Americans who I refer to as Black sartorial nationalists with whom they must occupy a common cultural space. These African Americans create ethno-religious distinctions through dress and adornment within the African American community to oppose Black Christian hegemony. Black sartorial nationalists often eschew (or reinterpret) Western dress in favor of African, Indian, or Islamic dress to emphasize a separate Black identity that is unhinged from Western Christian norms. The donning of African fabrics and styles, flowing Indian saris, and hijabs, khimars, and niqabs of orthodox Islamic practice are all examples of Black sartorial nationalist identity. All these choices speak of a heritage prior to enslavement in the western hemisphere. But clothing, like all aspects of culture, cannot remain static, and indeed is constantly in a fluid state of adaptation and reinterpretation by its wearers.

To illustrate this point, I draw upon my ethnographic work conducted between 2004 and 2010 in Philadelphia, Pennsylvania. There, I witnessed African American Muslim women wearing hijabs, khimars, and niqabs while also wearing designer jeans. Black Israelites and Sunni Muslim men wore cutoffs or rolled up pant legs that accentuated their pristine, butter-colored Timberlands while sporting a freshly coiffed "sunnah" beard, a distinct style based on Islamic tradition (i.e., the sunnah).[15] While visiting a North Philadelphia barbershop, I commonly heard the Arabic/Hebrew word *ahk* (brother) exchanged between African American Muslims, Hebrews, and "conscious" Black men. The largely African American orthodox Muslim community of North Philadelphia represented a refuge from Christian normativity that Black Israelites felt comfortable immersing themselves in as "brothers" of the Abrahamic tradition. These men, adorned with full black beards (sometimes dyed), in knitted kufis and black-and-white checkered kaffiyehs,[16] illustrate the porous nature of Black sartorial nationalism as practiced among religious communities who regard the Levant as the source of their spiritual and ethnic origins but who reside in America's urban meccas. What is to account for this occurrence?

Why would African Americans who identify as Jews and Israelites feel more comfortable dressing in full-sized knitted kufis and kaffiyehs, garments normally worn by orthodox Muslims, rather than the small black yarmulkes and fedoras reminiscent of Orthodox Jews who also lived throughout Philadelphia? This phenomenon was not relegated to just men: Black Israelite women adorned themselves in scarves, wore hijabs, and donned henna tattoos, nose rings, and other elements that they considered "Eastern" or "cultural" dress. Sa'ud Abdul Khabeer, a scholar-activist whose book *Muslim Cool* looks at the intersection of race, religion, and popular culture, discusses the impact of Muslim cultural chic via hip-hop, which only touches on the surface of cross-cultural religious identity. According to Khabeer, "Muslim Cool" is constructed through hip-hop and the performance of Blackness; it is a way of engaging with the Black American experience by both Black and non-Black young Muslims that challenges racist norms in the United States as well as dominant ethnic and religious structures within American Muslim communities.[17] Muslim cultural chic had poured over Philadelphia for decades and could be seen in the local hip-hop scene, which exported elements (the sunnah beard, men's capri pants) to the broader African American community. For Black Israelites, however, this shared Black sartorial nationalist ethos is designed to mark out a particular cultural and literal geography, as in the case of North Philadelphia's transplanted and "imagined" forced migrants from the Levant. In neighborhoods like North Philadelphia and Harlem, in New York City, the sons of Isaac and Ishmael have reconvened at barbershops, boutiques, and halal and vegan restaurants, dressing as they imagine their forebears did before the terrible fate of the Middle Passage.

However, the diversity of Black Israelite dress and adornment is not isolated to cross-cultural exchanges between Black Islam and Black Judaism. The Black church still resonates with some Black Israelites and their conceptions of modest dress. In the Mount Airy neighborhood of Philadelphia, a once isolated Black Israelite congregation has maintained a deep connection to its Afro-Pentecostal roots. For decades its congregants have dressed in dark suits and skirts during the fall and winter months and white clothing during the spring and summer, suggesting continuity with their Black Christian predecessors.[18] Traditionally, women were adorned in simple fashion and jewelry and wore a distinctive lace head covering called a "mantle," a practice also in continuity with Afro-Pentecostalism. The congregation's website requests that new visitors abide by the following rules: "Men are asked to wear a jacket and tie. Women are asked not to wear pants or shorts in the Sanctuary. *Cultural dress is acceptable for all genders, but it should be appropriate for service.* All worshipers are asked to cover their heads before entering the Sanctuary. This is done as a sign to honor the Torah and of humility. Men are asked to don a tallit during Torah service; women wear shawls."[19]

These practices have only recently been integrated with more overtly African forms of fashion by some members. However, the congregation retains its overall Holiness-Pentecostal character regarding dress and adornment. In this case we witness a congregation holding on to a style of dress more identifiable with African American Pentecostalism than with the Black sartorial nationalism of surrounding Israelite congregations. Whether from orthodox Islam or Afro-Pentecostalism, each of these sartorial markers is replete with genealogies of meaning that arose at specific times in African American religious history. When discussing the diversity of Black Israelite fashion in the present day, it is necessary to separate the strands that have become tangled over the years.

EARLY INFLUENCES: A BLACK ISRAELITE ORIENTALIST ODYSSEY

The sartorial choices of Black Israelite congregations in the early twentieth century reflected a combination of Masonic-inspired Orientalist themes and European Jewish stylistic norms. Rabbi Arnold J. Ford, for example, donned a white turban as the leader of Beth B'nai Abraham. Male members of his congregation were adorned in brimmed hats, turbans, and skullcaps, while they wore Western-style dark-colored suits. Female members wore shoulder-length head coverings and dark dresses. This mixture of Masonic, "Eastern," and Western dress would be the standard style for the Black Jews of Harlem and urban areas with significant Black Jewish congregations.

Another distinctive style belonged to the members of the Church of God and Saints of Christ (COGSOC), an early Black Israelite group heavily influenced by Masonic tradition. Men and women congregants wore dark uniforms with colored sashes and pillbox head coverings. Elly M. Wynia, an early researcher on Black Jewish congregations, documented the COGSOC's detailed dress code, which listed each item to be worn by female and male members. During the fall and winter months, women congregants were expected to wear the following:

> Black skirt with matching fabric belts
> White waist with white collar
> Black bow in hair
> Black oxford shoes
> Black shade hosiery
> White gloves[20]

During the summer months, the dress code changed to a summer uniform that consisted of

> White shirt waist dresses
> White shoes
> Blue bow (on front of dress)
> Blue fabric belt (to match bow)
> Blue bow in hair

> Church rosette
> Stockings
> White gloves[21]

Likewise, the uniforms for male members were equally detailed and specific, with dark-colored suits in the fall and winters and white suits, white shoes, and white gloves in the summer months. Wynia offers the following description of the liturgical significance of the colors and additional elements of the dress code:

> There are many different symbolic meanings for the style and color of the dress. The blue represents the sky, brown the earth, white is light, purity, joy, and glory. They also wear ribbons in a variety of colors ... Also of significance is the blouse has 72 tucks which represent the 70 elders of Israel plus Moses and Aaron. The brown shirt has 52 pleats which represents the 52 weeks of the year. The collar is stiff to remind the members of the stiff-heartedness of the Children of Israel.[22]

Wynia traced the origins of the dress code to the founder of the COGSOC, William Saunders Crowdy. Crowdy, a Prince Hall Freemason, offered two reasons for the dress code of the COGSOC: it ensured that everyone would be discreetly dressed so that no one would be distracted during the service by thoughts pertaining to "the flesh," and, by standardizing the mode of dress, that there would be no distinction between members based on something as superficial as clothing. Wynia attributed Crowdy's rationale to a desire to create a sense of separateness for his members while simultaneously encouraging an esprit de corps that prioritized commonality among members.

William S. Crowdy's emphasis on uniform and ritual was a result of his background as a Prince Hall Freemason.[23] According to historian of African American religion Jacob Dorman, Orientalist and Masonic themes influenced the early Black Israelite congregations as they sought to return to imagined "original" Eastern identities from the Middle East and Africa. Dorman documents that Crowdy and other early Israelite leaders were devout Masons. He states, "It is likely that Masonic texts as well as Masonic interest in the Holy Land and in biblical history helped ... formulate [Crowdy's] Israelite beliefs."[24] For Masonic-inspired religious leaders, the adoption of Hebrew, Arabic, and Yiddish was accompanied by styles of dressing to distance members from other African Americans or "so-called Negroes." The stylistic fashion of the Black church was discarded for uniform colors. At best, we can call these choices proto-Afrocentric, as they were largely still rooted in Western discourses of African identity and Western dress.

This period was marked by a dialectical tension between two overarching macro-identities in which Black Israelites found themselves situated during the early twentieth century America: the largely Protestant cultural milieu of African American Christianity, and the western European traditions of Ashkenazi Jews. To display a liturgical kinship, Rabbinic-oriented Black Israelites often dressed indistinguishably from their Euro-American Jewish counterparts while eschewing the aesthetic flashiness of their southern Christian racial brethren. The iconic church hats and sartorial flair that Gwendolyn S. O'Neal, scholar of African American religion and fashion, associates with the sacred cosmos of African American religiosity was replaced with veils, skullcaps, turbans, and fezzes.[25] While early twentieth-century ethnographers scandalously asserted that this amounted to racial mimicry on the part of Black Israelites, a similar processes occurred in the mid-twentieth century among Sephardic and Mizrachi (Middle Eastern) Jewish communities, who sought to accommodate themselves to hegemonic European Jewish stylistic norms after their immigration to the State of Israel.

This style of dress dominated Rabbinic-oriented Black Israelites for the next forty years, and its remnants are still present among older members and clergy. But as the 1940s and 1950s gave way to the more turbulent 1960s and 1970s, a cultural revolution that impacted African Americans in general would have profound and lasting effects on the smaller Black Israelite tradition while also creating new lines of demarcation.

The adoption of African and Indian styles of dress among Black Israelites mirrored the spread of African cultural norms in the larger Black community. Although IBOR member congregations had long considered themselves African people (i.e., Ethiopian Hebrews), their dress was distinctly Western Ashkenazi. If we presume a stylistic spectrum of fashion, early Black Israelites occupied some of the same territory as the Nation of Islam as "clean-cut Asiatics." Both groups emerged during the New Negro movement, which has come to be more popularly known as the Harlem Renaissance. While the term "Harlem Renaissance" accurately conveys the artistic and literary explosion among African American and Caribbean migrants, the New Negro movement provides a more expansive understanding of the degree to which African Americans saw themselves as refashioning their external identity. During that era a clean-cut image shorn of its southern flamboyance typified the sartorial choices of Harlem's Black Jews and Islamic groups such as the Moorish Science Temple and Nation of Islam. The surge of Black Power into inner-city America in the 1960s and 1970s would leave in its wake new cultural forms of Black Israelite religiosity, dress, and adornment that would challenge worshippers' dependency on the previous fashion regime.

One of the most impactful imports of the Black Power era was the ushering in of cultural nationalism and a reassessment of cultural standards and norms within the Black community. In her trailblazing retrieval of Black women's role in "fashioning" Black Power aesthetics, Black studies scholar Tanisha C. Ford documents the convergence of African independence movements along with the emergence of *soul* as a category of meaning in Harlem and other urban enclaves, which served as the critical juncture that birthed Black Power fashion aesthetics.[26] Nearly every facet of African American life would be impacted by the emergence of Black Power and its soul aesthetic. Music, dress, food, and religion would all be reassessed in the wake of Black Power. For the Black Israelite community, it would not take long for the soul aesthetic to complicate the community's notions of Blackness and Africanity.

THE HOLY DASHIKI

Perhaps the most visible difference between cultural-nationalist Israelites and their Rabbinic coreligionists is the wearing of a garment that would become synonymous with many cultural nationalists of the era: the dashiki. The *tzitzit* were moved from a liturgical garment to become an appendage of an article of clothing that perfectly symbolized the cultural-reclamation project of African Americans all over the country, the dashiki. The dashiki came to serve as a potent symbol for the rejection of Euro-American Jewish aesthetics for Israelites and those joining the Israelite "way of life."

By donning dashikis affixed with *tzitzit*, cultural-nationalist Israelites were connecting to the wider Black Power movement in aesthetic terms. It is worth noting that the origins of the African American interpretation

FIGURE 5.2 A Hebrew Israelite dashiki with fringes affixed. Image courtesy of the author.

of the dashiki occurred in New York City, which was home to the majority of cultural-nationalist Israelites. According to fashion critic Khanya Mtshali, the American dashiki was the product of Jason and Mable Benning, who wanted to reconnect with African culture.[27] The adoption of the dashiki by Black cultural nationalists such as Black Israelites served two purposes. First, it allowed Israelites to maintain sartorial connections to other Black nationalists with whom they shared similar a social and political outlook. Second, by affixing *tzitzit* to the dashiki, it continued a demarcation of ethno-religious identity for cultural-nationalist Israelites who were adopting a fashion trend that was largely secular. This act of sacralizing (making sacred) the dashiki was part of a larger liturgical reorganization of cultural-nationalist Israelite practice.

Amid the schism of the 1960s, cultural Israelites who adopted a theological position that would come be known as "Torah-only" not only eschewed the Rabbinic orientation to their Jewish identity but reoriented their aesthetic choices regarding music, worship, and dress. Prayer books and Rabbinic liturgy were replaced by extemporaneous prayers, extended teaching sessions, and African drumming. The dark suits, pleated skirts, and veils were replaced by dashikis, large-knit skullcaps, and flowing, African-style robes and *buba*-style dresses. Men wore turbans and women wrapped their heads in *gele*-style head wraps. The sartorial lines had been drawn: dashikis versus suits, satin yarmulkes versus knitted kufis and turbans. African clothing was placed in the service of reconnecting Black Israelites with African culture, albeit not necessarily Afro-Judaic culture.

The binary created by cultural Israelites fits a pattern of Afrocentric cultural nationalism in the areas of dress and clothing in the larger African American community. It was a partial and incomplete process; residue from the previous aesthetic regime was still to be found within the newfound cultural nationalism. As Van Dyk Lewis, a fashion designer, stylist, and art anthropologist, comments, "the way that black people use apparel in personal representations of self may differ and be dependent upon location and perspective. Afrocentric fashion is analogous to Western fashion. Both appropriate much from oppositional fashion expressions; consequently, both expressions are fragmented and perennially incomplete."[28]

Cultural Hebrew Israelites' approach to their sartorial evolution was part of a larger process called the "power to define." They claimed agency not only in matters of doctrine, but in the overall reconstruction of themselves as African albeit Hebrew people. They employed terms like "culture," "Eastern," or "African-Edenic" to distance themselves from the "religious Black Jews" who followed Rabbinic Judaism. However, this process lacked cultural cohesion, incorporating multiple African styles in its approach, none of them rooted in an actual Afro-Judaic cultural milieu. Again, Lewis is informative on this dissonance as he notes that,

> For Afrocentrists, Afrocentric dress is the norm; consequently Western dress is "ethnic" and therefore "exotic." For that reason, Afrocentric dress has become a virtuoso expression of African diaspora culture. Political and cultural activities like black cultural nationalism have adopted Afrocentric fashion for its visual symbolism. African and black identity and

black-nationalism are expressed by the wearing of African and African-inspired dress such as the dashiki, Abacos (Mao-styled suit), Kanga, caftan, wraps, and Buba. All of these items are cultural products of the black diaspora and are worn exclusively or integrated into Western dress.[29]

To illustrate Lewis's contention regarding the incompleteness of this sartorial regime change, the life of the cultural-nationalist Israelite leader Cohen Levi Israel is instructive. In recounting the life of Levi Israel, IBOR rabbi and historian Sholomo Levy discusses the theological tension that arose between traditionalists who believed adhering to Rabbinic traditions was essential, and cultural nationalists who wanted to eliminate Rabbinic and European Jewish cultural practices that were not found in the Hebrew Bible. Levi writes that by 1964, some leaders and members of New York's Israelite congregations desired a complete break with Rabbinic Judaism, both ritually and liturgically. This ritual/liturgical break was accompanied by a sartorial break as well.[30]

In Levy's account, Levi Israel was deeply involved in the social and political climate of 1960s Brooklyn. Levi Israel maintained friendships with Black nationalist leader Amiri Baraka, Kwanzaa founder Maulana Karenga, and local Brooklyn activist Sonny Carson. Levy notes some of the early sartorial changes that Levi Israel and his congregation instituted: "At first members of Hashabah [Levi Israel's congregation] rid themselves of the cookie-shaped yarmulkes that Jews wore on their heads and replaced them with knitted or crochet head coverings; they also wore West African garb with the addition of tzitzit (fringes) on the corners of their garments."[31] Also reflecting on the origins of their cultural-nationalist approach to Black Judaism, Uzziel Lewi, a Black Israelite community historian stated, "this is a tradition that we picked up as trying to separate ourselves. [Our teachers] looked at it as being passed down from the [Ashkenazi] Jewish man, so they wanted to have their own tradition and their own way of identifying with the tradition."[32]

Levi Israel and his congregation would soon drop the West African dress for what they considered a more biblical or "Eastern" mode of dress, one that harkened to the Orientalist days of its founders. Levy notes that Levi Israel and Hashabah "seemed to be aware that their West African attire did not match the eastern garb that Israelites wore in Biblical days. Slowly they began to adopt the turbans and long robes that had become the hallmark of a rival Israelite group called B'nai Zaken founded by Prince Yaakov and Navi Tate."[33] Although Levi Israel and Hashabah's foray into West African dress was brief, it represented a clear attempt to make a cultural, religious, and even a sartorial break with European Jewish standards and tradition. Other cultural-nationalist congregations would continue to wear West African dress as opposed to what they considered Western or "Jewish" sartorial norms. Members of these congregations began referring to the practice of wearing "Eastern" or African clothes as "wearing culture" or "being in culture." It would take a group of Black Israelites leaving the United States for a distinct Israelite style rooted in African cultural fashions to finally develop.

THE DIVINE GARMENTS OF THE AFRICAN HEBREW ISRAELITES

As a group known as much for their veganism and open embrace of polygyny as for their Afrocentric dress, the African Hebrew Israelites of Jerusalem (AHIJ) perhaps best signify the maturation of Black sartorial nationalism among Black Israelites. Based in Dimona, Israel, with satellites in the United States, the Caribbean, and Africa, the AHIJ have developed a distinctive style, with much of their theological and sartorial refashioning having occurred within the State of Israel.

The AHIJ argued that the collage of African cultures represented in most African American forays into Afrocentric fashion were not markers of what they called a "divine Edenic identity." Therefore, they set out to create a distinct African Hebrew Israelite aesthetic that would separate them from other African ethnicities and cultures. The leader of the AHIJ, Ben Ammi, defined divine culture as "the perpetual trademark that secures the identity of a righteous people and secures the existence of our eternal, living [God]."[34] For the AHIJ, clothing was not just a mundane covering of the body—it also communicated "present moral trends ... [as well as] remembrances of that society's nationalistic past. We have come to understand that today's outlandish, amorphous, eccentric, ever-changing fashions reflect a society ruled by materialism, controversy, and denigration."[35] Readily understanding that textiles carry both national and ethnic significance, the AHIJ decided to design and develop an

African Hebrew Israelite aesthetic referred to as "divine dress," which maintains ties with African styles but can be distinguished as "Hebrew Israelite" dress.

The rationale for what constitutes divine dress is described as follows: "Our determination of cultural dress is based upon [God's] laws and guidelines as defined in the Bible. If the garment complies with these laws and guidelines, then we designate it a *cultural garment*."[36] Hence a cultural garment is part of a larger framework the AHIJ refers to as the Divine Messianic Dress Code (DMDC). The DMDC outlines categories of appropriate clothing to be worn based on age, gender, and occasion. It is further broken down along the following categories: Full Cultural Attire, Proper Dress Wear and Outer Garments, Sports and Entertainment Wear, Sleepwear, Proper Skin and Hair Care, Shoes, and Miscellaneous. The DMDC is supplemented by children's cultural dress guidelines to be administered by parents and guardians, which includes the categories Shoes, Headwear, *Baneem* (Hebrew for "boys") and *Banote* (Hebrew for "girls") Dresswear, Hairstyles, Jewelry.[37]

The common themes to be found throughout the DMDC is the wearing of loose-fitting natural fabrics and the prohibition against unnecessarily exposing the body, wearing Western styles except when necessary (and with permission), and the use of most cosmetics and hair-care products except those approved by the community. In terms of style, the DMDC stresses that all cultural garments should conform to community standards. Hence, uniformity of color and style pervades the clothing worn by the AHIJ and meets the desired goal of being "set apart" from generic African clothing styles. The AHIJ concept of divine dress has been adopted by other Black Israelites and symbolizes a most potent refashioning of Black Judaism into a distinct cultural expression, however the AHIJ is by no means the only group with a distinctive style of dress.

RHINESTONE HEBREWS: THE CURIOUS CASE OF THE ICUPK

Perhaps no Black Israelite group is as identifiable by its dress as by its doctrine compared to the Israeli Church of Universal Practical Knowledge (ICUPK). Founded in 1969 by Abba Henry Bivens, the ICUPK and its offshoots have garnered significant media attention in the United States for

FIGURE 5.3 Members of the Israeli Church of Universal Practical Knowledge. Image courtesy of Wikimedia Commons/Creative Commons.

their controversial and abrasive street teaching demonstrations. However, equally intriguing is their unique style of dress, which has largely gone unexamined. Unlike other cultural-nationalist Black Israelites, the ICUPK eschews any identification with African culture in lieu of a biblical-futurist chic that combines leather outfits, rhinestones, bright colors, and head scarves; imagine Moses meeting Earth, Wind, and Fire. The ICUPK's distinct dress includes militaristic aspects along with other worldly elements through color coding to indicate tribal affiliation, rank, and an individual's position within the organization.

Some of its offshoots have modified the traditional ICUPK uniform to create a less-formal, warm-weather-friendly fringed T-shirt, which is worn as a uniform along with army fatigue bottoms and Timberland boots. The hip-hop-style clothing has become attractive among younger members, who are familiar with this more radical fringe of the Israelite community through social media outlets like Facebook and YouTube. Various versions of fringed T-shirts and tunics have become quite popular in the Black Israelite community. Websites like Etsy and Pinterest feature versions of the fringed tunic in variety of colors and styles.

BLACK BIBLICAL AESTHETICS

While the reclamation of African culture and identity plays a major role in the religious lives of most Black Israelites, Afrocentric fashion does not appeal to those Black sartorial nationalists who, like Cohen Levi Yisrael's earlier departure from West African clothing, believe that an even more radical approach to clothing and ritual observance needs to be taken, one that goes beyond simply wearing African clothes with ritual tassels. These Black sartorial nationalists look to historical reconstructions and archaeological relics to create a distinct style that I refer to as *Black biblical aesthetics*. Black biblical aesthetics represents an intersection of reconstructed biblical fashion with a Black cultural-nationalist consciousness. It represents an attempt to demarcate a Black identity that is distinct from generalized notions of African culture, and that emphasizes that the descendants of enslaved Africans are the "true Israelites" and should therefore dress in a manner consistent with biblical laws. Unlike the ICUPK or the AHIK's codified approach to dress and adornment, Black biblical aesthetics cannot be associated with any single group.

Examples of the Black biblical aesthetic can be seen on Hebrew Israelite–operated websites such as Fringez.net, an online clothing store that specializes in hand-sewn, ritually approved clothing for daily use and special occasions such as holy days. According to the website Hebrewisraeliteculture.com, clothing is of paramount importance and not something that God takes lightly. They cite Zephaniah 1:8, "And it shall come to pass in the day of the Lord's sacrifice, that I will punish the princes, and the king's children, and all such as are clothed with strange apparel." The website proceeds to raise the question of what constitutes "strange apparel." The implications are clear for this and similar Black Israelite groups, as they believe they should be clothed in a distinct manner. Hebrewisraeliteculture.com outlines six general principles detailing the proper dress for Israelites, one of which requires the wearing of fringes along with a purple cord/ribbon (*techelet*). The others include avoiding mixed fabrics, wool-and-linen mixtures, and unisex clothes and/cross-dressing, while the final principle makes reference to the special garments to be worn by priests. Before proceeding into the section on *tzitzit* and *techelet*, the website offers a rebuke to Black Israelites who follow Rabbinic tradition: "Please read the law below carefully, some believe women are not required to wear fringes & ribbon because they follow the Jewish Tradition when it comes to this law, but if you read carefully, it says 'Children of Israel' not only men."[38]

Once again, the issue of wearing *tzitzit* becomes a critical point of contention for Black Israelites. Congregations that regard themselves as Torah-only (non-Rabbinic) or messianic have taken to redefining what signifies contemporary Israelite dress and tradition, and they interpret the proper wearing of *tzitzit* according to specific criteria. Regarding these doctrinal disputes, the wearing of *tzitzit* and *techelet* becomes a site of contestation because of the underlying issues of race and agency. Using the "power to define" as a guiding principle, the parameters of the ritual observance are central to understanding why this goes beyond a doctrinal disagreement. The stance of the IBOR closely adheres to Rabbinic practice, with an exception for female participation. However, the IBOR does not feel that this choice places its adherents outside the pale of mainstream Jewish practice. They seek distinction within the larger body of world of Jewry. Torah-only and messianic Black Israelites, however, clearly

FIGURE 5.4 African Hebrew Israelites in divine dress. Image courtesy of Wikimedia Commons/Creative Commons.

regard the wearing of *tzitzit* in the prescribed Rabbinic manner as a betrayal of their agency, and more importantly a rejection of God's law in favor of man's (read: white man's) traditions.

To illustrate this issue further, the Black Israelite fashion retailer Bayadwa Baht-Yah offers advice on proper apparel for Israelites. She maintains a website, Hebrewgarments.com, and authored the book *Righteous Clothes Revolution*. Rather than simply repurposing African dress and affixing *tzitzit* to dashikis and dresses, she makes an argument that biblically acceptable clothing must be made with an intention to be worn by Israelites alone. In an informational YouTube video, Bayadwa Baht-Yah informs viewers that she has removed the fringes from her clothing made by non-Israelites and sewn her own garments so as to fulfill the requirements stated in the Hebrew Bible.[39] What these Black Israelites seek to accomplish is the creation of a distinct Israelite culture, identifiable through clothing as much as adherence to other aspects of their religious tradition. The visibility and social distinction created by clothing pushes these individuals to become more radical in their approach to Black sartorial nationalism, moving from an African cultural basis to a biblically centered notion of Black ethno-religious identity. For these groups and individuals, the dashiki is no longer sufficient to serve as a holy garment; instead, it represents a profane article regardless of its cultural importance to the wider African American community. In its place, these Black sartorial nationalists embrace more "authentic" sacred dress, as prescribed by biblical dictates, as their current and future direction.

In this chapter, I attempted to address the intersection between cultural nationalism and ritual adherence in the dress and adornment of Black Israelites. By charting the sartorial evolution of this religious community, I identified the aesthetic choices that Black Israelites attach to the adornment and ritual items they used to signify concerns about the reaffirmation of an African identity and its relationship to perceived notions of Jewishness/Israelite-ness. Beginning with Orientalist and Masonic impulses, the adoption of Israelite fashion was largely a matter of "appearing Jewish" in the urban centers of the United States. However, the critical departure from Westernized and Orientalist notions of Jewishness are represented in the adoption of the dashiki as a symbol of cultural awakening and ethno-religious particularism. This served as the beginning of a Black sartorial nationalist journey for this religious community.

The competing approaches of various groups to self-definition and cultural agency represented through Black sartorial nationalism pushed cultural Israelites to abandon normative expressions of Afrocentric fashion for an even more culturally and ritually specific approach to dress and adornment. It can be argued that a collective goal of these cultural Israelites is to be able to identity a Hebrew Israelite by their dress as a reflection of the wearer's understanding of the biblical text. Simply put, their desire is not to be mistaken for a practitioner of Rabbinic Judaism or orthodox Islam, or even as expressing a generalized notion of Africanness. For these groups, this requires dressing so distinctively as to stand out as the "children of Israel." This process is ongoing and reflects the continued reimagining that these groups of African Americans have engaged in around the meaning of Blackness as symbolized through dress and adornment.

NOTES

1. Jessica Strubel, "Dashiki," in *Ethnic Dress in the United States: A Cultural Encyclopedia*, ed. Annette Lynch and Mitchell D. Strauss (Lanham, MD: Rowan and Littlefield, 2014).
2. KJV, i.e., the King James Version. I use this version in this chapter as it represents the preferred English translation of most Black Israelite groups.
3. Eric Silverman, *A Cultural History of Jewish Dress* (New York: Bloomsbury, 2013), 132.
4. Sholomo Ben Levy, "Proposal for an Israelite Tzitzit," Blackjews.org, accessed March 21, 2017, http://www.blackjews.org/wp-content/uploads/2016/11/Proposal-for-An-Israelite-Tzitit-v1.pdf.
5. Levy, "Proposal for an Israelite Tzitzit."
6. Levy, "Proposal for an Israelite Tzitzit."
7. Edward E. Curtis IV, *Black Muslim Religion in the Nation of Islam, 1960–1975* (Chapel Hill: University of North Carolina Press, 2006), 96–8.
8. Lynne Humes's *The Religious Life of Dress: Global Fashion and Faith* (London: Bloomsbury, 2013) is a foundational text that concentrates specifically on the intersection of religions and dress. Linda B. Arthur's *Undressing Religion: Commitment and Conversion from a Cross-Cultural Perspective* (New York: Berg, 2000) consists of historical and ethnographic work showing

how religious and social systems are symbolically expressed through dress and how change occurs when a religion moves into a new culture. Also refer to Linda B. Arthur's edited volume *Religion, Dress and the Body* (New York: Berg, 1999), which investigates several American religious communities in which dress is shown to be a vital component of social control.

9. Algernon Austin, *Achieving Blackness* (New York: New York University Press, 2006), 27–30.
10. Curtis IV, *Black Muslim Religion in the Nation of Islam*, 109–18.
11. Linda B. Arthur, "Introduction: Dress and the Social Control of the Body," in Arthur, ed., *Religion, Dress, and the Body*, 3.
12. CERCL Writing Collective, *Embodiment and Black Religion: Rethinking the Body in the African American Experience* (Bristol, CT: Equinox, 2017), 97.
13. The phrase "so-called Negro" was used by African American ethno-religious groups at the turn of the twentieth century to denote that the term "Negro" was an ahistorical descriptor that lacked ties to any particular national or ethnic ancestry. Although popularized by the Nation of Islam, the phrase "so-called Negro" was adopted by various ethno-religious groups. See Sylvester Johnson's "The Rise of Black Ethnic: The Ethnic Turn in African American Religions, 1916–1945," *Religion and American Culture: A Journal of Interpretation* 20, no. 2 (2010): 125–63.
14. Challah is a bread of eastern European origin in Ashkenazi Jewish cuisine, usually braided and typically eaten on ceremonial occasions such as the Sabbath and major Jewish holidays.
15. For a fuller description of the rise and impact of the sunnah beard on hip-hop and African American men, see "The Sunnah Beard: The Latest Trend Amongst Non-Muslims in Philadelphia USA," Muslimvillage.com, August 24, 2011, https://muslimvillage.com/2011/08/24/13211/the-sunnah-beard-the-latest-trend-amongst-non-muslims-in-philadelphia-usa/. Also refer to Hisham Aida, "The Long Reach of the Philly Beard," Al Jazeera, January 17, 2015, http://america.aljazeera.com/opinions/2015/1/philadelphia-islamafricanamericanartmusicactivism.html.
16. The kaffiyeh is a traditional headdress that originated in the Arabian Peninsula and is now worn throughout the Middle East. Popularized by former PLO chairman Yasser Arafat, the garment has become commonplace among African Americans as both a symbol of solidarity with Palestinians and an expression of overall Muslim identity, and for others a chic fashion accessory. See popular discussions of the history of the kaffiyeh in "The History

of the Keffiyeh: A Traditional Scarf from Palestine," Handmade Palestine, September 24, 2018, https://handmadepalestine.com/blogs/news/history-of-keffiyeh-the-traditional-palestinian-headdress.

17. Sa'ud Abdul Khabeer, *Muslim Cool: Race, Religion and Hip Hop in the United States* (New York: New York University Press, 2016).

18. The color scheme worn by Congregation Temple Beth El may have origins in the Church of God and Saints of Christ. The liturgical color scheme shares similarities to the Church of God and Saints of Christ but can be attributed to its direct forerunner, the House of God, a Hebrew-Pentecostal organization. See "Brief History," House of God, accessed July 17, 2017, http://houseofgod.org/about/.

19. "Things You Should Know When Visiting Our Synagogue," Congregation Temple Beth'El, accessed July 17, 2017, http://www.bethel-ph.org/. Emphasis mine.

20. Elly M. Wynia, *Church of God and Saints of Christ: The Rise of Black Jews* (New York: Routledge, 1994), 65.

21. Wynia, 65.

22. Wynia, 66–7.

23. Prince Hall Freemasonry is a branch of North American Freemasonry for African Americans founded by Prince Hall, a free African American, on September 29, 1784. For a more complete history of the role and impact of Prince Hall Freemasonry in African American social, political, and religious movements, see Corey D. B. Walker's *A Noble Fight: African American Freemasonry and the Struggle for Democracy in America* (Champaign: University of Illinois Press, 2008).

24. Jacob Dorman, *Chosen People: The Rise of American Black Israelite Religions* (New York: Oxford University Press, 2013), 79.

25. Gwendolyn O'Neal, "The African American Church, Its Sacred Cosmos and Dress," in Arthur, ed., *Religion, Dress, and the Body*, 117–34.

26. Tanisha C. Ford, *Liberated Threads: Black Women, Style, and the Global Politics of Soul* (Chapel Hill: University of North Carolina Press, 2015).

27. Khanya Mtshali, "The Revolution Will Wear a Dashiki: How a 1960s Harlem Couple Popularized Afrocentric Fashion and Built a Community Where Black Power Thrived," Timeline, March 8, 2018, https://timeline.com/harlem-couple-afrocentric-fashion-dashiki-2e806f792794.

28. Van Dyk Lewis, "Afrocentric Fashion," in *The Berg Companion to Fashion*, ed. Valerie Steele (New York: Berg, 2010), 15.

29. Lewis, 15.

30. Sam Kestenbaum, "Can a Tzitzit Unify Hebrew Israelites?" *The Forward*, December 25, 2016, https://forward.com/news/356301/how-a-simple-ritual-tassel-brings-up-old-debate-for-black-israelites-about/.
31. Sholomo B. Levy, "Cohen Levi Ben Yisrael: His Life and Legacy," Blackjews.org, accessed March 12, 2021, https://www.blackjews.org/biography-of-cohen-levi-yisrael/.
32. Kestenbaum, "Can a Tzitzit Unify Hebrew Israelites?"
33. Levy, "Cohen Levi Ben Yisrael."
34. Communicators Press, *Tree of Life: African Hebrew Israelite of Jerusalem Absorption Manual* (Washington, DC: Communicators Press, 2003), 77.
35. Communicators Press, 77.
36. Communicators Press, 77; emphasis mine.
37. Communicators Press, 78–86.
38. "Hebrew-Yisraelite Clothing," Hebrew Yisraelite Culture, accessed June 16, 2017, http://hebrewisraeliteculture.com/clothing/.
39. Hebrew Garments, "Cutting Off My Fringes & Blue Ribbons Off My Clothes," YouTube, June 16, 2017, https://www.youtube.com/watch?v=Kd7Qp0uylUA&t=193s.

Six

REFINED BODIES

CLOTHING AS A VISUAL SIGNIFIER OF PIETY FOR MORMON WOMEN IN AMERICA

KATE DAVIS

ATTIRE ACTS AS a powerful tool for nonverbal communication. Clothing, as much as speech, is a means of social delineation and constitution. It is the introduction we make to the world, and the first means by which we establish identity in communal spaces. As sociologist Cornelia Bohn put it, "Not all texts are textiles. But all textiles are texts or at least textual components."[1] The body of the religious woman is the page upon which the cultural and religious expectations of her community are written into a solid identity, and clothing is one of the fundamental tools used in this creation. In this chapter I will make the case for Latter-day Saint clothing guidelines as veiled or implicit religious garb, paying particular attention to the guidelines for young women.[2] I argue that the cultivation of young women's own style constitutes what Judith Butler calls a stylized repetition of acts, with the aim of creating and maintaining a public performance of Latter-day Saint femininity.

The Church of Jesus Christ of Latter-day Saints, historically called Mormonism, is primarily led by laypeople, meaning that it is sustained by a volunteer force. Unlike some other Christian denominations that have professional clergy or that set apart monastic orders, all men over the age of twelve who are deemed worthy by the church can hold the priesthood.[3]

As such, leaders of the church are not distinguished by a priest's collar or a nun's habit, but instead follow guidelines both implicit and explicit to craft a religious wardrobe out of secular clothing. Although women cannot hold the priesthood, as members of the church they are still participants in this lay ministry and are instructed to act as representatives for the faith in their everyday life. For Latter-day Saint women everyday clothing is, in many ways, religious attire, and it is governed by church directives. As Bohn puts it, "fashion obligates individuals to negate themselves as individuals, as fashion standardizes the characters."[4] The women may shop at secular stores such as Target but will often seek out clothing with looser fits, longer hemlines, and options for layering (such as cardigans and blazers), with a goal of reflecting both modesty and femininity as a means of conforming their self-presentation to religious standards. Former church president Thomas Monson explained that, "when you [young women] dress modestly, you show respect for your Heavenly Father and for yourself. At this time, when dress fashions are styled after the skimpy clothing some of the current movie and music idols are wearing, it may be difficult to find modest apparel in clothing stores. However, it is possible, and it is important."[5] Modesty, in other words, is an inward virtue with outward signifiers. The modest woman does not wear miniskirts, not because she does not wish to be fashionable, but because to do so would be disrespectful to her heavenly father. In fact, the online "Dress and Grooming Guidelines for Sister Missionaries" in 2019 identified four key markers of modest clothing: it "is neither too tight or too loose, is not transparent or revealing in any way, does not draw attention to any part of the body, is not casual, wrinkled, sloppy, or faddish."[6]

This chapter will focus on young women within the church, in particular those between the ages of nineteen and twenty-five, the most common age for missionary work. This is also the age group most likely to be enrolled as traditional undergraduate students at the Latter-day Saint Church–affiliated Brigham Young University (BYU), as well as the age at which most young women in the tradition marry.[7] These life circumstances combine to place a lot of pressure on young women: pressure to perform (and conform to) femininity correctly; pressure to proselytize through both word and action; and pressure to represent and define the future of the church as (future) wives and mothers.

CONSTRUCTING A GENDERED IDENTITY

What does it mean to construct a gendered identity? Who is doing the constructive work, and what materials (or textiles) are they using? According to gender and queer theorist Judith Butler, gender is what humanizes individuals in our culture, it is what makes us recognizable, and we punish those who do not "do" gender right. Wearing gender-differentiating clothing is part of what it means to "do" one's gender. She suggests that "gendered bodies are so many 'styles of the flesh,'" or, put another way, gendered bodies are the foundation of nonverbal communication, the thing upon which everything else is built.[8] They are the subject indicated by clothing, the subtext of one's textiles. One can style a gendered body as masculine or feminine, or one can create what Butler calls "gender trouble" by styling a body that does not neatly fit into either of those two categories. It is essential to note that the different styles and fashions of gendered bodies, the things which are being signaled and indicated, do not, for Butler, exist as necessary or natural outside of culture. Instead, she argues, "these styles are never fully self-styled, for styles have a history, and those condition and limit the possibilities."[9] The gendered body is tied inextricably to the society that defines it, and it is created by the communications and texts that indicate its presence; it is not necessarily understandable outside of that context. Just as clothing is heavily constrained by gender differentiation before it even reaches the consumer, gendered performance and identity is already culturally defined before it is performed by individuals. As Butler puts it, "acts, gestures, and desire produce the effect of an internal core or substance, but produce this *on the surface* of the body."[10] Clothing indicates a particular style of gendered body, but for Butler it is an indication pointing to something that, outside of those indications, does not actually exist. Gender is created and maintained by and through culture, and gendered bodies are "naturalized but not natural," meaning that what is often perceived as a natural phenomenon (in this case, a gendered body) is in fact a constructed reality, performatively manufactured to appear naturally occurring, as in the case of a bowl of plastic fruit.[11]

Daily clothing choice is the summit, the culmination, of the largely hidden considerations of existential questions about identity and communication.

The daily ritual of putting together an outfit has become, for most, a largely unremarkable task. The more difficult task of putting together a wardrobe has already been accomplished, and the questions asked behind the curtains of the fitting room (*Does this shade of blue look good on me?*) have been answered. Unsurprisingly, those wardrobe choices are widely delineated by gender. From designer to factory to consumer, men's and women's clothing is differentiated by fabric, shape, construction, and color. These differences serve a purpose: they aid in the creation and maintenance of a visually gendered body. This gendered bifurcation happens long before the consumer, the wearer of the clothing, comes onto the scene. Thus our clothing choices are already and always being made within a constricted paradigm of binary gender, masked by superficial choices (*Do I want gray jeans or blue?*), giving the illusion of individuality and agency. Ultimately, our individual clothing choices become a ritualized reconstruction of gendered identity.

If we accept that gendered bodies and gendered identities are created and communicated outwardly on the body, as Butler asserts, we have to also acknowledge that there is a shared language of gender that makes these communications intelligible. Butler says that gendered performances make a body legible in society; legibility necessitates both a reader and a text (or subject) to be read. To communicate in the shared language of gender is to make oneself legible to a normative reader through a conforming presentation—or nonconforming, although that carries with it the risk of exclusion or even violence.

Thus, clothing is one of the tools through which individuals can communicate their status as a member of a particular group. To return to the idea of construction, one can utilize the tools of gender to build a socially recognizable gendered body, but one can only work with the tools available to them. As the saying goes, when all you have is a hammer, everything looks like a nail. For Latter-day Saint women, the tools can be utilized to craft an identity that is both highly gendered and religiously distinct, yet the options and range for differentiation are decidedly limited. By utilizing known and accepted self-selected cultural signifiers, or tools, such as clothing, hairstyle, and cosmetics, a Latter-day Saint woman is able to communicate very clearly her religious peculiarity.

THE PUSH AND PULL OF ASSIMILATION

Members of the Church of Jesus Christ of Latter-day Saints view themselves as a people set apart from the world, and they take pride in their peculiarity when compared to secular society. To be a religiously peculiar people means finding the delicate balance between assimilation and peculiarity, which Armand Mauss identifies as a key struggle for the church in the twentieth century. In 1974, Gordon B. Hinckley (who was at the time an apostle, although he would become president of the church in 1995) reflected on the church's changing role in public life.[12] Recalling the struggles of his forebearers in their quest for recognition and survival in the American religious landscape, he issued a call of warning and solidarity to his listeners: "Unless the world alters the course of its present trends (and that is not likely); and if, on the other hand, we continue to follow the teachings of the prophets, we shall increasingly become a peculiar and distinctive people of whom the world will take note."[13] He was both issuing a call for holding strong to faith and framing church history as out of step with secular society. Peculiarity in this sense means resisting cultural assimilation, embracing one's status as an outsider, and communicating that status in thought and deed. As Hinckley put it, "It is not always easy to live in the world and not be a part of it. We cannot live entirely with our own or unto ourselves, nor would we wish to. We must mingle with others. In so doing, we can be gracious. We can be inoffensive. We can avoid any spirit or attitude of self-righteousness. But we can maintain our standards. The natural tendency will be otherwise, and many have succumbed to it."[14]

Sociologist of religion Armand Mauss provides a helpful explanation of the particular relationship between the church and American society as one marked by oppositional waves of assimilation and retrenchment. As the church gained wider acceptance in the twentieth century, messages such as Hinckley's became increasingly prominent. Whereas previously the church faced both legal and cultural ostracism, leading to efforts to shed its outsider status as a means of survival, "Mormons have felt the need since the sixties to reach even more deeply into their bag of cultural peculiarities to find either symbolic or actual traits that will help them mark their subcultural boundaries and thus their very identities as a special people."¹⁵ According to Mauss's timeline, the church was the most sectarian in the nineteenth century, with a period of assimilation and increasing cultural acceptance from the early twentieth century until about 1949, when it entered a period of retreat and retrenchment, which persisted through the rest of the century. Into the twenty-first century, with the church's legal and physical survival now assured, members are faced with more existential questions about what it means to be a peculiar people within American society. The church stands in a place of tension. In the twenty-first century it has taken on a more conservative and wholesome demeanor, aided and abetted by the highly successful satirical Broadway musical *The Book of Mormon*, which portrayed young male missionaries as naive all-American boys, a far cry from the threatening portraits of a century earlier. The faith achieved a significant marker of acceptance through the 2008 presidential candidacy of church member Mitt Romney, which was a swing toward assimilation. However, the rise (since at least the 1970s) of Mormon feminism has exposed fissures within the church, disrupting its united facade.

Church leaders have been working to address these existential questions, and to figure out what it means to be a peculiar people who are in, but not of, the secular world. In response to cultural shifts, the family, and in particular the role of women, became major sites of contention. The rise of second wave feminism was seen as a particular threat to the Latter-day Saint family.¹⁶ Rapid changes in women's fashion in the mid-twentieth century provided a very visible symbol for the dangers of assimilation into the secular world. In 1951, while giving a talk at BYU, then elder Spencer W. Kimball (who would become president of the church in 1973) laid out the basis for the modern church's stance on female modesty, calling for what he termed "a style of our own" that would set Latter-day Saint women apart from their worldly counterparts. Kimball gave an impassioned warning to the women of the church: "I am positive that the clothes we wear can be a tremendous factor in the gradual breakdown of our love of virtue, our steadfastness in chastity."¹⁷ Here Kimball is acknowledging that clothing has constructive power. He is asserting that clothing *does* something with and to the wearer in that it not only communicates, but also creates or destroys individual and communal virtue. Clothing, in this context, becomes the most prominent sign of Latter-day Saint peculiarity. Women, then, must restyle their bodies as a bulwark against religious decline. "The Lord has promised to the valiant, 'All that

I have is thine.' To reach these lofty heights and limitless blessings, you must take no chances. Keep your lives sweet and clean and pure, so that there will never be any forfeiture. To do this, you will do well to avoid 'the very appearance of evil' and 'the very approach toward evil.'"[18] Kimball utilized scripture to remind the BYU students of the rewards and punishments available to them as God's chosen people. They must avoid even the slightest appearance of worldliness or evil, lest they forfeit their reward.

These guidelines from church leaders erase the distinction between religious and nonreligious garb. They effectively construct an unofficial uniform intended to present visual signifiers of inward piety and solidify the set-apart nature of Latter-day Saint women. This is most apparent when providing directions for young people partaking in mission work (discussed further below), where such guidelines move out of the realm of mere suggestion.[19]

CLOTHING AS RESISTANCE

Cultural peculiarity does not exist in a vacuum. Calls for retreat and retrenchment within the church increased in the 1960s, particularly regarding the roles of women.[20] The church sought to encourage modest dress as a means of creating and preserving femininity among Latter-day Saint youth while simultaneously rejecting cultural movements that were perceived to be at odds with their belief and culture, like feminism and the "hippie" movement. Thus, although hippie clothing could certainly be more modest than other popular female dress styles of the time, it was heartily discouraged, and young women were warned away from what was termed as "grubby" clothing (denim pants, shorts, sweatshirts, etc.).[21] Here we see the importance of peculiarity: modesty is not sufficient on its own, and one must also make a firm distinction between oneself and the other. This again points to the creative and constructive power of clothing for the constitution and maintenance of a gendered identity. The prohibited clothing communicated a dangerously androgynous style of body: one that was simultaneously unfeminine ("grubby") and sexually explicit (hip-hugging bell-bottom jeans, etc.). Such clothes do not allow women to "do" their gender in a way that communicates their peculiar status. Through the 1950s and 1960s the church hierarchy and BYU president

Ernest Wilkinson increased their efforts to curb immodest attire. Leaders began to develop what would become significant additions to the BYU Honor Code delineating proper behavior and appearance for students. Starting in 1965 Wilkinson embarked upon a personal crusade against countercultural movements and their associated fashions, stating that he did not want any "beatles, beatniks, or buzzards" on the BYU campus.[22] Wilkinson built on Kimball's ideas, drawing a clear line between what he perceived to be wrong behavior and wrong styles. As Kimball asserted, "[Mormons] must be different when there is a right and wrong. We need not do anything we do not wish to do. We can create our own styles and standards for costumes. We can also control or influence the patterns in many of our schools and help to develop proper community patterns."[23] The markers of difference must be both visible and intelligible in order to be an effective means of communicating group identification and rejecting offensive style affiliations.

Identifying with a group can help an individual to define their place in society, and to orient themselves to the world around them.[24] Additionally, there exist very real societal rewards for those who do their gender successfully. Gender-conforming clothing contributes to the "successful" creation of a gendered body according to rigid societal standards, and people who are perceived to be doing their gender well are also perceived to be more attractive, competent, and successful.[25] Latter-day Saint women experience these pressures and benefits on multiple levels. Those who perform well are rewarded within their social group and are perceived as being both more "natural" and more religiously obedient. Societally they can be rewarded for attractiveness, but they can also receive negative feedback if they do not conform to popular fashion norms.[26] As with many out-groups, perceived discrimination tends to strengthen individuals' determination to maintain and emphasize both the connection to the group and the signifiers of that connection.[27] By participating in a more peculiar and modest fashion, Latter-day Saint women partake in a process of self-selected segregation. Social identification with an out-group can become stronger when there is pressure (whether real or imagined) to conform to in-group norms. Thus, young women are willing to answer Kimball's call to create a style of their own, to embrace a peculiar identity, and to communicate this identity to the world, because it provides a means of self-understanding and positionality within the wider culture.

For Butler, gender is something that a person *does*, not something that a person *is*. It is always an act of production, of becoming. As such it is constituted through a highly rigid, regulated, and ritualized repetition of acts.[28] Rituals such as selecting and wearing clothing build up and reinforce the presentation of a gendered identity. If we think of gendered identity and presentation in theatrical terms, as Butler often does, the putting on of clothing becomes even more significant. As an actor chooses costuming and makeup, creating layers of identities useful for the telling of a particular story, so young women carefully select their wardrobes, looking out for the shape of a sleeve and the length of a hem. It is a carefully tailored expression meant to communicate a precise story to the audience. As Butler puts it, "there is no gender identity behind the expressions of gender; that identity is performatively constituted by the very expressions that are said to be its results."[29] To continue with the theatrical analogy, think of all the different actors who have played the character of Hamlet. Is Kenneth Branagh more authentically Hamlet than Mel Gibson or Laurence Olivier?[30] Is there a true Hamlet, or does he only exist because he is written and interpreted? Hamlet is performatively constituted by these acts (and actors), and there is no "true" Hamlet that can exist outside of these communications. Much in the same way, the creation of the persona of the Good Latter-day Saint Woman is just that: an act of creative enterprise. The identity is constituted by the creation itself, rather than reflecting some concrete, true body. Thus, in a very real sense, women are participating in the creation and maintenance of that ideal. That is not to say that they bear equal responsibility. Instead, their performance is tightly bound, with much of their script and setting determined before they arrive on the scene.

THE RITUAL OF MODESTY

There are two necessary elements to creating and maintaining a particularly gendered presentation: it must be both highly stylized and highly ritualized. Like layers of paint on a canvas, or rows of brick in a wall, each new act of gender builds upon, enhances, and reinforces the ones that came before it. The choice of particular clothing is never an independent act, but rather exists within the paradigm of socially mandated construction. Therefore the act of *putting on* becomes a ritual, imbued with sacred importance. For, as Kimball put it, "one contributing factor to immodesty and a breakdown of moral values is the modern dress. I am sure that the immodest clothes that are worn by some of our young women, and their mothers, contribute directly and indirectly to the immorality of this age."[31] Kimball again acknowledges the power of communication through clothing, not just for the wearer but also for the viewer. It is constitution and communication with consequences. Latter-day Saint women who do not "do" their gender correctly—correctly in this instance being in line with the peculiarity of modesty espoused by church leaders—are consequently a threat, not just to themselves but to the church community at large. As a result, young women are tasked with the maintenance and perpetuation of the church by stemming the tide of immodesty and societal degradation. Their identities as future mothers are impressed upon them at an early age, and they are expected to behave accordingly. As Gordon B. Hinckley said, "the example of our living will carry a greater influence than will all the preaching in which we might indulge. We cannot expect to lift others unless we stand on higher ground ourselves ... The home is the cradle of virtue, the place where character is formed and habits are established."[32] The home is, in Latter-day Saint discourse, the natural jurisdiction of the mother. This emphasis on the home and motherhood can be seen in the first article published in the church magazine *Ensign*, in 1971. Then member of the Quorum of the Twelve Apostles (he would become president of the church in 2008) Thomas Monson took aim at women's liberation by mounting a defense of women's role as a wives and mothers, arguing that, "what the modernists, even the liberationists, fail to remember is that women, in addition to being persons, also belong to a sex, and that with the differences in sex are associated important differences in function and behavior ... Recognizing the truth of this statement, may I issue to you three challenges for our times: first, *sustain your husband*; second, *strengthen your home*; third, *serve your God*."[33] Here Monson presents clear instructions, in line with both Hinckley and Kimball, for establishing oneself as a Good Latter-day Saint Woman in both thought and deed. It is perhaps curious that he orders these challenges in this manner, placing the sustenance of the husband in the prime spot and the service to God last, but this is possibly explained by what Monson perceives to be the divine gift given to women, "the power to influence for good the lives of their husbands."[34]

The act of creating and maintaining one's identity as a Good Latter-day Saint Woman is centered on the performance of modesty, an inherently subjective concept with continually shifting standards and objectives. Kimball stated it plainly when he mused, "I wonder if our young sisters realize the temptation they are flaunting before young men when they leave their bodies partly uncovered."[35] Young women, as future wives and mothers, are implored to begin assuming the responsibilities of those roles early. If, as Monson claimed, a woman's greatest gift is her influence on her husband, where does that influence start? The implication is that the bodily communications of young women need to be curtailed. In his 1951 speech Kimball elaborates on some of the specific ways in which young women fail to properly perform their modesty, stating that "I notice frequently where I go, the very tight-fitting sweaters, body revealing, form-fitting sweaters, and I think sweaters can be worn, but they don't need to be worn to emphasize the form of the girl who wears them."[36] A properly adorned Latter-day Saint body is thus gendered but not sexualized. As Butler put it, "the gendered body acts its part in a culturally restricted corporeal space and enacts interpretations within the confines of already existing directives."[37] In this instance, then, the gendered body of the young Latter-day Saint woman is interpreted within the confines of a peculiar modesty. She creates a body that is highly differentiated from both men and secular women. In this space the act of clothing is also an act of constitution, meant to delineate the space in which Latter-day Saint women must represent multiple feminine identities.

The job of maintaining a modest appearance is shared by both men and women, but women are placed under greater strictures in order to properly influence the young men around them. In a 2013 devotional address to BYU-Idaho, Tad Callister, elder and then member of the Presidency of the Seventy, said that "the dress of a woman has a powerful impact upon the minds and passions of men. If it is too low or too high or too tight, it may prompt improper thoughts, even in the mind of a young man who is striving to be pure."[38] This message of female culpability for male sexual sin espoused by Kimball in 1951 has remained consistent through the modern era of the church.[39]

DONNING THE SACRED UNIFORM

There is an established tradition of sacred attire for all laypeople within the church.[40] Temple garments are meant to be worn daily yet to remain hidden beneath clothing, but the shape and form of such garments necessarily impacts the outer layers. Clothing marks the boundaries and spaces of the social body, and in the case of temple garments, they become the soft frictions between what is hidden and what is revealed. In establishing clothing guidelines for women in the church, the indications and communications of the temple garments are in a fundamental way turned outward. The necessity of concealing temple garments eliminates wide swaths of women's fashion. The choice of clothing for Latter-day Saints, then, creates a coded message that can be deciphered if one has the key. These garments become vestments, or what Bohn calls vestimentary communications, a sacred uniform utilizing the tools of the secular world.

Though all individuals choose their vestments as a means of representation and introduction, Latter-day Saint missionaries are explicitly tasked with being the forward guard of the religion. The role of a missionary is akin to that of a salesperson, peddling religion door-to-door.[41] While most Latter-day Saint missionaries are young men, young women are increasingly represented in the mission field. From its founding the church has emphasized mission work, and the first single women to be called as missionaries served in 1899.[42] However women still only make up about one-quarter of the missionary force, even though those numbers have been steadily increasing since the mid-twentieth century.[43] In the late 1970s it became clear to the church hierarchy that there was a need for a fundamental restructuring of the rules of attire for the female salesforce.

Alice Buehner, BYU student and the wife of a former mission president, was up to the task. She set out to create an exhaustive guide for young women, not only giving them the tools to create a new wardrobe, but, in the style of many such secular fashion guides of the era, she framed her guide as an initiation into a secret club of women infiltrators of the professional world. From the 1960s to the 1980s there was a steady rise in the number of women working outside the home, and there was a concurrent rise in self-help-style books aimed at primarily middle-class working women.[44] Books like *The Women's Dress for Success Book* by John Malloy, published in 1977, provided performative advice for women, emphasizing a "fake it till you make it" and "dress for the job you want, not the job you have" mentality, coupled with extensive examples and diagrams to help women pass as acceptable businesspeople. Books like Malloy's provided secular advice but were found to be insufficient for Latter-day Saint women creating a style of their own that was suitable to the work and life of a set-apart people. Thus, Buehner and her coauthors set to work revamping the guidelines for lady missionaries to reflect the changing times and the ever-expanding options for feminine performance. As she explained in her final report, "it was therefore acknowledged by the First Presidency that an education program was needed to train lady missionaries in the art of projecting a professional image, the purpose of which was to enhance not only their own appearance—therefore building self-confidence—but also to improve the image of the Church as a whole."[45] The eighteen-page booklet titled *Clothing Guidelines for Lady Missionaries* was approved and printed in 1981, significantly expanding upon the previous church efforts: a single page listing suggested apparel types, which was deemed to be insufficiently specific for the needs of the modern church. Young women were discouraged from working outside of the home and were not in possession of the type of professional wardrobes that Buehner's research indicated were the most appropriate for lady missionaries. At the start of her study she indicates with despair that young Latter-day Saint women were woefully uneducated about such matters, some even showing up to missionary training in "the occasional mumu."[46] Buehner, in her master's thesis, engaged with the work of sociologists, anthropologists, and cultural theorists as well as popular science and psychology to develop a holistic pattern for lady missionaries.

Buehner advised, "Not only does the outward appearance of each individual sister communicate her own character and capabilities, but it also reflects upon the LDS Church as a whole."[47] The new clothing guide relied heavily on both textile analysis (the line and cut of garments, proportion, color, etc.) and textual analysis, carefully explaining what different clothing would communicate to potential spiritual customers. In this way the proper lady missionary was being constructed from the skin outward. As the physical representation of the church in the world, her corporeal style must be carefully tailored to her message. Inward characteristics must be made into outward signifiers, and they must become written upon the body in a way that is intelligible to her consumers. The palatability of a lady missionary is dependent upon her ability to do her gender correctly; in this case, "the overall appearance of lady missionaries should communicate order, cleanliness, neatness, tasteful femininity, freshness, reasonable stylishness, dignity and modesty."[48] The inclusion of "tasteful femininity" in this list is further indication of the cultural dichotomy through which binary gender is continually shaped and redefined over and against that which is unpalatable, distasteful, and thus unfeminine.

FIGURE 6.1 Cover of the booklet designed in part by Alice Buehner for the Missionary Training Center. From Alice W. Buehner, "The Communicational Function of Wearing Apparel for Lady Missionaries of The Church of Jesus Christ of Latter-Day Saints" (master's thesis, Brigham Young University, 1982), https://scholarsarchive.byu.edu/etd/4568.

Buehner's original guide formed the basis for missionary guidelines that are now updated every few years to reflect changes in fashion and culture. The current options in dress for female missionaries are carefully tailored to present a peculiar image. One of the first instructions they receive is that "clothing should be attractive, colorful, tailored to fit well, and conservative in style."[49] This is in stark contrast to the rule for male missionaries, who, while still subject to exacting clothing standards—all are expected to wear solid-black suits or suit pants, white button-down shirts, and a tie—are simply directed to avoid bright colors or bold prints. For example, in the guidelines for ties they are instructed to avoid nonstandard tie shape and are directed to "not, for any reason, wear ties that draw attention, appear unprofessional, and distract others from your message."[50] For male missionaries the main goal is uniformity of attire, removing distractions and individuality so as to better emphasize the message being delivered. And while both male and female missionaries are directed to dress in conservative, well-tailored clothing, nowhere are male missionaries directed to make sure that they are dressed attractively. Physical attractiveness is a marker of palatability, of tasteful femininity, of a properly done female body. Buehner cautions her readers on this point, reminding them of "the spiritual motivational aspect of looking attractive. Many LDS Church leaders have been concerned with women members dressing modestly and yet setting an example of stylishness."[51] Kimball made a similar point when he argued that not only could Latter-day Saint women create their own fashion, they could do it better than their worldly (perhaps distasteful) counterparts. In this view, proper fashion acts as a veil, concealing and modifying the body to downplay aspects of femininity that are perceived to be inappropriate or displeasing.

The online "Dress and Grooming Guidelines" lay out the guiding principle for lady missionaries as they prepare to serve: "Your appearance is often the first message others receive, and it should support what you say. Never allow your appearance or your behavior to draw attention away from your message or your calling."[52] With those instructions in mind, the "Dress and Grooming Guidelines" provides a parade of smiling young women modeling not only appropriate outfits but also the homogeneous hair, makeup, and demeanor expected of a Good Latter-day Saint Woman. Women are not, strictly speaking, required to wear makeup, but they are encouraged to, as makeup can help the lady missionary to "present a dignified, clean, well-groomed appearance and be feminine and professional in style."[53] The guidelines present a six-step makeup tutorial, with an emphasis on conservative and feminine applications in neutral or natural shades.[54] It is interesting to note that while there is some diversity among the hairstyle models, the same model is used for each step of the makeup tutorial, and the guidelines and color palate are particularly geared toward white skin, such as when they recommend that eye shadows should be in shades of light pink or cream, with no more than a subtle shimmer. This color palate presupposes a white subject.

FIGURE 6.2 Illustrated examples for full-figured lady missionaries. From Alice W. Buehner, "The Communicational Function of Wearing Apparel for Lady Missionaries of The Church of Jesus Christ of Latter-Day Saints" (master's thesis, Brigham Young University, 1982), https://scholarsarchive.byu.edu/etd/4568.

Of the 31 examples of appropriate hairstyles presented in these guidelines, 15 of them fall below the shoulder, 11 are at or near shoulder length, and 5 are styled as short or "pixie" cuts. While several of the models appear to have dyed hair, none have strayed outside of "natural" hair colors, with 20 in varied shades of brown/brunette, 7 blond, and 4 reddish-blond or brunette. The models in each of the pictorial guides are smiling and wearing subtle makeup, presenting expressions that are open and friendly.[55] All elements of their physical presentation are crafted to convey a specific religious message: attractive, wholesome, and pleasant, but not sexually tempting to young men.

In utilizing models to demonstrate proper attire, the online guides are able to provide not only physical representations of tasteful femininity but also useful examples of the consumerist aspects of social identity. An entire industry has sprung up to fulfill the needs of such young women. Clothing companies such as LuLaRoe, a company that utilizes direct sales (and that has heavily recruited stay-at-home moms as sellers), market products to Latter-day Saint women who wish to remain fashionable while still following religious guidelines. Additionally, religious fashion bloggers such as Karli Ellis (Everyday-Ellis.com) provide handy guides for modest fashion. Ellis provides seasonal guides for fellow faithful women who wish to, for instance, purchase a new swimsuit or find an appropriate dress for a company Christmas party. Fashion blogs supplement the official guidelines and provide the necessary templates that allow Latter-day Saint women to communicate their social identification while still maintaining an attractive countenance. After all, modesty is no excuse for frumpiness, and indeed one of the stated goals of Buehner's original guide is to "help them [lady missionaries] to realize that beauty is part of spirituality."[56] Group identities allow people to be simultaneously the same and different. Modeling these fashions for group identities provides women with options for maintaining personal style within a restrictive paradigm.

THE MEANING OF BECOMING

By carefully crafting an outwardly modest image, the Latter-day Saint woman can reaffirm her identity as set apart from the rest of the world, and the act of dressing takes on additional meaning in the performance of her gender. When she gets dressed a faithful woman dons the signifiers of her faith and places herself within the historical narrative of Latter-day Saint separatism vis-à-vis mainstream society. Covered knees and shoulders come to signify her moral and spiritual right(eous)ness and act as a means of identification and authenticity for other church members. The donning of specific types of modest clothing thus becomes an act of a particularly Latter-day Saint performance. This act of creating a female-gendered performance is necessarily rooted in the active pursuit of a historical conception of a feminine idea.[57] The act of becoming is perforce active; it is a series of actions that work to craft an identity that in this case fits within the established historical paradigm of Latter-day Saint culture. Choosing one's public presentation through clothing is thus an active means of both performing and creating Latter-day Saint femininity.

NOTES

1. Cornelia Bohn, "Clothing as a Medium of Communication," Researchgate .net, April 2012, https://www.researchgate.net/publication/328530889 _Clothing_as_medium_of_Communication. Original version published as "Kleidung als Kommunikationsmedium," in *Inklusion, Exklusion und die Person*, 95–127 (Konstanz, DE: UVK Verlag, 2006).
2. On August 16, 2018, the president of the Church of Jesus Christ of Latter-day Saints, Russell M. Nelson, released a statement in which he declared that the church would stop using abbreviations or nicknames (such as LDS or Mormon), and would henceforth be known as either the Church of Jesus Christ of Latter-day Saints or the Restored Church of Jesus Christ. In accordance with this declaration, they have retired older web addresses (such as lds.org, which was formerly the main church website) and have released a new style guide detailing how they would like the church and its members referred to, which includes refraining from calling members Mormons and instead referring to them as Latter-day Saints. This decision has not been met with universal acceptance from within or without, largely because of the cultural history behind these names and abbreviations. In recognition of this new policy, I have made efforts to utilize the new style guide throughout this chapter, although quotes and references that use the old language have been left intact.
3. It is not quite a priesthood of all believers as it is commonly understood in many Protestant denominations. Rather it is an endowment given to worthy men, often conceptualized as entrusting them with the keys to the

kingdom, and all of the privileges and responsibilities that come with them. Thus, those who hold the priesthood can perform duties such as blessings, healing the sick, teaching, and baptizing. The priesthood is split into two categories: the Aaronic priesthood, which is available to men as young as twelve and is sometimes seen as a sort of "preparatory priesthood," and the Melchizedek priesthood, which confers both greater authority and greater responsibility. A member of the Melchizedek priesthood can serve in the higher offices of the church, such as the First Presidency.

4. Bohn, "Clothing as a Medium of Communication," 99.
5. Thomas S. Monson, "Be Thou an Example," General Conference, Church of Jesus Christ of Latter-day Saints, April 2005, https://www.churchofjesuschrist.org/general-conference/2005/04/be-thou-an-example?lang=eng.
6. Church of Jesus Christ of Latter-day Saints, "Dress and Grooming Guidelines for Sister Missionaries," LDS.org, accessed May 17, 2019, https://web.archive.org/web/20190517234421/https://missionary.lds.org/clothing/sister/?lang=eng.
7. Jana Riess, "In Praise of Single Mormons," Religion News Service, October 12, 2018, https://religionnews.com/2018/10/10/in-praise-of-single-mormons/.
8. Judith Butler, *Gender Trouble: Feminism and the Subversion of Identity* (New York: Routledge, 1999), 190.
9. Butler, 190.
10. Butler, 185. Emphasis in original.
11. Butler, 9.
12. The Church of Jesus Christ of Latter-day Saints is led by a group known as the General Authority, which is then broken down further into several distinct groups: the First Presidency (made up of the president of the church, also known as the prophet of the church, and his two chosen counselors), the Quorum of the Twelve Apostles, and the Seventy General Authorities. The president/prophet is considered to be the leader of the church, and he takes the role of both administrator and seer/prophet, one who receives direct revelation from God. The president/prophet is always selected from the Quorum of the Twelve Apostles, much as the Roman Catholic pope is selected from among the ranks of the cardinals. The current president, Russell M. Nelson, is the seventeenth to hold that position, the first being Joseph Smith Jr.
13. Gordon B. Hinckley, "A City Set Upon a Hill," General Conference Talks, October 1974, https://www.churchofjesuschrist.org/study/general-conference/1974/10/a-city-set-upon-a-hill?lang=eng.

14. Hinckley, "A City Set Upon a Hill."
15. Armand Mauss, *The Angel and the Beehive: The Mormon Struggle for Assimilation* (Urbana: University of Illinois Press, 1994), 77.
16. This conflict came to national prominence with the church's outspoken opposition to the Equal Rights Amendment (ERA) in the 1970s. For many in the church, the ERA came to symbolize the inevitable divide between the church and American society, but the seeds of this conflict were planted much earlier.
17. Spencer W. Kimball, "Modesty: A Style of Our Own," in *Faith Precedes the Miracle: Based on Discourses of Spencer W. Kimball* (Salt Lake City: Deseret Book Co., 1972), 168. There are multiple versions of this speech, as Kimball revisited it many times over the years. All quotes in this chapter are taken from the version cited here.
18. Kimball, 168.
19. Youth in the church are encouraged to undertake a period of mission work, usually two years for men and eighteen months for women. This will most commonly happen around the age of nineteen. Mission work entails everything from serving as a guide or worker at a church site to door-to-door proselytizing or humanitarian relief work, and can be undertaken either domestically or internationally.
20. Katie Clark Blakesley, " 'A Style of Our Own:' Modesty and Mormon Women, 1951–2008," *Dialogue: A Journal of Mormon Thought* 42, no. 2 (2009): 27.
21. Blakesley, 24.
22. Bryan Waterman, "Ernest Wilkinson and the Transformation of BYU's Honor Code, 1965–1971," *Dialogue: A Journal of Mormon Thought* 31, no. 4 (1998): 88. Waterman is here quoting former BYU president Ernest Wilkinson. Wilkinson seems to be making a rhetorical point about the general unruly, unkempt, and uncivilized nature of these sorts of students (beatles and beatniks) by comparing them to buzzards, as, according to Waterman, he goes on to say, "we have on this campus scientists who are specialists in the control of insects, beatles, beatniks and buzzards. Usually we use chemical or biological control methods, but often we just step on them to exterminate them. For biological specimens like students, we usually send them to the Dean of Students for the same kind of treatment."
23. Kimball, "Modesty: A Style of Our Own," 165.
24. Jolanda Jetten, Nyla Branscombe, Michael Schmidt, and Russell Spears, "Rebels with a Cause: Group Identification as a Response to Perceived Discrimination

from the Mainstream," *Personality and Social Psychology Bulletin* 27, no. 9 (September 2001): 1205.
25. Samantha Kwan and Mary Nell Trautner, "Beauty Work: Individual and Institutional Rewards, the Reproduction of Gender, and Questions of Agency," *Sociology Compass* 3, no. 1 (2009): 49–71.
26. Kwan and Trautner, 63–65.
27. Jetten et al., "Rebels with a Cause," 1204.
28. Sarah Salih, "On Judith Butler and Performativity," in *Sexualities & Communication in Everyday Life: A Reader*, ed. Karen E. Lovaas and Mercilee M. Jenkins (Thousand Oaks, CA: SAGE Publications, 2007), 56.
29. Butler, *Gender Trouble*, 25.
30. There have also been several female actors who have tackled the role, and often with much acclaim, such as Sarah Siddons in the eighteenth century and Sarah Bernhardt in the nineteenth century.
31. Kimball, "Modesty: A Style of Our Own," 163.
32. Gordon B. Hinckley, "Opposing Evil," *Ensign* 5, no. 11 (November 1975), https://www.churchofjesuschrist.org/study/ensign/1975/11/opposing-evil?lang=eng.
33. Thomas S. Monson, "The Women's Movement: Liberation or Deception?" *Ensign* 1, no. 1 (January 1971), https://www.churchofjesuschrist.org/study/ensign/1971/01/the-womens-movement-liberation-or-deception?lang=eng. Emphasis in original.
34. Monson, "The Women's Movement: Liberation or Deception?"
35. Kimball, "Modesty: A Style of Our Own," 163.
36. Kimball, 162.
37. Butler, *Gender Trouble*, 526.
38. Tad Callister, "The Lord's Standard of Morality," *Ensign* 44, no. 3 (January 2013): https://www.churchofjesuschrist.org/study/ensign/2014/03/the-lords-standard-of-morality?lang=eng.
39. Although I should note that this sentiment is also present through much of Christian history.
40. Temple garments are articles of clothing worn underneath all other layers, against the skin. They are to be worn by members of the church who have participated in an endowment ceremony in the temple and are meant to act as a reminder of the covenants taken during that ceremony. Members are expected to wear these garments both day and night.
41. "In reality, missionaries, although not selling produce, can be likened to salespersons in that they are working to sell ideas and principles." Alice W.

Buehner, "The Communicational Function of Wearing Apparel for Lady Missionaries of the Church of Jesus Christ of Latter-day Saints" (master's thesis, Brigham Young University, 1982), 4.

42. Diane L. Mangum, "The First Sister Missionaries." *Ensign* 10, no. 7 (July 1980), https://www.churchofjesuschrist.org/study/ensign/1980/07/the-first-sister-missionaries?lang=eng.

43. Alyssa Litoff, "New Wave of Mormon Missionaries Is Young, Energetic and Female," ABC News, January 27, 2015, https://abcnews.go.com/US/wave-mormon-missionaries-young-energetic-female/story?id=27924269.

44. Starr, Martha A., "Consumption, Identity, and the Sociocultural Constitution of 'Preferences:' Reading Women's Magazines," *Review of Social Economy* 62, no. 3 (2004): 291–305.

45. Buehner, "The Communicational Function of Wearing Apparel for Lady Missionaries," 5.

46. Buehner, 6.

47. Buehner, 2.

48. Buehner, 40.

49. Church of Jesus Christ of Latter-day Saints, "Dress and Grooming Guidelines."

50. Church of Jesus Christ of Latter-day Saints, "Dress and Grooming Guidelines."

51. Buehner, "The Communicational Function of Wearing Apparel for Lady Missionaries," 58.

52. Church of Jesus Christ of Latter-day Saints, "Dress and Grooming Guidelines."

53. Church of Jesus Christ of Latter-day Saints, "Dress and Grooming Guidelines."

54. The six steps are: moisturizer/concealer, powder/blush, lipstick/gloss, eye shadow, eyeliner, and mascara.

55. Church of Jesus Christ of Latter-day Saints, "Dress and Grooming Guidelines."

56. Buehner, "The Communicational Function of Wearing Apparel for Lady Missionaries," 27.

57. Butler, *Gender Trouble*, 519.

Seven

THE CHRISTIAN TATTOO

MUCH MORE THAN SKIN-DEEP

JEROME R. KOCH AND KEVIN D. DOUGHERTY

A MONG THE EARLIEST school memories for many of us is "show-and-tell." We find something important to us, show it to others, and tell the story behind it. A rock from the yard. A picture of someone we love. A token of our achievement. But it's the story that matters most, and the rock, picture, or trophy are the punch lines.

In the prologue to his novel *The Gates of the Forest*, noted author, Holocaust survivor, and Nobel laureate Elie Wiesel tells a story from the tradition of the Jewish Hasidim, an eighteenth-century sect known for storytelling, and defined in part by other shared sensory experiences such as costuming and dance.[1] The story (abridged) is as follows:

> When the great Rabbi Israel Ba'al Shem-Tov saw misfortune threatening the Jews, it was his custom to go into a certain part of the forest to meditate. There he would light the fire, say a special prayer, and the miracle would be accomplished and the misfortune averted . . . The years passed. And it fell to Rabbi Israel of Ryzhyn to overcome misfortune. Sitting in his armchair, his head in his hands, he spoke to God: "I am unable to light the fire, and I do not know the prayer, and I cannot even find the place in the forest.

All I can do is tell the story, and this must be sufficient." And it was sufficient. God made man [and woman] because [God] loves stories.²

Stories are foundational to the human experience, perhaps especially so with respect to religion. It seems innately human that we situate ourselves within a larger, cosmic story that provides meaning and moral order.³ Cosmic stories are often told through religious symbols: the Christian cross, the Muslim star and crescent, the Jewish Star of David, the Hindu om. These are among the most recognizable images that anchor religion to culture and signify religious identity for individuals who wear them.

Sacred spaces are equally foundational. Michelangelo's painting on the ceiling of the Sistine Chapel recounts the story of the Creation. The twelve Stations of the Cross in Roman Catholic sanctuaries tell the story of Christ's atoning sacrifice and death. The Wailing Wall in Jerusalem is the holiest site for Jewish prayer, so named for the sadness and travail expressed throughout Jewish tradition by the storied destruction of the Temple. The Kaaba at the center of the Great Mosque is regarded as the holiest of holy places in Islamic faith and practice. Much like the Jewish tabernacle, it represents the dwelling place of God, and it is in the direction of the Kaaba that devout Muslims face when they pray throughout the day. Buddhists make pilgrimage to Bodh Gaya, the place where the Buddha received his enlightenment. Each of these places and practices embed the stories of religious history, tradition, hope, and mission within the lives of faithful people. Homogamous religious space engenders trust.⁴ Moreover, encounters and conversations can make otherwise secular space a sacred place for those so engaged.⁵

If, as believers insist, God loves stories, and the places and practices and traditions that show-and-tell them, God must *really* love tattoos. Tattoos are part of the storytelling that people use to make and convey meaning in their lives.⁶ Tattoos are a form of adornment that contain implicit stories. As sociologists Miliann Kang and Katherine Jones explain, "People use tattoos to express who they are, what they have lived through, and how they see themselves in relation to others and to their social worlds."⁷

Tattoo acquisition is a growing trend. The percentage of American adults that have at least one tattoo doubled from 14 percent to 29 percent in the past ten years, and nearly half of all millennials (born between the 1980s and the mid-1990s) are tattooed.⁸ While there is a growing body of research examining the antecedents, outcomes, and correlations for tattoo acquisition, there is very little written about Christian tattoos. This chapter analyzes and reflects upon these trends in four phases. First, we present a brief history of tattoos and tattoo behavior that sets the cultural context for tattoos today. We then discuss the evolving relationship between tattoos and religion in the United States, with particular attention to the beliefs and practices of the millennial generation and Generation Z (born after 1996). Next, we report findings from our research on the prevalence and meaning of Christian tattoos on college campuses, including photos of religious tattoos from one Christian university. Finally, we discuss the implications for the study of religion through the growing trend toward religious tattoo acquisition among emerging adults. Like a game of show-and-tell, religious tattoos are a form of adornment that communicate identity, affiliation, and transformation in ways that are both personal and public.

A BRIEF HISTORY OF TATTOOS

Humans have been marking their bodies with tattoos for millennia. The mummified remains of Oetzi the Iceman were found in the Italian Alps in 1991. His remains date to approximately 3250 BCE. Sixty-one separate tattoos, nearly all perpendicular lines, found in nineteen groupings adorn his body.[9]

Polynesian and South Pacific cultures have used tattoos as signs of affiliation, identity, and masculinity for centuries. Heavily tattooed men showed their strength and tolerance for pain by obtaining, over time, an outfit of ink from the knees up onto and through the torso. Culturally, this process was understood as the male equivalent to childbirth. It demonstrated forbearance and pain tolerance. Tattoos among Micronesian women were more lightly applied and signified ornate beauty and sensuality. Christian missionaries, with their harsh and sometimes deadly conversion tactics and punishments for apostasy, nearly ended the practice of cultural tattoos; it did not reemerge in full throughout the South Pacific until the 1980s.[10]

Tattoos in the United States show up first (more or less) among subgroups of individuals who are socially distinct. For example, returning sailors, others in the military, and criminals in prison are dehumanized in varying ways by the institution to which they are essentially confined (i.e., a ship, submarine, platoon, or prison cell). Tattoos became a way to uniquely adorn an identity, and also signify affiliation with the navy, merchant marine, or, more nefariously, a prison gang. Outlaw biker subcultures are still codified and solidified by specific tattoo images. And as early as the mid-1800s, numerous circus midways included the "Tattooed Lady" character among many other rather scornful displays of so-called human oddities. While scientific studies regarding tattoo acquisition, motivation, and meaning are only recently coming to the fore, early theories of crime and criminality regarded tattoos as indicative of a lower-order criminal mind and/or deviant personality. These ideas were also embedded in medical research that identified tattoos as signs of mental illness.[11] Few today would link tattoos to mental illness, but there remains a lingering bond between tattoos and crime. In a recent study of over 100,000 inmates in Florida state prisons, three-quarters had tattoos.[12]

Nevertheless, tattoos are not just for "sailors and jailers" anymore. One hardly ever watches an American concert, sporting event, or movie or television show absent visible, elaborate, and obvious tattoos on the performers or athletes. Significantly, these are the types of celebrities who stand as contemporary role models. Thus, while tattoos still signify subcultural identity among bikers, military personnel, and prisoners, tattoos have become mainstream in the United States, most noticeably for younger generations. Over a third (36 percent) of Generation X and 47 percent of millennials have a tattoo, as compared to only 13 percent of baby boomers.[13] The rising popularity of tattoos in the United States highlights the central importance of self-expression and individuality for Americans born since 1970.[14]

TATTOOS AND RELIGION: PAST AND PRESENT

The perception that religion prohibits tattoos is a lingering stereotype. Some people point to a divine prohibition against tattoos recorded in sacred scriptures, such as the following verse from the Jewish Torah and Christian Old Testament: "Do not cut your bodies for the dead or put tattoo marks on yourselves. I am the LORD" (Lev. 19:28). Christian missionaries used this text as warrant to control the behavior of converts, and it is still routinely considered prohibitive among conservative Jewish and

Christian groups. The cultural stigma toward tattoo wearers, and the attendant assumption that they are gang affiliated or otherwise socially deviant, seems especially prominent among conservative Catholics and other Christians in Latin America. Sociologist Robert Brenneman has detailed the experiences of gang members who convert to evangelical Christianity, finding that their gang tattoos become problematic as they seek a new identity and yet remain marked for life, as it were, as part of the gang they seek to renounce.[15] Tattoo removal is often sought, and offered, within the evangelical community.

Empirical evidence suggests a continued religious bias against tattoos and tattoo wearers. For generations, religious people in the United States have been among the least likely to be tattooed. A 2014 nationally representative survey of over fifteen thousand U.S. adults found that people without tattoos are more active churchgoers.[16] Thirty-one percent of Americans without a tattoo attended religious services weekly or more in 2014; only 14 percent of tattooed Americans reported that same frequency of attendance.

While the religiously based stigma associated with tattoos persists, an interesting change is now underway. One in five tattooed adults state that their tattoo makes them feel more spiritual.[17] For some, a tattoo is an expression of religious faith. Pop singer Justin Bieber, for example, has over fifty tattoos, including a full Bible verse on his shoulder: "Your word is a lamp for my feet, a light on my path Psalm 119:105." This is one of many tattoos with religious significance for Bieber. Other celebrities with religious tattoos are singer Mary J. Blige (a cross on her upper left arm), actor and rapper Nick Cannon (a massive crucifixion scene across his entire back), actress Angelina Jolie (text of a Buddhist prayer over her left shoulder blade), and English soccer star David Beckham (multiple depictions of Jesus and angels).

Younger generations of religious conservatives are finding their way to tattoo parlors as well. In her 2004 book *Born Again Bodies*, religious studies scholar Marie Griffith wrote, "Tattoos, once reviled by mainstream Anglo-Americans as seedy, low-class, and even satanic, now enjoy a refurbished reputation and are all the rage among growing segments of evangelical youth culture."[18] Others have observed this trend. Sociologists Lori Jensen, Richard Flory, and Donald Miller documented the popularity of religious tattoos among Gen X evangelicals. They described religious tattooing as "an extreme expression of an extreme faith."[19] These inked expressions of faith are championed by Christian tattoo parlors and professional organizations such as the Christian Tattoo Association and Alliance of Christian Tattooers.

TATTOOS AND RELIGION: ADORATION, ADORNMENT, TRANSFORMATION

Religious faith and practice connect us to a power beyond our selves, and often beyond our imagination. Yet that power is reflected in what we think, how we act, and how we let others know of those connections. Religion expresses and reflects adoration. Tattoos are adornment. Religious tattoos connect adoration and adornment to who we are and how we express ourselves.

Outward symbols of religious identity and affiliation are common. Necklaces with a cross or Star of David are customary pieces of jewelry worn by Christians or Jews. The various outer garments worn by Muslim women are vivid indicators of identity and affiliation. A clerical collar or nun's habit not only identifies professional clergy: the wearer also assumes responsibility for their behavior in keeping with this outward declaration of religious identity. Tattoos accomplish many of the same things: identity formation, group affiliation, and impression management. Without overstating its meaning, the trilogy of novels by Stieg Larsson featuring *The Girl with the Dragon Tattoo* illustrates the point. This is who she *is*.

Religious rituals combine adoration and adornment. Among liturgically minded Christians, the sacrament of Holy Baptism provides a literal answer to the question, "How shall this child be named?" The so-named child is immediately initiated into the Christian fellowship and, theologically, reborn, beloved of God. The broadly used liturgy for this seems to metaphorically anticipate contemplating tattoo acquisition: "[Name], child of God. You have been sealed by the Holy Spirit and marked with the Cross of Christ forever."[20] Candles are lit. Oil anoints the head of the initiate, symbolizing adoration and adornment.

Tattoos are social as well as personal. In their seminal study of global tattoo culture, Clinton Sanders and Angus Vail conceptualize tattoos as adornment of self in relation to others. Acquiring a tattoo involves "pleasure of place (exotic) . . . ritual (courage, self assertion) . . . positive response (admiration, praise, etc.)."[21] It is a familiar theme expressed by contemporary tattoo scholars and ethnographers. A survey of college students conducted in the 1990s found that self-expression was the dominant reason given for acquiring a tattoo.[22] Yet, tattoos also are affiliative—they connect individuals to others, be that a tribe, a gang, an organization, or a subculture. Religious tattoos hold comparable meanings: they serve functions of individual expression and group identity.[23] An example of religious tattoos expressing both affiliation and veneration is the regularly seen Catholic icon of the Virgin Mary inked on Latino prison inmates.[24]

Finally, we take special note of the congruent motivations and manifestations of religion and tattoos on the matter of transformation. Among the most ancient religious rites were prayers and liturgies for healing. Much public religious discourse recounts the story of an individual's transformation or conversion to a faith tradition. Even absent organized religion, twelve-step self-help programs are deeply spiritual and become pivot points for amendment of life and a forward movement away from strife. Similarly, researchers have noted the strategic use of body modification, especially among women, to reclaim identity, and also to engender a subcultural identity marking turning points in their lives.[25] These moments/events include, but are not limited to, coming of age, commemorating an achievement, memorializing a loved one, surviving a catastrophe, or recovery from illness. For example, survivors of sexual assault and other traumas are turning to tattoos to help them heal.[26]

Research has shown that the use of tattoos to mark turning points in life is not exclusive to women or the abused. A 2006 study found analogous patterns among tattooed men and tattooed women pertaining to other transitions in life—marriage, childbirth, loss of a loved one.[27] More recent work has provided additional evidence for the transformative application of body art among suicide survivors.[28] Yet other studies have moved this inquiry forward and have found specifically religious tattoos signifying transformation, memory, restoration, and hope.[29]

Not all tattoos are intended primarily for others to see. Psychologist Sam Gosling points out that the orientation of a tattoo on someone's body determines whether it is for others or for oneself.[30] Tattoos oriented to be visible, upright, and/or readable to the owner are self-directed identity claims. Tattoos that face out toward others, as most do, represent other-directed identity claims. We believe this distinction is particularly important in understanding religious tattoos as reminders of conversion or transformation.

All of the above frames our argument for the major purposes of religious tattoos. In short, we assert that the acquisition of a religious tattoo begins with a strong sense of the divine (adoration). The religious tattoo brings an emotional connection to life on the body (adornment). And in many cases, the meaning of the tattoo punctuates a life-changing experience (transformation).

MILLENNIALS AND RELIGION

A key driver of the evolution of tattoos and religion is generational change. Just as Generation X is more tattooed than boomers, millennials outpace Gen X in the acquisition of permanent body art. Our focus is the religious tattoos of the most heavily tattooed generation in American history: millennials.

To understand the meanings and motivations for their religious tattoos, we must first understand the religious beliefs and behaviors of this youthful generation. It is widely reported that millennials in the United States are less religious than previous generations. The evidence includes a higher percentage of millennials who claim no religious affiliation, lower rates of religious participation, and more pluralistic religious beliefs.[31] A study analyzing college-age emerging adults (eighteen to twenty-three years old) discovered that fewer than one in ten attend a place of worship on a weekly basis.[32] However, researchers dispute claims of widespread abandonment of religion by millennials.[33] Rather than a generational change away from religion entirely, sociologists Christian Smith and Patricia Snell conclude that emerging adults exhibit a "religious slump" that is more characteristic of their age than their generation.[34] They argue that millennials today are no less religious than previous generations at the same age.

What is widely accepted is millennials' emphasis on individualism, diversity, and equality. Millennials are distrustful of authority and tradition, including organized religion. Consequently, for many, personal spirituality is prized over institutional religion.[35] Like the tattoos that adorn their bodies, millennials' orientation toward faith is highly individualistic. Millennials are used to being told they are unique and special. Their own names reinforce this idea for them; as Neil Howe and William Strauss humorously observed in 2000, "Nowadays, you can go to a middle-school choir concert, peruse a program with two hundred names, and not see two first names spelled the same way."[36] Millennials expect and embrace this diversity, even in matters of faith.[37]

Yet, there is a minority of college-age millennials for whom religious beliefs and piety are central. Smith and Snell classify them as committed traditionalists and estimate that they represent about 15 percent of contemporary emerging adults in the United States.[38] In contrast to others their age who are indifferent (25 percent), disconnected (5 percent), or disdainful (10 percent) toward organized religion, committed traditionalists have an identity rooted in an established religious tradition.[39] It is on the bodies of these committed traditionalists that we might expect to see religious tattoos. However, for the 15 percent of emerging adults who Smith and Snell describe as spiritually open (15 percent), tattoos may also hold spiritual significance.[40]

A new generation is now entering adulthood. It is too early to know if Generation Z (born after 1996) is strikingly different from millennials. Research thus far points to shared values of individualism and inclusion as well as the continued turn from traditional, organized religion to personal, individualistic faith.[41]

NEW RESEARCH ON RELIGIOUS TATTOOS ON COLLEGE CAMPUSES

Our body of research on religious tattoos has been growing for over a decade. Jerome Koch has been studying body art on college campuses since 1999. Kevin Dougherty collaborated with Koch on data collection in the early 2000s. Dougherty followed the research with interest from its inception and eventually incorporated Koch's research into his teaching. The topic of religious tattoos became a focal point. After collecting hundreds of tattoo photos and survey data from thousands of college students, we have amassed a valuable vantage point from which to explore the understudied phenomenon of Christian tattoos on college campuses. The time frame of our data collection results in our study encompassing both late millennials and the front edge of Generation Z.

The bulk of our analysis comes from photos of tattoos taken at Baylor University, which is a useful setting for a study of specifically Christian tattoos. The university was founded as a Baptist liberal arts college in 1845. It has grown into a Christian research university of seventeen thousand students. Ninety percent identify with a Christian denomination: Baptist (26 percent), unspecified Christian (17 percent), and Catholic (16 percent) are the most prevalent religious affiliations of students.

In 2016 and 2017, students in Dougherty's large sections of Introduction to Sociology at Baylor participated in a semester-long research activity called the Campus Tattoos Project.[42] Students took photos of tattoos on campus and used them to write a series of papers about identity, groups, stratification, and social institutions.[43] We used photos from one paper assignment for our research. From fall 2016 and spring 2017, we collected 752 photos that students had used to compare tattoos by gender. We coded photographed tattoos for religion (overtly religious or not), location on the body, size (small, medium, or large), and content (image, text, or both image and text). Overtly religious tattoos appear in 145 photos (19 percent of the entire sample). Of these overtly religious tattoos, 72 are on women (49.7 percent) and 73 are on men (50.3 percent). The size and location of religious tattoos differ by gender. Men's religious tattoos are larger and in more readily apparent locations, such as the upper arm or forearm. Women's religious tattoos are small and more often on the wrist, foot, or back.[44]

In fall 2018, we extended data collection. With Institutional Review Board approval, we invited Baylor University students with religious tattoos to have their tattoos photographed for research purposes. An email invitation was circulated through Introduction to Sociology courses. Over several weeks in November 2018, a string of students visited Dougherty's office. They signed consent forms and then rolled up their sleeve, pulled down their sock, or otherwise shifted clothing as necessary to display their tattoo. Very quickly, we realized that the religious significance of a tattoo is not always immediately obvious to outside observers. The self-described religious tattoos of students included butterflies, light bulbs, maps, phrases, and abstract symbols. In fact, of the seventy-three photos we took in fall 2018, 41 percent are what we classified as "covert religious tattoos." They are religious to the owner, but these visible tattoos contained images or text that were not obviously or overtly religious to others. Thus, we realized that our previous coding of photos drastically undercounted the prevalence of religious tattoos at Baylor University. The photos shown in this chapter come from students in fall

2018 for whom we have received signed consent to use their tattoos in publications.

A third source of data that we will present in this chapter is from a survey of college students. From 2010 to 2013, Koch and several colleagues surveyed introductory sociology students at twelve universities across the United States. The purpose of the survey was to study religion, body art, and well-being among college students. Cooperating universities were big and small, public and private, Christian and secular. The final sample size was 3,521 students. Using questions about the number of tattoos and tattoo content, we coded respondents into three groups: no tattoo (84 percent of the sample), one or more nonreligious tattoos (12 percent), and one or more religious tattoos (4 percent). This college-age sample had a considerably lower incidence of tattoos compared to the general statistics noted above for millennials. The sample is not a random sample from the full population of U.S. millennials. As such, the demographics of the sample—disproportionately Anglo, female, aged eighteen to twenty, and in college—account for the discrepancy. Nevertheless, these data enable us to analyze the relationship between tattoo content and religiosity.

Below, we report our own version of show-and-tell. We show representative photos of religious tattoos at Baylor University and tell of ways that college students use religious tattoos to express (and perhaps to sustain) their faith. With images and words, we document religious tattoos as a form of adornment that expresses identity, affiliation, and transformation.

Presentation of identity

Tattoos convey meaningful messages about who individuals think they are, or who they want to be. Religious tattoos identify individuals as people of faith. The way students choose to express their religious identity through permanent ink varies greatly. We saw text and images of different sizes in different locations on the body: a tiny, two-dimensional cross or fish symbol (*ichthus*) below the sock line on a foot; a full Bible verse with multiple lines of text across the back or down the side torso. Some religious tattoos are monochromatic. Others have an array of colors. Fourteen different books of the Bible are referenced in students' religious tattoos. They come from the Old Testament and the New Testament. When full verses are used, they are taken from different translations of the Bible.

Amid this vast variation, there are patterns. Nearly three-fourths of the religious tattoos feature an image, either by itself (51 percent) or with text (21 percent). Figure 7.1 is representative of religious tattoos on college men in our photos. This male student has a cross tattoo with Jesus's face on his upper arm and the text from Romans 1:16: "For I am not ashamed of the gospel, because it is the power of God that brings salvation to everyone who believes . . ." The image and scripture reference communicate an identity claim. The individual is proclaiming to others his belief in Jesus as the crucified savior.

The tattoo shown in figure 7.2 depicts the evangelical identity of another student. The young woman in the photo believes that she must share her faith "to the ends of the earth." She has found a dramatic, personal image that implies an imperative for mission around the world. The tattooed map on her upper back gives permanence to her identity as a missionary.

Students' religious tattoos connect faith to other aspects of identity, such as gender or ethnicity. A woman has the first half of Psalm 46:5

FIGURE 7.1 Cross and Bible verse tattoo on upper arm of male student. Image courtesy of the authors.

FIGURE 7.2 World map tattoo on upper back of female student. Image courtesy of the authors.

tattooed on her upper back, stretching from her left shoulder to her upper spine. The monochromatic cursive script reads, "God is within her, she will not fall." The feminine pronouns in this verse actually refer to a geographic location: Jerusalem, "the city of God." This woman's tattoo personalizes the verse to capture a belief in the in-dwelling presence and power of God for women. Roughly a quarter of religious tattoos in our sample (28 percent) are composed entirely of text, and the verse that we encountered most often in students' religious tattoos also pertains to women: Proverbs 31:25. Four women have this verse or a reference to it tattooed on them. As seen on the right shoulder blade of one woman: "She is clothed with strength and dignity and laughs without fear of the future." In the New Living Translation, this verse is from a section of Proverbs labeled "A Wife of Noble Character." Hence, a tattoo from this passage of Christian scripture affirms a gendered religious identity that prizes marriage and motherhood for women.

Religious tattoos likewise overlap with ethnic identity, although not always in ways that we expected. Our Lady of Guadalupe, a popular depiction of the Virgin Mary, is tattooed on the forearm of a male student. The student is not Latino or Catholic. He is Anglo and attends a nondenominational Protestant church. He explained his choice of the Virgin Mary tattoo as a symbolic link to his mother's Italian heritage.

Affiliation

Religious tattoos also indicate affiliation. The constitutively Christian cross is the dominant religious symbol tattooed on Baylor students. Some variation of a Christian cross appears in 61 percent of the religious tattoo photos. Figure 7.3 shows a cross image that we saw repeatedly: a Coptic cross. This image has a very long history as a tattoo. Egyptian Christians (Copts) have distinguished themselves for centuries from Muslim Egyptians by getting a small cross tattoo, typically on their right wrist. In a

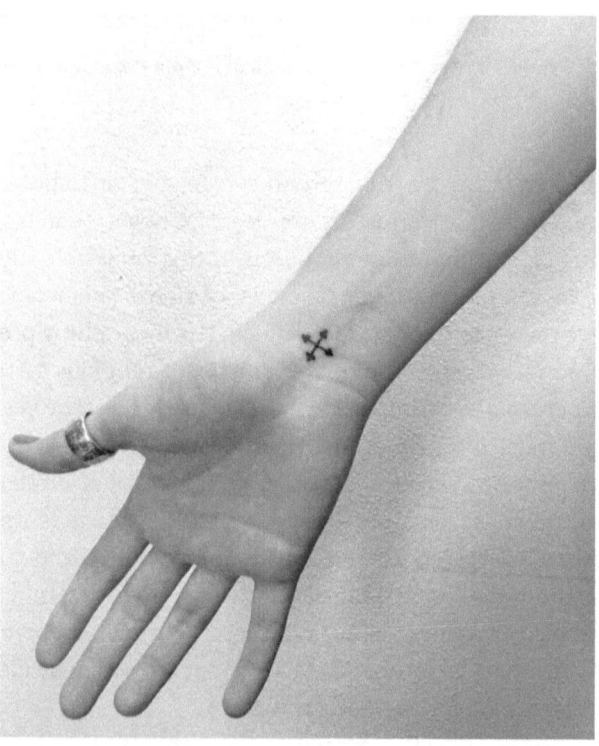

FIGURE 7.3 Coptic cross on wrist of college woman. Image courtesy of the authors.

country with a history of religious rivalry, Egyptian Christians use this religious marker to gain entrance into Christian churches and Christian schools. A small cross on the wrist was a favorite religious tattoo of women in our sample.

Another recurring symbol set that illustrates affiliation are the Greek letters *Chi* and *Rho*, as seen in figure 7.4. *Chi Rho* is a reference to Christ. These letters are one of the earliest symbols of the crucifix. It was used by Roman emperor Constantine in the third century. We saw these letters on men's legs, shoulders, and torso. Like the Coptic cross, *Chi Rho* locates an individual within the Christian religion. Not surprisingly for students at a Christian university, countless variations of the cross and other Christian symbols are tattooed on Baylor students.

Not all of the religious tattoos we observed are Christian. We saw several examples of non-Christian affiliation. A male student has a Hindu deity on his left shoulder. A woman has the *hamsa* hand, a Middle Eastern symbol of happiness and luck, covering the right side of her torso. The palm-shaped image represents to her a connection with Middle Eastern spirituality.

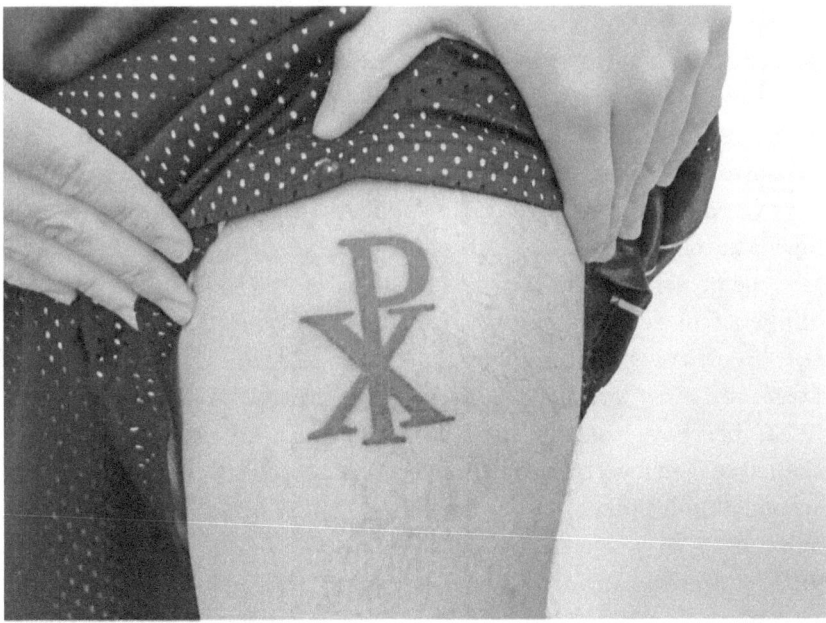

FIGURE 7.4 *Chi Rho* religious tattoo on upper leg of college man. Image courtesy of the authors.

In general, the religious tattoos of students reflect a broad affiliation with one or other religion. At Baylor, the affiliation expressed through religious tattoos is overtly Christian. Interestingly, we did not see any names or logos of churches or denominations. We saw other types of logos that convey affiliation to universities, sports teams, cities, and nations, but similar tattooed affiliations to religious organizations are absent. This finding matches what others have argued about the religious moorings of millennials and Generation Z. They embrace a faith that is more personal and individualistic than traditional and institutionalized.

Transformation

As indicated throughout our narrative, tattoos tell stories. We found repeated instances of religious tattoos revealing stories of transformation and healing. The tattooed symbols in figure 7.5 are a mathematical expression that mean God is greater than the highs and the lows. We saw similar tattoos in eleven photos. We do not know the origins of this tattoo or if it is exclusive to Christians, but we have learned subsequently that it has become popular as an expression of religious meaning.[45] In our photos, it is on men and women in varied places on the body, although the wrist is typical. The woman who has this tattoo in figure 7.5 battles depression. When things get dark for her, she looks at her wrist to remind herself that God is in control. The message faces her. It is a self-directed identity claim. We discovered that religious tattoos in our photos are more likely than nonreligious tattoos to face the owner. A quarter of religious tattoos (26 percent) face the owner, as compared to 18 percent of nonreligious tattoos. This difference in percentages is statistically significant. Other examples of self-directed religious tattoos on college women are "fear not" and "In God I trust" on inner forearms and "i am His" on the wrist. In addition to the wrist, men have self-directed religious tattoos tattooed on their upper arms. One man has an elaborate angel wing tattooed on his outer arm and shoulder. On his inner bicep is the following Bible verse: "For he will command his angels concerning you to guard you in all your ways. Psalm 91:11." It reminds the man of God's consistent protection.

Reminiscent of the mathematical expression in figure 7.5, other covert religious tattoos carry meanings of transformation. One young woman has a row of numbers and letters on her left forearm. They are the

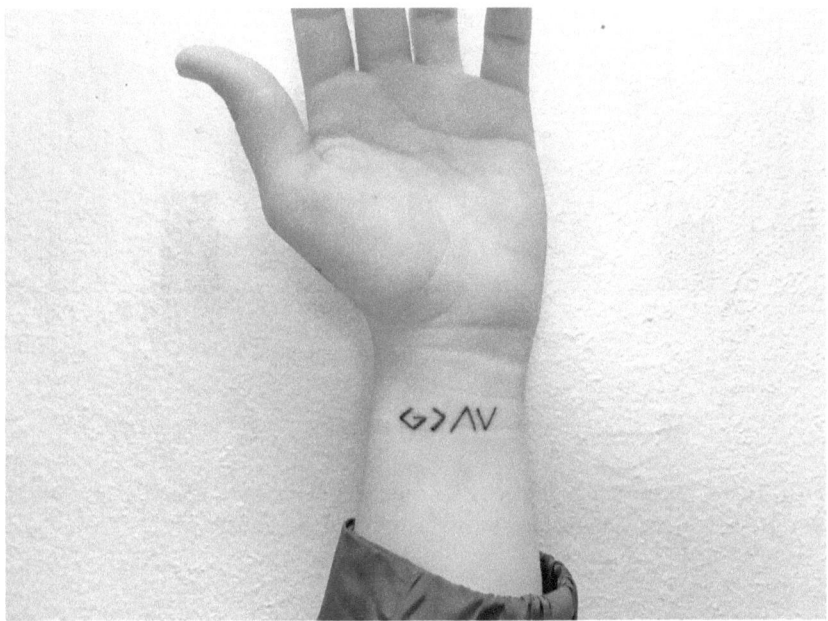

FIGURE 7.5 Self-directed religious tattoo of female student. Image courtesy of the authors.

latitude and longitude coordinates of her childhood home, where she saw faith modeled and embraced the faith as her own. The numbers and letters on her forearm encapsulate her conversion story. Others have commemorative tattoos to honor deceased loved ones, such as a cross with text below that states, "In loving memory of . . ." The story of these tattoos are stories of relationships, love, and loss.

Religious tattoos and religiosity

Using student survey data from twelve universities, we compared levels of religious faith and practice for three groups of students: those with no tattoos, those with religious tattoos, and those with nonreligious tattoos. The survey instrument employed questions from the well-known General Social Survey.[46] Respondents with religious tattoos were more than twice as likely to report a "very strong" religious faith compared to those with nonreligious tattoos. Those with religious tattoos also prayed more

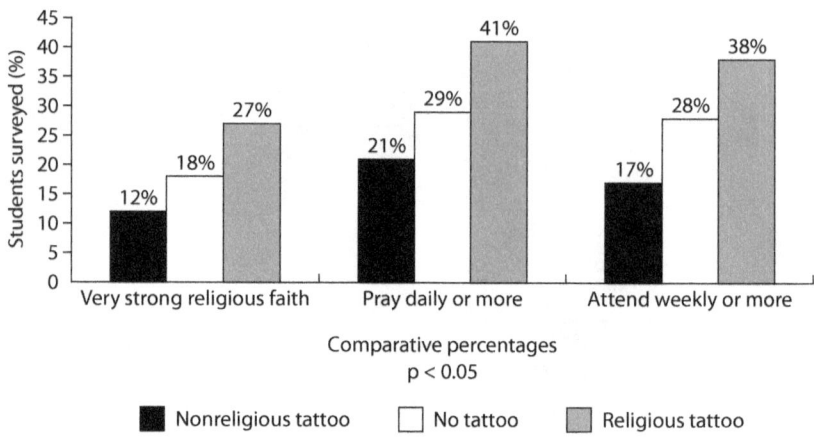

FIGURE 7.6 Comparing religiosity for college students with nonreligious tattoos, no tattoos, and religious tattoos. Image courtesy of the authors.

frequently and attended religious services more often. Figure 7.6 portrays these results. There is a familiar pattern in these graphs. People with religious tattoos report the highest levels of religious faith and practice; people with nonreligious tattoos report the lowest levels; and those with no tattoos are in the middle. College students with religious tattoos seem to fit the committed traditionalist category of Smith and Snell.[47] They are individuals with active faiths. Beyond private prayer and attendance at places of worship, college students with religious tattoos put their faith into action through body art. Yet, they also challenge the assumptions of Smith and Snell, as we discuss below.

FURTHER REFLECTION

We have learned that religious tattoos, as evidenced by the Christian ones demonstrated in these photographs, are much more than skin-deep. Displaying a religious tattoo is a show-and-tell event. Others see it and, either through conversation or conjecture, learn a story. Even tattoos that are concealed beneath clothing remind the wearer of who they are, and often to whom they are connected. Our analysis of religious tattoos on college campuses enables us to extend the show-and-tell game to speak about religion in the millennial generation and among the first wave of Generation Z. On first glance, the wide variety of tattoos on campus may suggest that young Americans' quest for individualism fully explains the choice of body art. Yet there are less obvious stories to be told. As sociologists, we look for patterns. These patterns tell us important things about the use of religious tattoos to express more than unique identity.

To help set the stage for this observation of patterns, we invoke the influential work of sociologist C. Wright Mills. Mills described what he believed we all have, and all use—even without knowing it by name—as the "sociological imagination." Briefly defined, this is a "Quality of the mind that helps us learn, and think through, what is happening to us and around us."[48] This raises crucial questions about our social being and sense of self, such as, "Who am I and what am I doing in my world?" Conversely, "What is happening in my world that shapes who I am and who I want to be?" Finally, "How does my life change the world?" There is much insight to be gained about ourselves and our world by examining the meanings and manifestations of religious tattoos within the latest generations, for whom tattoos are most prevalent.

We have learned that virtually every tattoo expresses something deeply meaningful about an individual's identity. Getting a tattoo involves a significant commitment of time and thought, self-reflection, pain, and, not trivially, money. When these complex processes result in a religious tattoo, an added dimension of the expression of faith brings added meaning to the symbols. Much as wearing a cross-shaped necklace identifies individuals as Christians, a cruciform tattoo adds to its meaning because it cannot be removed. The link between oneself and one's Christian faith cannot be taken away. Younger generations are forging this link in new ways, often outside the doors of religious congregations. Their religious tattoos highlight ways that they understand their faith, relate their faith to other salient aspects of identity, and practice their faith.

Belonging involves affiliation. Here we activate our sociological imagination to see the link between self and society. Imagery is at the heart of religious expression and culture. Religious art and sacred music link self and society. Images become anchors and touchstones to stories, histories, unifying experiences, and perseverance through crises. Imagine: the sound of the call to prayer in Mecca; reciting the Passover liturgy in a synagogue in Jerusalem; or singing "A Mighty Fortress Is Our God" on Reformation Sunday in Munich. Each of these events, repeated in similar fashion across the world and through the centuries, connects self and society. Similarly, we present the religious tattoo. A single image of a cross, a crescent, or a Star of David signifies not only a personal identity, but also one's belonging to a vast, historic tradition. For young Americans, religious tattoos characterize affiliation to broad religious traditions more so than a connection to any particular denomination or congregation.

A religious tattoo can also signify transformation. Religion is a source of solace, stability, and recovery for emerging adults whose lives have been disrupted by pain or brokenness.[49] Religious tattoos can be part of a therapeutic process. We recall again the strategic acquisition and display of body art to champion healing and hope.[50] On the student survey, one male respondent wrote that he obtained his religious tattoo after losing his virginity. The tattoo's purpose was to record and remind the young man of his recommitment to Christian faith and life.[51] That story, in microcosm, captures the power of a religious tattoo to depict and perhaps even drive personal transformation.

Herein lies another important insight about religious tattoos. They may serve to sustain higher levels of religiosity. Smith and Snell discuss causal mechanisms that explain why teens who are religious remain religious as college-age emerging adults.[52] One of the causal mechanisms they identify is the drive for identity continuity: "When people understand themselves to be the kind of selves for whom faith is highly important, the basic human interest in sustaining a continuously coherent identity will—all else being equal—tend to motivate them to remain highly religious into future years."[53] Religious tattoos provide an indelible marker of identity. If the natural tendency is for people to seek consistency in identity, the religious tattoo becomes a form of foreshadowing. We lack data about people with religious tattoos over time, but this is an intriguing line of research for the future. Does the presence of sacred symbols etched into a body prevent defection from the faith?

We have a caveat for Smith and Snell. They wrote that committed traditionalists "keep their faith quite privatized in a way that does not violate American society's broader 'culture of civility'; that requires tolerance and acceptance of difference."[54] Millennials and emerging adults in Generation Z with religious tattoos are committed traditionalists in terms of religious belief and religious behavior, but they are not practicing the type of private piety described by Smith and Snell.[55] Their tattoos represent a public proclamation of their religious identity, affiliation, or transformation. Jensen, Flory, and Miller observed the same among GenXers with religious tattoos and concluded that religious tattoos blur the line between public and private, sacred and profane.[56] Hence, overt religious tattoos may be personal but not private.

Another useful extension of our findings is in relation to everyday religion. The concept of everyday religion has gained popularity in recent years because it moves analysis of faith and spirituality outside the doors of religious organizations. It refers to the way average people experience faith.[57] Research on religious tattoos is a nice complement to studies of everyday religion. After all, people with religious tattoos, especially overtly religious tattoos, are expressing their faith in any social setting they enter. Religious tattoos help define individuals as religious people.

In sum, young Americans' interest in and acquisition of religious tattoos empower them with a visible sense of who they are and to whom they belong. These sacred images and texts can also signify pivot points of conversion and transformation. In all cases, religious body art reflects a level of adoration for the divine power in a person's life. The tattoo transforms adoration to adornment.

NOTES

1. Hasidic Jews are distinct because they wear unique clothing and maintain specific dietary, hygienic, and worship practices. Adopting a distinctive look and embracing a subcultural identity in the name of religion is quite akin to the motivation for and manifestation of religious tattoos, and the stories they represent.
2. Elie Wiesel, *The Gates of the Forest* (New York: Holt, Rinehart and Winston, 1966).
3. Christian Smith, *Moral, Believing Animals: Human Personhood and Culture* (New York: Oxford University Press, 2003).
4. Joey Marshall and Daniel V. A. Olson, "Local Religious Subcultures and Generalized Social Trust in the United States: Local Religious Subcultures and Generalized Trust," *Journal for the Scientific Study of Religion* 57, no. 3 (September 2018): 473–94.
5. Nancy T. Ammerman, "Finding Religion in Everyday Life," *Sociology of Religion* 75, no. 2 (2014): 189–207.

6. Anne M. Velliquitte, Jeff B. Murray, and Deborah J. Evers, "Inscribing the Personal Myth: The Role of Tattoos in Identification," *Research in Consumer Behavior* 10 (2006): 35–70.
7. Miliann Kang and Katherine Jones, "Why Do People Get Tattoos?" *Contexts* 6, no. 1 (February 2007): 42.
8. Larry Shannon-Missal, "Tattoo Takeover: Three in Ten Americans Have Tattoos, and Most Don't Stop at Just One," The Harris Poll, February 10, 2016, https://www.prnewswire.com/news-releases/tattoo-takeover-three-in-ten-americans-have-tattoos-and-most-dont-stop-at-just-one-300217862.html.
9. Marco Samadelli, Marcello Melis, Matteo Miccolo, Eduard Egarter Vigl, and Albert R. Zink, "Complete Mapping of the Tattoos of the 5300-year-old Tyrolean Iceman," *Journal of Cultural Heritage* 16 (2015): 753–58.
10. For a broader discussion of Polynesian culture, tattoos, and Christian religion, see Maarten Hesselt van Dinter, *The World of Tattoo: An Illustrated History* (Amsterdam: KIT Van Dinter, 2005).
11. Cesare Lombroso and Guglielmo Ferrero, *Criminal Woman, the Prostitute, and the Normal Woman*, trans. Nicole Hahn Rafter and Mary Gibson (1893; Durham, NC: Duke University Press, 2004); Richard S. Post, "The Relationship of Tattoos to Personality Disorders," *Journal of Criminal Law, Criminology, and Police Science* 59, no. 4 (1968): 516–24. For an elaboration of the historic association of tattoos with crime, deviant subcultures, and mental illness, see Beverly Yuen Thompson, *Covered in Ink: Tattoos, Women, and the Politics of the Body* (New York: New York University Press, 2015), 21–34. This work is nuanced in discussing the foregoing in light of gender roles and sexism.
12. "Prison Tattoos: A Statistical Analysis of the Art on Convicts' Bodies," *The Economist*, December 24, 2016, https://www.economist.com/christmas-specials/2016/12/24/a-statistical-analysis-of-the-art-on-convicts-bodies.
13. Shannon-Missal, "Tattoo Takeover."
14. Jean M. Twenge, *Generation Me: Why Today's Young Americans Are More Confident, Assertive, Entitled—and More Miserable than Ever Before* (New York: Free Press, 2006); Jean M. Twenge, *iGen: Why Today's Super-Connected Kids Are Growing Up Less Rebellious, More Tolerant, Less Happy—and Completely Unprepared for Adulthood* (New York: Atria, 2017).
15. Robert E. Brenneman, *Homies and Hermanos: God and Gangs in Central America* (New York: Oxford University Press, 2012).
16. A summary, codebook, and data file from the Relationships in America Survey 2014 are available at https://www.thearda.com/data-archive?fid=FS14.

17. Shannon-Missal, "Tattoo Takeover."
18. R. Marie Griffith, *Born Again Bodies: Flesh and Spirit in American Christianity* (Berkeley: University of California Press, 2004), 243.
19. Lori Jensen, Richard W. Flory, and Donald E. Miller, "Marked for Jesus: Sacred Tattooing Among Evangelical GenXers," in *GenX Religion*, ed. Richard W. Flory and Donald E. Miller (New York: Routledge, 2000), 28.
20. *Lutheran Book of Worship: Hymns* (Minneapolis: Augsburg Publishing House, 1978).
21. Clinton B. Sanders and D. Angus Vail, *Customizing the Body: The Art and Culture of Tattooing* (Philadelphia: Temple University Press, 2008), 59.
22. Judith Greif, Walter Hewitt, and Myrna L. Armstrong, "Tattooing and Body Piercing: Body Art Practices Among College Students," *Clinical Nursing Research* 8, no. 4 (1999): 368–85.
23. Jensen, Flory, and Miller, "Marked for Jesus," 15–30.
24. "Prison Tattoos: A Statistical Analysis," *The Economist*.
25. Margo DeMello, *Bodies of Inscription: A Cultural History of the Modern Tattoo Community* (Durham, NC: Duke University Press, 2000); Thompson, *Covered in Ink*.
26. December Maxwell, Johanna Thomas, and Shaun A. Thomas, "Cathartic Ink: A Qualitative Examination of Tattoo Motivations for Survivors of Sexual Trauma," *Deviant Behavior* 41, no. 3 (2020): 348–65.
27. Anne Velliquette, Jeff Murray, and Deborah Evers, "Inscribing the Personal Myth: The Role of Tattoos in Identification," *Research in Consumer Behavior* 10 (July 2006): 35–70.
28. Jerome R. Koch, Alden E. Roberts, Myrna L. Armstrong, and Donna C. Owen, "Tattoos, Gender, and Well-Being Among American College Students," *Social Science Journal* 52, no. 4 (2015): 536–41.
29. Jerome R. Koch and Alden E Roberts, "The Protestant Ethic and the Religious Tattoo," *Social Science Journal* 49, no. 2 (2012): 210–13; Patricia A. Maloney and Jerome R. Koch, "The Young Adult's Religious Tattoo: Respect, Reverence, Remembrance," *Sociological Focus* 53, no. 1 (2020); Kevin D. Dougherty and Jerome R. Koch, "Religious Tattoos at One Christian University," *Visual Studies* 34, no. 4 (2019), 311–18.
30. Sam Gosling, *Snoop: What Your Stuff Says About You* (New York: Basic Books, 2009).
31. Vern L. Bengston, Norella M. Putney, and Susan Harris, *Families and Faith: How Religion Is Passed Down Across Generations* (New York: Oxford University Press, 2013); "Religion Among the Millennials," Pew Research Center, February 17,

2010, http://pewforum.org/docs/?DocID=510; Christian Smith and Patricia Snell, *Souls in Transition: The Religious and Spiritual Lives of Emerging Adults* (New York: Oxford University Press, 2009).

32. Smith and Snell, *Souls in Transition*.
33. Neil Howe and William Strauss, *Millennials Rising: The Next Great Generation* (New York: Vintage Books, 2000).
34. Smith and Snell, *Souls in Transition*.
35. Bengston, Putney, and Harris, *Families and Faith*; Howe and Strauss, *Millennials Rising*; Smith and Snell, *Souls in Transition*; Twenge, *Generation Me*.
36. Howe and Strauss, *Millennials Rising*.
37. Bengston, Putney, and Harris, *Families and Faith*.
38. Smith and Snell, *Souls in Transition*.
39. Smith and Snell, *Souls in Transition*.
40. Smith and Snell, *Souls in Transition*.
41. Twenge, *iGen*.
42. Kevin D. Dougherty, Jake Kane, and Renae Wilkinson, "Campus Tattoos Project," assignment published in *TRAILS: Teaching Resources and Innovations Library for Sociology*, American Sociological Association, October 16, 2017, https://trails.asanet.org/article/view/campus-tattoos-project.
43. Students were instructed to ask verbal permission before taking photographs. As an instructional activity, we did not initially seek IRB approval. It was only after two semesters of the Campus Tattoos Project that we realized the research potential of the accumulated photos. We were retroactively granted permission to use student-submitted photos for analysis.
44. Dougherty and Koch, "Religious Tattoos at One Christian University," 311–18.
45. Carol Kuruvilla, "These 10 Tattoos Have Deep Spiritual and Religious Meaning," *Huffington Post*, November 9, 2015, https://www.huffpost.com/entry/these-10-tattoos-have-deep-spiritual-and-religious-meaning_n_56407716e4b0307f2cadf3ee.
46. Tom W. Smith, Michael Davern, Jeremy Freese, and Stephen L. Morgan, *General Social Surveys, 1972-2018* [machine-readable data file]. Principal investigator, Tom W. Smith; co-principal investigators, Michael Davern, Jeremy Freese, and Stephen L. Morgan, NORC ed. Chicago: NORC, 2019. 1 data file (64,814 logical records) + 1 codebook (3,758 pp.). (National Data Program for the Social Sciences, no. 25).
47. Smith and Snell, *Souls in Transition*.

48. C. Wright Mills, *The Sociological Imagination* (Oxford: Oxford University Press, 1959).
49. Smith and Snell, *Souls in Transition*.
50. DeMello, *Bodies of Inscription*; Thompson, *Covered in Ink*; Koch et al., "Tattoos, Gender, and Well-Being."
51. Jerome R. Koch and Alden E. Roberts, "The Protestant Ethic and the Religious Tattoo," *Social Science Journal* 49, no. 2 (2012): 210–13.
52. Smith and Snell, *Souls in Transition*.
53. Smith and Snell, *Souls in Transition*, 236–37.
54. Smith and Snell, *Souls in Transition*, 166.
55. Smith and Snell *Souls in Transition*.
56. Jensen, Flory, and Miller, "Marked for Jesus," 15–30.
57. See essays in Nancy T. Ammerman, ed., *Everyday Religion: Observing Modern Religious Lives* (New York: Oxford University Press, 2007).

Eight

"QUEENS OF THE EARTH"

THE MGT UNIFORM AS A FORM OF IDENTITY CREATION AND NATION BUILDING

KAYLA RENÉE WHEELER

IN 1966, Sister Linda X published a poem in the weekly news journal of the Nation of Islam, *Muhammad Speaks*, about the role Islam had played in helping her reconstruct her image of self, as a Black woman in the United States. The poem was entitled "The Queen of the Earth." Part of it reads, "The women in Islam are beautiful to see / Just the way I've wanted to be. / The clothes they wear are neat and clean, / The lengths they are befit a queen."[1] This poem reflects the emotions involved in the physical, behavioral, and spiritual transformation that Black women underwent after joining the Nation of Islam (NOI). I argue that clothing, specifically the Muslim Girls' Training (MGT) uniform, played a central role in completing this transformation. Black women in the NOI used the MGT uniform and the organization's gender ideology, which emphasized women's domesticity, modesty, and neatness, to challenge white supremacist images of Blackness. In providing a feminist qualitative discourse analysis of "The Woman in Islam" editorials featured in the NOI's official journal, *Muhammad Speaks*, I show how Black Muslim women played an active role in their own self-making, embracing a new identity as "Mothers of Civilization" that challenged Eurocentric beauty norms.

CENTERING BLACK WOMEN IN STUDIES OF THE NATION OF ISLAM

In providing a critical feminist qualitative discourse analysis of "The Woman in Islam" editorials featured in *Muhammad Speaks* from 1961 to 1975, I show how Black Muslim women played an active role in their own self-making by emphasizing sartorial modesty via the MGT uniform, thereby embracing a new identity as "Mothers of Civilization" that challenged Eurocentric beauty norms. Like the Black women's Baptist movement that began in the late 1800s, dress functioned as a form of respectability politics that challenged mainstream representations of Blackness and played an important role in communicating the NOI's commitment to Black racial uplift.[2] The MGT uniform, which is worn by all female members of the NOI and consists of a wimple scarf, a long sheath skirt that goes down to the ankles, and a mid-thigh-length tunic, functioned as a form of *affective dress*, which shapes the behavior of both the wearer and viewer. It helped discipline the body and mind of both the wearer and her audience, Muslim and non-Muslim alike. NOI women's clothed bodies were so powerful that they temporarily transformed public space. *Muhammad Speaks* writers reported that men stopped catcalling women and swearing when they saw a woman in an MGT uniform walking by, and in some cases, offered "salaams." Anthropologist Saba Mahmood observed the similar disciplining effect that the veil had on Muslim women in the Egyptian mosque movement, yet little has been written on how this disciplining effect shows up in non-Muslim-majority contexts.[3] The MGT uniform served three purposes in the NOI: identity creation and maintenance, nation building, and religious recruitment.

Scholarship on the NOI tends to privilege official male leaders, like the Honorable Elijah Muhammad and Minister Louis Farrakhan. In contrast, I focus on rank-and-file members, who did not have official leadership roles but who played an important role in shaping the NOI's public image. As historian Dawn-Marie Gibson notes, *Muhammad Speaks* was a space for Muslim women to challenge official teachings and articulate their own understandings of their religion and its mandates, and to communicate their ideas to NOI women across the country.[4] Even in instances in which women affirmed male leaders' views on modesty and gender norms, they often provided different rationales. Through their dress practices, Black women continued to challenge both white supremacist beauty standards and Arab-centrism in American Islam. For Black Muslim women, clothing becomes a space for community building as well as promoting entrepreneurship and economic empowerment.

I situate my work in conversation with the scholarship of Edward E. Curtis IV, Dawn-Marie Gibson and Jamillah Karim, and Ula Taylor, who have all explored the role the MGT uniform played in Black women's individual self-making.[5] Curtis highlighted the ethical self-making that Black people underwent when they joined the NOI. Gibson and Karim focused on the gender ideologies created by four male leaders of the organization: W. D. Fard Muhammad, Elijah Muhammad, Warith Deen Mohammed, and Louis Farrakhan. Taylor explored why Black women joined the NOI, which was committed to creating a Black patriarchy, during the rise of second wave feminism. By focusing on "The Woman in Islam" editorials written during Elijah Muhammad's tenure as leader of the NOI, I privilege Black women as the creators of Islamic knowledge and fashion as a source of Islamic knowledge. My work is also informed by fashion studies scholarship, specifically that of Joanne Entwistle, who argues that fashion plays a central role in constructing our race, gender, sexuality, and identities.[6] It is important to focus on the NOI's women's dress practices as fashion because the organization created the infrastructure that allowed for contemporary Black Muslim models, fashion designers, and stylists to succeed in both the modest and the mainstream fashion industries.

EARLY BEGINNINGS OF THE NATION OF ISLAM

While not all Black American Muslim fashion designers, models, or tastemakers are members of the Nation of Islam, they are indebted to the organization for creating a blueprint for Islamic fashion in the United States. Clothing has played an important role in the NOI since its inception. W. D. Fard Muhammad, the founder of the NOI, met many of his followers during his day job as door-to-door salesman selling raincoats and silk. He told potential customers that the silks he sold were the same kind that their people used to wear in their native countries, from which he had travelled to share the truth with his Negro brothers and sisters. He invited interested listeners to hear his message at a local meeting hall. He began his speeches by stating, "My name is W. D. Fard and I came from the Holy City of Mecca. More about myself I will not tell you yet, for the time has not yet come. I am your brother. You have not yet seen me in my royal robes."[7] According to Fard Muhammad, Black people in the Americas (or Asiatic Blacks, as his members often identified themselves) were members of the Lost Tribe of Shabazz, whose unique Asiatic language, religion, and cultural practices were forgotten during enslavement. The NOI provided a remedy to this by teaching members about their ancestral past: they were the Original People, who ruled the world before being enslaved by white people. Fard Muhammad implored his listeners to denounce Christianity, a religion of spooks and spirits that had been forced upon them by their captors. He explained that God was not a spirit in the sky: he was on earth in the form of the Black man. Instead of quietly suffering on earth in the hopes of earning a higher position in heaven, Fard Muhammad told his followers to create their own heaven on earth by building a strong, independent Black community. He also challenged racist gender ideology and upheld Black women as important contributors in this process, encouraging women to take public roles in the recruitment of new members and serve as leaders within the organization.

Because Fard Muhammad met most of his followers at his day job, many of the first NOI members, who are known as pioneers, were women. They were attracted to the NOI's emphasis on racial uplift and Fard Muhamad's gender ideology. Women in the NOI sought to disrupt what Patricia Hill-Collins calls the "controlling images" of Black womanhood, which had been used to justify their marginalization: Mammy, Jezebel, and Sapphire.[8] Respectively, these tropes can be described as the asexual caretaker who neglects her own children to take care of whites; the hypersexual maneater whose animal-like urges masculinize her; and the Black matriarch who emasculates Black men. These narratives, which were created in the 1800s and early 1900s, circulated in both the mainstream media and academia, and they had material consequences for Black women's well-being. In place of these stereotypical images, the NOI positioned Black women as the Original Woman, the blueprint for all other women, whose primary role was raising her children and introducing them to Islam. Through the Original Woman narrative, the NOI provided Black women with the femininity and respectability that white supremacy had denied them. According to official NOI doctrine, not only had Black people forgotten their original language, religion, and history during the transatlantic slave trade, they had also forgotten the original structure of their societies and women's role in it. The NOI helped them recover their lost identities by providing them with new names, aesthetics, worldviews, and politics that distanced them from racist images of rural poverty.

Following the disappearance of Fard Muhammad, one of his closest followers, Elijah Muhammad, took over the organization and moved the national headquarters from Detroit to Chicago. Although Elijah Muhammad challenged white supremacy in the United States, he encouraged his followers to replicate respectable middle-class white American aesthetics and aspirations. As Dawn-Marie Gibson and Jamillah Karim note, Muhammad's gender ideology was rooted in notions of American racial uplift, not exclusively in his reading of the Qur'an or other Islamic texts.[9] His gender ideology was divided into two areas: domestic relations and physical modesty. Women in the NOI engaged in the politics of respectability by focusing on proper grooming, cleanliness, and Victorian modesty, much like the Black Baptist church women that historian Evelyn Brooks Higginbotham studied.[10] Dress played a central role in NOI women's identity reclamation.

THE MGT UNIFORM

As the NOI grew to prominence, it began developing a distinguishable women's attire, distancing the organization sartorially from other Black American and Muslim organizations. The MGT uniform played an important role in communicating the NOI's commitment to Black self-determination and Black pride. The uniform resembled that of the Black Cross Nurses, a women's auxiliary group of the United Negro Improvement Association, a Pan-African organization founded by Jamaican political activist and writer Marcus Garvey. Many early NOI members were former Garveyites and saw the NOI as the heir of Marcus Garvey's dream for an economically independent Black nation sustained by thrift, entrepreneurship, and collective buying. The MGT uniform was central to reimagining what Blackness looked like on an individual and collective level as respectable, dignified, and civilized.

The MGT uniform was created in large part by two women: Mother Clara Muhammad, Elijah Muhammad's wife, who led the organization from 1942 to 1946, and their eldest daughter, Sister Ethel Muhammad Sharrieff.[11] Mother Clara designed the original uniform in the 1930s, and Sister Ethel standardized it in 1967. The original uniform encompassed a mid-calf-length skirt and a long blouse with a matching head scarf. The final version of the official uniform included a long skirt that stopped two inches above the ankle (two inches lower than Mother Clara's version), a high-collar blouse with sleeves that stopped below the elbows, and a head scarf that left the wearer's neck and ears exposed. Clara Muhammad served as one of the public faces of the NOI. She sought to distance herself from the typical Christian preacher's wife, who often wore expensive clothes to communicate their husband's professional success. She generally alternated between long, flowy white skirts paired with a loose-fitting white top or a long, dark-colored cloak that resembled an abaya.

Sister Ethel served as the supreme captain of the MGT-GCC, or Muslim Girls' Training and General Civilization Class, which is an all-women's training program through which members are introduced to NOI teachings and the organization's gender ideologies, including how to dress and comport themselves in public. In this position, she worked closely with her father to expand the roles of women within the NOI and to loosen some of the organization's dress restrictions to allow women to express their creativity. The MGT uniform was available in multiple colors, including pink, yellow, lavender, and lime. Women were expected to wear beige uniforms during the Saturday MGT-GCC classes and white uniforms for official NOI events, while male lieutenants and captains in the MGT often wore fezzes and capes during official functions.[12] The Vanguard, an elite group of women between the ages of sixteen and thirty who were tasked with protecting the community if Muslim men were unavailable, wore pink uniforms with maroon piping.[13] The color coding reveals how structured the organization was.

Sister Ethel founded the Temple No. 2 Clothing Factory in Chicago and the Clothing Factory Store, which were both on 79th Street, in the early 1960s. The NOI clothing factory and clothing store proved to be among the organization's most lucrative ventures. The store also sold jewelry, shoes, and modest everyday wear, which was purchased by both Muslims and non-Muslims. Women members were encouraged to buy their MGT uniform directly from the Temple No. 2 Clothing Factory as a means of keeping wealth within the Black Muslim community.[14] The uniforms produced in the NOI's factory and sold in their accompanying store ranged in price from $25.75 to $39.95. Women were encouraged to own two MGT uniforms to ensure they always had a clean one available. For the NOI's members, many of whom were poor or working class, these prices made the official uniform unattainable. This opened the door for women to draw on the sewing and dressmaking skills they had developed during their weekly MGT-GCC classes to create knockoffs for themselves and their families. Some women proved to be such skilled seamstresses that they were able to monetize their efforts and sell imitations of the uniform to other NOI members. There was also a growing market for everyday modest clothing.

Outside of temple events, women were still expected to dress modestly, wearing long skirts or loose-fitting pants, tops that covered their cleavage and their arms down to their elbows, and heels that were one inch or shorter. Many women started small fashion lines in their homes, working on pieces while their children were at school or sleeping. These small businesses provided a welcome income to these families while upholding gender ideologies that positioned men as working outside of the home and women as remaining in the domestic sphere to care for their families. Many of the NOI's poorest members could not afford to survive on a single income. Elijah Muhammad celebrated these small businesses as proof of the NOI's ability to lift Black people out of poverty, transforming them into respectable, productive community members. The NOI sponsored fashion shows at which entrepreneurs could highlight their brands and women could stay up-to-date with the latest fashion trends. Annual regional and national unity bazaars gave women in the NOI an opportunity to display and sell their products to the broader NOI community, and these products were highlighted in *Muhammad Speaks*. Additionally, the journal played an important role in teaching Muslim women how to dress and explaining to them the significance of modest dress.

CONSTRUCTING WOMEN'S FASHION IN *MUHAMMAD SPEAKS*

Muhammad Speaks, founded in 1960, was one of the main vehicles for spreading Elijah Muhammad's teachings. At the height of its popularity, it was one of the most widely read journals among Black Americans, with over 600,000 copies in circulation.[15] In addition to highlighting NOI teachings and successes, the journal covered national and international news. Early on it proved to be an important space for female members to share their opinions and religious interpretations, which sometimes subtly diverged from official NOI teachings. Women writers highlighted their unique perspectives as covered Muslim women, and they detailed their struggles of living as racial and religious minorities in a white supremacist, Christian-centric society, even though there were also times when they uncritically promoted the official teachings of the NOI. Three of the most prolific women writers in *Muhammad Speaks* were Margary Hassain, Tynetta Deanar (spiritual wife of Elijah Muhammad), and Anna Karriem (the first female managing editor of the journal), whose pieces I discuss below. For much of the journal's initial fifteen-year run, it featured a column entitled "The Woman in Islam" in which female staff writers discussed the benefits that Islam offered to Black women and the importance of following NOI mandates. Another frequently featured column, "What Islam Has Done for Me," invited guest writers as well as staff writers to describe how joining the NOI had positively affected their lives. Modesty and dress were popular topics in both columns. One major theme that emerged in the *Muhammad Speaks* columns was the belief that modesty is both a religious mandate and central to performing a unique religio-racial identity.[16]

According to NOI teachings, modesty is the natural state for Black women and other women of color, and it had been prevalent in most of the world until the early twentieth century. Women members in the NOI saw immodest dress not only as a personal failure, but as a symptom of society's moral decay, which had sweeping consequences for its citizens. In a 1969 newspaper column, Margary Hassain linked the Great Depression to changes in dress norms. She wrote, "The shorter, almost knee-length dress walked in, in the 1920's hand-in-hand with the depression, breadlines and stock market crash, a sign of American's national condition."[17] For Black people to become financially successful, they must first see themselves as civilized people and act accordingly. Hassain suggests that for Black women, this meant not only dressing modestly but also being well-groomed, neat, and aesthetically pleasing, as well as taking on feminine characteristics such as walking with poise, speaking softly, and displaying good manners. Modest dress helped to civilize society and spiritually cleanse individuals' souls. In a column later the same year, Hassain wrote, "With the Words of Truth, Messenger Muhammad cleanses us spiritually and enables the women in Islam to wage a constant fight against the physical, spiritual and moral pollution of this enemy environment, the world of the white race and his filthy civilization."[18] Like their Black Muslim contemporaries, including the Moorish Science Temple of America and the Black American members of the Ahmadiyya community, the NOI's early dress practices drew inspiration from the imagined Islamic East. This took many forms, including wearing satin robes and silk turbans with crescent pins, usually in red, green, or white, which were viewed as the official colors of Islam.

It is important to note that the NOI was not antifashion. While the organization promoted thrift, which meant limiting the amount of money members spent on their clothing, members were expected to be well-groomed and dress neatly in a way that made them readily identifiable as members of the NOI. As Tynetta Deanar urged in a 1961 column, "Develop styles of dress conforming to the personality of your own people! Then you will be loved, respected, and admired the world over. Remember that there is as much difference between white woman and black woman as night is from day!"[19] Outside of the official MGT uniform, women in the NOI were expected to wear long skirts or dresses, or loose-fitting pants paired with shirts that covered them from their collarbone down to and past their buttocks. Women in the NOI were encouraged to wear extravagant clothing that showed how financially successful the organization was, even during the Great Depression, when the organization first emerged, in a manner that mirrored the style of Christian preachers' wives.[20] The main difference between the two groups was that all Muslim women, not just ministers' wives, were expected to dress up every day and their clothing was part of a larger project of nation building, separating themselves from both the United States and non-Muslim Black people.

For members of the NOI, looking good was both a form of worship and an important recruitment tool. Unlike Christian women, who tended to reserve their fanciest clothes for Sunday services or religious holidays, members of the NOI were expected to dress their best on a daily basis. Margary Hassain wrote, "THE WORK of the Messenger of Allah is to reform the woman.... Whenever one's spirit was at a low ebb, a friend would advise them to go shopping and buy a new hat or dress. In Christianity, one dressed up on Sunday or some annual holiday, but ... we should always look our best, for every day is our day, for we are the Makers and Owners of the Planet Earth."[21] Dressing up helped created images of Black respectability that challenged racist depictions of Black women as ugly or masculine. Modest dress was supposed to emphasize Black women's natural beauty and help maintain their physical and spiritual purity. In another "The Woman in Islam" editorial, Hassain explained that "VISITORS to the Mosque will see the Muslim Sisters clothed in beautiful, glistening white robes and lovely tastefully matching jewelry (pearls or crystals), her natural face glowing with health and cleanliness of mind and body. The Bible, Jb. 29:14 verifies and teaches us, 'I put on righteousness, and it clothed me, my judgement was a robe and a diadem.'"[22] Of note here is the use of a biblical quote. The NOI accepted the Bible as a valid religious text but argued that only by embracing the teachings of the NOI could people fully understand the Bible's meaning. The Bible is used to affirm NOI teachings that modest dress can affect a wearer's behavior and how she is viewed by others. The MGT uniform was both a symbol of a Black woman's civilization and a means of civilizing her body.

NOI women's dress practices made them stand out in urban areas, acting as a form of affective fashion. Women in the NOI, especially those who wore the official MGT uniform, temporarily transformed public space into sacred space. Their presence changed their viewers' behavior. Modest dress communicated to people that the wearer was protected by the NOI and its men and that, if necessary, Muslim women were willing and able to defend themselves against harassment. For many Black women, joining the NOI provided them with a measure of safety in public that they had never felt before.[23] Some Black women were drawn to the NOI mainly because of how its female members were treated by Black men, both Muslim and non-Muslim alike. They believed that by joining the NOI they would be protected from disrespect and would attract righteous suitors who would be able to financially provide for them and lead them to salvation by embracing the NOI's teachings. It was important for the NOI to have a unique aesthetic because it visually symbolized the power and strength of its community.

REDEFINING BLACK AESTHETICS

In fact, by the mid-1960s, the official NOI message explicitly prohibited members from wearing Afrocentric clothing. In a speech entitled "Warning to M.G.T. and G.C. Class," Elijah Muhammad stated, "No style of dress is to be worn, but the style of the real Muslim people and the one that I am offering you. The head piece of traditional and tribal African people who are other than Believers of Islam is also forbidden for you to accept."[24] Five years later, in his book *The Fall of America*, Elijah Muhammad went even further, stating, "The Black man in America accepts the jungle life, thinking that they would get the love of Black Africa. Black Brother and Black Sister, wearing savage dress and hair-styles will not get you the love of Africa. The dignified people of Africa are either Muslim or educated Christians."[25] NOI members were prohibited from wearing Afrocentric clothing or hairstyles, which Elijah Muhammad believed were uncivilized and not the natural state of Black people. This sentiment was echoed by female writers in *Muhammad Speaks*. In 1971, Anna Karriem wrote the following in a "What Islam Has Done for Me" column entitled "A Salute to Black Women":

> In mathematics, you can't work with mixed numbers. They must be resolved into like compatible numerals if they are to be multiplied and transformed into a whole number and no longer mixed. So it is with the Black woman who wears the African Bush on her head as she expounds her alignment with Black awareness and Africa. But, when the world looks at her manner of dress, it sees the mini skirt and dress slacks and shorts that expose her body in the American style. Your head, Black Sister, tells the public one thing and your attire tells something else . . . Only with the TRUTH that God has given the Most Honorable Elijah Muhammad can the Black Woman be unified in mind and Body so that Allah can bestow upon her the dignity that will elevate her and restore her to her own in order that she be made WHOLE AGAIN.[26]

It was important for Black Muslim women to not imitate the fashion practices of either white American women or continental African women. Through imitation, members of the NOI were denying their "true" identity as Asiatic Blacks, Muslims who had once ruled the world. Afrocentric dress did not allow Black women members of the NOI to communicate their religio-racial identity, as it made it difficult to differentiate between those who were members of the NOI and those who were not.[27]

Why, during the rise of the Black Power movement, which in part was inspired by the NOI, did Elijah Muhammad instruct his followers to turn away from sub-Saharan Africa? It would be easy to pass these comments off as an example of anti-Blackness within the NOI. These anti-African sentiments certainly reflect broader normative American cultural trends in the mid-twentieth century, which viewed the African continent as the home of premodern savages. However, this organizational distancing could also be seen as an attempt to position the NOI as connected to *all* people of color in the world, not just Black people, which is evident in one of the original names for members of the NOI, Asiatic Blacks. The NOI wanted to inherit the whole world, not just the African continent. Additionally, as a growing organization, it was important for the NOI to continue to distinguish itself from other Black American organizations like the Black Panther Party and other majority-Black Muslim organizations such as Dar-ul Islam. One way to distinguish the NOI from other Black American organizations was to institutionalize the MGT uniform.

Elijah Muhammad's desire to differentiate members of the NOI also extended to hairstyles. Muhammad banned his members from wearing Afros in the mid-1960s, reversing an earlier declaration that encouraged members to style their hair in this way. Initially, the NOI celebrated the Afro as a means of embracing its members' "original selves," practicing thriftiness by not going to the salon, and engaging in healthy bodily practices by avoiding harmful chemical straighteners. However, by the mid-1960s as the Black Power movement was gaining steam, the NOI shifted its view, instead encouraging its members to use warm combs to straighten their hair since the use of relaxers remained prohibited. Straight hair was reimagined as a sign of neatness, beauty, and Black urbanity rather than Eurocentrism. Most importantly, straight hair was positioned as a sign of civility; an important step in helping members reclaim their rightful position as the so-called Mothers of Civilization. Straight hair also helped to further differentiate NOI members from other Black nationalist organizations.

The editorials in *Muhammad Speaks* reveal how the NOI resisted white supremacist logics—such as the Jezebel trope portraying Black women as sexually deviant—while simultaneously appropriating them. While the NOI certainly challenged Black women's position within the Eurocentric beauty hierarchy and created space for different types of women to be celebrated, it did not provide drastically different interpretations of femininity. In fact, in many instances, members of the NOI reified Eurocentric beauty norms. Fat women, poor women who could not afford to buy the official uniforms, and women who wore "natural" hairstyles were excluded from the NOI's definition of ideal womanhood. Additionally, the NOI's emphasis on sartorial modesty as a means for racial uplift made Black women themselves, rather than white supremacy, responsible for preventing their own oppression and exploitation. This narrative tension highlights how Black people can internalize white supremacist logics. Additionally, it shows the limits of using clothing as one's primary form of resistance; there will always be people and bodies who are unable to meet normative standards of dress.

HONORING THE NATION OF ISLAM'S LEGACY

Increasingly since the 2010s, scholars have paid greater attention to Muslim fashion outside of the traditional "veil" studies common in the field of anthropology. These scholars have sought to show the diversity of Muslim women's dress practices and to highlight the multiple parties that collaborate to create dynamic definitions of Islamic modesty. Despite their influence on American Muslim fashion, which can be traced back to the 1930s, and their political and religious ties to the global *ummah*, members of the NOI have largely been erased from Muslim fashion narratives. Part of this erasure can be explained by the narrow time frame that many Islamic fashion scholars deploy, often limiting studies to the post-9/11 and post-7/7 world and focusing on how Muslims interact with mainstream fashion industries. By emphasizing the relatively new embrace of modest fashion by the mainstream fashion industry, we run the risk of ignoring the Black Muslim trailblazers who helped make the rise of such fashion possible in the United States and who will remain here after modesty is no longer "in." While often ignored in Islamic fashion studies, the NOI played a central role in recreating the images of beauty and Islamic femininity in a way that centered dark-skinned Black Muslim women. The organization's commitment to Black economic empowerment and self-determination laid the groundwork for the modern Islamic fashion industry in the United States. It was the labor of Black women in the NOI that made it possible for contemporary Muslim fashion trailblazers like Halima Aden, Ibtihaj Muhammad, and Ayana Ife to rise to fame.

The erasure of NOI fashion trailblazers also points to the Sunni-centrism and anti-Blackness prominent among many Muslims. Elsewhere, I have described the phenomenon of privileging Arab cultural practices as the most *authentic* versions of Islam as "hegemonic Islam."[28] Islam is racialized as a "Brown religion." This racialization of Islam began in the early 1900s but was solidified after 9/11. Simply put, Black Muslims, especially those who are not Sunni Muslims, are not viewed as *real* Muslims. While early NOI members' beliefs diverged from many Sunni Muslims in terms of their notions of Allah and the line of prophets, this was the first introduction many non-Muslim Americans had to Islam and therefore helped construct the images of Muslims and Islamic dress. For women in the NOI, dress proved to be an important way to construct their new religio-racial identity and to represent the organization's commitment to self-determination.

NOTES

1. Linda X, "The Queen of the Earth," *Muhammad Speaks*, March 4, 1966.
2. Evelyn Brooks Higginbotham, *Righteous Discontent: The Women's Movement in the Black Baptist Church, 1880–1920* (Cambridge, MA: Harvard University Press, 1994).
3. Saba Mahmood, *Politics of Piety: The Islamic Revival and the Feminist Subject* (Princeton, NJ: Princeton University Press, 2006).
4. Dawn-Marie Gibson, "Nation Women's Engagement and Resistance in the Muhammad Speaks Newspaper," *Journal of American Studies* 49, no. 1 (2015): 1–18.
5. Edward E. Curtis IV, *Black Muslim Religion in the Nation of Islam, 1960–1975* (Chapel Hill: University of North Carolina Press, 2006); Dawn-Marie Gibson and Jamillah Karim, *Women of the Nation: Between Black Protest and Sunni Islam* (New York: New York University Press, 2014); Ula Y. Taylor, *The Promise of Patriarchy: Women and the Nation of Islam* (Chapel Hill: University of North Carolina Press, 2017).
6. Joanne Entwistle, *The Fashioned Body: Fashion, Dress, and Modern Social Theory*, 2nd ed. (Cambridge: Polity, 2015).
7. As quoted in Taylor, *The Promise of Patriarchy*, 12–13.
8. Patricia Hill-Collins, *Black Feminist Thought: Knowledge, Consciousness, and the Politics of Empowerment* (London: Routledge, 2000), 69.
9. Gibson and Karim, *Women of the Nation*.
10. Higginbotham, *Righteous Discontent*.
11. Kayla Renee Wheeler, "Clothes of Righteousness: The MGT Uniform in the Twentieth Century," in *Islam Through Objects*, ed. Anna Bigelow. (London: Bloomsbury Academic, 2021), 17–30.

12. Ajile Aisha Amatullah-Rahman, " 'She Stood By His Side and at Times in His Stead': The Life and Legacy of Sister Clara Muhammad, First Lady of the Nation of Islam" (PhD diss., Clark Atlanta University, 1999), 86; Gibson and Karim, *Women of the Nation*, 122.
13. Amatullah-Rahman, " 'She Stood by his Side,' " 86.
14. Curtis, *Black Muslim Religion*, 117.
15. C. Eric Lincoln, *The Black Muslims in America*, 3rd ed. (Trenton, NJ: William B. Eerdmans, 1994), 128.
16. Judith Weisenfeld, *New World A-Coming: Black Religion and Racial Identity During the Great Migration* (New York: New York University Press, 2017).
17. Margary Hassain, "The Woman in Islam," column, *Muhammad Speaks*, August 1, 1969, 22.
18. Margary Hassain, "The Woman in Islam," column, *Muhammad Speaks*, October 24, 1969, 18.
19. Tynetta Deanar, "Dress Should Identify Black Woman," *Muhammad Speaks*, July 19, 1961, 27.
20. Ula Y. Taylor, "As-Salaam Alaikum, My Sister, Peace Be Unto You: The Honorable Elijah Muhammad and The Women Who Followed Him," *Race and Society* 1, no. 2 (1998): 177–96.
21. Margary Hassain, "The Woman in Islam," column, *Muhammad Speaks*, May 23, 1969, 30.
22. Margary Hassain, "The Woman in Islam," column, *Muhammad Speaks*, November 26, 1971, 18.
23. Sonsyrea Tate, *Little X: Growing Up in the Nation of Islam* (Knoxville: University of Tennessee Press, 2005), 105.
24. Elijah Muhammad, "Warning to the M.G.T. and G.C.C," *Muhammad Speaks*, June 28, 1968, 4.
25. Elijah Muhammad, *The Fall of America*, reprint ed. (Phoenix, AZ: Secretarius Memps Publications, 2006), 150.
26. Anna Karriem, "A Salute to Black Women," *Muhammad Speaks*, November 19, 1971, 15.
27. Weisenfeld, *New World A-Coming*.
28. Kayla Renée Wheeler, "All Americanists Are Christian, All Muslims Are Brown, but Some of Us Are Brave," *American Religion* 2, no. 1 (Fall 2020): 37.

Part III

NEGOTIATED ADORNMENT

Nine

"YE SHALL BE NAKED IN YOUR RITES"

RITUAL ATTIRE AND RITUAL NUDITY (SKYCLAD) IN NORTH AMERICAN WICCA

MICHELLE MUELLER

Myself, I think that there must be some story to the effect that the goddess always wore a necklace; I believe that Astarte always wore one and was known as the Goddess of the Necklace, being otherwise "sky-clad," as they say in India. I have known one or two witches who wear talismans on their necklaces, but these are mainly astrological, being made for the owner only, and they bear no witch signs, so that I am inclined to think that the necklace itself is the important thing.
—GERALD GARDNER, WITCHCRAFT TODAY

*And ye shall be free from slavery; and as a sign that ye are really free, ye shall be naked in your rites; and ye shall dance, sing, feast, make music and love, all in my praise.
For mine is the ecstasy of the spirit and mine also is joy on earth; for my Law is Love unto all Beings.*
—DOREEN VALIENTE, THE CHARGE OF THE GODDESS

A TRADITION THAT EMERGED in Southern England during and after World War II, Wicca has become a global religion. Primarily recognized as a British-American tradition (with recent estimates of 12,000 Wiccans in England and Wales and 734,000 Wiccan/ Pagan Americans), Wiccan populations have flourished in Australia, Africa, Latin America, and elsewhere around the world.[1] Frequently described by the keywords "occult," "witchcraft," "Goddess religion," "paganism," "earth-based mysticism," and "European shamanism" (or "neo-shamanism"), the modern religion maintains unique practices of ritual attire and ritual nudity that can be traced to the biography of the religion's founder, Gerald Gardner. In addition to being an occultist, a world traveler, a government employee, and an avid reader, Gardner was a nudist.[2] Several eyewitnesses reported that he regularly frequented the Spielplatz naturist club in Hertfordshire, a historic English county north of London, and his correspondence records show his persistent interest in other naturist clubs.[3] Gardner's involvement with naturist clubs coincided with his initiation into occult traditions.[4] These social worlds were not separate for Gardner, and naturism played a significant role in his developing religious practices.[5]

As the subject of this chapter involves unique vocabulary from a religious minority, including terms that have had other meanings ("witch" and "witchcraft"), an explanation of how I will use these terms is necessary before continuing. In *Witchcraft Today*, Gardner's first nonfiction book about Wicca, Gardner referred to his initiators (and coreligionists) as "witches" and on occasion as "the Wica," whom he defined as "wise people, with herbal knowledge and a working occult teaching usually used for good."[6] Gardner used the term "witch" in a gender-neutral sense, a convention that persists across Wiccan traditions. Over time, the religion's spelling has changed from "Wica" to "Wicca." Today, "Wicca" refers to the religion, and "Wiccan" to a practitioner (or as an adjective for anything Wicca-related).[7] Additionally, whereas Gardner did not capitalize "witches," contemporary Wiccans usually do. In this essay, I capitalize "Witch" except in direct quotations from Gardner's work. "Skyclad," which is the key subject of this chapter, is an adjective, meaning any of: *clad with sky, adorned by nothing but the sky* (except, sometimes, a necklace and/or cord), or, simply, *naked, for religious purposes*.[8] Since there is no accepted noun in use for the state of being skyclad, I will use "skyclad" also as a noun for the Wiccan practice of ritual nudity.[9] One additional term requiring clarity is "tradition," as contemporary Wiccans and Pagans use this term to refer to what others might consider a "denomination" or "sect."[10]

The Witches of Gardner's coven (the term for a small congregation or working group) practiced religious rites skyclad almost exclusively.[11] The absence of clothing was believed to assist 1950s Witches in performing successful magical workings, which, they believed, mundane attire would prevent them from doing. According to Gardner, the Witches taught that clothing blocked the flow of magic.[12] Anthropologist Tanya Luhrmann, who did fieldwork with five covens in England in the 1980s, noted the effective distinction from mundane life that ritual nudity facilitated. She commented, "Whatever the reason for its [ritual nudity's] introduction, it marks the rituals as different."[13] In addition to contributing to practitioners' sense of separation from the mundane, skyclad has long been associated with freedom. The fourth verse of Doreen Valiente's *Charge of the Goddess*, a liturgical text delivered as a speech from the Witches' Goddess, links nudity with freedom: "And ye shall be free from slavery; and as a sign that ye are really free, ye shall be naked in your rites; and ye shall dance, sing, feast, make music and love, all in my praise."[14] An early Gardnerian text, Valiente's *Charge of the Goddess* has become a form of inspired gospel for contemporary Wiccans across traditions.

While the skyclad tradition's separation of the sacred (ritual practice) from the mundane (daily life) has been consistent, the general meaning and practices of Wiccan skyclad have otherwise been adapted during the brief history of this contemporary religion.[15] Through addition rather than opposition, contemporary North American Witches teach that being skyclad for special ceremonies facilitates a vulnerability, as practitioners are literally exposed, and that this vulnerability assists the practitioner in understanding what love and trust mean in the context of Wiccan ritual. In terms of practice, among the groups in North America—mostly those Gardnerian and Alexandrian covens[16] that have preserved ritual nudity for all inner court observances (those attended by initiates only) are the exceptions. The majority of North American groups have moved toward a practice of ritual nudity for degree initiations only. The Wiccan initiatory degree system is similar to those in other occult traditions, such as Freemasonry, Order of the Golden Dawn, and Aleister Crowley's Ordo Templi Orientis. Across these systems, each degree represents a level of knowledge or prowess—be it magical, occult, or spiritual—and each is met in succession.[17] Many British groups have altered the skyclad practice as well, but it is primarily within North America that the institutionalization of adjusted ritual nudity practices has occurred, the most common practice being ritual nudity exclusively for the initiand (the person being initiated) within the initiation ceremony.

On a broader scale, the Wiccan movement, particularly within the United States, has been transformed by wider discourses from feminism and LGBTQ political culture, and these same discourses have shaped the history of ritual nudity. Whereas British Wicca had emphasized the fertilizing relationship between Goddess and God and the complementarity of high priestess and high priest, later U.S.-based practitioners developed non-heteronormative Witchcraft traditions, including Minoan Wicca and Feri Witchcraft and even newer traditions (Pagan Polytheism and Reclaiming Witchcraft). These later American traditions offered alternative models that did not prioritize the coupling of male and female, or even a dyadic (binary) approach to gender. Scholars including Regina Smith Oboler and Christine Hoff Kraemer have discussed these changes.[18] Although ritual nudity required by traditional Gardnerians has also been compromised in younger Witchcraft traditions, this evolution has received little attention from researchers.[19]

In the same way that non-heteronormative and non-dyadic Wiccan/Pagan traditions provided possibilities for more inclusive religious experiences, generations of practitioners have made adaptations to skyclad ritual norms in alignment with socially progressive ideals of their time, particularly "consent culture" and inclusion. In their book *Pagan Consent Culture*, Christine Hoff Kraemer and Yvonne Aburrow described consent culture as a culture in which "seeking clear consent to social interactions, especially those involving touch or sexual contact, is the expected norm."[20] North American Wiccans' positive attention to consent has informed the adapted practices of ritual nudity, as newer rituals are constructed in ways that theoretically better include both those who choose to disrobe, and those who choose not to disrobe, in religious ritual. However, initiation ceremonies in North American Wicca are the ritual arts in which the relic of ritual nudity is most preserved. It is the preservation of ritual nudity at all, despite the fact of the groups' tendency away from the requirement of ritual nudity for all inner court circles, that interests me. How do contemporary Witches negotiate the heritage of naturism in the religion, their current religious beliefs, and their social values and arrive at the preservation of ritual nudity for initiands only?

This chapter interprets the history of Wiccan skyclad as an example of religious negotiation. Contemporary Wiccan skyclad practices bespeak a heritage that includes (but is not limited to) Gardner,[21] adaptation and invention in Wicca and Neo-Paganism, a history of evolving Wiccan/Pagan social ethics and social values, and a practice of negotiation common to religious populations. Contemporary Wiccans practice a partial orthodoxy as they negotiate around religious tradition, ritual tradition, religious/magical heritage, and contemporary social values. I aim to address the subject by providing a brief history of Gardner's nudism as it overlapped with the development of Wicca and the history of North American Wicca, in which popularization and commercialization are key, followed by an interpretation of Wiccan religious nudity (skyclad) in individual contexts, evidence linking popularization of North American Wicca with the standardization of ritual robes, and, finally, an analysis of theological negotiation in the history of Wiccan skyclad. This history should be understood as one example of members of a religious population negotiating between tradition and contemporary social influences that could be compared with the theological/liturgical negotiations of other religious populations.

GARDNER, NUDISM, AND THE ORIGINS OF WICCA

Gardner's upbringing was within an elite English family. He traveled the world as a child and youth, particularly to Southeast Asia and frequently with a governess who cared for him. Gardner's hagiography tells that he was a civil servant; he is almost always described by that term. But, details about his specific professional responsibilities as a British customs officer in Malaya are little known.[22] Historian Ronald Hutton reported that, in 1936, Gardner retired and relocated shortly thereafter to the New Forest of Southern England, which is where he encountered the Witches.[23] Gardner claimed to have been initiated there, in 1939, into a coven of Witches, who were modern-day English shamans. He said he "met some people who claimed to have known [him] in a past life" and "soon found [himself] in the [magic] circle [taking] the usual oaths of secrecy [associated with initiation]."[24] Gardner's lifetime of global traveling contributed to the development of Wicca. Throughout his writing, he described Wiccan practices in comparison with non-European religious and cultural traditions. This style established the aesthetic of European shamanism and global eclecticism that characterizes Wiccan religion and Wiccan identity today. As an example of this, in a 2004 reprint of *Witchcraft Today* with additions from scholars and Wiccan practitioners, priestess Judy Harrow noted that the word "shamanism" did not appear in Gardner's book; rather, he used synonyms for the same concept.[25] Harrow described a shaman as a "technician of the Sacred," "one who dreams, or trances, or explores the Otherworld in service to the People."[26] Simultaneously summarizing Gardner's observations and capturing the contemporary Wiccan worldview, she wrote, "We see that shamanism is widespread, a primal religious response. Logically, there is no reason for Europe to be left out."[27] Wicca, according to Gardner, was a European tradition that was informed and shaped by the world's religious and esoteric wisdom.

Then, in the mid-1940s, Gardner, with an associate, Reginald "Rex" Wellbye, purchased land in Bricket Wood, Hertfordshire, that was the former site of a social club called Fouracres. Gardner and Wellbye together envisioned developing the land into a nudist camp.[28] They renamed the land Five Acres since they had bought the original Fouracres land plus adjacent land.[29] The reinvented club's mission was described in a 1947 periodical as follows:

> This club ... aims at breaking new ground, making nudity a cultural agency, and so appealing to many not ordinarily attracted, or apt to be bored by "just nudism." As a social, recreational and cultural club on a nudist basis, it has as its object the bringing together of thoughtful and wellinformed [sic] people for play, conversation and such cultural activities (e.g. discussions, talks, dramatics, etc.) as can be most pleasantly associated with social nakedness.[30]

Five Acres was a stone's throw from "the Witches' Cottage," the meeting place for Gardner's new Bricket Wood Coven.[31] Five Acres and the Bricket Wood Coven were separate organizations, but many members of the coven chose to become members of Five Acres as well.[32] The early Gardnerian Wicca movement was shaped by this unofficial affiliation with the Five Acres nudist community.

POPULARIZATION AND GROWTH OF WICCA IN NORTH AMERICA, 1960s–2000s

Historians of Wicca and Neo-Paganism agree that the Neo-Pagan umbrella expanded in the United States as early as the 1960s.[33] Almost as quickly as Gardnerian Witchcraft arrived (high priest and author Raymond Buckland receiving the greatest credit), Americans founded new Wiccan/Pagan traditions. In New York, Eddie Buczynski, a gay man no older than thirty, founded the Minoan tradition. This tradition was named for ancient Minoan (Cretan) civilization—popularly known for Goddess worship and Goddess imagery—but was indeed a new tradition with modern LGBTQ-affirming sensibilities. Minoan tradition differed from Gardnerian Wicca, or British Traditional Witchcraft more broadly, in its central emphasis on women's mysteries and men's mysteries. Whereas Gardnerian rituals had been rites for women and men together, the Minoan tradition introduced women's circles and men's circles that met separately for Esbats (full moons) and jointly for Sabbats (the eight solar festivals). Eddie Buczynski's and Herman Slater's Magickal Childe, founded in the mid-1970s and lasting up until the 1990s, became one of many storefront headquarters for the developing Wiccan/Pagan community.[34] Leaders such as Starhawk, Zsuzsanna Budapest, and Oberon Zell (also known as Tim Zell or Oberon Zell-Ravenheart) developed popular communities in California; Rev. Selena Fox built up Circle Sanctuary and *Circle Magazine* in the midwestern states.

In the 1970s, North America became the birthplace of new feminist Wiccan traditions.[35] As the late journalist Margot Adler described, North American women united political consciousness-raising with Wiccan ritual practices.[36] Leaders Zsuzsanna Budapest and Morgan McFarland founded separate women's-only Wiccan traditions, both labeled "Dianic." Other groups practiced generic Wicca, or "eclectic Wicca," without joining Dianic or other denominational covens. The women's-only Dianic traditions and the Minoan tradition differed from each other in that the Minoan tradition had been founded by gay men and always included men. However, the Minoan tradition's observance of men's mysteries and women's mysteries in separate, single-sex covens meant that the Minoan tradition also offered Wiccan women women's space. Well-known high priestesses Phyllis Curott and Lexa Roséan trained and were initiated within the Minoan tradition. Women's politically conscious spiritual activity worked much the same way in Minoan women's covens as it did in the other traditions, which is evidenced in Phyllis Curott's autobiographical narrative.[37]

The largest growth of Wicca and Paganism, occurring in the 1990s, has been traced to new information being readily available through the Internet.[38] As new Wiccans were members of a minority group, sometimes without knowledge of any group in their vicinity, those of like mind found each other via each other's webpages and within AOL chat rooms. Witchvox.com—an online directory for individuals and groups that was founded by Clearwater, Florida, Wiccans Wren Walker and Fritz Jung—was a central hub in the 1990s and early 2000s.[39] Information about Wicca came to populate, if not dominate, New Age sections of leading commercial bookstores (these being Barnes & Noble and Borders), and smaller independent bookshops too, across the United States and Canada.

With the rapid growth of Wicca and Neo-Paganism in North America came a popularization of Wiccan traditions. Emerging leaders—spiritual teachers and influential authors—transformed the religious tradition to be more broadly accessible. The three-degree system is preserved in the culture of North American Wicca, but as Wiccan and Pagan events became much more accessible, the degree system became less necessary for Wiccan identity. Scott Cunningham's *Wicca: A Guide for the Solitary Practitioner* (1989) and *Living Wicca: A Further Guide for the Solitary Practitioner* (1993) popularized the practice of being a solitary Wiccan practitioner, or a Wiccan who practices alone—logistically, a Wiccan without a coven.[40] Cunningham encouraged a practice of self-initiation, thereby preserving initiation as a core ritual for Wiccan religious identity while eliminating the need for group practice and initiations by existing initiates. In North America, Wicca became a religion that anyone could join—with or without an existing community—whereas participation within a coven had been considered necessary in British Traditional Wicca.

With this growth came organization, efforts for recognition alongside other religious groups, and normalization. In the late 1990s, Wiccans made national news organizing at Fort Hood, the United States' largest military base, which is in Texas.[41] Wiccans and other Pagans joined and contributed to interfaith coalitions. Wiccans and other Pagans have participated prominently in the Parliament of the World's Religions since the 1993 parliament in Chicago, and following this, those in Capetown (1999),

Barcelona (2004), Melbourne (2009), Salt Lake City (2015), and Toronto (2018). The patterns of popularization and normalization contributed to practitioners making changes in their ritual attire customs.

FEMINIST WOMEN'S-ONLY COVENS AND THE POWER OF SKYCLAD

In the women's-only Wiccan groups originating in the 1970s, women took ownership of nudity, inherent to the Wiccan tradition, by reinscribing ritual nudity or partial nudity as feminist praxis. Whereas Gardner's naturism was likely shaped by an aesthetic of personal liberation, skyclad in women's circles became associated specifically with *women's* liberation. Skyclad in women's circles came to be associated with reclaiming one's body and sexuality as one's own in a patriarchal world where women were constantly deprived of ownership of both. In skyclad circles, women nurtured and grew their self-esteem through the vulnerability of being naked in front of others and through recognizing the Goddess in each and every woman around them. Being skyclad enabled the women to approach body-related political issues, as they unveiled natural blemishes, scars from childbirth, postmenopausal breasts, and a plethora of body types and weights. Issues such as body image, pregnancy, aging, and menopause were addressed holistically through the experience of being naked together.

Popular Pagan author Starhawk described a group of Wiccan women jailed after doing activism. She contrasted women's nakedness as a mechanism of women's disempowerment—"The women must undress in front of [the guards'] male eyes"—with empowerment: "Outside is a small exercise yard. The central California sun is hot. And we begin to take off our shirts to lie in the sun bare-breasted . . . We feel good about our bodies; we enjoy looking at each other. In that setting of corrugated iron and concrete, we are soft and alive and beautiful."[42] Starhawk includes a friend's takeaway in addition to her own: "'I never knew how many shapes and sizes women come in,' says a friend, whose life has not previously allowed her to hang out in the company of two hundred naked women. 'And we're all beautiful. Look at that woman there. She's like a sculpture—like a Venus of Willendorf, a Goddess.'"[43] The female practitioners Starhawk described experienced strengthened, renewed appreciation for the female body in all its diversity and for the spiritual beings inhabiting those bodies, this appreciation being a political force within a misogynistic society.

POPULARIZATION AND THE STANDARDIZATION OF RITUAL ROBES IN NORTH AMERICAN WICCA

With the popularization of Wicca and the solitary Wiccan movement came adaptations to the practices of attire and adornment for Wiccan ritual. Cunningham, a driver for the solitary Wiccan movement, emphasized the separation of the sacred from the profane and wrote that "Many Wiccans dress in special robes for worship [that] are usually worn solely for ritual observances" and that ritual jewelry "refers to jewelry worn only in the circle for ritual purposes." Cunningham reiterated the importance: "Remember: ritual jewelry isn't worn outside the circle. When it is, it loses its specialness and its direct links with ritual. Other pieces can be worn around the clock, but if you choose to use ritual jewelry, save it for the circle."[44] Cunningham's approach was very open-minded. He taught that there were many ways to be Wiccan and to practice Wicca, views that sometimes put him at odds with other British Traditional Witches but that contributed to the growth of Wicca in North America.[45] Cunningham acknowledged that "Some Wiccans worship naked," while providing other options. He described going skyclad or not as "a personal decision" and further recommended that every solitary Wiccan, even those who practice skyclad, "have a robe around somewhere, in case [they] ever [change their] mind, or are invited to a robed ritual . . . [for] it does happen."[46] He directed solitary Wiccans to find robes at occult shops or from mail-order businesses, or to make their own from natural cloth—"polyester and other synthetic fabrics will leave you hot and uncomfortable in circle, and will hardly connect you with the Deities of nature"—using patterns found in yardage shops.[47] Whereas the skyclad method put Witches very inexpensively in communion with the deities, later approaches, informed by modesty (or pragmatism if Witches were gathering at parks), required more purchases. Cunningham supports making ritual jewelry or robes oneself, which can save costs. Still, the need to keep ritual attire distinct from mundane attire meant procuring additional religious garments and jewelry or the materials to create them.

In his writing, Cunningham was recording changes that were happening in North American practice. Because of the new influx of Wiccans learning from books and the Internet, he was also contributing to a standardization of this new norm. Despite the religion's nudist past, the norm for religious attire among North American Wiccans became "ritual robes." The praxis of sewing one's own ritual robe became a magical act. One did not need experience and skill; to invest oneself in the design and labor imbued the robe with one's natural energy and power. Magical shops—including storefronts and online shops—carried ritual robes, of course, and many chose from the selections available for various reasons—convenience, preference, and lack of sewing abilities or sewing machine, for instance. In a time of acceptance-seeking, wearing ritual robes seemed more palatable for outsiders than the practice of religious nakedness.

THEOLOGICAL NEGOTIATIONS: RITUAL NUDITY IN CONTEMPORARY WICCAN INITIATION CEREMONIES

The majority of North American Wiccan groups have moved away from ritual nudity as the norm, but they have not absolved the practice of ritual nudity entirely. Most North American Wiccan groups have preserved ritual nudity for special circumstances. The most common practice is ritual nudity for the initiand in initiation ceremonies.[48] The key distinctions between this and the Gardnerian/Alexandrian standard are (1) the specificity of skyclad for initiation ceremonies only, and (2) the specificity of the initiand being skyclad in comparison with the existing coven members in ritual robes. Examples of this are found in the Assembly of the Sacred Wheel, a mid-Atlantic Wiccan organization; the Reclaiming tradition, a Bay Area–born ecofeminist Witchcraft tradition that now spans North America; and Bado's Merry Circle tradition, derived and adapted from British Traditional Wicca.[49]

This newer adaptation has made skyclad a less defining characteristic of Wiccan ritual at large, as it is less universally practiced; at the same time, the limitation of skyclad to initiation ceremonies has strengthened the significance of skyclad for contemporary Wiccans, as initiation is a particularly intimate rite of passage for a Wiccan's relationship to the coven and to the gods. In essence, the adaptation has simultaneously made skyclad *less important* and *more important* in the Wiccan tradition, as a case of quantity versus quality.

Post-Gardnerian Wiccans adapted skyclad because of outside social influences and their own social values. Whereas the early British Witches were focused on the creation of a radical, occult society within postwar Europe, younger generations of Witches have been concerned with raising children Wiccan/Pagan, gaining respectability in broader society, and sustaining an existing new religious movement. Skyclad all-ages rituals would be problematic for parents and for community members outside the families, except in rare cases of absolute-nudist families. Furthermore, naked rituals would likely be perceived as too extreme for potential members who are interested in the other aspects of Wicca such as mysticism and Goddess worship. Departing from skyclad-for-all rituals, younger Wiccan generations, specifically in North America, have been successful in growing and normalizing the religion. Additionally, younger generations of Wiccans have been increasingly mindful of fostering consent culture. As described earlier, nudity in Wiccan rituals can bring about feelings of liberation. However, the absence of options can infringe upon the personal freedoms of members or potential members.

As skyclad ritual practice has changed, so has theology. The driving force behind adaptations of skyclad seems to be interest in growth and normalization, with respect for varying social conventions. Because the community involved is a religious one, the practitioners have developed new theological (or, as some might prefer, cosmological) reasons to justify the skyclad-for-initiations practice. This evolution is in line with theories of ritualization in that rituals and their meanings are constantly evolving. Limiting skyclad to initiation ceremonies only enabled reformist Wiccans to preserve a characteristic unique to British Traditional Wiccan practice, thereby maintaining connections with traditional heritage. However, the very same limitation made the earlier rationale for skyclad—that clothing blocked the flow of magic—inapplicable because of the inconsistency.

Post-Gardnerian Wiccans then needed to create new understandings of skyclad in order to support the new practice. In contemporary North American Wicca, skyclad for initiations is interpreted as an aspect that makes the rite of passage effective for the individual but for reasons other than the flow of magic. Entering the circle skyclad, the initiand makes oneself vulnerable. The physical vulnerability of being exposed leads to psychological, emotional, and spiritual vulnerability. The initiand reveals all of one's physical self, facing every insecurity about the body and carrying onward, in perfect love and trust with the coven and the gods. The new meaning is relevant even within Gardnerian/Alexandrian covens or other groups that practice skyclad for inner court circles, for the initiation ceremony is the first instance of the initiate's skyclad experience within the coven.

Variations of this ritual meaning exist but are generally consistent with this baseline. For instance, theologian and ethnographer Jone Salomensen interpreted skyclad in ecofeminist Reclaiming covens: "Nudity is consequently, the material, bodily, ritualized symbol of [Witches' devotional attitude toward the Goddess], which, in a ritual context, is associated with pride, vulnerability, sensuality, honesty, and equality, as well as with the remembrance of how human life is brought into the world: as a naked body, through a naked body. Ritual nudity symbolizes that the participants, at a deep level, are one body, one being, one member, as it symbolizes the innocence of beginnings, of conversions, of being born again."[50] The emphasis here on birth and the circle of life is consistent with the Reclaiming tradition's ecofeminist sensibilities, which are at the center of its formative influences.

It is important to note that several of the newer North American traditions, which preserve a theology of ritual nudity for specific rites, keep membership and the tradition(s) accessible to candidates who do not choose nudity for any rites. For instance, one can be a member of a Reclaiming coven or an Assembly of the Sacred Wheel coven without ever becoming an initiate or having an initiation ceremony. This practice is different from British Traditional Witchcraft, wherein membership is established upon completion of the first-degree initiation ceremony.

In Bado's Merry Circle tradition, a close derivative of British Traditional Wicca, skyclad in the dedication ceremony is nonnegotiable. Bado reflected, "To my knowledge, no one has ever refused to take the rite because of ritual nudity, but it is certainly theoretically possible that a student would opt not to become dedicated within the Merry Circle's tradition if this were a critical issue."[51] Speaking to ritual ethics, she clarified that "ritual nudity is not sprung on the student as a surprise test . . . [and the student is informed well in advance] that . . . [they] will need to be skyclad."[52] In my own observations of American Pagans, I have not heard from individuals who refused initiation because of a nudity requirement either. I have met practitioners for whom skyclad/attire practices were one factor in their decision of which tradition to join. Bado's note about students being informed in advance supports this reality. Students who take issue with ritual nudity would likely have jumped ship and joined a different group well before their rejection of the dedication rite became an issue.

Even in cases where members have the option between being initiated (skyclad) or uninitiated, members' avoidance of their own ritual nudity inevitably limits their own progression within the tradition, and even their opportunities for community ritual and community bonding. In the vast majority of Wiccan traditions, only initiates of the present degree are permitted to attend another initiand's ceremony, meaning a first-degree initiation ceremony can be attended by the initiand and existing first-, second-, and third-degree initiates; a second-degree initiation ceremony can be attended by the initiand and existing second- and third-degree initiates; and so on. Not only would individuals reject their own ritual nudity, they would by extension exclude themselves from others' initiation rites.

The mainstreaming and desire for normalization are factors in adaptations to Gardner's nudist religion, in addition to North American Wicca being informed by second, third, and fourth wave feminisms in succession. While each historic feminist wave reflects particular circumstances and contexts, all have common interests in the protection of sexual freedom, the well-being and autonomy of bodies, protection against assault, and the development of consent culture in place of rape culture and domination models. Feminist principles of sexual liberation and sexual freedom have been continuous influences on North American Wicca. Whereas Gardnerian Witches' naturism was freeing in the 1950s, mandated nudity has become problematic for contemporary North American Wiccans, given the ideals of consent culture. The values of consent culture include, above all, consent, choice, and agency. Clothing-optional rituals offer greater individual choice than no-clothing rituals do. Greater flexibility with respect to ritual nudity expectations resulted from the feminist influence on North American Wicca.

Within all religious traditions, later generations have opportunities to reform, and usually they do in some way or another. Christianity alone has experienced changes in the rituals of baptism and the Eucharist, and the liturgical theology around these rituals has evolved accordingly. Nude baptism was normative in early Christianity.[53] In a less direct, though still relevant, example, the primacy of millenarianism has changed in Christian tradition after years of no recognized "Second Coming."

Gardner's religious experience was defined by the newness of the traditions. There was a novelty that shaped the experiences of early Gardnerians. Ritual nudity was avant-garde, which felt magical for mid-twentieth-century Witches, and does for many today, as evidenced by the continued practices and the newer theologies of skyclad as a test of vulnerability in a devotional rite of passage. But, contemporary Wiccans approach established traditions with a measured suspicion appropriate to later generations. In the 1950s, ritual nudity was likely freeing for members of the naturist community who were also Wiccan. But, the expectation or requirement of absolute ritual nudity is perceived of as too eccentric, or even oppressive, by contemporary North American Wiccans. This perception has led to the adapted practices of skyclad observed today, which include the rejection of skyclad and the limitations on skyclad observance to unique rites of passage. Even while rejecting the practice of skyclad for all inner court rituals, North American Wiccans preserve ritual nudity for the most magical rites, revealing an evolution of religious thought. Practices are adapted over time guided by changes in social values and social norms. But significant practices are not abandoned wholesale: the North American Wiccan community assigned new meanings to the skyclad tradition and preserved it with more restricted parameters.

NOTES

1. Massimo Introvigne, "The Rise and Rise of Wicca: The Astonishing Growth of Witchcraft in the US Is a Little-Understood Phenomenon," MercatorNet, December 5, 2018, https://www.mercatornet.com/above/view/the-rise-and-rise-of-wicca/22002.
2. See Philip Heselton, *Witchfather: From Witch Cult to Wicca*, vol. 2, *A Life of Gerald Gardner* (Loughborough, UK: Thoth Publications, 2012), 294.
3. Heselton, 294, 296, 309.

4. Heselton, 294, 296.
5. Heselton, 295–8.
6. Gerald B. Gardner, *Witchcraft Today*, new ed. (Thame, UK: I-H-O Books, 1999), 88. Prior to *Witchcraft Today*, Gardner wrote *High Magic's Aid* (1949), a novel that is now recognized as a semi-fictional depiction of what was (or what would become) Wicca. In *Witchcraft Today*, Gardner explained that he had been "permitted to write, as fiction, something of what a witch believes in the novel *High Magic's Aid*"; *Witchcraft Today*, he wrote, "has the same purpose, but deals with the subject in a factual way" (16). Common Gardnerian lore has it that the Witches gave Gardner the permission after long-standing anti-witchcraft laws were repealed in 1951, and that Gardner had to hurry before the Witches changed their mind. See Ronald Hutton, *The Triumph of the Moon: A History of Modern Pagan Witchcraft*, paperback ed. (Oxford: Oxford University Press, 2001), 206.
7. While no etymological origin is agreed upon by academics, popular Wiccan lore associates the term with "the wise" and/or "wicker" (the latter used to suggest that the name, Wicca, refers to the "bending" and "shaping" inherent in its magical practices).
8. Gardner attributed the term "sky-clad" to India, which has been verified: "sky-clad" is a literal translation of *Digambara*, the name for a sect of Jainism in which male ascetics reject property ownership and do not wear clothing. Gardner, *Witchcraft Today*, 126; *Oxford Dictionary of English*, 3rd ed. (2010), s.v. "Digambara"; "Skyclad (Nudity)," in *Encyclopedia of Religious Controversies in the United States*, ed. Bill J. Leonard and Jill Y. Crainshaw (Santa Barbara, CA: ABC-Clio, 2013), 751.
9. I join Jill Y. Crainshaw in this convention. See Leonard and Crainshaw, "Skyclad (Nudity)."
10. This chapter focuses on Wicca and Wiccanate Pagan traditions (those that have a distinctly Wiccan flavor), but the reader should note that a wider Pagan movement developed around Gardner's Wiccan religion. Recognition of non-Wiccan Pagan traditions is a significant priority of today's American Pagan community, the term "Wiccanate" actually having been coined by community members critical of Wiccan hegemony in information about American Paganism. Parsing out the distinctions between Wiccan and non-Wiccan Pagan traditions, a complex subject, is beyond the scope of this chapter. As a researcher, I am especially focused on the subjects of sexuality and the body, theology, and feminist ethics, and I am therefore compelled to theorize the unique doctrinal practice of ritual nudity in Wiccan liturgy.

I hope that readers versed in this area will be satisfied by my statement that this chapter focuses on the history of Wiccans' adaptation of the skyclad tradition without ignoring the fact that skyclad and naturism have found their own place and meaning in non-Wiccan Paganisms. Furthermore, attire and nudity at Pagan festivals is a much larger subject also worthy of attention but beyond the scope of this chapter. Other scholars have theorized about Pagan festival attire, and I refer my readers to those works while limiting my focus here. See, for instance, Sarah M. Pike, *Earthly Bodies, Magical Selves: Contemporary Pagans and the Search for Community* (Berkeley: University of California Press, 2001); Margot Adler, *Drawing Down the Moon: Witches, Druids, Goddess-Worshippers and Other Pagans in America*, revised and updated ed. (New York: Penguin Books, 2006); Helen A. Berger, Evan A. Leach, and Leigh S. Shaffer, *Voices from the Pagan Census: A National Survey of Witches and Neo-Pagans in the United States* (Columbia: University of South Carolina Press, 2003).

11. Dayonis, telephone conversation with author, July 9, 2019.
12. Ronald Hutton, "A Modest Look at Ritual Nudity," *Pomegranate: The International Journal of Pagan Studies* 17 (2001): 4–19. On the skyclad teaching, Gardner wrote, "Witches are taught and believe that the power resides within their bodies which they can release in various ways, the simplest being dancing round in a circle, singing or shouting, to induce a frenzy; this power they believe exudes from their bodies, clothing impending its release." Gardner, *Witchcraft Today*, 17.
13. T. M. Luhrmann, *Persuasians of the Witch's Craft: Ritual Magic in Contemporary England* (Cambridge, MA: Harvard University Press, 1989), 229.
14. Doreen Valiente, "The Charge of the Goddess," The Official Doreen Valiente Website, accessed July 7, 2019, http://www.doreenvaliente.com/Doreen-Valiente-Doreen_Valiente_Poetry-11.php#sthash.c7isZAzI.dpbs. See also Phyllis Curott, *Witch Crafting: A Spiritual Guide to Making Magic* (New York: Broadway Books, 2001), 284.
15. See Leonard and Crainshaw, "Skyclad (Nudity)," 751. The Witches of Gardner's time and of today also have in common the tradition of maintaining special ritual jewelry only worn for religious rites, again showing the use of attire (including the lack of attire) to separate the sacred from the mundane. It is interesting to note that Gardner himself espoused a liberal view on the necessity of skyclad for effective magic. He agreed with current Wiccan understandings of the power of magic residing most securely with belief, writing, "It is easy to imagine that a witch who firmly believes that it is essential to be naked could not whip up the final effort to attain the ecstasy

without being naked. Another, however, who did not share this belief might, though partially clothed, exert sufficient energy to force power through her face, shoulders, arms and legs, to produce some result; but who can say that she could not have produced twice the power with half the effort had she been in the traditional nakedness?" Gardner, *Witchcraft Today*, 17. Gardner upheld the stance that clothing limited magical flow with some room for doubt that skyclad was absolutely necessary.

16. See Shelley TSivia Rabinovitch, "Spells of Transformation: Categorizing Modern Neo-Pagan Witches," in *Magical Religion and Modern Witchcraft*, ed. James R. Lewis (Albany: State University of New York Press, 1996), 79; Leonard and Crainshaw, "Skyclad (Nudity)," 752; Luhrmann, *Persuasions of the Witch's Craft*, 43; Curott, *Witch Crafting*, 284.

17. Most Wiccan traditions, following British Traditional Witchcraft, use a system of three degrees, although there are exceptions such as the Assembly of the Sacred Wheel's five degrees, which end with the degree and title of "elder." Nikki Bado reported the British Traditional Wiccan tradition into which she was initiated having two known degrees and circulating "rumors of a third level, usually reached after several years as a High Priest or Priestess, and after experience leading more than one coven . . . [which is believed to be] assumed without ritual fanfare, and considered a private matter between the Witch and the Gods." Nikki Bado-Fralick, *Coming to the Edge of the Circle: A Wiccan Initiation Ritual* (New York: Oxford University Press, 2005), 44. What Bado described as a secret third degree seems equivalent to what other British Traditional Witches have called the status of "Witch queen" or "mage," a title assumed after similar accomplishments beyond the third degree.

18. See Regina Smith Oboler, "Negotiating Gender Essentialism in Contemporary Paganism," *Pomegranate: The International Journal of Pagan Studies* 12, no. 2 (2011): 159–84; Christine Hoff Kraemer, *Eros and Touch from a Pagan Perspective: Divided for Love's Sake*, (New York: Routledge, 2013); Yvonne Aburrow, *All Acts of Love & Pleasure: Inclusive Wicca* (London: Avalonia, 2014); Martin Lepage, "Queerness and Transgender: Identity Negotiations in the Pagan Community of Montreal," *Studies in Religion* 46, no. 4 (2017): 601–19. I myself addressed these changes in Michelle Mueller, "The Chalice and the Rainbow: Conflicts Between Women's Spirituality and Transgender Rights in US Wicca in the 2010s," in *Female Leaders in New Religious Movements*, ed. Inga Bårdsen Tøllefsen and Christian Giudice (Cham, CH: Palgrave Macmillan, 2017), 249–78.

19. In exception, Nikki Bado included analysis of skyclad in her auto-ethnographic description of the Merry Circle dedication ritual in *Coming to the Edge of the Circle*. Her data and findings are discussed later in this chapter.
20. Christine Hoff Kraemer and Yvonne Aburrow, eds., *Pagan Consent Culture: Building Communities of Empathy and Autonomy* (Hubbardston, MA: Asphodel Press, 2015), ii.
21. See Jone Salomonsen, *Enchanted Feminism: Ritual, Gender and Divinity Among the Reclaiming Witches of San Francisco* (New York: Routledge, 2002), 225; Luhrmann, *Persuasions of the Witch's Craft*, 229.
22. Adler, *Drawing Down the Moon*, 58; Luhrmann, *Persuasions of the Witch's Craft*, 43; Ethan Doyle White, "Review of *Witchfather: A Life of Gerald Gardner: Volume One—Into the Witch Cult* and *Witchfather: A Life of Gerald Gardner: Volume Two—From Witch Cult to Wicca*, by Philip Heselton," *Pomegranate: The International Journal of Pagan Studies* 14, no. 1 (2012): 172.
23. Hutton, *The Triumph of the Moon*, 205–6.
24. Gardner, *Witchcraft Today*, 16.
25. Judy Harrow, "Looking Forward: Gardner's Hunches," in *Witchcraft Today*, fiftieth ann. ed. (New York: Citadel Press, 2004), 184.
26. Harrow, "Looking Forward," 184.
27. Harrow, 184.
28. Heselton, *Witchfather*, 2:303–4.
29. Heselton, 298–99.
30. *Sun Bathing Review*, quoted in Heselton, 304.
31. Heselton, 331–32; Dayonis, interview.
32. Dayonis, interview.
33. Hutton, *The Triumph of the Moon*; Adler, *Drawing Down the Moon*.
34. Dinitia Smith, "Finding Personal Spaces in Public Places," *New York Times*, May 17, 1996, https://www.nytimes.com/1996/05/17/arts/finding-personal-spaces-in-public-places.html; "Read Us the Book of the Names of the Dead," *Secret Sun* (blog), August 22, 2016, https://secretsun.blogspot.com/2016/08/read-us-book-of-names-of-dead.html.
35. Scholars recognize the tradition of Wicca at large as a feminist religious tradition, but the label "feminist Wicca" has most often been used to refer to Dianic or other women's-only groups. See Michelle Mueller, "Constructing Wicca as 'Women's Religion': A By-product of Feminist Religious Scholarship," in *The Rowman & Littlefield Handbook of Women's Studies in Religion*, ed. Helen T. Boursier (Lanham, MD: Rowman & Littlefield, 2021), 123–41.

36. Adler, *Drawing Down the Moon*, 179–84.
37. Phyllis Curott, *Book of Shadows: A Modern Woman's Journey Into the Wisdom of Witchcraft and the Magic of the Goddess* (New York: Broadway Books, 1998).
38. The teen-oriented blockbuster movie *The Craft* (1996) has also been credited for growth of Wicca among female teenagers in the mid-1990s. Hannah E. Johnston and Peg Aloi, eds., *New Generation Witches: Teenage Witchcraft in Contemporary Culture* (Burlington, VT: Ashgate, 2007); Helen Berger and Douglas Ezzy, *Teenage Witches: Magical Youth and the Search for the Self* (New Brunswick, NJ: Rutgers University Press, 2007).
39. "Meet the Witches' Voice Staff," Witchvox Central, last accessed February 2, 1997, http://www.witchvox.com/va/dt_va.html?a=&c=twv&id=1927.
40. Scott Cunningham, *Wicca: A Guide for the Solitary Practitioner* (St. Paul, MN: Llewellyn Publications, 1989); Scott Cunningham, *Living Wicca: A Further Guide for the Solitary Practitioner*, 1st ed. (St. Paul, MN: Llewellyn Publications, 2000).
41. Hanna Rosin, "Wiccan Controversy Tests Military Religious Tolerance," *Washington Post*, June 8, 1999, https://www.washingtonpost.com/wp-srv/national/daily/june99/wicca08.htm.
42. Starhawk, *Dreaming the Dark: Magic, Sex, and Politics*, fifteenth ann. ed. (Boston: Beacon Press, 1997), 151–52.
43. Starhawk, 152.
44. Cunningham, *Living Wicca*, 110–11.
45. Cunningham disclosed that his writing on self-initiation had been the most controversial subject of *Wicca* in Cunningham, 27.
46. Cunningham, 110.
47. Cunningham, 110.
48. See Curott, *Witch Crafting*, 284; Leonard and Crainshaw, "Skyclad (Nudity)," 752.
49. The Merry Circle rite Bado described was labeled a "dedication ceremony." Bado-Fralick, *Coming to the Edge of the Circle*, 99.
50. Salomonsen, *Enchanted Feminism*, 225.
51. Bado-Fralick, *Coming to the Edge of the Circle*, 99.
52. Bado-Fralick, 99.
53. Everett Ferguson, *Baptism in the Early Church: History, Theology, and Liturgy in the First Five Centuries* (Grand Rapids, MI: William B. Eerdmans Publishing, 2009).

Ten

AMISH VOGUE

PERFORMING FASHION IN THE PLAIN WORLD

NAO NOMURA

The very first fabric-shopping trip with my Amish informants happened on a beautiful late summer afternoon. I offered them a ride for shopping as a thank-you for letting me stay for a weekend. As Miriam, a mother in her mid-thirties, needed to get some fabric for winter clothes for the family, Miriam, Mary, the oldest teenage daughter, and Sarah, a preschool-aged youngest daughter, and I decided to go to a fabric store. When we were getting ready, I noticed that both Miriam and Mary had changed their dresses. "Why did you change your dress?" I asked innocently. To a novice ethnographer in the Amish community, their solid-color dresses looked the same and I didn't understand why they had to change their dress before going out. "I don't know. It was old-fashioned, I guess. Sleeves were a little short too," Miriam answered. "Old-fashioned? But they all look the same," I thought to myself. I felt a bit confused but did not say anything.

—Field note, September 20, 2010[1]

THE OLD ORDER Amish are often portrayed as devout Christians who value preserving a premodern lifestyle within modern society. The seemingly pastoral way of Amish living, manifest in their selective acceptance of advanced technology, use of horse and buggies, and community-sanctioned solid-color dress, does not necessarily evoke an image of the Amish as active consumers. Anthropologist of religion Lynne Hume has posited that "Religious dress is a visible signifier of difference," and the uniform-like, plain dress of the Amish demonstrates this.[2] Their dress embodies their religious identity, signifying their emphasis on thrift, tradition, and obedience to the community and to God, while constructing visual and symbolic boundaries between Amish and mainstream society. Any adornment is forbidden—including makeup, jewelry, wedding bands, and even wristwatches. To the casual eye, all Amish clothing may appear identical, which naturally leads to an assumption that fashion is absent from Amish society. However, my ethnographic fieldwork indicates that Amish women, particularly younger women, are very conscious of what they wear and how they look, and often use clothing to subtly express individual tastes.

It is certainly true that Amish church guidelines determine the overall style of clothing, thereby socially controlling adherents' bodies.[3] Leading scholars on the Amish emphasize Amish clothing as a physical and symbolic separator that maintains their "public ethnic identity."[4] It communicates "the biblical values of humility, modesty, self-denial, simplicity, and separation from the world," and serves as an indicator of whether one conforms to "church standards" or is "liberal or conservative."[5] While Amish teenagers may occasionally ask their mothers for certain colors of fabric, compared to their mainstream counterparts they are free from being preoccupied with the latest fashion trends.[6] Expert on the Old Order Amish Donald B. Kraybill has noted that "there is some freedom for flexibility" within the strict regulations, such as colors for young boys' shirts or the style of young women's aprons, but these variation are often invisible to outsiders.[7] On the other hand, scholars Jean A. Hamilton and Jana M. Hawley argue that fashion is not "a foreign concept" to the Amish, noting changes in dress styles over time in a midwestern Amish community. I, too, observed that Amish women in Lancaster County, Pennsylvania, consciously select what to wear on a daily basis, creating an inconspicuous fashion system operating within the strict dress code.[8] A close examination of their dress clearly shows subtle differences in details such as the bodice, cuffs, necklines, and even pearl-headed pins used as jewelry on the religiously constrained dress. Such nuanced playfulness in otherwise modest clothing, coupled with a wide array of dress materials available in countless colors and fabrics from local stores, suggests that clothing selection is a deliberate and measured process. In contrast to the dominant scholarly view that the Amish renounce "the right to use dress as a major tool of self-expression," my ethnographic research demonstrates that Amish women achieve a means of creating their own vogue while conforming to church restrictions, a process of which Amish women themselves may not be fully aware.[9]

In order to understand how the Old Order Amish practice their faith through clothing while simultaneously embracing fashion, I explore the sartorial practices that constitute a significant part of Amish consumer culture. By playing an active role in producing their visual representation, Amish women have defined and redefined the presumed boundaries of Amish attire, resulting in the understated expansion of perceptions of the Old Order Amish at large. In contrast to the stereotypical image of the Amish as devout people who detach themselves from worldly temptations, I argue that Amish women negotiate their religious identity with their fashioned bodies by manifesting personal style and taste within the constraints of church regulations, which makes each Amish seamstress—that is, most Amish women—a creative designer of her own wardrobe. The Amish ways of fashion serve as a catalyst for women to construct a visual identity within church constraints, allowing them to actively exercise their agency through their sartorial consumption practices in a highly gendered society.

This research is based on ethnographic fieldwork conducted in Lancaster County, Pennsylvania, which is home to one of the largest Amish communities. I lived with an Old Order Amish family for ten months in 2010–2011, followed by multiple short-term visits between 2012 and 2019. I met many Amish people, including my host family's extended family and members of their church district, and I interacted with church members on a regular basis for social gatherings and volunteer work.[10] My primary informants were my host family—a husband, wife, and six children, and I spent time with them helping around the house, joining family gatherings, going to Amish church, visiting gardens and zoos, and most importantly taking them out for shopping in my car.[11] I had numerous opportunities to accompany my Amish informants not only to local Amish stores but also on long-distant shopping trips to retail chain stores, outlet and shopping malls, and thrift stores.

WHO ARE THE AMISH?

Before delving into the details of Amish dress, it is helpful to provide an overview of Amish history, culture, and society to better understand the context of Amish attire and fashion. The Amish date their origins to the sixteenth-century Protestant Reformation in Europe, wherein some radical Christians denied the validity of infant baptism and began baptizing each other to express a voluntary decision to follow Jesus Christ. They came to be called Anabaptists, stemming from the Latin word *anabaptismus*, or "second baptism," because they would have been baptized as children.[12] The Amish church emerged in Alsace in 1693 under the leadership of Jacob Amman, who emphasized separation from worldly society. The Amish established communities in Alsace (in present-day France), the Palatinate (in present-day Germany), and Switzerland, and gradually migrated within Europe and to North America to seek religious freedom and economic opportunities. By the mid-eighteenth century, the first group of Amish moved to Pennsylvania, and more families were quick to follow their coreligionists in the following decades.[13] Since then, their settlements have spread across thirty-one states in the United States, four provinces in Canada, and to Argentina and Bolivia, with the total of approximately 374,000 adherents.[14]

In contrast to the popular image of the Amish as a homogeneous religious group, recent scholarship emphasizes the diversity of Amish among different settlements.[15] While it is difficult to generalize about them, there are some shared principles and characteristics. Ten practices that are shared among Amish groups are "rural residence, German-based dialect, eighth-grade education, church services in homes, small local congregations, lay ministers, church-regulated dress, selective use of technology, horse-and-buggy transportation, and nonparticipation in the military."[16] The Amish church itself is not a centralized institution; instead, the different needs of local Amish communities inform differing interpretations of how to live separately from the world.[17] The *Ordnung*, a set of guidelines that manifests the teachings and practices of the Amish church, varies in each church district (congregation). In Lancaster County, Pennsylvania, there is a shared *Ordnung* across the settlement.[18] This unwritten code that defines a "traditional way of going about life" has slowly evolved over time, allowing for gradual change.[19] Indeed, the Amish are not relics from the past. The *Ordnung* is reviewed and reshaped when the church is confronted with new issues, such as the introduction of new technologies, and changes in local and state laws.[20] More subtle changes, although they may or may not be controlled by the *Ordnung*, can also be observed in the Amish faith-based dress code.

THE AMISH WOMAN'S CLOTHING

There are stylistic differences in clothing among Amish settlements.[21] In the Lancaster settlement, Amish women's fundamental wardrobe consists of *Kapp*, or heart-shaped, white organdy head coverings, black bonnets, solid-color dresses, *Hals Duch* (neck cloth), or capes, aprons, black cardigans, black jackets, and black shawls. Church authorities will occasionally warn youth who they feel are dressing inappropriately; otherwise, each individual is left to make her own judgment when interpreting the prescriptive grammar of Amish sartorial practices. A close examination of how women are dressed at various social scenes suggests that an unstated dress code exists within Amish society. In fact, Amish dress quietly conveys social meanings such as age, gender, and marital status.[22] Amish women's appearance is the reflection of constant negotiation and affirmation of church expectations as well as the pursuit of personal desire in terms of both faith and individuality.

The Amish woman wears an ankle-length dress. It closes in the front with snaps or pins to the waist, and there are two pleats on the front and six in the back with a small peplum called the *Leppli* (tab) at the back of the waistline.[23] The *Leppli* has no functional purpose, but serves as a symbolic reminder of the wearer's religious identity as a committed Christian woman. Miriam laughingly explained that "It comes from a scripture that women's bottom should be covered with a large piece of cloth. . . . Now it has become just a small flap!"[24] She found it amusing that what women tried to cover up their bottoms with now remains as only a small piece of cloth. But Amish women faithfully conform to the system of plain clothing as a time-honored tradition that embodies their understanding and manifestation of a Christian way of living based strictly on the teachings of the Bible.

Women's body contours are concealed by the loosely fitted dress with voluminous sleeves, further layered by an apron for modesty. The cape, a triangular-shaped cloth with a slit in the middle, is also slipped over the dress for formal occasions such as church. Depending on the wearer's age, the cape is either black or made of fabric that matches the dress. Miriam joked about her sister's reaction to her changing the color of the cape to black: "Women start wearing a black cape when they become middle-aged.... I started wearing it when I turned thirty-five. My [younger] sister freaked out because she didn't want to become a middle-aged woman in a couple of years.... Amish women become middle-aged earlier than English, I guess."[25]

As this anecdote suggests, a woman's age has a significant influence on her choice of dress material. When choosing maroon-colored fabric for a new set of matching winter shirts and dresses for the family, Miriam picked a less lustrous fabric for herself. I asked why she didn't want the same material for her dress. "I don't know ... [the fabric] was too nice for me, I guess," she answered vaguely.[26] She clearly knew, as a middle-aged mother and wife, that she should refrain from fancy fabric. The design, material, and the very act of wearing the dress makes a woman acutely conscious of the humility her body is supposed to reflect in Amish society. As this interaction shows, Amish women serve as indispensable social agents by producing clothes that make the Amish *look* Amish to outsiders while simultaneously maintaining their socioreligious identity.

Women's hair and head coverings further reinforce their understanding of female identity based on a literal interpretation of the scriptures. Amish women's hair remains uncut and covered, based on their understanding of the biblical mandate in 1 Corinthians: "Every woman that prayeth or prophesieth with her head uncovered dishonoureth her head: for that is even all one as if she were shaven. For if the woman be not covered, let her also be shorn: but if it be a shame for a woman to be shorn or shaven, let her be covered.... But if a woman have long hair, it is a glory to her: for her hair is given her for a covering" (1 Cor. 11:1–16, KJV).[27] Through an almost ritualistic practice of combing and caring for their hair every morning, Amish children develop a strong sense of religiously grounded gender identity at a very young age. When their hair grows long enough, the forelock is tied into small buns called "bobbies" on either side of the forehead, using polybands or twist ties. "Oh, you have bobbies in your hair. You are such a big girl!" Levi praised his youngest daughter when she wore bobbies to church for the first time.[28] As a girl's hair gets longer, it is neatly center-parted, combed, and pulled into a bun in the back

FIGURE 10.1. Somber-colored dresses and black aprons on clotheslines in the screened porch of an Amish home. Image courtesy of the author.

with the side hair twisted into a roll from about the temple to behind the ear.[29] At the dinner table, eleven-year-old Naomi hesitantly yet amusingly told her father about her end-of-semester picnic: "Dad, you would not want to hear this, but we trimmed Susan's hair just a tiny bit when we were playing Indians today.... We pretended that her hair was scalp to prove that we captured her." The hair-cutting incident was a big deal for an innocent Christian girl.[30] Her father, however, did not seem to be bothered by this incident, perhaps because Naomi's concern proved that she clearly understood the Amish rules.

The head covering is usually made at home with sheer, white organdy fabric to perfectly fit the wearer's head. Most women own several sets of head coverings in different conditions—from old ones to wear at home, to crisp ones for church. Because of the delicate material, these are difficult to launder and keep white and stiff. My Pennsylvania informants envied Amish women from Ohio, whose head coverings are made of stronger fabric that hold up in washing. However, Lancaster Amish women are unwilling to compromise the clean look of their coverings. To stiffen these coverings and keep their shape, they use spray adhesive that is promoted at the local hardware store as "Ideal for coverings (caps)."[31] More recently, new organdy material that withstands washing has been introduced in Lancaster County, which made many fashion-conscious women happy because this allowed them to always keep their head coverings crisp and white. The entirety of an Amish woman's wardrobe, with the prescribed dresses and head coverings, puts both her religiosity and gender identity on visual display.

SOCIAL CONTEXT CONVEYED THROUGH CLOTHING

"They [Amish people] will understand," Miriam assured me as she helped me put on a cape over my Amish dress before church. The only waistband apron I owned had snap fastenings which clearly was not suitable for church attire. It should be fastened with silver straight pins as Amish women have always done to secure their dress in place. As an outsider, however, I did not have to conform to their dress code requirements.

—Field note, October 31, 2010

The Amish dress code communicates various social meanings, including those of gender, age, marital status, and level of compliance/conservatism.[32] Although Amish themselves might simply see it as "the way our people dress," more details become visible the more versed one becomes in Amish sartorial culture.[33] The *Ordnung* dictates uniformity of Amish garments, but women do not always dress in the cookie-cutter manner that might be assumed. On the contrary, there are various ways in which women carefully coordinate prescribed clothing items depending on the type of social and private activities taking place. For example, while snaps have replaced traditional straight pins as dress fasteners, one might still see a woman in a dress fastened with straight pins, an indication that she comes from a conservative family or church district.[34] If an older woman wears a dress with snap fasteners hidden under the fly front, it could suggest that she is a change-minded person.[35] My informant Miriam sometimes referred to "those *conservative* families in our church," a group

FIGURE 10.2 Amish women use commercial adhesive spray to keep their organdy head coverings stiff and crisp. Image courtesy of the author.

identifiable by the straight pins fastening the wives' dresses. Conservative young women also tend to choose somber colors such as forest green, navy blue, maroon, and purple, instead of bright colors popular among youth in Lancaster County, such as mint green, raspberry pink, and pumpkin orange. The wide spectrum of colors reflect social distinctions and subtle diversity among Amish women.

As church is the most important and authoritative institution in Amish society, the most formal attire is expected for church-related activities including Sunday service, meetings, and weddings, as well as for family gatherings on Sundays, Easter, Thanksgiving, and Christmas. For these occasions, women put on a complete set of formal clothing—the head covering, long-sleeve dress with a cape, waistband apron, black stockings, and black lace-up shoes—regardless of the season.[36] They save their best, most crisp white head covering, select a dress in some subdued color, and keep their shoes polished. For church service, single girls wear a cape and waistband apron made of sheer, white organdy, the same material for the head covering, symbolic of their virginity.[37] Straight pins are preferred for the waistband apron, even for young girls in church.

Many women dress "down" for work, shopping, or casual gatherings with friends and families. The essential casual attire still includes a head covering, yet young women might choose brighter colors than they would for their church attire.[38] The sleeve length for Amish dress is never too short because of the belief in modesty; therefore, even casual summer dresses have sleeves that fall just above the elbow. The selection of shoes and outerwear are entrusted to individuals, within the bounds of Amish common sense; women often wear black flip-flops or rubber "croc" sandals in summer and comfortable sneakers all year round.[39] Homemade or store-bought black cardigans—lustrous chenille cardigans with bead-embroidered designs would be a good choice if she is fashion-conscious—and jackets are worn over the dress for warmth in winter. These casual footwear and clothing items in black and other somber colors are available locally at both Amish-owned and non-Amish-owned stores.[40]

The Old Order Amish use attire as a measurement to discern whether one is Amish or not. Some Amish people would even call solid colors "Amish colors" to distinguish themselves from their religious cousins and neighbors the Mennonites, who are allowed to wear floral patterns and other dainty designs. "Is she Amish?" Naomi asked her mother in a surprised voice when she saw an Amish girl in a bright-red dress at a market. By "Amish" she meant the Old Order Amish, her own kind. "Yep," replied her mother, but not with the sound of condemnation. She probably knew who the girl was. The color of the dress did not really matter. What was most shocking was the color of her apron—it was in the matching red fabric, rather than the community-governed black apron.[41] The girl may have been acting rebellious during the *Rumspringa* period by violating the church regulations and being fashion-forward in an Amish way. Naomi seemed utterly surprised but did not ask further questions.

Although Amish women's clothing might appear plain, restrained, and identical at first sight, in fact the dress code is nuanced and complex, challenging the idea that there is a single definition of Amish clothing. Rather, many Amish women actively and creatively take on different modes of expression according to an unstated dress code that subdivides their wardrobe into formal, casual, and work clothes. Closer attention to detailed design elements reveals that their dress also shows individual tastes as well as fashion trends in Amish consumer culture. Amish fashion further elucidates covert desires for individualism, material possessions, and women's agency in the patriarchal Amish society, ironically enabled by the production of their plain attire.

MODESTLY FASHION-FORWARD: PERFORMING FASHION IN THE PLAIN WORLD

"You might notice that some girls dress very differently at this wedding," Miriam said as we were driving to her niece's wedding in my car on a rainy November morning. She continued to explain that her niece belonged to an unsupervised youth group, the Dominoes, during *Rumpsringa*. Some unbaptized Amish youth might experience worldly practices that the Amish church prohibits such as driving cars (but very rarely, contrary to the popular image of *Rumspringa* depicted in the 2002 documentary film *Devil's Playground*), and that many girls who belonged to such a group would often wear flashy dresses. It still sounded strange to me that Amish girls could stand out as "different."

—Field note, November 4, 2010[42]

Despite this warning, the young girls were all dressed in the church-prescribed Amish clothes from head to toe, but these conveyed discreet fashion statements. Miriam was right. Some girls looked clearly different from the ones I had met. Their long hair was covered by a *Kapp*, but with a string of hair hanging loose on either side, a subtle sign of disobedience. Dresses with capes in bright neon colors of blue, green, pink, and yellow dazzled in an otherwise dim and bare workshop that had been turned into a temporary wedding venue.[43] Some sleeves were tightly fitted around upper arms with flared cuffs cut on a bias fluttering around the elbows, while others covered their arms loosely with decorative cuffs embellished with delicate white lace, ribbon trimmings, or ornate buttons. Capes were tucked and pinned high at the shoulders, giving some dresses a flamboyant accent by forming more distinct folds. Some girls even put a pearl-headed pin in the center of their capes as a jewelry-like accent. As the Amish are not allowed to wear any jewelry—not even a wedding band or wristwatch as these are considered too ostentatious—a pin is one of very few ornamental options. Appearing with this little piece of jewelry on a sacred day was a sign of the wearer's fearlessness. Light-colored stockings were another indication of resistance to the Amish norm, which requires women to wear black stockings. Instead of traditional lace-up shoes, many were wearing feminine high heels or slip-ons with chunky soles to match their fancy dresses. Some girls even had makeup on, an act that would be simply out of the question for their conformist counterparts. In the context of a wedding, one of the most important rituals in Amish society, these style-conscious and creative girls challenged their community's strict boundaries. They performed and enacted a social identity of membership in an extreme youth group by making an explicit fashion statement through slight alterations to the uniform.[44]

Yet these rebellious young girls are not the only ones who lead the Amish fashion world. Girls who have not started the *Rumspringa* period, and who therefore have less opportunities to socialize with their peers, are also interested in experimenting with the details of their dresses. Sleeve cuffs serve as another creative canvas for Amish seamstresses. "Let me know if you have good ideas for sleeves. I am always looking for new designs for sleeves," Mary said as she was meticulously forming a bow-like design by tucking a box pleat in the cuff and pinching the center of the pleat with matching-colored thread.[45] This new dark-purple dress would be another addition to her closet, which was already filled with an array of colorful dresses with various cuff designs, suggesting her conscious desire and interest in always wearing something new and different. In addition to the bow-like element, pleated or gathered ruffles that ripple around the sleeves are also popular; small brass buttons or charms embellished on the cuff can give a subtle accent; and those who have access to a state-of-the-art computerized sewing machine might add intricate floral, foliage, or geometric embroidered stitches to the cuff or back of the dress.[46] While the Amish reject modern technologies, including electricity sourced from the public grid, they selectively and strategically adopt modern developments that they fell will not jeopardize their values or lifestyle. The sewing machine is one such example as it is a practical item that is indispensable for the Amish, who produce most of their clothing items. Miriam also sometimes used decorative stitches as she likes "to have a little design" on her dresses.[47] Although scholars have in the past dismissed this phenomenon of dress alteration as simply being indicative of "the home in which they are raised," it was clear from my informants that women—teenagers in particular—are actively engaged in the production of Amish fashion.[48] When Amish dress is examined within their media-free fashion world, rather than within a framework of mainstream fads, this becomes more evident.

Sleeves not only showcase women's originality and creative sewing skills, but also reflect changes in contemporary Amish fashion. When Mary received hand-me-down dresses from an aunt, she immediately altered them by trimming off the cuffs, thereby giving them a jagged edge and making them less voluminous. The teenager could not stand the "old-fashioned" dresses with sleeves that were "too puffy" for her taste, a style that would have been popular when her aunt was young. Although these dresses were made with exactly the same traditional pattern that she would use for her own dresses—six pleats in the back with a peplum in the center and two pleats in the front—Mary was too embarrassed to wear them as they were, even for everyday work clothes. It might take several years or even a decade for something to go out of fashion, but Amish women, particularly young ones, are slowly and independently producing new design elements by replacing outdated sleeve styles.

Although it is not as distinct as the sleeve variations, the necklines and bodice closures of dresses have become another focus for Amish fashion. The bodice is often covered under the bib apron or the cape, so it is only noticeable when paired with a waistband apron. Fashion-conscious young women have recently begun to make dresses with the front bodice seamed together in the center, rather than fastening it in front with snaps under a layer of fabric. The center-seamed front bodice creates a flat, clean line while imitating the appearance of the conventional style, but it requires a low neckline in order to slip the dress on over the head. Because the Old Order Amish believe that women's bodies should be covered for modesty, some mothers frown on this new bodice design. When Mary first wanted a dress with the seamed bodice, her mother was not happy about it. She finally gave in and made a "center-seamed" dress for Mary's seventeenth

FIGURE 10.3 An Amish teenager's wardrobe, showcasing different sleeves and cuff designs. Image courtesy of the author.

birthday. After the first, it did not take too long for Mary to fill her closet with more of these dresses.[49] Along with the sleeve designs, such small changes continue to gradually update Amish fashion culture.

Fabric also serves as a significant marker for one's sense of style. It might not be comparable to the mainstream fashion world, but in my first fabric-shopping trip with my informants I was quite overwhelmed by the countless numbers of colors, patterns, textures, weaves, and weights available. Amish women are familiar with the range and characteristics of fabric and they carefully, often after much hesitation, select those that will reflect both their fashion taste and their social identity. Particularly for an Amish teenager, picking the right fabric is crucial. "It'll be easy this time. I know exactly which fabric I want to get," Mary confidently told me with a small swatch in her hand. On our previous shopping trip together, she had a hard time choosing the perfect fabric in the color she wanted because different types of fabric would give completely different impressions.[50] For example, according to Mary stretchy double-knit fabrics that are usually available in a limited dark color palette such as forest green, navy blue, and eggplant purple are considered "so old-fashioned ... like grandma's dresses." Double-knit fabric is durable but easily ravels, thus is not suited to experimentation with details and intricate sewing. In contrast, fabrics preferred by young Amish girls are available with more variations in color and texture than an outsider would likely imagine for Amish clothing.

Miriam and Mary would often tell me which fabric was popular among their social group. During another fabric-shopping trip with a fellow researcher, Martha, who wanted to make an Amish dress, Miriam and Mary helped her pick a fabric. She decided to get dark purple in a fabric called "Zenus." Mary quickly responded to her choice: "This fabric is really popular now ... it's been around for a couple of years." Miriam also commented that it was "a very popular fabric.... It feels very soft. Naomi has a dress in that fabric. Actually, she was wearing that today." Martha also wanted to get material for the apron and picked a striped fabric which looked solid black from distance. "That's a good fabric. I like that one. It stays black," Mary said. "Is there difference in black fabrics?" Martha and I both immediately asked. "Yes. This one fades to almost red," Mary said, as she pulled out a bolt of black fabric and compared it to the apron she was wearing.[51] Neither of us had any idea that black fabrics could be so different. Certainly, when I looked around the black fabric section, I found that a plain looking fabric can actually have subtle plaids, stripes, or floral patterns. Black fabric for aprons might have floral print in black that is only noticeable under closer inspection, or fine, lustrous yarn woven in that glows in the reflection of light. Even simple black fabrics for the apron come and go out of favor on the Amish market.

New materials constantly capture Amish consumers who are particular about their clothes, and sometimes even get them into trouble. "Would the bishop talk to you if you were not dressed appropriately?" I asked Miriam. "Yes, he would. It would not happen very often, but one time, we had a young girl who would not dress properly. He had to talk to her about it."[52] According to Miriam, there is no written guideline for colors, but church authorities define and redefine their judgment as new colors and materials become available on the market. I wondered how "inappropriately" the girl was dressed. To my question about her color preference, Miriam replied matter-of-factly that "We dress on a darker side. I know people who live to the south of us wear lighter colors that we would not wear—like yellows and greens. We wear light colors sometimes, but we are always on the darker side.... We wear those [light] colors sometimes.... Children often do. Like Sarah. But I would not make another pink dress for her, I don't think." I could not quite agree with her evaluation of her family's dress preference—yes, they certainly dress on the "darker side," including mauve, navy blue, and purple, but their children have dresses in fuchsia, lime green, and sky blue. Furthermore, over the course of my fieldwork, I noticed that the colors of their dresses were becoming brighter. It was still important for Miriam to remind herself that they favor traditional colors in order to demonstrate that her family are faithful Christians who do not fall for fancy colors. In any case, it was evident that Miriam's color palette was accepted by her congregation.

Mothers, including Miriam, would often give advice to their daughters to stay away from trouble when selecting new dress materials. Teenagers and younger women are less pressured in selecting colors, but there seems to be an implicit collective understanding of what colors are acceptable for church and formal occasions, and what colors are acceptable for social occasions. One time, Naomi begged her mother to make a new dress with pale pink fabric, saying, "I promise I will not wear this to church." Even at the age of eleven, an Amish girl is fully aware of the Amish dress code. By their own intuition, females of all ages know exactly which materials conform to church expectations. After all, most dry goods stores that carry dress materials are operated by and cater to religiously conservative customers. Local businesses are aware of their customers' expectations, and thus their selection of fabrics would not be that far off from typical Amish norms, as conservative suppliers and consumers mutually "screened" these fabrics.

NEGOTIATING MAINSTREAM CONSUMER CULTURE

In spite of the strict church regulations and peer pressure, the Amish have always adopted and adapted new materials into their prescribed garb.[53] "We loved it. We loved it when polyester came out. We jumped on it," one elderly Amish woman recalled of the period when polyester became available in the late 1950s.[54] This new type of fabric immediately took over the Amish wardrobe because it required little care compared to natural fibers

FIGURE 10.4 A popular fabric store in Lancaster County, Pennsylvania, that carries a wide array of fabrics and attracts Amish from neighboring states. Image courtesy of the author.

such as cotton and wool. It did not shrink, bleed, or wrinkle, and did not require ironing with an old-fashioned steel iron; the price was also better. In contrast to the popular and idealized image that the Amish dress in a "homespun" way, most contemporary Amish embrace synthetic dress materials.[55]

As new synthetic fabrics continued to flood the Amish market, Amish seamstresses came to be better connoisseurs of their dress materials. Some materials may not be as practical as others because they launder and fade differently, so Amish women pay careful attention to fabrics that need special care. "I wouldn't even put this in a wringer. It wrinkles like everything," Mary would often say during her morning laundry chore, using an old-fashioned wringer-roller washing machine and a Maytag washer converted into a spinner.[56] Surely, Amish tenets teach not to be "in" the world—that is, mainstream, secular society—but Amish women are still conscious of how they look within their own standards.

Some Amish women went further for their search for better fabric and began to use nylon bathroom curtains to make Sunday aprons for girls. Miriam was not immune to this trend and purchased a set of curtains when we stopped at a Walmart one day. She explained to me that "It's been around for a few years. . . . Walmart curtains are stronger than nylons from Zook's. Someone started it and it quickly spread around."[57] When Miriam told Naomi that she had made a set of church aprons and capes, Naomi was thrilled. "I don't have to wear organdy aprons. . . . Oh, I am so excited!" Miriam smiled and said, "Oh, I just made her day. She doesn't have to wear the organdy apron to church because I made her new nylon aprons for Sunday." I asked if nylon aprons were better than organdy ones. Miriam replied, "Oh, much nicer. Organdy ones wrinkle so badly and nylon aprons last longer. . . . Girls at a certain age, well, I guess it's not really the age when we decide to wear organdy. . . . When Naomi started going in to church with the girls, she wore organdy aprons. But young girls can wear nylon aprons."[58] Here, Amish women appropriated a mainstream consumer product into their faith-based fashion system.

Amish also carefully adopt retail clothing items into their faith-based sartorial practices. Mary found a lightweight quilted jacket in black at a local general store. Miriam approved her daughter's selection and said, "It looks fine. I can even sew darts in the back to give it a shape, you know." They also bought black buttons to replace the zipper on the new jacket. Miriam simply told me that "we don't really do zippers."[59] After we returned home, Miriam got busy "Amish-ifying" Mary's new jacket. She swiftly removed the zipper, put buttons on, created buttonholes, and added darts in both the front and back for a fitted look. The entire process was baffling to me because Mary already owned a zip hoodie that she sometimes wore to work, and the zipper on the jacket did not seem to stand out. But because she would probably wear the jacket to church and other formal occasions, it needed to fulfill church expectations.

The shift to synthetic dress fabric, the unexpected use of household commodities (curtains from Walmart and spray adhesive for head coverings), and the ingenious makeover, or "Amish-ification," of store-bought clothes further corroborates the claim that Amish women actively participate in consumer culture through their faith-based fashion system. As the primary consumers of the household, Amish women are empowered as significant cultural agents who appropriate and negotiate with mainstream consumer culture to modestly and strategically expand their bodily expression in a highly gendered society. At the same time, this also suggests that Amish women are often exposed to worldly temptations that could potentially challenge their religiosity. Their conscious or unconscious negotiation with mainstream consumer culture is ultimately a conflict between their strong religious belief and desire for consumerism.

Back in the field visiting my Amish host family, I witnessed another small but pivotal change in their dressmaking practices. Mary was ironing her white organdy church apron and cape by the kitchen stove. She told me that it was a new kind of fabric that recently became available at local stores and now everyone uses it for Sunday aprons, capes, and head coverings. "The company made a mistake or something and it was not supposed to be like this [soft]. It is sort of like organdy, but it is different. It is so much better because it does not wrinkle. I mean it still wrinkles, but not as bad as the ones that we used to wear. We even make our head coverings with this fabric now." I asked her if I could feel her head covering. "Sure," she said as she kept ironing the apron. It was stiff and its shape was intact. She might be right. It might have felt a little bit different, but to be honest, I was not able to discern that much of a difference. "It's been around for about a year now. That is probably one of the big changes around here," she laughed. But I noticed that Mary's dress was a much brighter color than the ones I used to see when I started my fieldwork several years ago. "It [the new organdy-like material] became really popular.... It feels different.... We often used spray [adhesive] to keep it stiff, now when it gets wet or dirty, we just wash it and it's fine. If the head covering made of the old organdy got wet, you know that was it."

"Yes, I know. I remember that you envied Ohio women's head coverings because they were washable," I said.

"Last year, we were worried that we would not able to get the same fabric anymore, but the company managed to keep the fabric. We were so happy."

—Field note, August 31, 2015[60]

As this research shows, fashion plays an important role in Amish society as a sign of individuality and group identity. Although the demonstration of Amish self-expression through clothing might seem insignificant compared to the latest cutting-edge fashion in mainstream society, Amish women, and young women in particular, convey their sense of identity by wearing subtly distinctive dresses. They willingly consume dressmaking materials in order to produce clothes that meet their personal tastes. Within the inconspicuous yet complex code that dictates Amish sartorial behavior, an internal code of fashion—the plain fashion system—exists, fostering a creative outlet for Amish women. Paying close attention to design details such as sleeves, necklines, and front bodice closures, as well as to the materials used in Amish dress, proves that the Amish fashion system is not static, but rather changes and evolves over time, just as mainstream fashion does. Change might occur very slowly, but there are trends in Amish dress that highlight aesthetic, practical, and social factors. In this way, fashion thrives in Amish communities through the constant negotiation of members' desire for self-expression within an environment characterized by church regulations and social pressure.

NOTES

1. All informants mentioned in this chapter have been assigned pseudonyms.
2. Lynne Hume, *The Religious Life of Dress: Global Fashion and Faith* (London: Bloomsbury, 2013), 1. On the role of dress as a visual boundary in ethno-religious

communities, see Linda B. Arthur, "Dress and the Social Control of the Body," in *Religion, Dress and the Body*, ed. Linda B. Arthur (Oxford: Berg, 1999), 1–7.
3. Beth Graybill and Linda B. Arthur excellently delineate the sartorial control of conservative Mennonite women's bodies in "The Social Control of Women's Bodies in Two Mennonite Communities," in Arthur, ed., *Religion, Dress and the Body*, 9–29.
4. Donald B. Kraybill, Karen M. Johnson-Weiner, and Steven M. Nolt, *The Amish* (Baltimore: Johns Hopkins University Press, 2013), 125.
5. Kraybill, Johnson-Weiner, and Nolt, 127, 128.
6. Kraybill, Johnson-Weiner, and Nolt, 129–30.
7. Donald B. Kraybill, *The Riddle of Amish Culture*, 2nd ed. (Baltimore: Johns Hopkins University Press, 2001), 60.
8. Jean A. Hamilton and Jana M. Hawley, "Sacred Dress, Public Worlds: Amish and Mormon Experience and Commitment," in Arthur, ed., *Religion, Dress and the Body*, 31–51.
9. Kraybill, Johnson-Weiner, and Nolt, *The Amish*, 127.
10. I conducted fieldwork in Lancaster County, Pennsylvania, in 2010–2011 through a Fulbright Doctoral Dissertation Research grant funded by the Japan-U.S. Educational Commission. The follow-up research from 2014 to date has been supported by the Japan Society for the Promotion of Science, KAKENHI Grant Numbers 15K01863 and 17KK0020.
11. The Old Order Amish are not allowed to drive cars but are willing to ride in one driven by a non-Amish person. In more conservative communities, riding in a car is restricted to emergencies.
12. Steven M. Nolt, *A History of the Amish*, 3rd ed. (Intercourse, PA: Good Books, 2015), 9–10.
13. Nolt, 50–64.
14. For details on statistics of the Amish population, see "Amish Population, 2022," Young Center for Anabaptist and Pietist Studies, Elizabethtown College, accessed September 8, 2022, https://groups.etown.edu/amishstudies/statistics/population-2022/.
15. For discussions of diversity among the Amish, see Steven M. Nolt and Thomas J. Meyers, *Plain Diversity: Amish Cultures and Identities* (Baltimore: Johns Hopkins University Press, 2007); Kraybill, Johnson-Weiner, and Nolt, *The Amish*, 137–54. My research, too, does not aim to represent the Old Order Amish as a whole. Rather, it tries to provide a nuanced account of the Old Order Amish in Lancaster, Pennsylvania, as a case study.
16. Kraybill, Johnson-Weiner, and Nolt, *The Amish*, 14.

17. Kraybill, Johnson-Weiner, and Nolt, 172.
18. Nolt and Meyers, *Plain Diversity*, 9–10, 52.
19. Nolt, *A History of the Amish*, 164.
20. Kraybill, Johnson-Weiner, and Nolt, *The Amish*, 277–81.
21. Stephen Scott found more than three hundred differences in clothing among Amish settlements. Stephen Scott, *Why Do They Dress That Way?* (Intercourse, PA: Good Books, 1997).
22. Kraybill, *The Riddle of Amish Culture*, 59–60.
23. The wearing of *Leppli* is a distinctive feature of the Lancaster County Amish settlement. Scott, *Why Do They Dress That Way?*, 100.
24. Field notes, November 15, 2010. In contrast to Miriam's understanding that the *Leppli* comes from a scripture, Kraybill, Johnson-Weiner, and Nolt have written that "clothing regulations are usually not tied to specific Scriptures." *The Amish*, 127.
25. Field notes, October 26, 2010. Amish refer to non-Amish Americans as "English."
26. Field notes, September 20, 2010.
27. KJV, i.e., the King James version. The Amish traditionally use this as their preferred English translation.
28. Field notes, December 5, 2010.
29. While Amish women's hair is always put into a bun, there are differences in hairstyle in each settlement, just as there are in dresses. This particular hairstyle, with the twisted rolls on the side, is distinctive of the Lancaster County Amish.
30. Field Notes, May 12, 2011. Susan, about fifteen or sixteen years old, was then the teacher's assistant at the school my host family's children attended. At Amish schools, teachers and their assistants also have only an eighth-grade education. Some start teaching full-time as young as age sixteen.
31. Miriam laughed when she saw the sign and said, "They must get a lot of questions. 'Which one is for the covering?'" Field Notes, December 17, 2010.
32. Kraybill, Johnson-Weiner, and Nolt, *The Amish*, 128.
33. Kraybill, *The Riddle of Amish Culture*, 59.
34. According to Kraybill, Amish, who eschew the use of buttons on women's dresses, adopted snap fasteners as "a compromise between the patterns of tradition and the interests of convenience." Kraybill, *The Riddle of Amish Culture*, 69.
35. Miriam's mother, Elizabeth, often wears the "hidden snap fasteners" style that looks like the front bodice is closed with straight pins.

36. In some church districts in Lancaster County, single girls wear black head coverings for church. The head coverings designs differ in each settlement.
37. When women do not marry, they make a voluntary decision around the age of thirty to switch to a cape made of the same dress material or black fabric.
38. I observed that older and conservative women often wore the formal attire even for casual occasions.
39. I observed that many youth shopped for popular shoe brands such as Keds, Nikes, Reeboks, and Skechers.
40. There are outlet malls and big-box stores such as Costco, Target, and Walmart in Lancaster, Pennsylvania, where some Amish people enjoy shopping.
41. Lancaster Old Order Amish wear black aprons, while other Amish affiliations, including car-driving Spring Garden and Beachy Amish, wear aprons in the same colors as their dresses.
42. Field Notes, November 4, 2010. The wedding is one of the most important religious rituals for the Amish. Kraybill, Johnson-Weiner, and Nolt, *The Amish*, 232.
43. The wedding is held at the bride's house, with the family's large barn or workshop often turned into a temporary ceremonial hall. The bride's family, relatives, and church members prepare meals, snacks, and beverages for these all-day events.
44. Before taking the baptismal vow, children born into an Amish family are not technically Amish, and thus are not disciplined by church authorities. A 2002 documentary film, *Devil's Playground*, extended popular myths about *Rumspringa* as a period to experience "the world," which rarely happens in reality.
45. Field Notes, October 30, 2010.
46. Bernina, a high-end brand for sewing machines, is popular among Amish women. Many women own a portable, computerized sewing machine, which they hook up to batteries with an inverter/converter.
47. Field Notes, October 30, 2010. Miriam has a non-electronic Bernina sewing machine with a few decorative stich options that operates with air pressure.
48. Kraybill, Johnson-Weiner, and Nolt, *The Amish*, 128.
49. Most of Mary's new dresses are now of the center-seamed style. Field Notes, March 8, 2012.
50. Field Notes, October 25, 2010.
51. Field Notes, November 15, 2010.
52. Field Notes, October 11, 2010.

53. Kraybill, *The Riddle of Amish Culture*, 69.
54. Field Notes, August 2011, Aylmer, Ontario. The woman grew up in Lancaster County, Pennsylvania, and later moved to a more conservative Amish settlement in Canada.
55. An anonymous caller asked why Amish clothing did not show a "homespun, simple nature. . . . something like cotton or wool or natural fabric." "10 Things You Don't Know About the Amish," *Smart Talk*, podcast, October 27, 2010, WITF Radio. During my fieldwork, I met one woman who preferred cotton and wool dresses. She ran an organic greenhouse and was considered an expert on herbs by her Amish friends. Her friends' reaction to her natural fiber dresses were not very positive. They could not believe that she would go through the effort to pay more money for a fabric that would take extra time to care for. From my outsider's aesthetic point of view, her cotton and wool dresses hanging in the bathroom seemed much more exquisite than ordinary polyester dresses.
56. My host family installed large solar panels to produce "Amish electricity" around 2015. During my fieldwork in the summer of 2015, they asked me to drive to a local appliance store to purchase an automatic washing machine.
57. Field Notes, November 8, 2010. Zook's is a fabric store in Intercourse, Pennsylvania.
58. Field Notes, December 2, 2010.
59. Field Notes, December 2, 2010.
60. Field Notes, August 31, 2015.

Eleven

"YOUR RELIGION IS SHOWING"

NEGOTIATION AND PERSONAL EXPERIENCE IN MORMON GARMENTS

JESSICA FINNIGAN AND NANCY ROSS

JOSEPH SMITH, THE founder of Mormonism, instituted the practice of wearing what members of the faith call "garments" in the nineteenth century. These early garments looked like single-piece, wrist-to-ankle long underwear but evolved to the two-piece, short-sleeved and legged versions that members of the Church of Jesus Christ of Latter-day Saints (known as the LDS Church or the Mormon Church) wear today.[1] Garments are articles of clothing that represent the ritual spaces of the religion's most sacred places—temples—and heavenly places for believing Mormons.[2] LDS temple rituals prompt Mormons to envision the afterlife as real and connect the wearer to the Creation story, God, biblical figures, and angels.[3] During these ceremonies, Mormons make commitments, termed "covenants," to obey God. Outside of the temple, garments connect wearers to those rituals and the afterlife in a way that is ever present.[4]

Mormons receive garments in the sex-segregated initiatory ceremony in LDS temples, which confers spiritual power upon the wearer.[5] Prior to the ritual, individuals receive instructions to wear the garment throughout their lives, day and night, with few exceptions, and not to alter the form of the garment.[6] Individuals are also invited to seek personal spiritual guidance on questions regarding garment wearing.[7] Further discussion of garments, including their symbolism, wearing, and temple connections, is taboo. Historian John-Charles Duffy sees the relative silence surrounding garments and the flexibility in garment-related instruction as empowering Mormons to create individualized meanings for their garments, but others note that the limited discourse requires wearing garments continually.[8]

Because of this taboo, some researchers, like Duffy and Colleen McDannell, limit their academic discussions of garments to official LDS Church sources.[9] Mormons often explain that their garments are "sacred, not secret," meaning that some sacred topics are off-limits for discussion. Many elements of LDS temples also fall under this "sacred, not secret" taboo. Mormon temple practices derived from secret Masonic rituals, and Masonic symbols are still sewn into garments today. Mormons inherited the same ban on open discussion of rituals from Freemasonry. As the LDS Church has tried to ally itself with Christian conservatives in the twentieth and twenty-first centuries, the taboo has served to make Mormons appear more mainstream.

Garments serve as community markers and symbolize the religious commitment of the wearer.[10] The wearing of garments is linked to an adult LDS Church member's high standing within their community.[11] Periodically, church members are interviewed by local ecclesiastical leaders, who ask them questions about beliefs and practices in relation to official Mormon teachings and standards of behavior. To pass this "temple recommend" interview, which is required for Mormons to receive permission to enter the group's temples, Mormons must, among other beliefs and practices, affirm that they wear garments night and day. Passing the interview is also a formal requirement for many volunteer jobs within the church organization and is the main criteria for being deemed a good practicing Mormon.[12] Hence, the wearing of garments (or lack thereof) has social and religious ramifications for individual Mormons.

Garments reflect the power that the LDS Church has over Mormon bodies. Official instruction about the garment identifies it as a symbol of private religious commitment.[13] In Mormon communities, the lines of the garment are often visible through one's outer layers, and this serves as a public symbol of orthopraxy and orthodoxy,[14] a clear marker of one's insider status,[15] and also of moral and sexual purity.[16] The lace trim on women's garments create noticeable raised lines that are visible through several layers of clothing. Men's garments are fully hemmed and resemble a traditional men's undershirt. They are conspicuous only when worn beneath a white shirt. Mormons are adept at spotting even subtle markers.[17] In this way, garments become a marker of personal righteousness that is continually visible in Mormon communities.[18]

AGENCY AND NEGOTIATION

The requirement to wear garments night and day, their dual function as symbolic ritual clothing and underwear, and their visibility to others in Mormon communities can create tensions around issues of choice (agency). These issues cause wearers to live out their choices in ways that force them to weigh their personal needs against community expectations (negotiation). The wearing of garments presents a peculiar problem: Wearing prescribed underwear is interpreted as an ongoing act of religious devotion and a sign of both public and private commitment to the Mormon community.[19] While many wear garments without difficulty, some Mormons experience physical irritation, encounter health problems, or struggle with psychological discomfort at the idea of allowing the LDS Church to dictate adherents' underwear choices. Not wearing garments causes a Mormon to be "unworthy," a technical term that indicates that one is not spiritually or morally ready to enter an LDS temple, as they would not be able to pass a temple recommend interview.

The decisions that Mormons make about garment wearing are laden with social, familial, and spiritual costs. For example, in our personal experience—and this is also borne out in the survey data from our study—it is common for family members (especially mothers and mothers-in-law) to ask about garment wearing, to make unvoiced visual observations related to garment wearing, or to rub one's shoulders to try and detect the presence of garments. These encounters serve as informal religious tests in addition to the more formal temple recommend interviews.

Mormon discourse also references the concept of agency, though it is invoked in a way that is different from the way that feminist scholars use the term. Within Mormonism, individual actions and choices are judged within a framework of agency, where the concept is more akin to the broader Christian idea of free will. Individuals can choose between a set of options. Mormon discourse frames agency as a mutually exclusive dichotomy: there is typically a good choice and a bad choice, with morally complex choices viewed as negative ones.

As used in this chapter, the term "agency" denotes the ability to choose to wear or not wear garments. If agency is a broad umbrella concept, negotiation is a somewhat narrower idea that speaks to the ways in which individuals navigate their inner values, needs, and desires in relation to community values and expectations. With Mormons and their garments, negotiation theory offers a more refined framework for understanding the complexity of the choices made by religious people, rejecting the resistance/observance framework of traditional agency literature in favor of a more nuanced understanding of how individuals navigate and negotiate personal and social costs.

The literature on agency focuses on the choices of women in gender-traditional religions. This grew out of assumptions by secular feminist scholars that these women experienced a lack of agency,[20] but eventually developed into a more nuanced discussion that centered the experiences of women in these traditions.[21] Men are typically left out of the discussion, perhaps because of an assumption that gender-traditional religions do not limit the agency of men. Yet research on Mormon men shows that their agency with regard to grooming is indeed limited.[22] In looking at the agency of men and women in our study, it is clear that the people we refer to as "non-conforming men," in addition to women, experience limitations on their agency.

STUDY OVERVIEW

We wanted to conduct a study that would gather a large number of individual experiences with garments.[23] The initial hypothesis of this study was that Mormon men would be largely satisfied with their garments. Mormon garments were designed to fit male bodies and largely resemble secular men's underwear. From anecdotal evidence, we thought that Mormon women would be unhappy with their garments because they were not designed to fit women's bodies. We participated in many online conversations about garments with Mormon women. Personal experience and the complaints from other Mormon women about their garments led us to become interested in this topic as an area for further study.

Garment design follows twentieth-century trends in men's underwear, which does not always meet the needs of women. Men and women, whose bodies experience many different changes throughout the life cycle, can have diverging experiences with their garments. When we tried to understand the range of women's experiences with their garments, we found that separating the men and women out by belief type (conforming/nonconforming) correlated with different kinds of survey responses. In recent years, sociologists have moved away from studying belief type, but the LDS Church has its own embedded belief test, known as the temple recommend interview, the details of which are published in a handbook for church leaders.[24] Using a similar test in the survey allowed us to address concerns about researchers evaluating belief statements.[25] Adding belief types into the gender groupings gives greater insight into the survey data and helps to explain the range of responses within gender groupings.

Previous studies about agency have used in-depth personal interviews from a narrowly bounded geographic location.[26] None of these previous studies contains a representative sample of Mormons either in the United States or internationally. Historically, the closed nature of the LDS community and the sensitive nature of sacred practices related to the temple has made it difficult to recruit study participants.[27] In order to collect a large number of personal narratives, overcome historical limitations, and maintain the anonymity of participants, we conducted an online survey.

We posted our survey on June 3, 2014, to multiple progressive and conservative Mormon social media pages; we utilized a similar approach in other surveys we have conducted.[28] Participants then shared the survey in their social media. In order to capture the complex relationship with garments across a wide demographic, the survey was open to all adult individuals who self-identified with the LDS Church, including those who have never worn garments, those who currently wear them, and those who have ceased the practice. The survey consisted of a multiple-choice questionnaire to capture basic demographic and religiosity information, and open-ended qualitative questions that explored a wide range of experiences related to body, theology, and garments. The online format allowed for the collection of personal narratives from a geographically dispersed population. The survey closed on June 9, 2014, with 4,559 responses.

Nearly all of the participants were from the United States, with just sixty-one people from outside the country. Seventy-five percent of respondents were between the ages of eighteen and forty. Ninety-four percent identified their race and ethnicity as "white," with the second-largest group being "Hispanic/Latino," at 2 percent. Seventy-five percent of respondents reported themselves as married and in their first marriage, with the second-largest group being single Mormons, who constituted 11 percent. Seventy-seven percent of respondents were parents. Thirty-five percent of respondents reported that their yearly household income is between $50,000 and $90,000 per year and a further 35 percent reported an income greater than $90,000. The people who responded to the survey were highly educated. Forty-three percent reported that their highest level of educational attainment is a bachelor's degree and a further 28 percent have masters and/or doctoral degrees.

While a small and growing body of scholarly literature investigates the history and theology of LDS garments, only two studies examine Mormons' experiences with their garments specifically, both of which use interview methodologies with relatively small sample sizes.[29] The analysis and conclusions in this chapter come from survey data that constitutes the garment study with the largest sample size to date (n=4,559). We found that two variables correlate with Mormons' experiences with their garments: gender (men/women) and belief type (conforming/nonconforming).

Conforming believing participants are those who answered the belief test (temple recommend) questions by agreeing with all standard LDS belief and practice statements. It is important to note that these statements are mainly about agreeing with the LDS Church's particular constructs of belief and faith, and not about a broader idea of Christian faith. The LDS Church claims that it is the one true church,[30] and does not support faith development beyond its own teachings. In contrast, nonconforming believers are Mormons who did not meet this high threshold.[31] The next few sections document the ways in which these four groups of Mormons negotiate their garments.

CONFORMING MEN

Conforming men were the smallest (n=389) and least racially diverse of the four groups, with 94.7 percent of respondents in this group identifying as white. About 92 percent of respondents in this group report attending church every week, the highest in the study, and these respondents were also the most likely to report that they were wearing garments regularly at the time of the study (95 percent).

Conforming men are at the center of the LDS Church. They are decision makers at every level of church governance and oversee the committee tasked with garment design. When asked about church teachings related to their bodies, they are likely to respond with positive affirmations. One conforming man wrote, "I am created in the image of God, my body is a temple to be respected, kept clean and fit, and a gift. I should take good care of it, but God loves me regardless." Another conforming man went further:

> As a man I have been taught I should keep the Word of Wisdom because my physical body is a blessing I sought in the preexistence but I don't remember ever hearing any teachings that would make me feel ashamed of my body. We played shirts and skins basketball games at the church for Mutual.[32] Away from the church we went skinny dipping at scout camp and laughed at the guy whose suit came off when the scouts were water skiing but never thought there was any modesty issue about these. They were naughty the same way fart jokes are naughty but revealing our bodies didn't have anything to do with our morality.

These comments reference the Mormon health code (the Word of Wisdom), which forbids Mormons from drinking coffee, tea, or alcohol. In LDS Church doctrine, "preexistence" references a life with God before this life, where individuals had bodies made of spirit but not flesh and blood. While Mormons are supposed to wear garments day and night, the commonly understood exceptions to this rule are for sex, swimming, and exercise. These conforming men's bodies are connected to God and the sacred spaces of the temple, beloved of God, and without shame.

Men in this group responded to the question of "Why do you wear garments?" by consistently discussing God's commandments and temple covenants to wear them night and day. One conforming man offered three justifications for his choice:

> 1. Because I've made a covenant to do so, and I believe in that promise that I made and the promises made to me in the temple. 2. Also because it is one of the temple recommend questions and my continued attendance at the temple is important to me. 3. Social pressure is just as big a reason,

however; it is immediately very obvious in LDS social situations who is not wearing their garments. And there's a stigma that goes with that.

Only a few reported wearing garments for other reasons. Men in this group were unlikely to reference their spouse or children in their answers, though a few mentioned the "social pressure" indicated above.

When asked "What do garments mean to you?" conforming men were likely to repeat LDS Church teaching about garments. One conforming man answered, "[They are an] outward show of inward covenants. They are a protection from temptation." These kinds of statements come from some of the few authoritative talks that reference garments.[33] Another conforming man elaborated: "I take the commandant and the blessings associated with the garment very literally. The garment is a symbol and reminder of sacred covenants I have made with the Lord. And in turn, they provide protection for me against the power of the adversary." Here, the "adversary" is a reference to Satan and evil. This theme of protection came up in all four groups. While some, like the conforming man above, indicated that garments were a protection from supernatural forces, other conforming men talked about self-control. One conforming man answered this same question with the response, "I can control and master my physical and mental self."

Researchers asked respondents "How does wearing garments make you feel?" Because this question does not have an official LDS Church response, participants were able to offer a greater variety of answers. Some men expressed varying kinds of satisfaction and comfort in wearing their garments. A number of conforming men gave one-word responses: "great," "comfortable," "safe," "good," "protected," "worthy," or "obedient." One conforming man wrote, "Kind of an odd question. How does wearing any underwear make you feel? Normal." To this last respondent, the answer to this question seems obvious: garments are normal. Similarly, another wrote, "Like I fit in with Utah society," and another responded, "I love wearing garments. I would wear some kind of underwear anyway and I consider garments to be very convenient and also—attractive." This same question also received a few unanticipated answers, such as "confined," "never thought about it," "hot," "uncomfortable," "unsexy." These types of responses were rare, however. For the overwhelming majority of conforming men, garment wearing was somewhere between a neutral and a positive experience. As a group, conforming men did not have to spend energy figuring out how to make garments work for them, either physically or psychologically. Garments fit into the lives of these men in a way that many of them saw as normal, and they rarely mentioned other groups of people who needed to be considered in the discussion of garments.

The open-ended responses from this survey show that, overall, conforming men do not appear to be doing much negotiation of belief or garments. They rarely report experiencing physical or psychological issues as a result of their garments. They did not have to negotiate their beliefs or their wearing of garments because they wholeheartedly embrace the teachings of the LDS Church and they do not, except for a few rare cases, experience physical changes in their bodies that cause problems with garments. Conforming men rarely reference other groups of people within Mormonism (women, children, teens) and their responses show little awareness of other groups within the church.

NONCONFORMING MEN

Nonconforming men were the second-smallest group in this study (n=525) and the second-most racially diverse group, with almost 8 percent of participants identifying as people of color and/or multiracial. As a group, nonconforming men attend church less often than conforming men do, with 42.3 percent of respondents attending church weekly. They also wear garments at a lower rate, with only 45.1 percent of respondents wearing garments at the time of the survey.

When asked about church teaching related to their bodies, nonconforming men gave a much wider variety of responses than conforming men did. Some of the responses echoed conforming men and official church teaching, like "[my body is] a gift from God, that it's something to protect and keep sacred," and "it's a temple." A number of comments reflected the tension between the desires of the body and church teaching. One nonconforming man wrote "that it is to be covered and that my body and its needs are inherently evil," and another wrote "that our bodies are exceedingly fragile temples that are beautiful albeit irreparably broken." Nonconforming men were more likely to reference the Word of Wisdom's restrictions on coffee, tea, alcohol, drugs, as well as prohibitions on tattoos, revealing clothing, masturbation, and sex outside of marriage. One nonconforming man wrote,

It is a gift from God, I could not progress without it. I must respect it, not misuse it sexually (adultery, fornication, masturbation) and by the things that I take into my body (coffee, alcohol, tobacco, or drugs). Each of us must harness the desires of the "natural man," which is inclined toward lust, overindulgence, selfishness and addiction. I should eat good foods. I will be resurrected to a state of perfection.

Some respondents indicated that they were made to feel shame about their bodies and sexuality. One participant wrote that he was taught to feel "ashamed of my own sexual responses and to feel a need to suppress all sexual response until after marriage. That I shouldn't masturbate, that if I was having an erection then I was already in a spiritually suspect state of mind." Many of these responses identify one or more activities that participants sacrifice because of their beliefs, particularly the promise of a better place in the afterlife. They are more likely than conforming men to list their sacrifices and express negative feelings about church teaching.

Nonconforming men gave a broad range of responses to the question "Why do you wear garments?" Like the conforming men, some responded with answers like "obedience to my covenants and for the spiritual protection they provide." Others gave responses that referenced the role that their wives and others played in the decision to wear garments. One nonconforming man wrote that he wore garments due to "fear of judgment from [my] spouse as well as others and second because I made a covenant to." Nonconforming men were more motivated by marital and social considerations than their conforming counterparts. Others responded that they wore garments out of "habit," "tradition," and "custom."

In response to the question "What do your garments mean to you?" the responses of nonconforming men overlapped somewhat with those of conforming men. Some men gave short answers like "covenant reminder," "sign of my commitment to God," and "they are a physical connection to the spiritual." Nonconforming men were equally likely to give more cynical responses. Some answered, "a choice that I was pressured into by my parents," "control by an organization," and "nothing." One man gave further explanation:

I dislike them very much. They are a symbol of a religion that brings me a lot of heartache. I hate how easily they get dirty, how hard they are to clean, and how much trouble you have to go through to get rid of them.[34] They are ugly and expensive. I'm not opposed outright to purchasing expensive underwear, but when it's something that is a forced purchase then it becomes a problem.

Many men emphasized that the wearing of garments was a mechanism for the LDS Church to control their bodies, and they expressed discomfort with that.

Nonconforming men were more negative in response to the question "How do you feel about your garments?" A few men responded with simple statements like "fine," "good," "great," and "normal," but these were in the minority. Short responses also revealed a variety of challenging situations: "ambivalent," "angry," "a little annoyed," "apathetic," "awkward," "chained," "ugly." Many of these men claimed more affirming meanings for their garments, but ultimately felt few neutral or positive feelings about wearing them. In longer responses, some indicated the tension between their nonconforming status and the belief that is embodied in garments. One man wrote, "[I feel] like a liar. Because I'm not that convinced of the gospel, wearing them seems like an affront." Many expressed feeling physically hot in their garments. One man wrote, "I don't notice, except when it's hot and then they feel stifling."

In sum, nonconforming men are often conflicted about garments. They are more aware of what they are sacrificing to be in good standing in the LDS Church. Some men in this group identify spiritual meanings for their garments but resent having to wear them. Some experience physical issues of discomfort related to wearing an extra layer under their shirts, or psychological discomfort because the LDS Church is trying to control their bodies. Nonconforming men describe garments as a potential source of tension as they navigate their place in the community. Some nonconforming men resent the garment as a symbol of the LDS Church's control over their bodies. Other men report continued wearing of the garment to please their wives. In referencing spouses, this group is more likely than conforming men to talk about others in the negotiation of their garments.

CONFORMING WOMEN

Conforming women were the largest group (n=1,946) in this study. Conforming women respondents were 93.4 percent white, with less than

7 percent identifying as women of color. The church attendance for this group was nearly equal to the conforming men, with more than 92 percent attending every week. Fewer conforming women reported wearing garments at the time of the survey (91.4 percent) than conforming men (95.0 percent).

Conforming women were trying to maintain their commitment to the church while identifying problems with garments and church messaging about women's bodies. In response to being asked "What does the church teach you about your body?" women gave many different kinds of answers. Two of the most common kinds of responses reflected church teachings and in this sense were similar to men's responses: "it is a temple," and "it is sacred." Many other responses included variations on these statements, but with additional commentary unique to this group. One conforming woman wrote,

> I don't like being told that showing a little skin, cleavage, leg is wrong. I don't like that girls are taught that if they dress "sexy" they are causing impure thought in the opposite sex. I do like the idea that my body is a temple and is special just for me. I do like a discussion that I had with other women about the amazing ability our bodies have to create life and how that makes us closer to the Savior.

When these women expressed complaints, they were likely to return to elements of the practice that work for them. Conforming women do not tend to make critiques of the LDS Church without also making statements that demonstrate their loyalty to the institution. Because of this, conforming women wrote lengthier responses than men to open-ended survey questions and showed a greater awareness of how other women might also respond differently to the same question. A conforming woman captured this when she answered, "I feel super lucky that modesty teachings did not make me feel ashamed of my body. The church has taught me that I should respect my body and by some miracle I retained that instead of shame or feeling like I needed to cover up or that my body was sinful. Not sure how I got so lucky?" Even as she stated that she was taught to respect her body, this conforming woman showed an awareness of the body shame that many other Mormon women carry. Only a small minority of responses to this question referenced the harm of church teaching without including loyalty statements. A conforming woman wrote that she learned her body "is shameful, lust inducing, something to hide and a burden to overcome." It is interesting to note that while the LDS Church discourse places an enormous emphasis on motherhood, only a handful of women mentioned motherhood in their responses to this question.

In response to the question "Why do you wear garments?" about 68 percent of respondents referenced commitments, commandments, promises, or covenants. These women felt bound by the things they agreed to during temple ceremonies. A typical response read, "As a reminder of my temple covenants." Another woman elaborated on the way her garments symbolize her faith and enforce modesty: "Because of faith. The Lord has told me to and they are a symbol of the covenants I've made with him, which means a lot to me. I also appreciate the fact that when I wear them I have a guideline for a certain level of modesty. That makes things easier sometimes." Other women referenced the idea of physical or spiritual protection, with answers like "As a protection and reminder of my spiritual side." A few respondents referenced other people in their decision to wear garments. A conforming woman wrote, "Because it's part of Heavenly Father's plan. Because I want to be obedient and live up to my covenants. Because I have been reprimanded by my mother-in-law and husband when I do not. It would be socially unacceptable if I felt otherwise and followed those feelings." Conforming women tended to frame their choice to wear garments as a personal commitment to the divine, with few references to social and familial pressure.

Conforming women constructed the meaning of their garments in terms of LDS Church messaging and connection with God. In response to the question "What do your garments mean to you?" conforming women gave the following insights, which represent common themes in the responses: "they are a reminder of the temple for me and the peace I have felt there along with the presence of heavenly parents"; "they are a representation of who I am, a covenant-keeping person"; "they are a symbol of my faith"; and "they are a symbol of the atonement that Christ is lovingly clothing and sheltering me." For conforming women, their garments were a material symbol of intangible faith and divine realities. Other women expressed feeling bound by their commitments, even if they did not have these same positive experiences. One conforming woman wrote, "I really don't like them. I would stop wearing them if it wasn't part of my temple covenant."

As with the conforming men, the conforming women's responses to the question "How do you feel about your garments?" were revealing. There were a number of solidly positive responses to this question: "good," "comfortable," "protected," "normal," and "safe." These women felt physically and spiritually connected to God through their garments and the blessings of obedience that came from wearing them. One conforming woman wrote, "They are a reminder of the covenants I have made and the promises The Lord has given me. They also feel normal and comfortable after all these years. I feel uncomfortable when I don't have them on." Other women had many positive things to say about the spiritual associations with their garments, but expressed negative feelings about the garments as clothing. One woman wrote,

> I appreciate the significance of garments on an emotional and spiritual level. They help me remember sacred covenants and serve as an outward expression of my devotion and dedication to my beliefs. However, physically they often feel uncomfortable or that they take great effort to conceal due to the cuts of fabric being so different than modern day clothing.

A few others mentioned issues that went beyond physical discomfort or overheating, referencing yeast infections and urinary tract infections that resulted from wearing garments day and night. A woman reported feeling "uncomfortable, overweight/lumpy, frustrated, irritated (skin and emotionally), gives me yeast infections, hot, sweaty, restricted." Many of these stories recounted difficulties navigating garment wearing during pregnancy, breastfeeding, and menstruation. A number of responses indicated that women felt additional discomfort with garments during these stages of life. The LDS Church offers maternity and nursing garments, but these styles have fewer fabric options, and many respondents complained of poor design. One woman wrote, "Garments are frustrating during pregnancy and the nursing years, which is always since I nurse my children through toddlerhood. They make it that much more cumbersome to nurse in public, which is a major reason many moms wean early. It's just too hard. Nursing in public is hard enough by itself, then add the struggle of yet another layer." Another woman wrote that garments were

> Horribly uncomfortable during pregnancy. Also difficult since there was only one style maternity top and it was too big until late pregnancy, then

too small by the very end. No options in fabric made for hot summers! Nursing tops complicated the process and created weird lines that were visible through the bra and shirt because of the flaps. Eventually I switched to Carinessa[35] tops and just pull down the neckline to nurse.

While conforming women interpret their garments as sacred reminders of commitments made in temples, and often have positive experiences with their garments, this question about feelings reveals some women's complicated relationship to garment wearing. Conforming women were likely to tell stories about their garments and garment wearing, something few men did. These stories tried to reconcile the sacred meaning of garments while acknowledging the physical irritations created by poor design and fabrics.

For conforming women, concerns about salvation, spirituality, and orthopraxy supersede physical discomfort and medical concerns surrounding garments. These women negotiate their garments through their belief, with the goal of meeting community expectations to wear garments night and day throughout their lives. To these women, garments are important symbols of the temple, spirituality, and God's favor. Conforming women affirm community expectations, with an emphasis on problem solving within a framework of fabric options and rules.

NONCONFORMING WOMEN

Nonconforming women were the second-largest group in the survey (n=1,699). This group was the most racially diverse, with 90.7 percent identifying as white. This group was also the most detailed in their racial identification, selecting the most combinations of racial identities. Nonconforming women have the lowest rates of garment wearing, with only 36 percent reporting that they wore garments consistently at the time of the survey. Nonconforming women reported a rate of weekly church attendance (43.3 percent) similar to that of nonconforming men.

Of all four groups, nonconforming women had the biggest range of responses for every question. Their answers included the repetition of LDS Church teaching, but also included far more critical comments. In response to the question "What does the church teach you about your body?" some respondents wrote, "it is a temple," or "it is sacred." Like conforming women, nonconforming women gave responses that were critical of modesty culture within the LDS Church, which teaches that girls and women are responsible for men's sexual responses when they wear revealing clothing. These responses were more critical than those of conforming women and did not typically contain additional statements demonstrating loyalty to the LDS Church. A nonconforming woman wrote,

> Cover up! My shoulders, breasts, legs, even arms should be covered. I am going against God if I do not follow these "laws." That if I dress provocatively, I am responsible for men and their sexual reactions. That I deserved to be raped because of the way I dressed. That men can dress how they like, but women have multiple rules about their dress. If I wear anything other than a dress or skirt at church, I am being disrespectful and even disobedient.

This respondent was not the only nonconforming woman to tie modesty teachings to rape. Another woman wrote,

> As a rape victim that was disciplined for my rape, by my bishop, and then told to read the *Miracle of Forgiveness*,[36] I have a lot of issues with church teachings about women's bodies, modesty, and rape/chastity. The intense focus on my virginity/virtue belonging to my future husband was very damaging both before and after my rape. My growing relationship with my Heavenly Mother has helped me to accept my body and my life as a powerful gift that can change and have much more power to create, beyond children and sexual desire in my husband.

This woman is healing the relationship with her body by creating a relationship with Heavenly Mother. In the LDS Church, God the Father has a wife, known as Heavenly Mother, but talking about her is taboo. In this comment, this nonconforming woman is claiming faith and a relationship with the divine that is outside of church norms, even a bit transgressive. By claiming her faith in this individualized way, she is demonstrating independence from LDS Church discourse.

This last response also referenced the power of women's bodies to create children. While few conforming women referenced babies, children, or pregnancy in their survey responses, many more nonconforming women did. One nonconforming woman wrote, "as a woman your body is for making babies." Typically, these comments reflected a tone that was critical of that expectation. Another woman wrote, "[My body is] chewed up gum. Ruined cake. Sacred. Not to be shown. Not to be aroused. Enemy of God. . . . For making babies." The gum comment is a reference to a standard object lesson that teenage girls receive in the LDS Church that uses chewed gum to demonstrate the way in which sexual experience prior to marriage decreases Mormon women's value and desirability. This comment, and many others from this group, stand in stark contrast to what men and conforming women reported.

In response to the question "Why do you wear garments?" about 67 percent of nonconforming garment-wearing women referenced commitments, commandments, promises, or covenants, a similar percentage to conforming women (68 percent). Short answers that did not reference these words included "because I said I would," "because I was told to," and "guilt, fear of punishment." A nonconforming woman answered, "Cultural pressure. I don't want to be socially ostracized if it becomes apparent that I do not have [a high level of belief in] the LDS Church." Another woman offered the further explanation that,

> Currently, I wear garments only when I am around my parents or at church meetings. I wear them with my parents because I am afraid of them knowing about my changes in beliefs and behaviors because I was always the "righteous" child and I am afraid of breaking their hearts. I wear them to church when I attend partially to avoid gossip and awkward questions and also to show respect to the traditions of the faith I grew up in and though I don't believe completely, I still see some positive attributes.

These comments also reveal that clothing designated as underwear, and presumably private, is highly visible in the Mormon community, something that Mormons look for as an outward sign of commitment.

Nonconforming women addressed the question "What do your garments mean to you?" with a wide variety of responses. One nonconforming woman wrote, "Garments have become a symbol of broken promises to me. Although I love the church and am grateful for the things it has taught me and the social supports it has given me, I feel lied to about many things. I am not hostile about it, just sad." In a state of nonconformity, the garment that once symbolized promises transforms that meaning into broken promises, and that transformation is associated with feelings of betrayal and sadness. A nonconforming woman had another take on the meaning of her garments: "They mean I'm trying. Even though I'm not sure of just about anything, I'm trying very hard to be obedient in this. I was molested from age 10 and raped when I was 14, and so to me they also offer a shield between my body and the world." This woman found hope in the symbol of the garment as a protective force in her life, even as she was unsure about her belief. For another woman, garments had a very different meaning:

> Honestly, they are a reminder of my first temple experience where I blindly entered into a bunch of covenants that I was unprepared for, and all the doubt and uncertainty I have felt since that point in my life. I still get emotional about my temple experience even though it was almost three years ago. I wear my garments every day because I covenanted to God that I would.

This woman felt bound by her commitments, but her garments became a symbol of doubt instead of a symbol of faith. The reminder was not about furthering a relationship with God, but about being caught in a moment of unpreparedness. The difficulty of this first temple experience imprinted itself onto her garment and was a constant reminder of that. The meanings of nonconforming women's garments are more complex than for other groups, and this is expressed not in simple statements that relate to LDS Church discourse, but in the intricacies of lived experience, often articulated as stories, that these women describe.

Many women talked about physical discomfort in response to the question "How do you feel about your garments?" Like conforming women, some nonconforming women feel content with the meaning of garments as reminders of their commitments, but describe the garment as physically uncomfortable. One woman explained that,

> Emotionally, wearing garments is comfortable, a nice reminder to search for truth and keep the commandments (namely the first and second great commandments), though admittedly I don't always have these thoughts on my mind. But they are comforting to wear. Physically, though, they are very uncomfortable. They are often hot and uncomfortable, or they shift a lot when I wear them, or I'm tugging them all over the place to avoid them showing around the edges of my clothes. In these aspects, garments make me very uncomfortable.

Another nonconforming woman described having the opposite problem, using language that compares the necessity of garment wearing to a disability: "Crippled. I feel like I hate them even though they are comfortable. I fear others will JUDGE me if they notice I'm not wearing them. They hold no spiritual significance for me, they just help me keep my friendships intact." This woman felt compelled to wear them and resented the wearing of garments as a social necessity.

Nonconforming women were much more likely to report experiencing medical problems as a result of their garments, mentioning infection three times more often than conforming women. One woman reported that garments made her feel

> Frumpy. I feel good about my body, until I have to start adding layers to cover my garments. I get stressed and upset because I have short legs so garment bottoms sit really low on my legs. It's so hard to find things to wear—shopping is brutal and demoralizing. Also, I get yeast infections frequently, which my doctor suspects is a result of my garments. If God loves me why does he make me wear underwear that makes me so uncomfortable?

Many nonconforming women reported urinary tract infections, skin rashes, yeast infections, and other conditions, in addition to experiencing difficulty when wearing garments during pregnancy and nursing. In this response, the nonconforming woman identified garments as a source of infection and went on to question why a loving God would require this of her. This was a pattern that played out repeatedly with nonconforming women: physical issues stemming from garment wearing sometimes led to questions about faith or preceded a faith transition.

Nonconforming woman told many stories of the transformation of their faith and the role of garments in that transformation. While many nonconforming women navigated the problems with their garments by stopping the practice of wearing them, others continue to live, either happily or unhappily, with these constant reminders of faith and doubt. Nonconforming women navigate garments by naming the problems with them and finding appropriate solutions to those problems, without the ultimate goal of conforming to community expectations. When nonconforming women continue to wear garments in the face of challenges, they often do so out of fear of losing relationships or breaking their commitments to God.

A number of nonconforming women told stories about their garments in which physical discomfort, incompatibility with breastfeeding or pregnancy, and medical issues played a role initiating a faith transition from a place of conforming belief to a place of nonconforming belief. Unlike the conforming women, many nonconforming women were not able to come to satisfactory adaptations or solutions to their garment problems. More than participants in other groups, these women were the most likely to write lengthy responses to our open-ended questions, which gave insight into their negotiation processes. Many of these women made considerable efforts in trying to make garments work in their lives but were ultimately unable to do so.

The initial hypothesis for this study was that men and women probably have very different experiences with their garments. The study has confirmed that hypothesis and introduced the idea that an individual's belief type impacts their lived experiences in significant ways. The intersection of gender and belief type created four groups of participants, each of which negotiated their garments in different ways as they addressed questions about their meaning and significance.

There was a gender divide on the question of what the church teaches people about their bodies. Men reported receiving largely positive or neutral messages about their bodies. They told us that their bodies were temples and that they were made in the image of God. Women gave answers with much more detail and their responses were more mixed, with some reporting that the church taught them positive things about their bodies, in line with the responses from men, and others reporting very negative teachings. Negative responses often described the sexualization of women's bodies and their framing as sexual temptations to men. Women of color were more likely to discuss the sexualization of their bodies in church teaching, regardless of belief type, and this is an area for further study.

On the question of why people wear garments, the divide was biggest between conforming and nonconforming believers. Whether male or female, conforming believers framed their decision to wear garments in terms of covenant keeping, closeness to God, and obedience to God, and they were likely to view the decision as individual and personal. In contrast, nonconforming believers tended to cite social and familial reasons for wearing garments, demonstrating significant awareness of the social consequences of wearing or not wearing garments.

There was also a big divide in the way that conforming and nonconforming believers approached the question "What do your garments mean to you?" Conforming men and women gave answers to this question that were similar to the ones they gave for the question of why they wear them. For conformers, garments meant that they were keeping temple covenants and demonstrating obedience to God. Many felt that garments had a positive impact on their lives and referenced feelings of safety and security, which is part of the official church messaging on garments. In contrast, nonconforming men and women gave more mixed responses. Many nonconforming believers talked about their individual experiences with garments, which they said complicated the meaning of wearing them. Some nonconforming believers felt that the LDS Church used garments to control them.

Finally, in terms of their feelings about their garments, conformers connected garment wearing to positive spiritual benefits, though conforming women also sometimes noted frustration or discomfort with garments as underwear. Nonconforming believers had complicated feelings about garments. They saw garments as indicating membership in a community and many reported negative physical, emotional, and sexual impacts of wearing garments. Once again, the biggest divide was not between gender groups, but between those with differing types of belief, suggesting the importance of religious belief when it comes to understanding dress choices.

This study raises additional questions about further breakdowns by identity and how different subgroups experience their garments and what messages they absorb from the LDS Church about their bodies. Women of color were also more likely to report that garments did not fit their body types. Ideas of marriage and partnership are integrated into the meaning of garments, as marriage is essential for entry into the Celestial Kingdom, the highest place in Mormon heaven. Due to this, the wearing of garments by single people requires further investigation, as does the wearing of garments by LGBTQ+ Mormons. The theological construction of bodies within the LDS Church as able, white, heterosexual, cisgender, and partnered creates a number of problems when bodies do not match these ideals. Each of these identities are referenced in the garment data in one form or another, and further study will give more insight into the negotiation processes of Mormons.

NOTES

1. Adam J. Powell, "Covenant Cloaks: Mormon Temple Garments in the Light of Identity Theory" *Material Religion* 12, no. 4 (2016): 457–75.
2. Tona Hangen, "Lived Religion Among Mormons," in *The Oxford Handbook of Mormonism*, ed. Terryl Givens and Philip Barlow (Oxford: Oxford University Press, 2015), 209–23.
3. David John Buerger, "The Development of the Mormon Temple Endowment Ceremony," *Dialogue: A Journal of Mormon Thought* 34, nos. 1–2 (2001): 75–122.
4. Powell, "Covenant Cloaks," 457–75.
5. John-Charles Duffy, "Concealing the Body, Concealing the Sacred: The Decline of Ritual Nudity in Mormon Temples," *Journal of Ritual Studies* 21, no. 2 (2007): 1–21.
6. Carlos Asay, "The Temple Garment: 'An Outward Expression of an Inward Commitment,'" *Ensign*, August 1997, 18–23, https://www.lds.org/ensign/1997/08/the-temple-garment-an-outward-expression-of-an-inward-commitment?lang=eng.
7. Church of Jesus Christ of Latter-day Saints, *Handbook 1: Stake Presidents and Bishops* (Salt Lake City: Church of Jesus Christ of Latter-day Saints, 2010), 3.4.5.
8. Asay, "The Temple Garment," 18–23; Armand L. Mauss, *The Angel and the Beehive: The Mormon Struggle with Assimilation* (Urbana: University of Illinois Press, 1994), 89.
9. Duffy, "Concealing the Body, Concealing the Sacred," 1–21; Colleen McDannell, *Material Christianity: Religion and Popular Culture in America* (New Haven, CT: Yale University Press, 1995), 198–221.
10. Jean A. Hamilton and Jana Hawley, "Sacred Dress, Public Worlds: Amish and Mormon Experiences and Commitment," in *Religion, Dress and the Body*, ed. Linda B. Arthur (Oxford: Berg, 1999), 31–52.
11. Douglas Davies, *The Mormon Culture of Salvation* (Aldershot, UK: Ashgate, 2000), 119.
12. Edward L. Kimball, "The History of LDS Temple Admission Standards," *Journal of Mormon History* 24, no. 1 (1998): 135–76.
13. Asay, "The Temple Garment," 18–23.
14. Hamilton and Hawley, "Sacred Dress, Public Worlds," 31–52.

15. Buerger, "The Development of the Mormon Temple Endowment Ceremony," 75–122.
16. Clate W. Mask, "Standing Spotless before the Lord," *Ensign*, May 2004, 92, https://www.churchofjesuschrist.org/study/liahona/2004/05/standing-spotless-before-the-lord?lang=eng.
17. McDannell, *Material Christianity*, 198–221.
18. Powell, "Covenant Cloaks," 457–75.
19. Hamilton and Hawley, "Sacred Dress, Public Worlds," 31–52.
20. Kelsy C. Burke, "Women's Agency in Gender-Traditional Religions: A Review of Four Approaches," *Sociology Compass* 6, no. 2 (2012): 122–33.
21. Orit Avishai, "'Doing Religion' in a Secular World: Women in Conservative Religions and the Question of Agency," *Gender & Society* 22, no. 4 (2008): 409–33; Saba Mahmood, *Politics of Piety: The Islamic Revival and the Feminist Subject* (Princeton, NJ: Princeton University Press, 2005), 5–10.
22. Michael E. Nielsen and Daryl White, "Men's Grooming in the Latter-day Saints Church: A Qualitative Study of Norm Violation," *Mental Health, Religion & Culture* 11, no. 8 (2008): 807–25.
23. The results of this study were surprising to us, as we have had more than two decades of garment-wearing experience between us, including the experience of wearing garments through a combined six pregnancies and breastfeeding relationships.
24. Adam B. Cohen, Gina L. Mazza, Kathryn A. Johnson, Craig K. Enders, Carolyn M. Warner, Michael H. Pasek, and Jonathan E. Cook, "Theorizing and Measuring Religiosity Across Cultures," *Personality and Social Psychology Bulletin* 43, no. 12 (2017): 1724–36; Church of Jesus Christ of Latter-day Saints, *Handbook 1*, 3.3.3.
25. Cohen et al., "Theorizing and Measuring Religiosity Across Cultures," 1724–36.
26. Alexandria Gale Griffin, "(In)visible Piety: Reading Mormon Garments Through the Hijab" (master's thesis, Claremont Graduate University, 2014), 15; McDannell, *Material Christianity*, 198–221.
27. McDannell, *Material Christianity*, 198–221.
28. Jessica Finnigan and Nancy Ross, "'I'm a Mormon Feminist:' How Social Media Revitalized and Enlarged a Movement," *Interdisciplinary Journal of Research on Religion* 9 (2013): 12; Nancy Ross and Jessica Finnigan, "Mormon Feminist Perspectives on the Mormon Digital Awakening: A Study of Identity and Personal Narratives," *Dialogue: A Journal of Mormon Thought* 47, no. 4 (2014): 47–75.

29. Griffin, "(In)visible Piety," 15; McDannell, *Material Christianity*, 198–221.
30. *The Doctrine and Covenants of the Church of Jesus Christ of Latter-day Saints* (Salt Lake City: Intellectual Reserve, 2013), 1:30.
31. James W. Fowler, "Faith Development Theory and the Postmodern Challenges," *International Journal for the Psychology of Religion* 11, no. 3 (2001): 159–72.
32. The youth program for teenage boys used to be called the Young Men's Mutual Improvement Association, or "Mutual" for short.
33. Asay, "The Temple Garment."
34. Official instructions for the care of garments indicate that the symbols on the garments need to be removed and destroyed prior to throwing them away. Church of Jesus Christ of Latter-day Saints, *Handbook 1*, 3.4.8.
35. Carinessa is a stretchy, formfitting fabric option for women's garments.
36. This book is infamous in the Mormon community for making people feel guilt and shame. Spencer W. Kimball, *The Miracle of Forgiveness* (Salt Lake City: Bookcraft, 1969).

Part IV

ACTIVIST ADORNMENT

Twelve

DRESSED FOR GLORY

WHITE UNIFORMS IN AFRICAN AMERICAN CHURCH TRADITIONS AS VISUAL POLITICAL THEOLOGY

ELAINA SMITH

FOR FOLKS RAISED in African American church communities there is often a set of salient, evocative symbols that function as a reference point about what it means to attend or "do" Black church, aesthetically and theologically. Maybe it's tambourines, a sweaty glass of orange juice by the pulpit, church fans, lap cloths, the procession of altar calls and prayer, or a red hymnal. Surely it can be the starched, pressed white uniform of an usher, who presides over the sacred sanctuary space. These images and rituals may flow directly from personal experience and current community, or they may flow from memories of elders and ancestors, providing foundation for current liturgical moments. As much as traditions and symbols may have strong positive associations, especially for descendants and participants, the same symbols and traditions may be derided by others—including those with no community knowledge or those who have left a church tradition for their own reasons—as limiting, vapid, or indicative of what outsiders may consider an oppressed state. An act such as wearing a starched white uniform may be negatively viewed by some as simplistic, repressive, or merely a result of habit. However, a close examination of this tradition, with consideration of the intentions and claims of those who participate in it, reveals a complex and nuanced history that defies such limiting assumptions.

This chapter examines the wearing of white uniforms by African American church women in specific roles, in a way that *believes* the participants in the tradition. This means believing in the agency and intentionality of individuals; believing in the aesthetic practices of African American church traditions as both political and theological; and believing that the dividing lines, if indeed there are any, between aesthetic, political, and theological concerns depends on who is asked. While there may be occasions where uniforms can be applied in harmful ways, as well as moments where they may be applied in edifying or liberative ways, this chapter does not intend to declare one or the other to be "correct." Rather, it intends to land in a place that creates space for thinking about the theological claims of those who engage in the practice. Critically examining one ritual—the wearing of white uniforms—equips us to think critically about other rituals in ways that are theological, and not merely ethnographic or descriptive, taking seriously these rituals as active theological statements rather than mere passive habits.[1] Reflecting on the wearing of the white uniform as a visual, political, and theological act acknowledges and uplifts one way that Black church women encounter the gaze of God and their own embodiment in this world.

This research focuses primarily on the experiences of African American Protestants, though there are a number of connections involving the use of white clothing to be made across the African Diaspora. It is also important to note that this chapter takes its primary mode of analysis from theory and theology: this is meant to be neither prescriptive nor ethnographic; instead, it is a Womanist-informed stance of taking experiences seriously as appropriate sites of revelation and theological reflection.[2] Great attention could be paid to the suits of gospel quartets, to triptychs of Martin Luther King Jr., Jesus, and John F. Kennedy, to church punch and fellowship halls as profound theological statements mapped in aesthetic forms. We can approach this specificity of dress and visual aesthetic through a particular tradition, deeply churchy: the wearing of white uniforms.

THE WHITE UNIFORM

In African American Protestant churches there are a few main figures who embrace the white uniform. Most often the tradition is connected to ushers, and to women who occupy denominational roles such as district missionary or superintendent, heads of the women's board, or, on occasion, the board as a whole. Additionally, all-white dress may be worn by the women of the church as a collective, most frequently on special occasions such as Women's Day or Resurrection Sunday. White is also a frequent color for baptism, and in some traditions for funerals.[3]

Though not necessarily present in every church, the usher holds a prominent place in African American church structure and imagination. To receive affirmation from an usher is to receive a community seal of approval, and to be scolded by an usher is to be deemed gravely out of order and in need of correction. Ushers provide programs, fans, and tissues, and they quite literally control the doors to the sanctuary, restricting or permitting the flow of traffic based on the moment of service. Typically, the white uniform worn by ushers consists of a starched white blouse, a white skirt, stockings, and white shoes. It may include a white sweater, blazer, or jacket, and the shoes may be soft (like a medical professional's shoes) or heeled. In some instances, the ushers wear what are essentially medical-style pressed white garments, giving the appearance of a group of nurses guarding the sanctuary. This particular combination of role and uniform is almost always exclusively female. Some churches may have ushers whose roles are less heavily gendered and who may wear a more sedate combination of black suiting, or white shirts with slacks, and perhaps a name plaque. In very small churches, such as the one I grew up in, there may be no ushers at all, only a greeter who takes their seat once the service starts; however, an annual gathering such as a local convention may see the elevation of temporary ushers to allow for a more orderly experience.

Ushers are not the only women who wear these white uniforms. Sociologist and Womanist scholar Cheryl Townsend Gilkes describes the dress practice in Sanctified churches,[4] wherein female evangelists wear white uniforms to signify their leadership identity and to project dignity. These uniforms are worn at conventions, for travel, and at Sunday services. In addition, women who occupy certain denominational roles, such as the district superintendent or district missionary, or women who are participants in their church's women's guild, may also wear all-white uniforms if instructed by their leadership.[5] A pressed all-white uniform is also frequently worn by pulpit "attendants," who are responsible for insuring the preacher has water, orange juice, and a handkerchief in the preaching moment. This latter role is something like an usher, and may indeed be fulfilled by an usher, though it is in fact a different role/identity.[6]

When it comes to determining exactly what percentage of churches in African American communities have ushers or attendants, what denominations do so most prominently, or what percentage of women in these roles wear pressed white uniforms, statistical data is not readily available. Neither is there information on exactly how many Sanctified churches continue the tradition of white uniforms for evangelists and other female leaders. Such information would be helpful for a more ethnographic-style study. However, by engaging with the theoretical and theological works available about Black church aesthetics and women's practices, this chapter offers a preliminary consideration of the ways the aesthetic practice of wearing white uniforms constitutes a theological act.

AESTHETIC LANGUAGE

In the preface to *Black Religion and Aesthetics*, ethicist and humanist scholar Anthony B. Pinn argues that the core aesthetic of the Diaspora is religious: that the rituals that form and signify aesthetics flow from, and then reify, spiritual beliefs and positions. The fashioning of Black aesthetics, the commitment to styles and ways, is part of a spiritual commitment and identity. To consider the implied theologies of the Diaspora aesthetic one must understand aesthetic acts as religious; this understanding must include a more robust and complex concept of "the religious" than mere connection to a known religious group. Aesthetic acts become, and are, religious precisely because they anticipate and act in expectation of a spiritual and/or psychosocial reality that is signified, articulated, and embraced by the gestures happening in the physical realm. Put differently, there is no art for art's sake and no dress just to be flashy, but rather art, dress, and other aesthetic mechanisms serve as signifiers because they have real spiritual impact and individuals anticipate and expect this impact.[7] According to Pinn and others, clothing choices and other aesthetic tactics do real work in defining self, displacing the unjust external gaze, and creating or sustaining efforts at liberation.[8] This need to define the self while disrupting external judgment and disproving stereotypes is a unique need for the African American church. Both Pinn and Gilkes address this need directly, Pinn with a theory-based explanation and Gilkes by providing an account of historical tactics aimed at meeting this need, as well as a structural model explaining the ways Black churches support healthy psychosocial functioning.

Pinn's understanding of Black church aesthetics starts by locating the Diaspora as a continued "something that is in transition": African Americans are within this ongoing sense of movement or suspended state.[9] The aesthetics of the African American church reflects this liminality. Pinn invokes the claim of anthropologist Donald Carter that "rather than seeking 'assimilation' as a goal, diaspora is a way of being 'other' among the established, of keeping alive the drama of the voyage of 'otherness' in worlds that seek sameness and homogeneity."[10] Those within the Diaspora can neither return to the past and its type of resolution or total-ness, nor move into or take on (or in) the presented alternatives of colonial cultures in other places. Aesthetic mechanisms in African American churches hold this tension of sustaining "otherness" between landing points, retaining and remembering elements of the past/tradition, fending off the impositions of hegemonic structures, and fashioning selfhoods that reflect this continued "voyage." Pinn places the "aesthetic representation and expression of religion in the African diaspora" as "connected intimately to the body and issues of embodiment."[11] Diasporic aesthetics and religion are always—at least partially if not primarily—concerned with the movement (voyage) of the body as part of the total self through a homogenous-aspiring world that demands assimilation.[12] Put differently, Diasporic aesthetics and religion must always be with the body. They *must* be, in response to a body-repressive, and Black body–antagonistic, context of social assimilation where this retention of connection to and affirmation of embodiment is critical to individual and group survival. An aesthetically derived contestation for life is therefore inclusive of movement, of dress, of food, of vocal cadence and speech patterns, and of rhythm.[13] As Pinn writes, "Aesthetic representations of religiosity involve a *re-presenting* of Black bodies counter to the discourse, logic, and sociocultural representatives of white superiority."[14] This re-presentation moves and functions as a mode of the movement characteristic of the Diasporic voyage of otherness and is contained within it. It remembers a past, sees and anticipates a caricature offered by assimilation and oppression, and then devises a response.

It might be helpful, especially for folks outside of the tradition or for folks who do not invest much meaning in clothing, to consider the usher's uniform in conversation with other uniforms in Diasporic locations. Robert Beckford, a scholar-activist and documentary filmmaker, writes about the specifics and optics of a Black man in a suit and about the role of dress more broadly in Diasporic churches. Beckford argues that "dressing up for Sunday worships symbolizes ... conflict, a double-speak of personal empowerment and social passivity."[15] It is possible for the gestured response to contain a sort of deception that uses elements of a hegemonic aesthetic (white America or colonial Britain, for example), and repurposes and refashions them in a way that edifies and testifies to the histories, personalities, whims, and values of the wearer and their community.[16] In Beckford's eyes, dress contains within it a "semiotics of active radicalism," whereby ritual and its components can go beyond "social passivity" and take on, by way of deception and/or signifying, a liberative praxis.[17] Dress and other aesthetic mechanisms (dance, speech, etc.) then become an enactment or reflection of what Pinn terms "aesthetic grammar—notions of wholeness, beauty, balance, meaning, integrity," in ways that are also about relationship to history and a means by "which lived experience is formed and shaped."[18] Just as grammar in a linguistic context guides communication, an aesthetic grammar allows for a cohesive creation and presentation of ideas and concepts using the individual elements of style, tradition, texture, memory—to make a paragraph you need sentences, and to make sentences you need both words and an agreed-upon order that allows the words to take on meaning beyond their individual definitions. Aesthetically, how one individual or group wears something, or does something, relies upon aesthetic grammar to explore and articulate a more elaborate, nuanced meaning.

Wearing a white uniform holds a parallel to the wearing of a suit. The uniform is composed of pieces deemed acceptable and normative by hegemonic colonial structure, and is seemingly devoid of elements from other coasts and from the past. It contains in it the conflict of gestures, with the wearer putting on an image of power that could be read as placating the push for assimilation, but which may also be a deception or inversion that allows for a Diasporic motion to take place, so that something "other" is fashioned in a way that creates affirmation for the wearer.

AESTHETIC ACTION

Turning to the work of Gilkes can help us understand how this view of aesthetic mechanisms and aesthetic grammar works to affirm identity and culture specifically in African American churches, while deflecting or proving wrong external, white impositions. In *The Black Church as a Therapeutic Community*, Gilkes outlines four major therapeutic functions of the Black church: the articulation of suffering, the location of persecutors, the provision of asylum for "acting out," and the validation of experiences (both communal and individual). Gilkes argues that "an understanding of the therapeutic function of the black church would be beneficial not only for advancing an understanding of the essence of black culture but also an understanding of how the healing functions" of churches and other community institutions "can be better explained."[19] Within the community of the church and the space of its ritual, individuals are safe enough to "give accounts of the saddest and most troubling aspects of their personal lives without fear of punishment."[20] If we return to Pinn's use of Carter's understanding of the Diaspora, then we might consider this set of four therapeutic functions to be reflective of an awareness of the "worlds that seek sameness and homogeneity" via assimilation.[21] The provision of space to "act out" and to have one's experiences validated as real, important, and viable sites for spiritual thought and formation reflect the ongoing process of "keeping alive the drama of the voyage of 'otherness,'" in other words, the creation and sustenance of variations of an unconquered, unassimilated self.

A more nuanced appreciation of white uniforms emerges in the light of this discourse. Black church women assembling and wearing uniforms function in way that is similar to Robert Beckford's suit: personally empowering yet also reading as socially passive to hegemonic culture, and containing in the act itself the capacity to develop and/or signify radical intention. Beckford's suit draws power and salience as a symbol due to the uniformed history of earlier movements, like the Nation of Islam and Black Power movements in the United States and the United Kingdom. Rather than recreating or paralleling the monotony of assimilation, the cultivation of uniform in Diasporic traditions signals and sustains the "otherness" identified by Carter and Pinn in a way that leaves space for both personal flair and coded understanding within community.

Cheryl Townsend Gilkes charts the commitment to white uniforms as rooted both in beliefs around holiness and sanctification, and in a social, political gesture along the lines described by Pinn, Beckford, and others.[22] The intentionality of dress is also affirmed by historian of African American religion Anthea D. Butler, who documents the wearing of white at

Women's Day conventions, as well as the wearing of white each Sunday by church mothers in some Church of God in Christ (COGIC) churches. However, Butler notes that within COGIC the practice was not exclusively a political gesture; purity columns from COGIC newsletters emphasize the importance of Sanctified women presenting a pure image that would not lead their brothers into lust or cause sin. Although this theology was not exclusive to Sanctified settings, in this context it was also heavily emphasized that women were not to be seen in the color red, which belonged to Jezebel, or wearing makeup or earrings, which indicated an oncoming moral death.[23] This does not necessarily negate Gilkes's position concerning the wearing of a uniform as a resistant act, but it does establish context and nuance, underscoring that no one interpretation speaks to the intentions of all women wearing such a uniform.

Gilkes considers the function of uniforms within a context of ideas concerning the visibility of "holiness." This may also be described in some settings as evidence of sanctification. Depending on the church or tradition, purification may come before sanctification, or they may be concurrent.[24] Sanctification here includes a sense that the visible life of the saints should reflect internal and external changes, such that the saints look and act differently from those who are not among the elect.[25] Being set apart from the world includes being set apart from the racist stereotypes and hegemonic attempts of dominant culture. As Gilkes writes, "In order to counter the stereotypes used as rationales for the abuse of black women, Sanctified Church women were encouraged to 'dress as becometh holiness.'"[26] This encouragement puts forth a "challenge" to "the construction and confinement of Black bodies (as metaphor and material) through the mechanisms of slavery, colonization, and continued hardship."[27] The origins of the Sanctified Church, including the national conventions to which many women in leadership traveled, took place in an era characterized by segregated travel, legalized Jim Crow, and blatant stereotypes concerning Black women, their bodies, and sexuality. Cultivating a general code of dress for Sanctified women served as a sort of social armor:[28]

> [Lay] women wore black or uniformlike dress, and evangelists and church mothers devised a uniform or "habit" called "the Saint" to wear in services and on trains. At regional or national meetings, the highest ranking woman—the district missionary, the district supervisor, or the national

supervisor—determined the dress of all other women present and decided whether they wore white on a particular day. While this may seem a rather trivial matter, the problem of discipline was not, and clergymen were required to adhere to equally stringent dress codes.[29]

By cultivating and donning this uniform, "the women . . . achieved such a position of respect and autonomy that they defined the content of their own roles."[30]

The idea of the uniform as a sign of professionalism is not incidental: the women of the Sanctified Church made a calculated choice as to what would allow them to move through the world with a relative sense of freedom and enable them to take up leadership roles in which they could use their own gifts and insights. Within the Sanctified Church, women were engaged in important educating, organizing, and leadership efforts in the church and community. The wearing of white became not just a political aesthetic, it was also a theological comment, supposing a wrestling with scripture and interpretation, including scriptures about the role of women in church leadership.[31] Particularly, it became theological as a statement of the relationship between women and God, and what roles, or "calls," women can have in and on their lives as emissaries of God and the gospel. Later paralleled in Black and Womanist theology, the Christology that emboldened Sanctified women to take up authority and white robes seems to suggest that God is on and at their side, rather than removed and accessed only via male power or external rites of approval. Their own experiences of conversion and transformation were enough to declare themselves sanctified. This aesthetically performed theology was and is political, both in its refutation of oppression and in its ability to pave ways to new structural and social orders. By developing the uniform, "these women have legitimized the image of the 'professional' woman throughout the church. As a result, women . . . have established a more differentiated model of social mobility and occupational aspiration than have the men."[32] Wearing the pressed white uniform becomes a statement, then, that women can be both holy and in charge, devout without being voiceless.

Ethicist, Womanist, and pastor Cheryl J. Sanders writes about wearing white for Women's Day—a less denominationally tied practice—to express a sense of surrender to God. Sanders maps this surrender as a radical practice that actually creates freedom and strength for believers, empowering them to separate from and resist the hurtful impulses of the physical world, and to receive a sense of value and identity from God and release from the version of self that the world has offered.[33] Women in church who are uniformed declare their primary orientation and commitment to be to God, freeing them of the gaze of racism and patriarchy, and granting them the space to take up or develop new roles as part of a divine call. Because wearing white is connected to sanctification and holiness, it signifies that the women are already worthy in the eyes of God, and are prepared to do holy work. Scripturally, the white uniforms, like the robes of baptism, prefigure the biblical book of Revelation's dispensation of new robes for the saints, and culturally signifies expectations that after suffering "(we're) gonna put on (our) robe(s) and tell the story."[34] The uniform creates and affirms an alternate space, like the liminal ongoing creation of otherness of the broader Diaspora aesthetic, wherein Black women negate the constriction of hegemonic expectations (racist images, patriarchal denial of women taking up roles) and avoid constructing a false binary or mirrored opposite, developing instead an opportunity for newness and the option of "other."

The uniform, then, acts upon both the wearer and the person who sees the wearer; it is something that is done as well as something that is witnessed or seen. In church parlance it might be said the wearer is testifying (by talking/doing via wearing) and that those who "get it" (who see it and process the layers of what is happening) are witnesses; those who see without comprehension are the uninitiated, the non-elect. Being seen by the surrounding world outside the community does not make the act "real" or valid; the Diasporic religious aesthetic assumes both the sight of community (including ancestors) and the sight of God resting upon the doer. Returning to Pinn, it can be argued that the sight of the aesthetic practice—wearing white uniforms—does real work on the wearer and on the viewer, including addressing the spoken or unspoken perceptions that are brought to bear before, during, and after the visual moment.[35] Gilkes suggests that Sanctified women chose to wear their uniforms during travel precisely because it would disrupt the racialized, stereotyped gaze—in other words, that it would interject and disrupt the way the women were seen. Cultivating a uniform is a recognition that there is a disconnect in the way Black women see themselves and each other, and the ways that they are seen by white supremacists, by patriarchal forces, and by colonial power structures. Donning a uniform does not erase these violent, external perceptions, functions of "worlds that seek sameness and homogeneity," which by default render Black and Brown bodies external and whose primary aesthetic is constructed in favor of the colonizer and in opposition to the colonized.[36] However, the uniform does signal that Black women, countering the colonial aesthetic, see themselves as valuable, professional, capable, and sanctified. Though it cannot force a conversion of dominant (i.e., white) ways of seeing, the uniform challenges the preconceived notions of white sight to see differently, in part by playing with the elements of respectability and "appropriate" performance expected by the hegemonic external, and then making something new, something Diasporic.

In creating a uniform, Black church women address a number of limited "sights," ranging from white racism, which would not see them as holy, to patriarchy, which would not see them as authoritative. On one level, the wearing of white uniforms anticipates the problem of sight and interpretation skewed by bigotry, and develops a response that attempts to disrupt the pattern. But if we believe that this gesture is performed not in assimilation but in a Diasporic ethic/aesthetic of otherness, then we must believe that Black church women are also invoking other lines of sight, including self-perception and divine gaze. To see differently requires a belief in some other, less literal seeing, which could include the fantastic or the supernatural, or could also involve an active effort to see in a way that takes account of one's internalized biases and that seeks to imagine or search for alternate perceptions.

WHITE UNIFORMS AS POLITICAL THEOLOGY

In reflecting on sanctification, it is worth expanding on the idea of the wearing of white robes as prefiguration of the Revelation promise of new robes for the saints. This concept provides an opportunity to consider the wearing of white uniforms in a way that is overtly theological, or overtly concerned about God and humanity together. Besides an awareness of the limited sight of the material white gaze, Black church women anticipate and respond to a divine gaze in ways that say something about how God sees Black church women, and about how Black church women are obligated to respond, in their view of themselves and each other, and in aesthetic performance. Being and beingness are then conferred not by the limits of the material gaze but rather from a stream of divine immanence, starting with the first "it was/is good" of the first verses of Genesis. This gesture then contains multiple levels of sight as well as a transgression of time, collapsing the temporal and the expected eternal.

Several verses in the book of Revelation are concerned specifically with the wearing of white robes and/or white linen by the saints. Revelation 6:11 describes robes being given to those under an altar, who have already died as martyrs, as they are told to hold out a little longer before the final resolution. Revelation 7:9–17 describes a great multitude, "of every nation and tongue," dressed in white linen and declaring the goodness of the Lord. Revelation 19:14 describes Jesus's triumphal final battle, the son of God riding out in a white tunic dipped in blood and surrounded by an army wearing clean white linen. As a whole, Revelation is ripe with reference to new names, new robes, white clothing, and folks receiving these things as part of their transformation and welcome into a post-evil eternal existence.[37] It is possible to consider the creation of starchy, professional white uniforms in light of these scriptures as an intentional claim about who the saints are, and how Black church women are seen by God, as part of this great sainthood and a mighty army arriving to depose evil. To dress as though already in the promised attire given to those who "endure unto the end" is to signify that one expects to be received by God and that one is already in active relationship with God. Moreover, because the outfits of Revelation come from God, it supposes that God sees and actively looks upon the wearer in order to bestow the new robes. Even if one takes the more sedate interpretation, mentioned in Revelation 19:8, that the linen is at times representative of the good actions and deeds of the saints, God's gaze is still implied and even expected, as it is believed that God gazes upon the just. To dress oneself in this manner, then, assumes that God looks upon the wearer favorably and with pleasure, and that the one so adorned deserves or has earned this new robe. It also biblically underscores the claims of authority that the uniform makes, linking the wearer to those who have undergone persecution as martyrs and to those chosen by Jesus to wage war against evil, symbolized in Revelation as Babylon.

The assumption of God's gaze also connotes value: that God sees not the stereotypes of this world but rather the spiritual capacity of the person, and the *total* creation, meaning the body along with this spiritual capacity. If the Revelation scriptures are read as reflecting folks who are dressed in their ultimate identity, then to wear a version of this identity on earth is to proclaim that one sees oneself as this ultimate identity rather than through the expectations of this world or its stereotypes. Butler has highlighted this position, writing, "sanctified clothing was not only a sexual deterrent; it also expressed purity and consecration ... White attire ... represented the surrender of all marks of personal style and distinctiveness in favor of total identification with the worshipping community and God. White attire was also an eschatological symbol, suggesting that the believer was the bride of Christ."[38] Sanctified clothing aims to project the biblical image in the temporal world, as a proclamation and act of faith; in addition to firm beliefs about the necessity of holiness in the believer's life, the clothing and aesthetic itself become signifiers of this holiness. One's state of beingness is placed, then, not in the hands or eyes of the hegemonic, assimilationist world, but rather in the eyes of God, who sees those who seek God and Godself as triumphant, as martyrs to be blessed, as bold soldiers overthrowing a demonic empire, as extravagant tailors whose deeds drape the heavens.

In order to hold this belief, one must trust in one's experiences of God, in the knowledge shared by elders and peers, and in one's own salvation and revelation experiences. Individuals' experiences must serve as appropriate sites from which to do theological interpretation. In other words, one is situated to believe the sincerity of God among the people, and to believe one's own experiences to be enough to know God without human interjection, and to be true.[39] To share this uniform with others indicates one's belief that though there are many roles for different individuals, ultimately there will be a multitude of celebrants seen and adorned by God. To take one's robe now is to signify utter assurance, and a refutation of the limitations of this world in favor of the citizenship of heaven. Yet this theological gesture is not solely an "otherworldly" one: by draping and presenting the self, by wearing the white uniform, one insists that there is value in the present world, in the living body, and in embodiment as part of spiritual identity. If the body were a mere distraction, it would make sense to ignore or dismiss it, to cloak it in a way that would draw no attention from an uncharitable material gaze. If Black church women wholeheartedly believed the lies of the colonial, hegemonic world around them, bodies would be seen as an obstacle to salvation, rather than a benefit within it deserving to be cloaked in white linen. Rather than shunning embodiment as a hindrance, the creation and cultivation of aesthetic practices like wearing uniforms demonstrates a belief that care for the body, the adornment of the body with signifiers of spiritual identity, is not only good but necessary in the process of creating a liberative experience in the midst of social constructs of limitation.

By considering the theoretical claims (all aesthetic action of the Diaspora is inherently a spiritual gesture), the sociopolitical implications (dress contains "semiotics of radicalism" that offer a deflection of oppression and an opportunity or at least contribution to liberation), and the historical political specifics of function (wearing a white uniform provided protection to Black church women while traveling and a visible sign of authority in church), we can conclude there is a lot more to wearing a white uniform in African American churches than simply an abstract desire to look nice. We might extend the theological possibilities of this particular action further, to ask what theologies speak from choir robes, from pocket squares, from the linens that drape the communion table. If anything, hopefully we are encouraged to understand that rituals and traditions contain active political theologies, and that we can look to the aesthetics of African American Protestant traditions and find therein significant God talk.

NOTES

1. Significant ethnographic work about African American and Black churches has been done by Black folk, and is crucial, important work. This is not meant to dismiss such work; rather, I am deeply aware that we need such work, and more of it. My claim is that the work of the archive, the work of ethnographic, sociological, and other statistical forms, can and does then compel us to ask philosophical and/or theological questions, while giving us the tools we need to document or 'prove' validity to those who are intent on devaluing. In many cases the works of historians and ethnographers have served to preserve and declare valuable, to protect the practices and traditions they write about, an impulse often shared by theologians. We might understand the impetus to document and explain religious ritual and habit first, as it is out of these experiences that we do our theologizing and look for the

theologizing of other folk. In a way, this impulse and logic underpins not only Charles Long's work but also of womanist theology, and guides Anthony B. Pinn's emphasis on a spiritual "norm" in the Diasporic aesthetic, rather than seeking prevailing theological claims.

2. There is good reason for this lack of overt exploration of habits, patterns, and traditions, principally a fear of "decoding," or offering up to white audiences a thorough explanation of African American choices and patterns. To decode or provide too much information is to endanger the self and those you love. This ethic continues today, with good reason.

3. Annie Staten and Susan Roach, "Take Me to the Water: African-American River Baptism," in *Delta Pieces: Northeast Louisiana Folklife*, ed. Susan Roach and Maida Owens (Baton Rouge: Folklife in Louisiana, 2013), http://www.louisianafolklife.org/LT/Articles_Essays/creole_art_river_baptism.html; National Geographic, "Rare Footage: Hundreds Gather at a 1920s African-American Baptism," YouTube, October 30, 2016, https://www.youtube.com/watch?v=akaAMYGJ44k; Arthur Huff Fauset, *Black Gods of the Metropolis: Negro Religious Cults in the Urban North* (Philadelphia: University of Pennsylvania Press, 1971), 26, 63, 104.

4. "Sanctified" refers to churches that were born out of the Holiness movement or the doctrine of total sanctification. This includes what is today the Church of God in Christ, Church of God (i.e., the Sanctified Church), and other churches that have or currently define themselves as aspiring to holiness and sanctification as evidence of their salvation. This doctrine emphasizes the indwelling of the Holy Spirit that works with the washing of the believer in the blood of Jesus to clean and perfect the believer. One can learn more about some of these church denominations directly through their websites and social media, where you can also read doctrinal statements and other materials. See, for example, the Church of God in Christ (https://www.cogic.org/, accessed June 7, 2021), Original Church of God (https://www.originalchurchofgod.org/, accessed June 7, 2021), and the Christ Holy Sanctified Church of America (https://www.chschurch.org/history/, accessed June 7, 2021). See Sherry S. Dupree, *African-American Pentecostal Holiness Movement: An Annotated Bibliography* (New York: Routledge, 1996), for details on denominational traditions and statistics. See also Zora Neal Hurston, *The Sanctified Church* (New York: Marlowe, 1998).

5. Cheryl Townsend Gilkes, "'Together and in Harness': Women's Traditions in the Sanctified Church," *Signs: Journal of Women in Culture and Society* 10, no. 4 (1985): 685.

6. Cheryl J. Sanders, "African-American Worship in the Pentecostal and Holiness Movements," *Wesleyan Theological Journal* 32, no. 2 (Fall 1997): 111, 114.
7. Anthony B. Pinn, "Introduction: The Black Labyrinth, Aesthetics, and Black Religion," in *Black Religion and Aesthetics: Religious Thought and Life in Africa and the African Diaspora*, ed. Anthony B. Pinn (New York: Palgrave Macmillan, 2009), 9.
8. Pinn, 8, 9.
9. Pinn, 3.
10. Donald Carter, "Preface," in *New African Diasporas*, ed. Khalid Kaser (New York: Routledge, 2003) x; Pinn, "Introduction," 3. See also M. Shawn Copeland, "Blackness Past, Blackness Future, and Theology," in *South Atlantic Quarterly* 112, no. 4 (2013): 625–26.
11. Pinn, "Introduction," 3–4.
12. In other words, the body as a material component of a total or whole identity, rather than the Euro-normative mind-body divide.
13. Pinn, "Introduction," 4.
14. Pinn, 7; emphasis mine.
15. Robert Beckford, "Black Suit Matters: Faith, Politics, and Representation in the Religious Documentary," in Pinn, ed., *Black Religion and Aesthetics*, 137.
16. Pinn, "Introduction"; Beckford, "Black Suit Matters."
17. Beckford, "Black Suit Matters," 138.
18. Pinn, "Introduction," 7.
19. Cheryl Townsend Gilkes, "The Black Church as a Therapeutic Community: Suggested Areas for Research Into the Black Religious Experience," *Journal of the Interdenominational Theological Center* 8, no. 1 (Fall 1980): 32.
20. Gilkes, 36.
21. Carter, "Preface," x.
22. Gilkes, "'Together and in Harness.'"
23. Anthea D. Butler, *Women in the Church of God in Christ: Making a Sanctified World* (Chapel Hill: University of North Carolina Press, 2012), 83.
24. Walter Pitts, "Keep the Fire Burnin': Language and Ritual in the Afro-Baptist Church," *Journal of the American Academy of Religion* 56, no. 1 (Spring 1988): 86; Sanders, "African-American Worship in the Pentecostal and Holiness Movements," 107.
25. Use of the word "sanctified" is more common in Pentecostal, Holiness, and Sanctified traditions. Churches associate themselves with these words via denomination, church name, and in their creeds or professed beliefs. For churches that retain a connection to Baptist or other traditions, the word

"sanctified" may or may not be invoked, but a process of purification and initiation may be reflected in rules or talk about appropriate spiritual maturity. Scriptures used often in sanctification talk include "work out your own salvation with fear and trembling" (Phil. 2:12), "be conformed to the likeness of Christ" (Rom. 12:2–3), and others.
26. Gilkes, "'Together and in Harness,'" 685.
27. Pinn, "Introduction," 9.
28. Rules about dress that are connected both to a group understanding of holiness and to a desire to refute racist assumptions are also documented in the development of other African American religious groups. For example, the Mount Sinai Holy Church also required that members should "dress holy," the Moorish Science Temple had rules around dress and styling of the body (no cosmetics, men must wear a fez, etc.), and the United House of Prayer for All People had a more general warning about "beautifying the person" unto vanity. See Fauset, *Black Gods of the Metropolis*, 20, 51, 30. This is important for later reflections about dress as an intentional, theological statement; while not literally the same as white uniforms, there is a connection here and a similarity of intent grounded in a shared Diasporic aesthetic, without which the particularity of specific rituals cannot be understood.
29. Gilkes, "'Together and in Harness,'" 685–86.
30. Gilkes writes extensively on how evangelists functioned as preachers, though they were not formally given that title. Evangelist was a gendered role for women, to "teach," and men were given to "preach," though the effects of the evangelists' teaching was not discernibly different from preaching. Gilkes ties the uniform into the process of role creation and women developing and sustaining power in the Sanctified Church. Note that "evangelist" in other traditions does not automatically assume gender, nor a specific uniform. Gilkes, "'Together and in Harness,'" 688–89; quote at 686.
31. Gilkes, 687–89.
32. Gilkes, 689.
33. Sanders, "African-American Worship in the Pentecostal and Holiness Movements," 113.
34. This line, rendered in variation across spirituals and folk songs, as well as more recent treatments of "I Shall Wear a Crown," reflects popular expectation of both heaven and the relationship between folks/saints and Jesus. Rather than distant, Jesus is someone to sit down with and talk directly. See also James Cone, *The Spirituals and the Blues: An Interpretation* (Maryknoll, NY: Orbis, 1992).

35. Pinn, "Introduction," 8–9.
36. Pinn, 6.
37. Even in the same denomination there is considerable variation among individuals on whether this is a singular heaven (a separate place) or simply a new world and new total life in which evil is completely obliterated.
38. Butler, Women in the Church of God in Christ, 83.
39. See James H. Cone, *God of the Oppressed* (New York: Seabury Press, 1975); Cone, *A Black Theology of Liberation* (Philadelphia: Lippincott, 1970); Delores S. Williams, *Sisters in the Wilderness: The Challenge of Womanist God-Talk* (Maryknoll, NY: Orbis, 1993); Ada Maria Isasi-Diaz, *En la Lucha/In the Struggle: A Hispanic Women's Liberation Theology* (Minneapolis: Fortress Press, 1993).

Thirteen

"THE HARE KRISHNA LOOK"

ISKCON ADORNMENT AS RELIGIOUS ACTIVISM

BENJAMIN E. ZELLER

FOLK SINGERS Pete Seeger and Arlo Guthrie provided the musical accompaniment to much of the 1960s and 1970s counterculture. One of their more popular songs, "Old Time Religion," satirized the identically named nostalgic paean to the Christian tradition, but substituting other "old time" religions, such as Buddhism, Zoroastrianism, Druidism, and Greek Paganism, for the original song's Christianity. They played it live, so the verses often changed. But most versions of the song included a verse on the Hare Krishnas, the alternative religious movement that swept through the counterculture at the time. The Hare Krishnas, they sang, "dressed in saffron, with hair that's only half on." Two things are remarkable about the song's treatment of the Hare Krishnas: first, Seeger and Guthrie recognized the "old time" antiquity of the movement, which, while it was formally incorporated in 1966 in New York City, traces its point of origin to ancient Hindu tradition. But more importantly for our purposes, the verse's content entirely revolves around the image of bodily adornment.

The Hare Krishna propensity to adorn the body differently, donning Indian garments and hair styles considered aberrant by mainstream culture, attracted wide popular attention. Seeger and Guthrie pointed to adherents' saffron robes and the *sikha* (shaved head with a small ponytail lock, which they described as "hair that's only half on"). The "Hare

Krishna look" indeed became an identifying feature, often tied to the group's activities, such as book distribution and public chanting and dancing, almost always performed while religiously adorned. Media frequently highlighted devotees' physical appearances. The first major newspaper to note the arrival of the Hare Krishna movement into the countercultural scene, the *New York Times*, went to the trouble of including an image of the saffron-clad devotees in its first article on the movement, in October 1966. The image, in fact, covered as much of the page as the text did.[1] The pattern was repeated in one of the first major Christian polemic articles against the new movement, "The Eastern Mystics Are Out to Take You In," published in the *Moody Monthly*. A full-page color illustration of a Hare Krishna devotee in full religious garb led the three-page article in this fundamentalist Protestant magazine.[2] This set the mold for later coverage. How Hare Krishna devotees dressed seemed to attract almost as much attention as what they believed or did.

While one can analyze Hare Krishna adornment patterns in a variety of ways, especially by looking at treatments in the press or pop culture, one of the more notable developments within the movement involves their own turn toward conceptualizing and explaining their adornment choices. While early devotees adorned themselves in the "Hare Krishna look" for a variety of reasons, by the early 1970s the movement's leaders increasingly deployed their bodily adornment as a means of positioning themselves within broader culture, critiquing mainstream society, and carving a niche for themselves as a source of alternative religious legitimacy. Hare Krishna bodily adornment functioned as a form of cultural activism, challenging broader norms and providing an alternate perspective. This chapter looks to how Hare Krishna members themselves talked about their clothing, primarily by analyzing over sixty years of written material in their official magazine, *Back to Godhead*, a publication that was read internally by members and distributed externally as a form of proselytizing and publicity.

THE HARE KRISHNA MOVEMENT AND COUNTERCULTURAL RELIGION IN POSTWAR AMERICA

The rise of new and alternative religion was an indelible part of the youth counterculture of the 1960 and 1970s. Among these new religions, one of the most notable was the Hare Krishna movement, formally called the International Society for Krishna Consciousness (ISKCON), which was founded by the Indian monastic A. C. Bhaktivedanta (1896–1977), called by the honorific "Prabhupada" by his followers, and also by the title "Swami," a traditional Hindu honorific for a guru or yogic master (hence, his full title, A. C. Bhaktivedanta Swami Prabhupada, shortened to Bhaktivedanta here).[3] Bhaktivedanta promulgated a Bengali form of devotional monotheistic Hinduism that falls within the broad category of Gaudiya Vaishnavism, a sixteenth-century Hindu reform movement emphasizing devotionalism (or *bhakti*, meaning devotion) over other forms of practice.[4] This religion calls for devotional service to the god Krishna,[5] understood by his devotees as the "supreme personality of Godhead," in the words of ISKCON. As in broader Hinduism, Krishna takes multiple avatar forms and can be venerated in any of these, but adherents believe Krishna is his true form. Bhaktivedanta's specific movement called for public singing, processions, and preaching, and unlike most other Hindu groups, endorsed proselytizing.

Sent by his spiritual master to North America, Bhaktivedanta hoped originally to appeal to educated elites, like his predecessors the swamis Vivekananda (1863–1902) and Yogananda (1893–1952), Hindu proponents who successfully formed American associations of upper- and middle-class spiritual cosmopolitans in the first half of the twentieth century. Yet Bhaktivedanta arrived in the mid-1960s in New York City, the heart of the East Coast counterculture, rather than among the earlier moneyed bohemian classes. His public preaching, literature distribution, chanting, and giving away of free Indian food in New York City's Bowery district, and later in Haight-Ashbury, the heart of the San Francisco counterculture, attracted primarily hippies and aging beatniks. Beatnik poet Allen Ginsburg was briefly a proponent, as was a decade later George Harrison of the Beatles.

The hippies who flocked to Bhaktivedanta and with him instituted ISKCON formed part of what scholar of religion Harvey Cox has called the "turn East," the tendency among American spiritual seekers during this period to look to Asian religious traditions for alternative forms of spiritual fulfillment.[6] Bhaktivedanta and his Hare Krishna movement offered an entirely alternative subcultural identity, and called for replacing most aspects of Western mainstream society with their vision of ancient Indian religious-cultural society. Calling this "Vedic civilization," a reference to the ancient texts undergirding the Hindu religion, the Hare Krishnas hoped to supplant Western civilization with a Vedic alternative.

Religious veneration of Krishna (*bhakti*) functioned at the heart of what ISKCON understood to be its Vedic model. But ISKCON's Vedic vision also included numerous social norms, including social structures, family relations, gender norms, educational systems, and governmental standards. ISKCON not only called for replacing these norms in broader society, but also attempted to model how to do so within its own subculture. The movement's Vedic approach also extended to cultural patterns, such as food and cooking, art, and music. Importantly, clothing, and bodily adornment in the widest sense, crossed over into all these categories: as religious practices, social norms, and cultural expression. Devotees' embrace of Hare Krishna adornment practices was therefore not only a personal spiritual act, but a political one, part of the movement's activist agenda to transform Western society as a whole, one person at a time.

THE "HARE KRISHNA LOOK": ISKCON ADORNMENT IN THE EARLY YEARS

In her study of women's veiling in the Islamic tradition, religious studies scholar Elizabeth M. Bucar cautions against too narrow a focus on the "politics or ethics" of adornment practices and ignoring the "aesthetic dimensions" of the clothing and other adornments themselves.[7] Taking a nod from Bucar, students of the ISKCON aesthetic must recognize the adornment style itself, and not just its political resonance. The aesthetics of ISKCON adornment, labeled "the Hare Krishna look"[8] by an editor of the movement's *Back to Godhead* magazine, act in a powerful manner on not only outsiders, but on devotees as well. While widely associated with saffron robes and shaved heads, Hare Krishna sartorial aesthetics display far greater variability.

Because ISKCON devotees envision themselves as reconstituting Vedic religious civilization, they look to India to shape both their wardrobe and adornment practices as well as the religious norms of the wider Gaudiya Vaishnavism sect of Hinduism of which they are a part. But the 1960s and 1970s counterculture also left an indelible impact on the movement. Devotees' clothing and other adornment choices vary according to not only gender but the particular stages of life, or *ashramas*, through which individuals pass. This worldview, drawn from and shared with the broader Hindu tradition, divides life into four categories: children and young adults, called *brahmacharyis*; householders concerned with raising families, known as *grihasthas*; retirees looking beyond worldly pursuits toward spiritual self-fulfillment, or *vanaprasthas*; and religious renunciates, or *sanyasis*, sometimes also called monks or nuns. Within ISKCON, individuals—almost always men, though women had an alternative path—might progress directly from one of the earlier categories to the last stage, becoming a renunciate, or *sanyasi*, rather than starting a family or pursuing a gradual retirement. Widows represent another category, somewhat similar to the retirees in terms of their turning away from the world. Men and women in each of these categories adorn themselves differently, both in the broader Hindu tradition and also within ISKCON. Furthermore, devotees' adornment practices vary depending on the extent to which they have dedicated themselves to the ISKCON movement—that is, whether they are members of the movement but have not undergone formal religious initiation, have undergone an initial religious initiation, or are fully initiated and have therefore made lifetime vows of dedication and service.

Formal adornment requirements aside, those attending Hare Krishna temples as visitors reflect their immediate (sub)cultural context. Guests to ISKCON temples or other religious services typically adorn themselves in whatever style they prefer. During the movement's first decades, when it attracted primarily hippies, such guests often arrived adorned as other members of the counterculture, whereas today's visitors generally dress in a more contemporary manner. Some counterculturally oriented guests, both then and now, adopted elements of Asian adornment; as Cox noted, many of the young people attracted to the Hare Krishna movement looked to Asia for inspiration.[9] Guests arriving in the 1960s and 1970s already bedecked in saris, dhotis, Nehru jackets, or other Indian garments would have felt immediately at home. Today's guests may arrive dressed in business casual, Asian-inspired fashion, or clothing identified with other subcultural identities, such as punk, straight edge, or freegan. While uninitiated members were under no formal compunction to dress in the ISKCON style, frequent attendees—even before formally joining—were encouraged to do so. Scholar of the movement E. Burke Rochford noted that adherence to the movement's clothing norms served as a requirement for new recruits during the 1960s and 1970s, and even today it is often assumed before a new devotee becomes initiated into the movement.[10] Rochford's interviews with devotees indicated that most already had existing spiritual inclinations and had explored Asian alternatives to Western religions.

Once a person declared their formal intent to become a member of ISKCON, they could become initiated, meaning that they became a formal student of Bhaktivedanta (or after his death, other ISKCON gurus), and therefore adopted the regulative principles of membership in the movement. This included accepting religious regulations on everything from diet to sex, vowing to recite prayers at certain times, and being granted a new Sanskrit name within the movement. It also entailed accepting a set of adornment norms, some of which were formal religious requirements, while others were not officially required but nevertheless sanctioned by the movement as part of the "Vedic culture" they sought to promulgate.

Most importantly, initiated members vowed to adorn themselves with the *tilaka* marks, U-shaped clay marks applied to the forehead. Those applying *tilaka* follow specific requirements: the two arms of the u start just above the eyebrows, and reach to the top of the forehead, about as wide as a thumb's width. At their base, they join in an inverted teardrop shape said to resemble a leaf of the sacred *tulasi* plant. The marks symbolize aspects of the Vaishnava theology, and their application therefore represents an inscription of the movement's central theological claims upon the body. A contemporary ISKCON teachers explains the marks in this way: "The upper part of this tilaka, shaped like the prongs of a tuning-fork, represents Lord Krishna's footprint, and the leaf-shaped part on the nose represents a leaf of the tulasi, Krishna's favorite plant. The two lines also represent the walls of a Radha-Krishna temple, and so the space between the lines is Radha and Krishna's abode."[11] Skilled devotees can apply the *tilaka* at home, though neophytes and children may need assistance. The process takes some time, as the movement's principles call for preparing the paste each day using clay from one of several sacred lakes and rivers in India. Importing or purchasing such clay functions as a form of religious devotion for Hare Krishna members, though ordinary clay is permitted if such sacred clay is unavailable or if one lacks the ability or funds to procure it. Bhaktivedanta taught that devotees should recite the movement's central "Hare Krishna" mantra as they prepare and apply the

IMAGE 13.1 An ISKCON devotee with the *tilaka* mark. Image credit: Sipa USA via AP Images.

paste, which marks the bodily practice as not only an adornment rite but also a meditative one.

In keeping with the norms of Gaudiya Vaishnavism, Bhaktivedanta taught that application of *tilaka* served as a mandatory part of devotional service to Krishna. It also served as a visible sign for all to see of one's devotional service and identity. In his *The Nectar of Devotion*, a translation and summary of a sixteenth-century devotional manual, Bhaktivedanta explained that "One should decorate the body with tilaka, which is the sign of the Vaiṣṇavas. (The idea is that as soon as a person sees these marks on the body of the Vaiṣṇava, he will immediately remember Kṛṣṇa. Lord Caitanya said that a Vaiṣṇava is he who, when seen, reminds one of Kṛṣṇa. Therefore, it is essential that a Vaiṣṇava mark his body with tilaka to remind others of Kṛṣṇa.)"[12] The meditative function combines with this public role of reminding oneself and others of Krishna, meaning that *tilaka* also serves an evangelistic purpose, sharing Krishna consciousness with others. The entirely private, meditative, personally meaningful aspects of the *tilaka* adornment cannot be separated from *tilaka* as a form of cultural activism, spreading the awareness of Krishna into the public sphere.

The *tilaka* mark served as the most important ritual adornment practice for an initiated member of the Hare Krishna movement, but it was not the practice that attracted the most attention, nor did ISKCON members discuss it at great length. This is for two reasons. First, from an insider perspective, the practice was simply assumed as a requirement, and had very little variance from one individual to another. There was not much to say once one learned how to apply it. But second, and from an outsider perspective, the *tilaka* is small and, while hard to ignore, is far less noticeable than the clothing worn by devotees. ISKCON clothing therefore assumed most of the attention of both insider and outsider discussion of Hare Krishna adornment.

Bhaktivedanta provided changing and context-specific guidance on clothing during his lifetime. On one hand, he modeled for his devotees a tireless focus on the culture of Krishna consciousness. Bhaktivedanta eschewed Western dress, just as he did Western food, music, and literature, wearing exclusively the saffron robe appropriate for his station as a *sanyasi* (monk). Those of his disciples who also took monastic vows did the same and continue to do so to this day. Yet even among disciples who did not take the *sanyasi* vow and lived as either students or householders, most adopted Indian dressing styles. Since their guru taught that Vedic civilization ought to supplant Western civilization, this is hardly surprising. Most men in the movement adopted the practice of wearing the dhoti, a stretch of cotton fabric, usually white in color, wrapped around the bottom half of the body. They often paired this with a kurta, a light-weight Indian shirt. Women tended to wear saris: long drapes of fabric, generally colorful, wrapped over most of the body. Men and women also wore traditional Indian undergarments appropriate for dhotis and saris. Indian garb was, in other words, the norm.

Interestingly, Bhaktivedanta did not mandate this practice. In a 1968 epistle written to the president of the New York City temple and sent from San Francisco, where the group was then expanding, the swami offered guidance on adornment:

> Householders may wear dhotis in the Temple, or as they like, but not of the saffron color. They may wear white, yellow, or whatever. Outside the Temple they may wear American gentleman's dress, with *tilaka*, flag, and beads. It is not required to wear dhotis, as this society does not understand, so

IMAGE 13.2 ISKCON women in saris. Image courtesy of Wikimedia Commons/Creative Commons.

outside the Temple dress suit is more socially acceptable. If they so desire, for ceremony, they can dress in dhotis for Kirtana [sung worship].[13]

Here Bhaktivedanta prescribes (for non-*sanyasis*) only the *tilaka* and proscribes only the saffron color identified with formal renunciates. He permits Western clothing outside of formal worship, and even allows it for devotional service. While he did not explicitly address women's clothing choices—the swami tended to assume a male audience[14]—his guidance held for women as well. Bhaktivedanta seemed to understand that cultural adaptation to the norms of North America required abandoning some aspects of Vedic culture. Yet on the other hand, his advice was highly situational. Writing just two years later to a disciple about to depart for India, he suggested that he "embark the plane wearing western clothes but to be sure to disembark wearing a dhoti."[15]

The Hare Krishna founder also seemed to recognize that his movement's adornment practices functioned as a political act, a form of cultural activism. Cultural studies scholar Mary Lou O'Neil, writing of the clothing choices in contemporary, globalized Turkey, explains that "clothing and appearance are deeply rooted in politics at all levels from that of the state to the grass roots. Clothing can be used to protest, assimilate, and/or pass in an attempt to negotiate various situations ... All of these are deeply rooted in the politics of power."[16] O'Neil argues that modern Turks wear their political and social sentiments on their bodies, adorning themselves in ways that mark them as identifying with particular social and political movements. The ISKCON adornment norms functioned similarly, and for similar reasons. Like the Turkish moderns that O'Neil studies, ISKCON adherents identify themselves as living on the threshold of two cultures, the Western and a non-Western alternative. For Turks, the alternative is a fusion of Ottoman styles, pan-Islamic clothing, and imagined nostalgic tradition. For Hare Krishna devotees, it is the Indian adornment practices they associate with Vedic civilization and culture, which they hope will one day supplant that of the West.

Bhaktivedanta frequently contrasted his own disciples' adornment practices, which he identified as part of proper Vedic civilization, against the adornment norms of the West, which he envisioned as corrupting and sinful. In a public address in London in 1970, he railed against "fashionable dresses" as markers of people concerned only with their sex lives, comparing these items to "atom bombs" that are indicative of only the basest forms of animal existence, concerned with procreation and protection.[17] This remarkable comparison reveals the extent to which the swami disapproved of Western adornment practices that he believed emphasized bodily pleasure or display, despite permitting "gentlemen's dress" to his (male) devotees. As other scholars have noted, Bhaktivedanta assumed a highly patriarchal approach to gender relations and understood female sexuality as requiring careful management and curtailing. In associating "fashionable dress" with sexuality, he equated the two. Those who wore such clothing, he indicated, "are no better than the animals."[18]

The swami clearly recognized the persuasive political power of adornment, not unlike O'Neil's Turkish subjects. In 1977, shortly before his death and after the massive growth of ISKCON had slowed, several disciples approached the swami about forming a musical band to aid in outreach. These disciples, American converts to the movement, hoped that the Krishna band would book television appearances and therefore had a keen eye to their physical presentation. They suggested they dress like other rock bands of the day. But when they asked the elderly swami if the band members might wear wigs so as to cover their shaved heads, or wear clothing other than their robes, their guru rejected this plea. "That must be there," he said. When pushed, he avowed that the band members might "dress like gentlemen." But above all, he insisted that they not dress "like hippies," with colorful costumes or long hair.[19] He emphasized the need to present his movement to a television audience as either refined and sophisticated, or authentically Vedic. Unsurprisingly, his devotees abandoned the proposal.

ADORNMENT IN *BACK TO GODHEAD*

When Swami A. C. Bhaktivedanta died in 1977 his senior disciples took over the movement. For some time, the group experienced fragmentation and even chaos in some quarters,[20] but one of the important forces maintaining integrity was the group's official magazine, *Back to Godhead*. Bhaktivedanta actually began publishing *Back to Godhead* in India in 1944 as an English-language Gaudiya Vaishnava publication, and after forming ISKCON in the United States, handed off the publication to his disciples in 1966, who transformed it from a leaflet to a professionally produced glossy magazine. Importantly, devotees used and continue to use the magazine in two ways: they read it internally as a guide for ISKCON practice, thought, and culture, and they also distribute it to the broader public as a form of religious proselytizing and exposure. In the 1970s and 1980s the movement also used distribution of *Back to Godhead* for fundraising, asking for a few dollars for each copy of the "free" magazine. (They curtailed this practice after much bad press.)[21] Therefore, there have always been two parallel audiences for each *Back to Godhead* article: the committed Hare Krishna devotee, and the outsider, who is at best a potential convert but perhaps simply a donor or friendly sympathizer.

The vast majority of the articles in the magazine consider the basic devotional practices of the movement, most notably the chanting of the Hare Krishna mantra that gives the group its name ("Hare Krishna, Hare Krishna, Krishna Krishna, Hare Hare, Hare Rama, Hare Rama, Rama Rama, Hare Hare"). Other articles describe the group's activities, such as its agricultural settlements, charitable acts, music festivals, public food distribution, and worship events. A few articles detail elements of the movement's theology. A great many articles are reprintings of Bhaktivedanta's writings or edited transcripts of his public addresses. References to bodily adornment are scattered throughout.

Examining *Back to Godhead*'s treatment of adornment during the first sixty years of its publication reveals three interconnected but competing ideas, each of which are explored below.[22] Some of the articles describe adornment as unimportant, deferring to the theological notion within the movement that the material world must assume a secondary position to the spiritual world. A second theme actually contradicts the first, positioning bodily adornment alongside other material acts as forms of embodied devotion, and therefore deeply spiritual and meaningful. A third theme is that of female sexuality and the control of female bodies, a concern that the movement has continued to emphasize even after its leader's passing.

Like Mary Lou O'Neil and her treatment of globalized Turkey, Lynn S. Neal has argued that American adornment choices function equally as political and social statements. In her analysis of T-shirts conveying anti-Muslim sentiments, Neal argues that sartorial choices offer an arena for the individual to express religious and political opinions in a manner appropriate to American individualism. Yet fashion choices represent not only "individual ideas and unique expressions," they are also part of "American democratic discourse—free speech, individual expression, selling, and shopping."[23] They tie the wearer to broader discourse. Choosing to wear (or not wear) certain clothing, or to advocate for or against such clothing or other adornment practices, is not just an individual fashion statement, but an activist strategy to influence culture. The Hare Krishna authors writing for *Back to Godhead* knew this and wrote accordingly.

Antimaterialism: Adornment as unimportant

The Hare Krishna philosophy emerged from a long-developed set of texts and traditions within the broader Hindu religious world. Hindus take a variety of perspectives on the nature of the physical world, with some (monists and non-dualists) envisioning God and the material world as one, and others (dualists) envisioning a strict separation between the material world and the divine. ISKCON falls more toward the latter, positioning the material world as distinct from that of the divine self (i.e., Krishna).

The material world, and therefore our material bodies and the material adornments of said bodies, exist distinct from the divine or spiritual realm. "We are not these bodies," explained Bhaktivedanta in the first chapter of his book *Beyond Birth and Death*. The self is "a spirit soul," the swami wrote, and must be overcome. "Kṛṣṇa therefore encourages us to transcend the bodily conception of existence and attain to our actual spiritual life."[24] Given the need to transcend the body, from this perspective any sort of bodily adornment offers at best a distraction from one's spiritual goals, and at worst can cause one to become mired in the error of identifying with gross materialism. ISKCON authors in *Back to Godhead* tend to deploy this approach when describing the adornment practices of outsiders.

Typical of this sort of understanding of adornment, early Hare Krishna leader and *Back to Godhead* contributor Hayagriva das Adhikari wrote in 1969 of the dangers of sensual attachment as it related to adornment in his article "States and Attributes of the Creation," an introduction to the movement's philosophy that assumes an external audience unfamiliar with the basics of the group's core doctrines and practices. Under the heading "Self Control," Hayagriva warns that "Our hands and sense of touch will make us buy expensive clothing to cover our bodies and make us hunt for sexual partners."[25] This connection of bodily adornment with sexuality repeats as a theme throughout much of the movement's literature, with *Back to Godhead* authors often drawing such a connection between the desire for nice clothing and the desire for sexual gratification. Under this explicit rejection of the notion of sexual desire lurks a similar suspicion of broader sensual gratification.

Yet the rest of the issue serves as counterpoint to Hayagriva's argument. The cover featured a full-color image of over two dozen ISKCON devotees posing in exuberant joy, all dressed in the Hare Krishna style. Most visibly, at the top of the image seven *sanyasi* men stand aloft in their saffron robes, signifiers of their status as monastics. Several men clad in white dhotis, rows of women in colorful saris, and a few other *sanyasis* sit beneath them. The colorful image highlights their Hare Krishna clothing and *tilaka* adornment. A six-page black-and-white photo spread at the center of the magazine shows additional images of devotees adorned in the movement's clothing and style, serving effectively as a photo-essay on the group's recent public events in New York City. While a textual explanation of the images follows, indicating the sort of prayers and devotional service in which their subjects were engaged, the immediate impact is made by the pictures of Hare Krishna devotees and their clothing.[26]

The dismissal of adornment as theologically unimportant or distracting, and a simultaneous contrast with Hare Krishna adornment practices, follows throughout the magazine's run. Thirty-five years later, Caitanya Carana Dasa[27] writes in a 2004 article, "Are We Special?," that "fancy hairstyles, fashionable clothing, hi-tech mobile phones, flashy cars, and so on" represent only "external," material desires.[28] Deploying the logic of his guru, Caitanya Carana compares the focus on such externals as no different than the desires of animals. While half his list contains truly external objects (i.e., phones and cars), the first two items in fact represent bodily adornment: hairstyles and clothing. Here Caitanya Carana represents a notion within ISKCON that such adornments are at the heart of such animalistic materialist distractions.

If clothing served as only an unimportant external element, how did Hare Krishna devotees rectify this position with their overall embrace of Asian religious garb, and the "Hare Krishna look"? A 1980 article in *Back to Godhead* addressed that concern by reprinting an edited transcript of a

IMAGE 13.3   ISKCON men in dhotis. Image courtesy of the author.

New York news conference Bhaktivedanta held before his death. The article does not provide a date or much context for the swami's exchange with reporters, framing the content rather than context as important. Bhaktivedanta's overall argument about clothing—a rebuttal to the criticism that, far from ignoring adornment, his movement emphasized it—effectively held that Hare Krishna adornment functioned for proselytizing purposes, and that audiences should not confuse the ad with the product:

> REPORTER: Swamiji, your movement has received much attention because many of your followers dress in what, for the West, is an odd fashion. Why have you asked your followers to dress in this fashion and play drums on the streets?
>
> SRILA PRABHUPADA: This is our preaching method—somehow or other to draw people's attention, so that they may have the opportunity to revive their eternal relationship with God...
>
> REPORTER: But I mean, Swamiji, is this manifestation—dressing in this fashion, playing drums, and dancing in the streets the only way to be spiritual?... Can't people be spiritual without dressing in this fashion and dancing in the streets?
>
> SRILA PRABHUPADA: Oh, yes. Oh, yes. You can become spiritualized in the clothing you are wearing now. You simply have to learn about spiritual life from the books. Dress is not a very important thing. Still, in the material world one person is dressed in one way; another, another way.
>
> REPORTER: The way we ordinary people dress lets us move in all circles. But the way your disciples dress...
>
> SRILA PRABHUPADA: The thing is, to signify that one is performing a particular job, he may dress differently. For example, a policeman is differently dressed, so that others can understand that he is a policeman. Similarly, we are also differently dressed, so that everyone may understand that we are Hare Kṛṣṇa people.[29]

Here, Bhaktivedanta indicates that Hare Krishna bodily adornment functions primarily to attract attention from outsiders, and does so alongside the other public practices for which devotees were well-known during the first decade of the movement's history—namely, public prayer and devotional performance. The swami dismisses dress as "not a very important thing," and indicates that adornment serves only to identify devotees as such. The overall argument seems to be that any adornment practice must exist secondary to more spiritual pursuits.

Given the movement's emphasis on adornment practices, this seems somewhat disingenuous. Yet it did seem that Bhaktivedanta viewed adornment in this manner. The movement recorded many of the swami's conversations with visitors and has made such transcripts publicly accessible. During informal conversations Bhaktivedanta often took the approach of minimizing the value of adornment. When a visiting guest asked if people could become more Krishna conscious "without wearing a *dhoti* and shaving our heads," the swami replied that the adornment practices themselves "are not very important things ... You can remain in your coat and pants."[30] This would seem to convey rather clearly that adornment functions on a secondary level compared to other forms of devotion. Adornment represented materialism, and as the leader of a movement embracing a dualistic philosophy emphasizing what were described as spiritual rather than material ends, the Hare Krishna founder called for devaluing adornment and adornment choices.

On the other hand, the reporters and guests to whom the swami indicated that adornment was not very important could not have avoided noticing that the swami and his students all wore Indian dress and religious garb, and that all initiated members of the group did likewise. In various recorded informal occasions, Bhaktivedanta also made clear that Western attire was not associated with the culture of Krishna consciousness. In one such conversation, Bhaktivedanta pointed to religious iconography as a principle for how and why devotees dressed as they did. "Just see [an image of the God] Viṣṇu. He has no coat-pants [*chuckles*]."[31] Adornment was confined to the secondary, material realm, yet devotees nevertheless adhered to a strict set of adornment principles.

Bhakti: Adornment as devotion

While Swami A. C. Bhaktivedanta gave mixed messages about the place of adornment in his movement, many of his followers seemed to embrace the "Hare Krishna look." Those who did might point to a variety of philosophical notions about the state of the immaterial spirit in a material world, but far more often they simply assumed that bodily adornment functioned as a form of religious devotion, or *bhakti*. The Hare Krishna movement understands such *bhakti* as its core religious practice, and therefore devotees who understand adornment as such position their bodily adornment practices as core parts of their religious experience. In effect, adornment and clothing serve as devotional paraphernalia. Religious studies scholar Elizabeth Bucar, in her study of Islamic dress, calls such religious practices "virtue ethics, with a particular emphasis on the relationship between practices, the physical things a person does, and piety, an individual's religious devoutness and morality."[32]

Nagaraja Dasa embraces such virtue ethics in his description of his "typical day" as a Krishna devotee, published in a 1988 issue of *Back to Godhead*. He explicitly rejects the notion of Hare Krishna devotees as "otherworldly" in orientation and emphasizes the joyful bodily experiences of his day, from the clothing he wears to the food he eats.[33] Nagaraja, an associate editor for the magazine and therefore quite attuned to the orthodox positions of the official movement, carefully notes that his article does not support the "bodily consciousness" of the secular world, with its nightclubs, restaurants, and theaters. He eschews the body and sensual experience more broadly. However, because he emphasizes the place of food, dress, dance, music, and performance within the Hare Krishna movement, his article actually undercuts the idea that sensual enjoyment distracts from spiritual pursuits. Rather, he implicitly argues that embodied sensual practices performed with spiritual intentions serve valuable devotional roles. Nagaraja offered guidance on adornment:

> After rising, I shower, then apply tilaka (sacred clay) to my forehead and twelve other places on my body. By consecrating my body with tilaka, I remind myself that Kṛṣṇa is within my body as the Supersoul, and that my body is meant for serving Him. Afterwards, I dress in the traditional Vaiṣṇava (devotee of Kṛṣṇa) clothes, a dhoti and kurta.[34]

Nagaraja begins his day with a bodily adornment practice, one that serves a role of "reminding" and "serving" the divine. His emphasis on the body as a means of devotional service in fact undergirds his entire approach to bodily adornment. Unlike the perspective that adornment is simply a uniform, a proselytizing tool, or a distraction, Nagaraja approaches *tilaka* and clothing as a form of devotion.

Several other Hare Krishna writers follow the same patterns of concentrating on bodily adornments as forms of spiritual devotion, or *bhakti*. Devotee Kaumudi Rau describes attending an ISKCON festival in Durban, South Africa, and being attracted to four of the main sites: three of these were the tent housing the movement's cow protection service (cows are sacred within the Hare Krishna movement), the group's food stall, and the parade-like chariot procession that marked the festival's culmination. Yet the fourth, which Rau indicates was second only to the cow protection service as his favorite, centered on adornment materials. "My next favorite was the gift tent. Stuffed to the brim with devotional paraphernalia, it was a veritable feast for the eyes. If I were richer, I could have bought CDs, jewelry, clothing from India, or even tiles for my altar room, but I was still able to find some treasures I could afford."[35] While stressing the devotional aspect of the items in the gift tent, a sensual pleasure is still evident in Rau's description of this visual "veritable feast," with jewelry and clothing especially noted.

Closer to *Back to Godhead*'s office in North America, Drutakarma dasa describes a similar sort of experience in the movement's new "Govinda" temple-restaurant complex in San Diego, where he reveled in the attached gift shops: "The boutiques and gift shops adjoining each restaurant offer transcendental literature, Indian fashions, silk paintings, oriental rugs, incense, and even Indian spices and bulk grains and flours for those interested in duplicating their favorite Govinda's restaurant recipes." While the various sensual aspects cannot be unraveled in Drutakarma's description, with bodily adornments alongside food and household items, a theme of sensual pleasure percolates through the description, albeit mediated through the conception of devotional *bhakti*.[36]

Gender: Adornment and the danger of female sexuality

The status of women in the Hare Krishna movement represents one of the most contentious issues within this religious group. A. C. Bhaktivedanta emerged from a highly patriarchal religious culture and imprinted his perspective on the movement. As sociologist E. Burke Rochford notes, "Prabhupada emphasized that restrictions should be placed on women, that they should be grouped with other socially inferior classes (low-class *sudras* [servants]), and, because women are alluring sex objects, men should scrupulously avoid them."[37] While religious studies scholar Kim Knott has noted that more recently, the movement has attempted a "renewal" by opening itself to the "full participation" of women in leadership roles, the pattern set by its founder has had a lasting influence, especially on how devotees think about bodily adornment and gender.[38]

For many *Back to Godhead* authors, adornment—and especially clothing—is a stand-in for the dangers of female sexuality and the need to control that sexuality. This is the case in Mathuresa Dasa's article retelling the story of Saubhari Muni, a fabled monastic who fell from spiritual grace because he witnessed two fish copulating, leading the monk to break his vows of celibacy. Mathuresa uses women's clothing to emphasize the point that in Saubhari Muni's time, monastics were generally able to avoid such sensual distractions. "There were no attractive girls in designer jeans strutting along the river bottom, no ads for cigarettes, beer, or fashionable clothing to divert the attention," he writes. For this ISKCON writer, "attractive girls in designer jeans" represent the dangers of sensuality, but also the dangers of female sexuality. He transitions in his article from describing Saubhari Muni to calling for people to join ISKCON and thereby avoid "the distractions of modern life." While assuming as normative a male heterosexual readership, Mathuresa links the idea of young women and their bodily adornments (in this case designer jeans) as sex objects with that of limiting access to such young women so as to achieve what he calls "spiritual perfection."[39]

Other ISKCON devotees are even more explicit. Visnu-jana Swami, one of the Bhaktivedanta disciples who took *sanyasi* orders from the elder monk, authored an article in a 1970 issue of the magazine identifying what he called "major problems in all levels of society." One of these, in a list that ranged from "the fever of sense gratification" to "alcohol, drugs, frivolous sports," is his objection that "girls dress in an overly attractive fashion."[40] Like Mathuresa Dasa, Visnu-jana associates women's sexuality with their bodily adornment, treating it as a "major social problem." The pattern of male heteronormativity is also evident here, since it is effectively assumed that women's bodily adornment is a problem because it serves as a sexual distraction to men. Little attention is paid in this account to women's experience of their own adornment.

As was the case for other thematic approaches to bodily adornment, *Back to Godhead* sometimes deployed the founder's words in its connection of bodily adornment to the dangers of female sexuality. A 1982 article reprinted a conversation between the swami and some of his disciples on the topic of the words of a devotional song he had taught them. Yet the conversation was far-ranging, departing from an explanation of a simple verse on the need to worship Krishna in favor of a theological explanation of Krishna's relationship with his avatar's human mother (roughly analogous to the relation of Jesus to Mary in the Christian tradition, as Bhaktivedanta noted in this dialogue). Contrasting motherly love with other forms of love, the swami offered an aside on the topic of sensual pleasures. "People are trying sense gratification in so many ways, and now they have come to the last point: the naked dance and . . . what is that called—that short skirt?," he asked his disciples. "Miniskirt," answered a devotee. "Miniskirt, yes. [*Laughs*.] So, because in the material world the basic principle is sex," he surmised, before returning to the topic of divine avatars.[41]

On the one hand, this brief digression seemed apropos of nothing, unimportant and unrelated to the actual conversation about the Hindu theological concepts of *bhakti* and avatars. Yet, the swami's interjection actually shows how deeply he and the movement he founded came to associate women's clothing with the dangers of female sensuality and sexuality, and therefore distraction from spiritual matters. Bhaktivedanta seems to equate some sort of orgiastic nude dancing with women's choices to wear miniskirts, conflating female adornment practices with forbidden sexual practices. Of note, at no point in nearly sixty years of the *Back to Godhead* run could I find any similar condemnation of men's adornment practices as somehow indicative of dangerous sexuality.

CONCLUSION: ADORNMENT AS ACTIVISM

Each of the above-noted themes expressed in *Back to Godhead*—the anti-materialist approach to bodily adornment, the devotional *bhakti* approach, and the association of women's bodily adornments with dangerous sexuality—represent forms of what one might call *adornment activism*. By adorning one's body in particular ways, choosing not to adorn it in other ways, and rhetorically positioning certain types of adornment as good or bad, the Hare Krishna devotees engaged in a form of social action. The movement as a whole called for what scholar Kim Knott labeled a "return to a Golden Age . . . the lifestyle and values of another time," and its adherents held to what I have described as an ethos of "replacing" Western social and cultural norms and practices with those that they understand to derive from ancient Indian (i.e., Vedic) civilization.[42] The overall thrust of this activism aimed to utilize what they present as Vedic fashion and adornment as means to establish Vedic civilization in the present. Scholar of religion and dress Lynn S. Neal notes that such use of fashion to advocate social messages, while it "relies on visual cues rather than vocal utterances to make a point," nevertheless expresses a clear set of ideas.[43] Yet unlike some of ISKCON's more overt attempts to influence the public, such as public chanting, mass food distribution, and the sale of books and other literature, the promulgation of the "Hare Krishna style" comes across as less threatening, though no less obvious. Such fashion choices represent a form of communication that is "simultaneously aggressive and subtle, transparent and acceptable," explains Neal.[44]

At times, *Back to Godhead* and ISKCON devotees display a rather clear self-reflexivity about their use of adornment as a form of activism. The "Dressed for Spiritual Success" article, authored by one of the movement's senior female religious thinkers and teachers, Urmila Devi-Dasa, and published in 1987, represents such a case. An adornment advice article, it opens with a full-page color image of a male and female devotee smiling, walking hand in hand, wearing ISKCON clothing (no *tilaka* marks are visible), the woman in a lovely blue patterned sari and the man in tan dhoti and kurta. The article's lede notes the "spiritual advantages of the sari and the dhoti," and Urmila highlights the role of bodily adornment, specifically clothing, in *bhakti*. "A sari, being traditional Vedic attire, helps us remember Kṛṣṇa," she explains.[45] Urmila offers advice on specific colors, fabrics, and styles of sari and dhoti appropriate for different occasions or climates. Yet her article ultimately addresses the non-devotee, making clear that these pieces of clothing represent a manner by which she hopes to engage a potential convert, as well as spread her vision of Krishna consciousness to a broader audience: "We urge everyone interested in reviving his or her natural spiritual position of love of God to constantly chant His holy names. And for simplicity and natural elegance, why not try on a *sari* or *dhoti* when you get up tomorrow? That will help you remember Kṛṣṇa, who always wears a yellow silken dhoti, and bring you one step closer to loving Him."[46] Urmila rather clearly presents Hare Krishna adornment as an activist strategy for outreach and personal spiritual transformation, and by extension for broader social transformation as well. In a follow-up article several years later, she makes this even more explicit: "The magic of dressing as we do is that when people see us they chant and think of Kṛṣṇa without feeling we're forcing them or bothering them."[47]

Urmila Devi-Dasa as a professional educator stands apart in terms of the intentionality with which she writes about the activist power of Hare Krishna adornment, but her position reflects the broader trends of the devotees writing in *Back to Godhead*. One of the first academic books on the Hare Krishna movement, Kim Knott's *My Sweet Lord*, began with the observation that outsiders look at devotee adornment and come to the immediate conclusion that "we look normal and they do not."[48] Knott argued that this unique appearance represented "the need to be distinctive, to be recognized, to 'stand up and be counted,' " but that it was also a way "to interest people."[49] It is that last intention that I think is most important. Hare Krishna devotees are and have been less interested in being unique and more in attracting outsider attention in order to transform society. Adornment is their form of activism.

NOTES

1. James R. Sikes, "Swami's Flock Chants in Park to Find Ecstasy," *New York Times*, October 10, 1960, 24. Held at American Religions Collection, ARC Mss 1, Department of Special Collections, University Libraries, University of California, Santa Barbara.
2. Irvine Robertson, "The Eastern Mystics Are Out to Take You In," *Moody Monthly*, July–August 1973, 24–27. Held at American Religions Collection, ARC Mss 1, Department of Special Collections, University Libraries, University of California, Santa Barbara.
3. "Bhaktivedanta" is the religious name of the man originally named Abhay Charan De, akin to "Mother Theresa" being the religious name used by the woman born as Anjezë Gonxhe Bojaxhiu. In keeping with academic norms, I use his preferred religious name here.
4. For more on the movement's Hindu origins and the contextualization of its theology, see Edwin F. Bryant and Maria L. Ekstrand, eds., *The Hare Krishna Movement: The Postcharismatic Fate of a Religious Transplant* (New York: Columbia University Press, 2004).
5. Or "Kṛṣṇa" when spelled with diacritical marks. ISKCON is inconsistent with its usage of diacritical transliterations. In my writing I have therefore utilized alternative transliterations to those without diacriticals, e.g., "Vishnu"

rather than "Viṣṇu," and "sari" rather than "sārī." I have maintained the use of diacriticals within direct quotes.

6. Harvey Cox, *Turning East: Why Americans Look to the Orient for Spirituality—and What That Search Can Mean to the West* (New York: Touchstone, 1977).
7. Elizabeth M. Bucar, "Secular Fashion, Religious Dress, and Modest Ambiguity," *Journal of Religious Ethics* 44, no. 1 (2016): 68.
8. Jayadvaita Swami, "Hare Kṛṣṇa: Sticking with It," *Back to Godhead* 28, no. 4 (1994): 3.
9. Cox, *Turning East*. See also E. Burke Rochford, *Hare Krishna in America* (New Brunswick, NJ: Rutgers University Press, 1991), 55–56.
10. Rochford, *Hare Krishna in America*, 13.
11. Rohininandana Dasa, "Tilaka: The Mark of God," Krishna.com, accessed August 19, 2019, http://www.krishna.com/tilaka-mark-god.
12. A. C. Bhaktivedanta Swami Prabhupada, *The Nectar of Devotion: The Complete Science of Bhakti-Yoga* (Los Angeles: Bhaktivedanta Book Trust, 1970), 54.
13. The "beads" refer to prayer beads, used to count repetitions of the mantra. His "flag" likely refers to the tuft of hair worn as part of a male ISKCON member's adornment. See "Letter to: Balia" (March 12, 1968), Bhaktivedanta Vedabase, accessed August 19, 2019, https://vedabase.io/en/library/letters/letter-to-balai-4/. The context of this letter is interesting, as it is part of a series the swami sent to the New York temple, offering instruction on everything from food offerings to the meaning of particular practices.
14. Bhaktivedanta's treatment of women and his understanding of gender has been extensively treated. See especially Susan Jean Palmer, *Moon Sisters, Krishna Mothers, Rajneesh Lovers: Women's Roles in New Religions* (Syracuse, NY: Syracuse University Press, 1994), 15–43.
15. "Letter to: Jayapataka," (April 17, 1970), Bhaktivedanta Vedabase, accessed August 19, 2019, https://vedabase.io/en/library/letters/letter-to-jayapataka-17/.
16. Mary Lou O'Neil, "You Are What You Wear: Clothing Appearance Laws and the Construction of the Public Citizen in Turkey," *Fashion Theory* 14, no. 1 (2010): 66–67.
17. A. C. Bhaktivedanta Swami, "London Town Hall Lecture," *Back to Godhead* 1, no. 32 (1970): 4.
18. Bhaktivedanta, "London Town Hall Lecture," 4.
19. "Conversation on Train to Allahabad" (January 11, 1977), Bhaktivedanta Vedabase, accessed August 19, 2019, https://vedabase.io/en/library/transcripts/770111ttida/.

20. Bhaktivedanta left a series of contradicting oral and written succession instructions, a problem further exacerbated by the youth and relative inexperience of his several successors. See chapters in "Post-Bhaktivedanta Controversies of Lineage," part 3 of Bryant and Ekstrand, eds., *The Hare Krishna Movement*, 147–238.
21. E. Burke Rochford, "Airports, Conflict, and Change in the Hare Krishna Movement," in Bryant and Ekstrand, eds., *The Hare Krishna Movement*, 273–90.
22. In 2005, the editors of *Back to Godhead* released a digitized archive of their sixty-year print run, greatly increasing access to the material. I have used this collection in my research. International Society for Krishna Consciousness, *60 Years of Back to Godhead Magazine*, CD-ROM (Los Angeles: Bhaktivedanta Book Trust, 2005). I have cited individual articles by their original publication date, since they can be accessed either through this digital collection or more typical archival means.
23. Lynn S. Neal, "The Ideal Democratic Apparel: T-shirts, Religious Intolerance, and the Clothing of Democracy," *Material Religion: The Journal of Objects Art and Belief* 10, no. 2 (June 2014): 202.
24. A. C. Bhaktivedanta Swami Prabhupada, *Beyond Birth and Death* (Los Angeles: Bhaktivedanta Book Trust, 1979), 6.
25. Hayagriva das Adhikari, "States and Attributes of the Creation," *Back to Godhead* 1, no. 29 (1969): 21.
26. "New York Samkirtan," *Back to Godhead* 1, no. 29 (1969): 8–25.
27. ISKCON Devotees take Sanskrit names generally ending in "Dasa" or "Das" (for men), or "Devi Dasa" (for women). This final part of their name means "servant of," and the first part of the name reflects either a saint, some aspect of the divine, or another religious concept. In subsequent references, I drop the suffix.
28. Caitanya Carana Dasa, "Are We Special?," *Back to Godhead* 38, no. 3 (2004): 27
29. "Srila Prabhupada Speaks Out: 'Why Do They Seem So Strange?,'" *Back to Godhead* 15, nos. 1–2 (1980): 14. Ellipses in the original.
30. "Room Conversation" (October 6, 1972), Bhaktivedanta Vedabase, accessed August 19, 2019, https://vedabase.io/en/library/transcripts/721006r1ber/. See also "Garden Conversation with Professors" (June 24, 1975), Bhaktivedanta Vedabase, accessed August 19, 2019, https://vedabase.io/en/library/transcripts/750624gcla/.
31. "Room Conversation" (April 11, 1969), Bhaktivedanta Vedabase, accessed August 19, 2019, https://vedabase.io/en/library/transcripts/690411r1-new-york/.

32. Bucar, "Secular Fashion," 71.
33. Nagaraja Dasa, "Won't You Join the Dance?," *Back to Godhead* 23, nos. 2–3 (1988): 5–7+.
34. Nagaraja Dasa, 7.
35. Kaumudi Rau, "My Day at the Durban Rathayatra," *Back to Godhead* 37, no. 5 (2003): 54.
36. Drutakarma dasa, "Spiritual Places: A New Spirit in San Diego," *Back to Godhead* 20, nos. 2–3 (1985): 29.
37. E. Burke Rochford, *Hare Krishna Transformed* (New York: New York University Press, 2007), 126.
38. Kim Knott, "Healing the Heart of ISKCON," in Bryant and Ekstrand, eds., *The Hare Krishna Movement*, 305.
39. Mathuresa Dasa, "The Yogi in the River," *Back to Godhead* 20, no. 6 (1985): 33–34.
40. Visnu-jana Swami, "From Poverty to Bliss Through Kṛṣṇa Yoga," *Back to Godhead* 1, no. 46 (1970): 9.
41. "The Final Point for the Bubble of Illusion," *Back to Godhead* 17, no. 12 (1982): 4.
42. Kim Knott, *My Sweet Lord: The Hare Krishna Movement* (San Bernardino, CA: R. Reginald/The Borgio Press, 1986), 86; Benjamin E. Zeller, *Prophets and Protons: New Religious Movements and Science in Late Twentieth-Century America* (New York: New York University Press, 2010).
43. Neal, "The Ideal Democratic Apparel," 200.
44. Neal, 201.
45. Urmila Devi-Dasi, "Dressed for Spiritual," *Back to Godhead* 22, no. 7 (1987): 9.
46. Devi-Dasi, "Dressed for Spiritual": 9
47. Urmila Devi-Dasi, "Schooling Kṛṣṇa's Children," *Back to Godhead* 28, no. 3 (1994): 19.
48. Knott, *My Sweet Lord*, 19.
49. Knott, 21.

Fourteen

RELIGIOUS DRESS, THE CHURCH OF BODY MODIFICATION, AND THE FIRST AMENDMENT

MARIE W. DALLAM

IN MODERN SOCIETY, religious dress may take a wide variety of forms beyond clothing that covers or enhances the body, and it can even include adornments of the body itself. For members of the Church of Body Modification (hereafter CoBM), a small international religious organization, acts of adornment and manipulation of the body are key to personal spiritual development and, often, connections with the divine. Members explore the transcendent via acts performed on their physical bodies, and the resulting adornments serve as sacred markers of the ritual experience as well as declarations of one's religious self. However, these adornments can also cause problems for church members in formal settings, as their religiously marked bodies come into conflict with mainstream expectations for dress and appearance. As a result, each ritual of body modification must be seen as not merely a private expression of religion but also as a political choice through which church members publicly reveal their religious identity. Even more, in the United States church members unwittingly become activists for their faith as they are sometimes forced to mount legal challenges in order to demand their right to religious free expression by fighting regulations that require them to hide their modified bodies. This essay will consider how religious dress has been regulated by American laws and courts in order to examine the distinctive challenges faced by CoBM members, which push at the traditional boundaries of First Amendment application even as they remain circumscribed by those boundaries.

RELIGIOUS ATTIRE AND THE LAW

As the chapters in this volume demonstrate, theologically significant adornment is found in all religious traditions, so there is scarcely a religious group that has escaped a conflict over such issues. History has shown that attire and adornment falling outside of sartorial norms can become particularly contentious in four specific institutional settings: schools, workplaces, the military, and prisons. Through the court systems of the United States, the right to wear specific, religiously defined clothing in these settings has been sought by Muslims, Sikhs, and members of numerous Christian denominations, many of whom are concerned with issues of modesty.[1] The right to not cut head and/or facial hair has been fought for by Christians, Muslims, Jews, Sikhs, Hindus, Rastafarians, and members of Native American religions, and most of these groups have also challenged restrictions on religious head coverings. As well, religious jewelry has at times been subject to challenge, varying from cross pins to prayer beads and everything in between, as has additional religious paraphernalia such as the kirpan (sacred dagger) that Khalsa Sikhs must wear at all times. Religious adornments of the body itself, whether a tattoo of a cross or a cicatrized pentagram, have also caused problems in institutional settings. Issues faced by CoBM members, then, must be situated within this broader context, even though their religious adornments differ significantly from the dress patterns of most other religious traditions.

In fact, religious dress is but one small example in a long history of case law relating to the free exercise of religion. Courts use various lines of inquiry to make determinations about whether a religious practice must be allowed, depending on the institution involved, the specific aspect of religion in question, and the law being called upon.[2] Among the points that the legal system potentially examines are the centrality of the practice to the religion; the sincerity of the believer; whether the religious person has an alternative way to fulfill their religious obligation; whether there is a reasonable accommodation that can be made for the religious practice that will not cause additional problems for the institution; whether the rule that limits religious practice is neutral and generally applicable to everyone; and whether the rule serves a legitimate, perhaps even compelling, purpose. Furthermore, a court may focus on one of these questions more than another, deeming it most relevant to the particular situation.[3] Because of these foci and the varying ways that courts have interpreted the law, rules about the accommodation of religious dress in institutional settings have lacked consistency.

One recurring concern has been distinctive religious clothing worn by classroom teachers in public schools. Examples have included teachers who are Catholic nuns and wish to wear habits; teachers who are Muslim and wish to wear head scarves; and, in one particularly well-known case, an Oregon teacher who wanted to wear an all-white outfit and turban in keeping with her Sikh faith.[4] In the school context, a special circumstance arises that often overrides the common set of questions a court might address: children are regarded as more impressionable than adults. Therefore, the argument goes, undue religious influence could be imparted if children see an authority figure wearing religious clothing on a daily basis. Furthermore, by allowing a teacher to wear a particular piece of religious attire, a school could be seen to endorse that religion, which would violate the First Amendment's establishment clause. Since the 1800s the wearing of religious garb by teachers has been repeatedly banned, both through laws and court cases upholding them, and only within the past few decades has this begun to change—state by state, and district by district. In contrast, distinctive religious clothing worn by students has generally been permitted, though compromises and negotiations with local school dress policies are not uncommon. What may not be immediately obvious to students is the distinction between dress that exercises religious beliefs (such as a yarmulke or a khimar) and dress that expresses religious beliefs (such as a T-shirt bearing a religious slogan). Restrictions on the former would be an issue of religious freedom, while the latter would be an issue of free speech, and therefore more likely to be delimited by school dress codes.

In workplace settings, there has been no shortage of conflicts about religious attire and adornment. These have included restrictions at well-known companies such as Red Robin Burgers, where a server was told to cover his religious tattoo, and at both Disneyland and the New York City

Transit Authority, where workers were forbidden to don religious headwear.[5] Employers have defended dress limitations based on a variety of concerns including hygiene, uniformity of appearance, company branding, safety, and maintaining a congenial work environment. However, in both hiring and employment, religion is a federally protected category via Title VII of the Civil Rights Act of 1964, which indicates that employees' religious needs should be accommodated unless doing so creates "undue hardship" for the employer.[6] Both the boundaries of accommodation and exactly what constitutes "hardship" are unclear, and for those reasons many of these conflicts enter litigation. Legal analyst Dallan F. Flake has observed that on the question of religious dress, the most consistent ruling has been that employers can proscribe the appearance of employees who work directly with customers, such as by prohibiting facial hair, head coverings, and—in the case of one CoBM member discussed below—facial jewelry.[7] But there are cases that have gone the other way, in which employers were sanctioned when they failed to prove that it would burden them to accommodate an employee's religious attire. Perhaps the most well-known of these is the Supreme Court case *EEOC v. Abercrombie & Fitch*. In this 2015 ruling, the clothing retailer, which has an extensive "look" policy for its employees, was penalized when it failed to hire a Muslim woman for the sole reason that the store manager wished to avoid making an accommodation for her head scarf.[8] It is possible that over time this ruling will become an influential precedent on questions of religious attire in the workplace because it is one of very few dress cases that has been adjudicated at such a high level.

Another institutional setting in which religious dress is often limited is within branches of the U.S. military. Although its members could be viewed as employees, and therefore protected by Title VII, the military is also set apart as an institution with its own sets of rules, regulations, and governance, and it has a record of stringency around appearance relating to all forms of attire and adornment. A single case, decided by the Supreme Court in 1986, continues to stand as the judicial guideline for religious dress arguments within the military. In *Goldman v. Weinberger*, an air force officer wore a yarmulke in work settings for several years until a superior officer filed a complaint that it violated the dress code prohibiting unauthorized headgear. The court, deciding against Officer Goldman, recognized that the "Air Force's strong interest in discipline justified the strict enforcement of its uniform dress requirements."[9] In other words, military regulations were permitted to supersede constitutional rights in the interest of uniformity. Based on the wording of the opinion, the court did not wish to open the door for similar complaints, preferring such decisions to be made internally by the military; indeed, since that time very few related cases have been adjudicated, and none by the Supreme Court. Individual servicemen and -women have successfully gained religious exemptions from dress policies both informally and through formal petitions within their own branches, and this in turn has led to incremental changes to regulations on attire and adornment in the military.[10]

The final example of an institutional setting where dress has been both regulated and adjudicated is American prisons, where one can find significant variation in the implementation of religious attire policies. The differences stem from factors beyond rights and laws, including whether the prison is a state or federal institution, whether it is privately run, whether it is a men's or women's prison, who happens to be in charge of prison security at any given time, and the ability of inmates to file formal complaints. Often, when regulations are challenged, the heightened need for order and security demanded by incarceration is considered a compelling interest that easily trumps the rights of individual religious expression. Thus, for example, dress that could become a hiding place for contraband can be restricted even if it is religious in nature, including head coverings, long hair, and facial hair. Religious jewelry and paraphernalia may be forbidden because both can be weaponized. As well, issues of identification may be raised by prisons: for instance, religious exceptions to dress codes might inadvertently support gang activity, or exceptions to existing rules could make identifying individuals more difficult. Furthermore, prisons may need to consider the cost and inconvenience of allowing individual exemptions within such a tightly controlled setting. While there are certainly many allowances made for the general practice of religion in prison, such as provisions for gathering space, leadership, and religious literature, religious dress continues to be curtailed more often than not. This broad overview of dress regulation in institutional settings and its support via jurisprudence provides a framework for understanding issues faced by CoBM members, even though the nature of their religious adornments distinguishes them in significant ways.

THE CHURCH OF BODY MODIFICATION

CoBM was founded about a decade before its formal U.S. incorporation in 2008, when it earned classification as a 501(c)3 nonprofit religious organization. Its early leaders included people well-known within the "BME community," such as Steve Haworth, a specialist in three-dimensional implants, and the late Rick Frueh, a professional piercer.[11] Its most recent leaders have worked in a variety of professions both within and outside of the body arts, and they are predominantly located within the United States.

At the core of CoBM is a belief that physical modification of the body has the potential to bring individuals closer to the divine. Ritualized modifications can include tattoos, piercings, scars, brands, and implants, while manipulation practices might include binding, corsetry, fire walking, and suspension;[12] in many cases the ritualized practice involves both manipulation and modification. To outsiders these rites are often unfamiliar and may even be considered extreme because they push the body past socially accepted limits of pain and often involve permanent physical changes. For members, however, such activities constitute a method of personal spiritual engagement and therefore have the potential to bring about direct contact with a power greater than themselves. As the CoBM website explains, "Practicing acts of body modification and engaging in body manipulation rituals strengthens the bond between body, mind, and soul ... We believe these rites are essential to our spirituality."[13]

The church has doctrinal statements, ministers (also called "spiritual guides"), a board of advisers, and bylaws, all of which are found on its website.[14] The CoBM's statements on faith, vision, and mission are not specific about the nature of the divine, but they implicitly acknowledge the existence of a supernatural world and a power greater than humans.[15] One can see in these statements an emphasis on ethical behavior in the present world, with references to positivity, respect, responsibility, safety, and integrity, all of which are echoed in the church's "Code of Ethics for Spiritual Guides." Of the nine points in the church's faith statement, two relate to members' status as public representatives of the practice of body modification. Unlike many other religious groups, CoBM does not have a central sacred text, nor any regular meeting times for its membership. It does not emphasize community rituals, although there are occasions when some members meet at both in-person and online gatherings. Because the religious practices are individual and personal, and members conceive of and describe divine power in a variety of different ways, CoBM precludes easy classification based on theology or tradition. However, its emphasis on unity through religious practice makes it notably different from Christianity, the dominant religion in the United States, in which the community of believers is united by beliefs about God and salvation.

One of the primary ways that CoBM members communicate is online, including through a semipublic discussion forum that was active from approximately 2011 to 2016. There, members could discuss matters both abstract and concrete, including any aspect of modification and manipulation. Many used it as a space to express how they conceived of these acts as sacred and/or to give personal testimony. As one contributor wrote, "For me getting pierced is the essence of spirituality. The sensation of the piercing brings me to a sense of awakening, almost. Essentially I feel as if there is a wave of calm and inner peace."[16] Another wrote, "I knew as a child, when I was told my body was a temple for God, that I had to decorate my body, that I had to wear my worship on my sleeve, literally."[17] A great many of the postings, regardless of the topic at hand, lay bare the personal spiritual nature of body modification practices. Some people made explicit religious references by framing their modifications in relation to traditions including shamanism, Paganism, Buddhism, Christianity, and Odinism; others made more generic references to a form of God or divine energy; and some wrote about acts of body modification as a way to unite body and spirit. Taken collectively, the posts demonstrate members' conception that body modification leads to religious experience, but that it manifests in a wide variety of ways.

In forum posts members sometimes disagreed about whether to call acts of modification "rituals," but this appeared to be primarily a debate about semantics more than a disagreement about the potential power of the acts themselves. For instance, one writer said that while modifications can spur spiritual experiences, to be "rituals" the practitioner would need intent for a specific outcome. In his view, a modification that randomly caused a mystical experience could not be considered a ritual. Elsewhere this same poster urged his fellow CoBM members to explore how and why a given modification causes mystical experience, so that one could learn how to recreate—and thus ritualize—such experiences.[18] In contrast, another poster suggested that "ritual body modification" means the person has "taken a step deeper, to internalize those modifications and not use them simply for aesthetics but for mind and spirit altering changes."[19] From that point of view, the lack of divine connection during a particular modification did not undercut its significance as a ritualized act within the broader context of that person's religious life. Intention and outcome, then, did not always go hand in hand.[20]

The online forum is no longer available, so in recent years communication among members has become more individual and private. CoBM has sometimes held virtual meeting sessions that could take the form of a lesson or roundtable discussion. For instance, sessions held in 2011 included "Communicating with Employers, Administrators, and Family Members," "Ministership," and "Religious Experience." Occasional barbecues in California have served as social gatherings for church members and their friends from the BME community. But the individual nature of CoBM practice has meant that communal activities are sporadic. Like any young religious group, CoBM has struggled with leadership, organizational structure, and maintaining momentum. It has also ridden small waves of controversy, including alleged financial mismanagement that caused some early supporters to distance themselves, as well as the 2016 removal of a minister after allegations of abuse, assault, and other criminal acts.[21] The decentralized nature of CoBM likely exacerbates many of these problems as well as making resolution more difficult to achieve.

At its core, CoBM is a virtual community of like-minded individuals who find deep significance in the process and results of personal body modification. Membership in the church provides them with a heightened sense of dignity, legitimacy, and pride. Notably, CoBM holds legal status as a religious organization in the United States, and its members share in constitutional protections. But because the essence of their religious practice is often difficult for outsiders to comprehend, members have not always been treated equally regarding the right to religious adornment. The nature of the CoBM religion, which inherently prevents members from being able to conceal their religious identity, forces them to become public activists on its behalf.

To date, only a handful of individual CoBM members have been involved in court cases related to their freedom of religious adornment in institutional settings, and most of these have followed precedential paths. For example, a church member incarcerated in Vermont filed a First

Amendment claim after he was forced to remove the jewelry from his eyebrow and tongue. Ultimately the prison's concerns for managing the health and safety of inmates outweighed his right to religious free expression.[22] Theoretically, one should be able to use dress precedents related to schools and the military to anticipate how CoBM members might fare in those settings, whereas the workplace is a less predictable context. Notably, the CoBM website explicitly instructs potential members not to misperceive the church as being a shield for those who seek exemption from institutional dress codes. The church FAQ warns, "If a person attempts to join the Church as a ploy to gain legal protection, they will not be accepted." It specifically advises those who have modification-based conflicts with employers to seek legal assistance, especially since the additional protections of Title VII may strengthen their cases. In the online forum, members sometimes counseled one another about modification-related conundrums. Many suggested a path that balanced demonstrating pride in one's own body with compromise about appearance requirements, particularly in the workplace. For example, when someone asked for advice regarding her employer's disapproval of her new hair color, several people were dubious that it was truly religious in nature and discouraged her from pursuing a claim. As one judiciously counseled, "My hair color has nothing to do with my beliefs. My piercings on the other hand were a different story. I fought for and received accommodations for them."[23]

CoBM has occasionally gotten more directly involved with regulations related to modification. For instance, a 2003 Illinois House bill attempted to outlaw tongue-splitting surgery—a procedure in which a portion of the tongue is divided, like that of a snake—except in cases of medical necessity. CoBM president Rick Frueh spoke out against the law, arguing that it targeted one specific form of cosmetic surgery rather than any other optional appearance-changing surgeries, such as breast enhancements or tummy tucks.[24] The bill eventually became a law that requires tongue-splitting surgery to be performed by a licensed medical or dental professional, though it no longer includes the phrase about medical necessity.[25] At that time CoBM was still in its early stages of development, but its name was drawn into the press when people affiliated with it mounted protests against the Illinois bill as well as similar proposals in other states. It was not long before it found itself entangled in cases more directly related to its members and their religiously based adornments.

CoBM AND RELIGIOUS ACTIVISM

Two instances of CoBM members publicly fighting dress regulations are worth examining in detail due to their surprising outcomes. The first was argued through federal courts while the second, though it did enter the court system, primarily played out in the press. The first situation involved a woman named Kimberly Cloutier, who challenged an employee dress code.[26] Cloutier had four tattoos and eleven ear piercings when she was first hired to be a front-end assistant at a Massachusetts Costco in 1997. Her job entailed checking prices, reshelving, and other similar tasks. Her adornments presented no problem until the following year when she was working in the deli department and was told that the store's updated dress code now prohibited food handlers from wearing jewelry. Because Cloutier refused to remove her earrings, the store transferred her back to her former position. For the next two years, Cloutier continued to engage in body modification, a process she later described to the court as personally meaningful albeit not associated with the practice of a particular religion at that time. She engaged in cutting and scarring as well as getting more tattoos and piercings, some of which were visible in the workplace, including the eyebrow ring she got in 1998. All the while, she was working in front-end positions at the store, earning a promotion to cashier in 2000.

Cloutier first heard of the CoBM in January 2001, and she sought to learn more about it both from the website and through communication with members. In March she attempted to apply for membership, but she later discovered that her online application had not been processed correctly. She resubmitted a paper copy in June and was accepted as a church member in July 2001. During this same period, Costco again revised its dress code policy such that cashiers were now forbidden from wearing facial jewelry. On June 25, 2001, Cloutier received a verbal warning that the dress code forbade her eyebrow ring. The following day she received a second warning because she was still wearing the jewelry, but this time she responded by handing her supervisor documents relating to the religious beliefs and practices of CoBM and explaining that the adornment was a religious requirement. The supervisor told her to remove the jewelry or go home, so Cloutier left. The following day she filed a Title VII–based complaint with the Equal Employment Opportunity Commission (EEOC), which set in motion a long process through which the agency attempted to mediate a resolution.

Three days later, when Cloutier went in for her next shift, she was again told she could not work unless she removed her eyebrow ring. She met with a manager, to whom she also gave CoBM documents, and she volunteered the idea that instead of removing the ring she could just wear a Band-Aid to cover it. The manager rejected her suggestion and sent her home, telling her not to return until the store responded to the EEOC paperwork. Cloutier did not hear anything further until July 14, when Costco sent her a notice that she was being terminated due to unexcused absences. All parties later agreed that, although the absences were the technical reason for her termination, the disagreement about her facial jewelry was the real cause.

As noted earlier, the history of dress cases in workplace situations has been somewhat mixed. Title VII implies that if an employee's nonregulation dress practice is based on a sincerely held religious belief, and the employer has been properly notified, the employer must offer a reasonable accommodation. The employee, in return, is expected to be cooperative in efforts to resolve the situation. However, if accommodating the employee would cause undue hardship for the business, that typically wins out over incidental infringement on religious freedom—a common example of this is when religious hairstyles interfere with necessary safety equipment. In Cloutier's situation, she was not offered any accommodation, and then she was fired. As the EEOC determined the following year, Costco clearly engaged in religious discrimination, violating both federal and state laws. Despite this, when the case reached federal District Court the ruling went against Kimberly Cloutier, and that decision was affirmed by the First Circuit court of appeals. This is because of an interaction that had occurred a few weeks after Cloutier was fired, discussed below, in combination with an "unclear" question that the appeals court noted but put aside. By choosing to ignore this significant issue the court came to an easy judgment against Cloutier's religious dress.

Although she had already been fired, in August 2001 Cloutier was contacted by Costco as an outgrowth of the EEOC complaint. Costco presented her with an offer: Cloutier would be allowed to return to her job if she agreed to either cover her facial jewelry with a Band-Aid, as she herself had originally suggested, or if she removed the eyebrow ring and wore a clear plastic retainer in the hole during work time. The store indicated that its public image would be tarnished by exempting Cloutier from its dress code policy, and therefore having her hide her "unprofessional" facial jewelry was the only option they considered appropriate. Cloutier refused, saying that her religion required her to display the jewelry at all times. In this, she was invoking parts of the CoBM faith statement that indicate members will "share [their] experiences openly and honestly" and "act as positive role models for future generations."[27] This belief is reinforced by the church Vision Statement that looks to a future in which "we may practice our rituals and body modification without prejudice or discrimination."[28]

Cloutier, as a new member of the church, would have been involved in a process of exploration and growth as she came to understand aspects of CoBM faith more deeply. Recent converts to any religion are characteristically overt enthusiasts, eager to demonstrate their new religious identity and often being particularly strict about their own religiously based conduct.[29] Cloutier's testimony indicated that throughout this period she was actively engaged in a process of connecting with CoBM members online and having new conversations about the meanings of body modification; it is therefore entirely plausible that the idea of covering her piercing with a Band-Aid had seemed reasonable to her in June but, two months later, felt like an insincere way to represent her faith.

The court took note that Cloutier had refused a reasonable offer of accommodation, and based its decision against her on that fact. But what the court overtly failed to address was the fact that Costco *had already fired* Cloutier; the accommodation was only offered many weeks later, as part of the EEOC mediation process that would have allowed her to get her job back. While one might fault Cloutier for not being receptive to this compromise, Costco clearly made the first error by refusing to offer any religious accommodation before terminating her. The appeals court expressed surprise that the lower court had not considered this fact, pointing out that Costco's end run around Title VII regulations for accommodation served to invalidate the entire purpose of Title VII. Although the appeals court could have made this issue substantive in its own considerations, it instead bracketed the question and suggested that someday, courts should really decide whether post-termination offers of accommodation are legally aligned with the spirit of Title VII.[30]

The depth of Costco's religious discrimination was even more evident from documents submitted to the court. In the termination notice

Cloutier received in July, Costco indicated that "the CBM was not a religion as the term is defined in state and federal antidiscrimination laws. Moreover, even if the CBM were a religion, Costco did not believe that CBM doctrine required Cloutier to wear her facial jewelry *at all times*."[31] In other words, Costco had made itself the arbiter of what religion is and is not, and had also assumed the authority to interpret church doctrine. Presumably, this is why it initially felt no need to offer Cloutier any accommodation for her religious practice. The courts were not much better, stating that they were not evaluating or even questioning the sincerity of Cloutier's beliefs, but then providing comments that indicated otherwise. For instance, the opinions contain multiple references to Cloutier's response to the Band-Aid idea, saying that her position had "evolved over time" and calling that change "notable." The inclusion of any comments about Cloutier's beliefs indicates that the courts were considering them, and they implicitly reveal that they found her stance change to be indicative of insincerity. In tandem, the appeals court pointed out that she had never protested wearing the store shirt that covered tattoos on her arms, implying that she was insincere about the display of her adornments overall. It appears that they did not consider the possibility that some, but not all, of Cloutier's bodily adornments were religious in nature. Had they more thoroughly interrogated the sincerity of her beliefs, as is common procedure in many cases of free exercise, they would have been unable to dismiss her request for accommodation so easily.

The unfortunate precedent set by the Cloutier case is that a business can assert, without a need to provide evidence, that a given dress practice hurts its public image, and therefore it can legally forbid that practice for its employees even if the dress is religious in nature. In subsequent years numerous employer-litigants have referenced the Cloutier decision claiming that they would suffer a hardship if forced to make accommodations for the religious needs of a single employee. Many of these cases have been successful for the employers despite the hypothetical nature of their anticipated hardships. The precedent of Cloutier has contributed to decisions against Title VII–based accommodations in nearly two dozen cases on issues such as Sabbath observance and workplace vaccinations, as well as cases specifically related to the religious attire and adornment of Muslims and Rastafarians.[32] For Cloutier herself, who stood her ground that only a complete exemption from the dress code would suffice, her job was not restored. Considering all of these ramifications, the case was a loss for many people.

The second significant case involving a CoBM member occurred in North Carolina nearly a decade after Cloutier's problem first arose. The circumstances were strikingly similar despite occurring in a very different setting. Fourteen-year-old Ariana Iacono joined CoBM, following in the footsteps of her mother, Nikki, who had joined a year earlier, and Ariana got a nose piercing to mark the occasion. On her first day of high school in August 2010, she was told that the nose stud violated the school's dress code. Over the next several weeks the mother and daughter met with school officials multiple times to discuss the situation, but all parties held their ground. Ariana refused to remove the jewelry because she believed her religion dictated that she should wear it at all times, and she pointed out that the school policy generically referenced exemptions for dress practices related to religion. The school's principal asserted that CoBM doctrine did not require the nose piercing to be worn at all times and said the best the school could offer was to permit her to wear a bandage that covered the piercing. Because Ariana refused, the school suspended her and recommended that she be transferred elsewhere.[33]

The American Civil Liberties Union filed a case on Iacono's behalf, citing constitutional violations and asserting that the alleged accommodation of having a minor wear a bandage on her face every day was unreasonable. In the meantime, a federal judge ordered the school to reinstate Ariana and permit the nose piercing until the matter could be resolved. The following spring, the case was settled out of court as a victory for Iacono: she was allowed a religious exemption for her nose piercing, and a clarified policy forbade school officials from claiming the authority to interpret religious doctrine when applying the dress code to any student.[34] However, because of the private nature of the settlement, this was not a victory for CoBM as a religious institution; it did not lead to a court precedent that acknowledged bodily adornment as a protected religious right for CoBM members in school settings. Though Iacono's story received national news attention at various points in its development, ultimately hers was only a personal victory that had little wider impact. Two years later a church member in New Mexico dealt with a similar situation involving her daughter but was unsuccessful when she showed school officials articles about the Iacono case; according to the parent, the school superintendent made reference to state case law that would support the school's policy of no facial jewelry.[35] Without a clear precedent, the bold stance taken by Iacono may have to be refought again and again by individuals—most likely minors—claiming their right to free exercise.

·····

The path that religious dress has traversed through the American legal system in recent decades indicates that it remains vulnerable to powerful entities. A stringent uniformity of appearance as dictated by corporate America, the military, prisons, and even schools tends to win out over the seemingly harmless religious adornment choices of individuals. What often goes unacknowledged is the Protestant orientation of jurisprudence on these and other issues of religious free exercise, which is a byproduct of Christianity's ideological dominance in the United States. Because Christianity emphasizes belief as its most defining feature, in a Christian-heavy society there can be an assumption that *all* religions value belief over practice. Constitutional scholar Stephen Feldman has zeroed in on this tendency, commenting that, "From a Christian standpoint, the potential for uncoerced belief in Christ must be protected in order for salvation to be possible, but the protection of this-worldly conduct is unnecessary because such conduct is largely unrelated to salvation."[36] This set of assumptions has had practical effects on laws and courts, and in turn on members of minority religions.

In fact, for decades Feldman and other scholars have observed that courts at all levels have appeared to conceive of "religion" not only in Christian terms, but more specifically in Protestant terms.[37] The evidence for this is found in the way opinions are worded and the way questions are framed, which demonstrate that well-intentioned judges essentially try to superimpose an unfamiliar religion onto a template of "religion" with which they are already familiar. Religious studies scholars Courtney Bender and Jennifer Snow say that Protestantization is seen not only in court decisions that give primacy to belief over practice, but also in the emphasis on individuals rather than collective communities and assumptions about the privacy of religion. They add, "The courts' language of rights . . . neatly dovetails with Protestant definitions of religion that give conscience and individual self-determination a central place."[38] In the specific case of CoBM, it is only the emphasis on belief over practice that is likely to undercut members' freedom of religious adornment, but for Sikhs, Hindus, Buddhists, Pagans, Native Americans, and many others, the translation of their religion into a Christian framework may cause significant distortions about numerous points of religious practice.

Given this broader question of what aspects of religion are held sacrosanct by the American legal system, as well as the influence of institutional power structures, it is unsurprising that Kimberly Cloutier was told that her permanent religious bodily adornments were disruptive to a company's public image. What needs to be recognized is that decisions such as these fail to protect religious practices even as they tout the protection of freedom of belief. Until American society develops more widespread cultural familiarity with the breadth of the world's religions, this tendency to make analogies with Christianity as a way to understand other religions will persist, preventing public understanding of non-Christian religions on their own terms. Religious dress, disregarded as expendable, will likewise only be protected if religious believers continue to step up as ambassadors of the central practices of their faith, forcing them into activist roles. For CoBM members the stakes may be heightened: in contrast with religions in which one's identity can be concealed by the quick removal of religious attire, CoBM members cannot easily hide.[39] They have permanent adornments and their core religious commitments anticipate that they will proudly show and explain these modifications. CoBM members are faced with a difficult choice as they are compelled to be constant representatives of their faith but told that the markers of their faith are simply unacceptable.

NOTES

1. For an overview and examples of these kinds of cases, see Ruthann Robson, *Dressing Constitutionally: Hierarchy, Sexuality, and Democracy from Our Hairstyles to Our Shoes* (Cambridge: Cambridge University Press, 2013), especially ch. 6. Also of interest are other more specific contexts, not discussed in this chapter, such as questions about religious attire in the courtroom and religious attire in government identification photos.
2. Cases involving the prohibition of religious dress may be filed in relation to a wide variety of legal principles, including state and federal antidiscrimination laws, constitutional concepts like the free exercise of religion or equal protection, or particular statutes such as Religious Land Use and

Institutionalized Persons Act (for inmates) or state Religious Freedom Restoration Acts. In other words, they are not all simply First Amendment claims about free exercise, even though this language is most often used to explain them.

3. These foci are also influenced, though not dictated, by precedents. For example, free exercise decisions between 1963 and 1990 often leaned on the *Sherbert* precedent that protected religious practice, whereas decisions after the 1990 *Smith* case were more likely to emphasize that generally applicable laws override individual religious needs.

4. Public school cases are typically state-level issues. See examples at O'Connor v. Hendrick, 184 N.Y. 421 (1906); United States v. Board of Educ. for School Dist., 911 F. 2d 882 (1990); Cooper v. Eugene School Dist., 301 Ore. 358 (1986).

5. See examples at EEOC v. Red Robin Gourmet Burgers, Inc., 2005 U.S. Dist. LEXIS 36219; Complaint, Boudlal v. Walt Disney Corp., No. 12-01306 (2012), available online at https://www.retaillaborandemploymentlaw.com/files/2014/07/Boudlal-v-Walt-Disney.pdf; Muhammad v. N.Y. City Transit Authority, 52 F. Supp. 3d 468 (2014). In the resolutions of both the *Red Robin* and *Transit Authority* cases, the employees were granted accommodation for their religious attire and adornment. The *Disney* case was settled out of court.

6. All text relating to employment practices, including subsequent updates, can be found in 42 USCS § 2000e–2000e-17. Title VII is further supported by EEOC guidelines, which advise employers against taking any actions that will impede religious dress.

7. Dallan F. Flake, "Image Is Everything: Corporate Branding and Religious Accommodation in the Workplace," *University of Pennsylvania Law Review* 163, no. 3 (2015): 699–754.

8. EEOC v. Abercrombie & Fitch Stores, Inc., 135 S. Ct. 2028 (2015).

9. Goldman v. Weinberger, 475 U.S. 503 (1986). From 1958–81, there was an explicit religious exception to military dress code policy for Sikhs; see Khalsa v. Weinberger, 779 F. 2d 1393 (1985).

10. See discussions in Singh v. McHugh, 109 F. Supp. 3d 72 (2015); Singh v. Carter, 168 F. Supp. 3d 216 (2016); Chad Garland, "Air Force Issues New Guidelines for Beards, Turbans, and Hijabs," *Stars and Stripes*, February 11, 2020, https://www.stripes.com/news/air-force/air-force-issues-new-guidelines-for-beards-turbans-and-hijabs-1.618346; Corey Dickstein, "More Bearded, Turbaned Sikhs Join Army as Pentagon Reviews Religious Articles Ban," *Stars and Stripes*, February 24, 2017, https://www.stripes.com/news/more-bearded

-turbaned-sikhs-join-army-as-pentagon-reviews-religious-articles-ban-1.455730.
11. BME refers to the Body Modification Ezine, a website started in 1994 that became a social, professional, and informational hub for people involved with all forms of body modification and manipulation.
12. Suspension involves piercing the skin so that the body can be physically hung. There are many different methods of suspension. For more information, see the website of the International Suspension Alliance, https://suspension.org.
13. "About," Church of Body Modification, accessed June 5, 2018, https://uscobm.com. This website is now defunct because it became infected with malicious code and could not be fixed. In late 2018 almost all of the content was reproduced and relaunched on a new church website (http://churchofbodmod.com); the old url now automatically redirects to the new website. The website does not include a "forum" section for members to communicate with each other.
14. "About Us," Church of Body Modification, http://churchofbodmod.com, accessed 7 August 2019.
15. The FAQ specifically states that the church believes in God, although other names may be preferred by individual members, such as Universal Truth or Goddess, among others. "FAQ," Church of Body Modification, accessed June 5, 2018, https://uscobm.com.
16. Forum post, "Religious/Spiritual Experience," April 6, 2011, Church of Body Modification, https://uscobm.com. All forum posts are from the original website, but when the site moved in 2018 the forum section did not move with it. Monikers have been deleted to protect the privacy of those who posted.
17. Forum post, "When did you know?," April 4, 2012.
18. Forum post, "Ritual vs. Non-Ritual Body Modification," March 9, 2012; forum transcript of class, "Mysticism," September 12, 2012.
19. Forum post, "Ritual vs. Non-Ritual Body Modification," March 8, 2012.
20. A similar difference of opinion was evident in a 2013 forum thread related to the use of mind-altering substances. Some felt that the loss of control would undercut the point of a religious ritual, while others felt it could intensify the experience and open up new spiritual channels.
21. Chris Carter, email message to author, August 16, 2017; "Church News," Church of Body Modification, November 4, 2016, https://uscobm.com.
22. Brandt v. Pallito, 2014 Vt. Unpub. LEXIS 83.
23. Forum post, "Dress Code Issue at Work. (Hair Color)," November 18, 2012.

24. "House Acts to Restrict Surgery to Split Tongues," *St. Louis Post-Dispatch*, March 27, 2003; "Illinois Bill Would Ban Tongue-Splitting," Associated Press, May 13, 2003.
25. Illinois Public Act 093-0449, effective 2004. Nearly identical laws were quickly passed in Delaware and New York; Texas had passed a similar law the previous year. In several other states, similar bills have not passed the legislature.
26. Cloutier's case was filed in federal District Court in Massachusetts in 2002 after the EEOC determined that Costco had engaged in religious discrimination. The opinion was rendered in early 2004 and affirmed by the First Circuit court of appeals in December of that year. Information about this case, including all quoted material, is taken from the two opinions: Kimberly M. Cloutier v. Costco Wholesale, 311 F. Supp. 2d 190 (2004), LEXIS 5128, and Kimberly M. Cloutier v. Costco Wholesale, 390 F. 3d 126 (2004), LEXIS 24763.
27. "Statement of Faith," Church of Body Modification, accessed August 14, 2018, https://uscobm.com.
28. "Vision statement," Church of Body Modification, accessed August 14, 2018, https://uscobm.com.
29. Eileen Barker, "What Are We Studying?" A Sociological Case for Keeping the 'Nova,'" *Nova Religio* 8, no. 1 (2004): 88–102; Phillip Charles Lucas, "Enfants Terribles: The Challenge of Sectarian Converts to Ethnic Orthodox Churches in the United States," *Nova Religio* 7, no. 2 (2003): 5–23.
30. The specific language from the opinion reads as follows: "We question the district court's dismissal of this timing difficulty.... The question of whether a post-termination offer extended during the EEOC mediation process can be a reasonable accommodation raises difficult issues. We have yet to consider this question directly and decline to do so here on the limited summary judgment record."
31. Cloutier v. Costco, District Court Opinion, at *194. Emphasis in original.
32. Bobby T. Brown v. F. L. Roberts, dba Jiffy Lube, 419 F. Supp. 2d 7 (2006), LEXIS 8394; and Aissatou Camara v. Epps Air Service, 292 F. Supp. 3d 1314 (2017), LEXIS 187913.
33. Iacono v. Croom, 2010 U.S. Dist. LEXIS 108153.
34. "Judge Returns Student to Class," *Smithfield Herald* (NC), October 13, 2010; Associated Press, "NC Student Can Continue to Wear Nose Stud in Class," June 6, 2011. The following year the school board changed its policy to allow facial jewelry.

35. Forum post, "Our Struggle with a Close Minded Community," August 17, 2012. However, this parent's posting showed that she erroneously thought the issue had been decided by a federal court, when in fact the only thing a federal court did was order the student's reinstatement.
36. Stephen M. Feldman, *Please Don't Wish Me a Merry Christmas: A Critical History of the Separation of Church and State* (New York: NYU Press, 1997), 248.
37. See examples of such discussions in Feldman, *Please Don't Wish Me a Merry Christmas*, ch. 9; Winnifred Fallers Sullivan, *Paying the Words Extra: Religious Discourse in the Supreme Court of the United States* (Cambridge, MA: Harvard University Press, 1994), ch. 5; and Courtney Bender and Jennifer Snow, "From Alleged Buddhists to Unreasonable Hindus: First Amendment Jurisprudence After 1965," in *A Nation of Religions: The Politics of Pluralism in Multireligious America*, ed. Stephen Prothero (Chapel Hill: University of North Carolina Press, 2006), 181–208.
38. Bender and Snow, "From Alleged Buddhists," 197–98.
39. Granted, for many people the removal of religious attire or adornment would be a moral transgression, and they would not choose to do so.

DISCUSSION QUESTIONS

1. SEVENTH-DAY ADVENTIST DRESS: "AN INDEX TO THE HEART"

1. In what ways did Adventist approaches to dress reform align with and converge from the normative dress standards for women in America in the nineteenth and early twentieth centuries? What might this tell us about the relationship between sectarian and mainline movements?
2. White's visions for dress reform changed over time. In a community in which faith was a necessary precursor to Christ's Second Coming, imagine some of the potential consequences for not following through with what God had prescribed.
3. How did conflicting views about women's clothing relate to other social reforms taking place in the same era?
4. White was one of several prophets in nineteenth-century America. What conditions in the American "religious marketplace" allowed for prophets, visions, and new religious movements to flourish at that time?

2. CLOTHING SPIRITUAL REALITY: THE SARTORIAL STYLES OF MARY BAKER EDDY

1. Why do you think material concerns such as physical healing and clothing were so important for Mary Baker Eddy, who taught that ultimate reality was above all spiritual?
2. What do you think of the claim that clothing and physical appearance reflect spiritual assumptions and attitudes?
3. What does Eddy's attitude toward the people who worked for her at Pleasant View reveal about how Eddy understood the importance of appearances?
4. If Mary Baker Eddy were alive today, how do you think she might dress?

3. FAITH, FASHION, AND FILM IN THE JAZZ AGE: CATHOLIC VESTMENTS ENCOUNTER THE ROARING 1920S

1. What social factors influenced the way Americans perceived the Eucharistic Congress in 1926?
2. What role does gender play in Catholic clerical clothing?
3. What are the advantages and disadvantages of clergy wearing distinctive dress when in worship? How about when in public?
4. What impact might Prohibition (1920–33) have had on the developments discussed in this chapter?

4. POWER BEFORE THRONES OF GOD AND MAN: WOMEN, ADORNMENT, AND PUBLIC LIFE IN WHITE AMERICAN PENTECOSTALISM

1. How do women of various religious traditions use attire to signal messages about their faith?
2. In what ways do men use attire to signal messages about faith? Are these noticeably different from women's signaling?

3. In what ways might attire be linked to a feeling that one is part of a religious minority?
4. How might women's use of clothing be interpreted and/or misinterpreted outside of their religious communities?

5. HOLY DASHIKIS! BLACK SARTORIAL NATIONALISM AND BLACK ISRAELITE RELIGION

1. In what ways have Black ethno-religious groups used dress to redefine the Black body as free versus enslaved?
2. Considering Black sartorial nationalism, what role does attire and adornment play in establishing a Black ethno-religious identity?
3. Discuss the phenomenon of "appearing Jewish" for Black Israelites. What factors might lead African Americans who identify as Jewish or Israelite to want to be publicly identified as such through their dress and adornment?
4. Is the "power to define," as an example of agency, evident in the attire or adornment practices of other religious traditions you are familiar with?

6. REFINED BODIES: CLOTHING AS A VISUAL SIGNIFIER OF PIETY FOR MORMON WOMEN IN AMERICA

1. What is religious peculiarity? Why do you think so much emphasis has been placed on cultivating a peculiar identity for Latter-day Saints?
2. What specific things differentiate religious and nonreligious attire?
3. Judith Butler says that "gender is the cultural meanings that the sexed body assumes." How are "cultural meanings" arrived at? What cultural meanings do you see ascribed to gendered bodies?
4. The rules for female missionaries are significantly more in-depth than the rules for male missionaries. Why do you think that is? What cultural meaning(s) can we infer from this?

7. THE CHRISTIAN TATTOO: MUCH MORE THAN SKIN-DEEP

1. Do you think the trend of tattoo acceptance and acquisition will continue, or will the pendulum swing in reverse? What factors might affect this?
2. Do religious groups risk their theological or spiritual integrity by accommodating the cultural mainstreaming of tattoos, and even openly endorsing religious tattoos?
3. Religious people ritualize their sense of belonging to one another; for example, a New Testament name for Christianity is "The Body of Christ," a phrase that is also used in the worship celebration of Holy Communion. In what ways are the photographs of religious tattoos found in this chapter evocative of Christian rituals?
4. The chapter suggests tattoos—and perhaps especially religious tattoos—mark or memorialize turning points in the lives of individuals. Consider the turning points in your own life so far, or imagine the future: Which of these if any, or other such life events, might be significant enough for you to consider getting a tattoo? What might the design look like?

8. "QUEENS OF THE EARTH": THE MGT UNIFORM AS A FORM OF IDENTITY CREATION AND NATION BUILDING

1. What are some of the key beliefs of the Nation of Islam, and which beliefs relate to attire and adornment?
2. What made the Nation of Islam so attractive to Black people in the early 1930s?
3. How did the MGT uniform help Black women construct their identity?
4. How did the Nation of Islam's relationship to Afrocentric clothing change over time?

9. "YE SHALL BE NAKED IN YOUR RITES": RITUAL ATTIRE AND RITUAL NUDITY (SKYCLAD) IN NORTH AMERICAN WICCA

1. Why do some contemporary Wiccans preserve the practice of ritual nudity?
2. In what ways might ritual nudity be liberating and in what ways might it be oppressive?
3. What does the reassignment of meaning onto the skyclad tradition tell us about the adaptability of religious cultures and traditions more broadly?
4. Can you identify other types of negotiations related to material objects/culture that religious populations do during their lifetimes?

10. AMISH VOGUE: PERFORMING FASHION IN THE PLAIN WORLD

1. For Amish women, what values are embedded in making their own clothing?
2. What are some of the differences and similarities between Amish fashion and mainstream fashion?
3. How do the Old Order Amish, especially young people, negotiate church regulations when making a fashion statement?
4. Do you think it is accurate to think of this discussion of Amish clothing evolution as a study of "fashion?" Why or why not?

11. "YOUR RELIGION IS SHOWING": NEGOTIATION AND PERSONAL EXPERIENCE IN MORMON GARMENTS

1. What does this study of garments tell us about Mormons and belief?
2. How does gender identity help shape Mormons' views of their garments?

3. Why do you think that conforming and nonconforming believers perceive their agency in different ways?
4. How do popular narratives about garments or representations of them in the media misrepresent the meaning of garments for Mormons?

12. DRESSED FOR GLORY: WHITE UNIFORMS IN AFRICAN AMERICAN CHURCH TRADITIONS AS VISUAL POLITICAL THEOLOGY

1. Consider a community to which you personally belong. Is there an outfit or type of clothing that you can understand as having a multiplicity of meanings? What claims or values does that clothing or outfit convey?
2. One of the sub-threads of the uniform discussion is an idea of separation, which can include a resistance to assimilation. Is this different from personal style and individualism? How so?
3. Where/how do you see political use of aesthetics and/or aesthetic dress today? How do you feel this use contributes to social conversations?
4. There are other uniforms, both historical and current, that one could consider in conversation with the usher uniform described in this chapter. What are some other "uniforms" that come to mind? How do they function—spiritually, politically, socially? What would be an "impactful" use of a uniform in your mind?

13. "THE HARE KRISHNA LOOK": ISKCON ADORNMENT AS RELIGIOUS ACTIVISM

1. What is the "Hare Krishna look," and what are the different reasons for leaders and adherents within ISKCON to adopt that look? What did it mean to them?
2. What is the political power of adornment? How can adorning oneself in a particular manner, which might seem like just an individual spiritual or aesthetic choice, actually be an activist act?

3. Why did Bhaktivedanta and other leaders in ISKCON focus so much on women's clothing and adornment? What is the connection between adornment and gender and sexuality?
4. There is a tension between dress and adornment as a practice and as a symbol. Are the clothes and other material culture (jewelry, *tilaka* marks, etc.) important in and of themselves, or rather as symbols of something else?

14. RELIGIOUS DRESS, THE CHURCH OF BODY MODIFICATION, AND THE FIRST AMENDMENT

1. Can you articulate a clear distinction between clothing that expresses religion and clothing that exercises religion? Are there articles of attire that fall into a gray area?
2. Is it appropriate for secular institutions to evaluate the "legitimacy" of a religion when deciding if its practices are acceptable in the institutional context? What problems might arise from such evaluations?
3. What differences do you think are necessary for regulations on attire and adornment in these four institutional settings: schools, the military, prisons, and the workplace? What regulations, if any, seem unnecessary or outdated?
4. Considering what you have learned from the situations discussed in this essay, if you were Kimberly Cloutier's supervisor today, how would you handle her request?

SUGGESTED READING LIST

Almila, Anna-Mari. *Veiling in Fashion: Space and the Hijab in Minority Communities.* London: I. B. Tauris, 2019.

Almila, Anna-Mari, and David Inglis, eds. *The Routledge International Handbook to Veils and Veiling Practices.* London: Routledge, 2018.

Anderson, Cory. "The Undistinguished Scholar of the Amish, Werner Enninger, -or- Has the Time Yet Come for Rigorous Theory in Amish Studies?" *Journal of Amish and Plain Anabaptist Studies* 5, no. 2 (2017): 196–238.

Arthur, Linda B., ed. *Religion, Dress, and the Body.* Oxford: Berg, 1999.

———. *Undressing Religion: Commitment and Conversion from a Cross-Cultural Perspective.* Oxford: Berg, 2000.

Asay, Caros. "The Temple Garment: 'An Outward Expression of an Inward Commitment.'" *Ensign,* August 1997, 18–23.

Barnard, Malcolm. *Fashion Theory: An Introduction.* London: Routledge, 2014.

Batten, Alicia J., and Kelly Olson. *Dress in Mediterranean Antiquity: Greeks Romans, Jews, and Christians.* London: T & T Clark, 2021.

Beckford, Robert. "Black Suit Matters: Faith, Politics, and Representation in the Religious Documentary." In *Black Religion and Aesthetics: Religious Thought and Life in Africa and the African Diaspora,* edited by Anthony B. Pinn, 135–51. New York: Palgrave Macmillan, 2009.

Blakesley, Katie Clark. "'A Style of Our Own': Modesty and Mormon Women, 1951–2008." *Dialogue: A Journal of Mormon Thought* 42, no. 2 (2009): 20–53.

Bohn, Cornelia. "Clothing as a Medium of Communication." Researchgate.net, April 2012. https://www.researchgate.net/publication/328530889_Clothing_as_medium_of_Communication.

Bucar, Elizabeth M. *Pious Fashion: How Muslim Women Dress.* Cambridge, MA: Harvard University Press, 2017.

———. "Secular Fashion, Religious Dress, and Modest Ambiguity." *Journal of Religious Ethics* 44, no. 1 (2016): 68–90.

Burns, E. Jane, ed. *Medieval Fabrications: Dress, Textiles, Clothwork, and Other Cultural Imaginings.* New York: Palgrave Macmillan, 1994.

Butler, Anthea. *Women in the Church of God in Christ: Making a Sanctified World.* Chapel Hill: University of North Carolina Press, 2007.

Butler, Judith. *Gender Trouble. Feminism and the Subversion of Identity.* New York: Routledge, 1999.

CERCL Writing Collective. *Embodiment and Black Religion: Rethinking the Body in African American Experience.* Bristol, CT: Equinox, 2017.

Coakley, Sarah. *Religion and the Body.* Cambridge: Cambridge University Press, 1997.

Cogan, Francis B. *All-American Girl: The Ideal of Real Womanhood in Mid-Nineteenth-Century America.* Athens: University of Georgia Press, 1989.

Covolo, Robert. *Fashion Theology.* Waco, TX: Baylor University Press, 2020.

Cunningham, Patricia A. *Reforming Women's Fashion, 1850–1920: Politics, Health, and Art.* Kent, OH: Kent State University Press, 2003.

Cunningham, Patricia A., and Susan Voso Lab, eds. *Dress in American Culture.* Bowling Green, OH: Bowling Green State University Popular Press, 1993.

Curtis, Edward E., IV. *Black Muslim Religion in the Nation of Islam, 1960–1975.* Chapel Hill, NC: University of North Carolina Press, 2006.

Duffy, John-Charles. "Concealing the Body, Concealing the Sacred: The Decline of Ritual Nudity in Mormon Temples." *Journal of Ritual Studies* 21, no. 2 (2007): 1–21.

Dwyer-McNulty, Sally. *Common Threads: A Cultural History of Clothing in American Catholicism.* Chapel Hill: University of North Carolina Press, 2014.

Elliott, Dyan. "Dressing and Undressing the Clergy: Rites of Ordination and Degradation." In *Medieval Fabrications: Dress, Textiles, Cloth Work, and Other Cultural Imaginings,* edited by E. Jane Burns, 55–69. New York: Palgrave Macmillan, 2004.

Enninger, Werner. "The Design Features of Clothing Codes: The Functions of Clothing Displays in Interaction." *Ars Semeiotica* 8, nos. 1–2 (1985): 81–110.

———. "The Semiotic Structure of Amish Folk Costume: Its Function in the Organisation of Face-to Face Interaction." In *Multimedial Communication*, vol. 1, edited by Ernest W. B. Hess-Luttich, 86–123. Tubingen, Germany: Gunter Narr, 1982.

Entwistle, Joanne. *The Fashioned Body: Fashion, Dress, and Modern Social Theory.* 2nd ed. Cambridge: Polity, 2015.

Finch, Martha L. *Dissenting Bodies: Corporealities in Early New England.* New York: Columbia University Press, 2010.

———. " 'Fashions of the Worldly Dames': Separatist Discourses of Dress in Early Modern London, Amsterdam, and Plymouth Colony." *Church History* 74, no. 3 (2005): 494–533.

Fischer, Gayle V. *Pantaloons and Power: A Nineteenth-Century Dress Reform in the United States.* Kent, OH: Kent State University Press, 2001.

Flake, Dallan F. "Image Is Everything: Corporate Branding and Religious Accommodation in the Workplace." *University of Pennsylvania Law Review* 163, no. 3 (2015): 699–754.

Ford, Tanisha C. *Liberated Threads: Black Women, Style, and the Global Politics of Soul.* Chapel Hill: University of North Carolina Press, 2015.

Gibson, Dawn-Marie, and Jamillah Ashira Karim. *Women of the Nation: Between Black Protest and Sunni Islam.* New York: NYU Press, 2014.

Gottschalk, Stephen. *Rolling Away the Stone: Mary Baker Eddy's Challenge to Materialism.* Bloomington: Indiana University Press, 2006.

Greenspoon, Leonard J., ed. *Fashioning Jews: Clothing, Culture, and Commerce.* West Lafayette, IN: Purdue University Press, 2013.

Griffin, Alexandria Gale. "(In)visible Piety: Reading Mormon Garments Through Hijab." Master's thesis, Claremont Graduate University, 2014.

Griffith, R. Marie. *Born Again Bodies: Flesh and Spirit in American Christianity.* Berkeley: University of California Press, 2004.

Hebdige, Richard. *Subculture: The Meaning of Style.* London: Routledge, 1979.

Higginbotham, Evelyn Brooks. *Righteous Discontent: The Women's Movement in the Black Baptist Church, 1880-1920.* Cambridge, MA: Harvard University Press, 1994.

Hume, Lynne. *The Religious Life of Dress: Global Fashion and Faith.* London: Bloomsbury Academic, 2013.

Jensen, Lori, Richard W. Flory, and Donald E. Miller. "Marked for Jesus: Sacred Tattooing Among Evangelical GenXers." In *GenX Religion*, edited by Richard W. Flory and Donald E. Miller, 15–30. New York: Routledge, 2000.

Joselit, Jenna Weissman. *A Perfect Fit: Clothes, Character, and the Promise of America.* New York: Metropolitan, 2001.

Joseph, Nathan. *Uniforms and Nonuniforms: Communication Through Clothing.* Westport, CT: Greenwood Press, 1986.

Khabeer, Su'ad Abdul. *Muslim Cool: Race, Religion, and Hip Hop in the United States.* New York: NYU Press, 2016.

Klassen, Pamela E. "The Robes of Womanhood: Dress and Authenticity Among African American Methodist Women in the Nineteenth Century." *Religion and American Culture* 14, no. 1 (Winter 2004): 39–82.

Koch, Jerome R., and Alden E. Roberts. "The Protestant Ethic and the Religious Tattoo." *Social Science Journal* 49, no. 2 (2012): 210–13.

Kraybill, Donald B. *The Riddle of Amish Culture.* 2nd ed. Baltimore: Johns Hopkins University Press, 2001.

Lewis, Reina. "Modest Body Politics: The Commercial and Ideological Intersect of Fat, Black, and Muslim in the Modest Fashion Market and Media." *Fashion Theory: The Journal of Dress, Body, & Culture* 23, no. 2 (2019): 243–73.

———. *Muslim Fashion: Contemporary Style Cultures.* Durham, NC: Duke University Press, 2015.

Lewis, Reina, ed. *Modest Fashion: Styling Bodies, Mediating Faith.* London: I. B. Tauris, 2013.

Lowe, Scott. *Hair.* London: Bloomsbury Press, 2016.

Marzel, Shoshana-Rose, and Guy Stiebel, eds. *Dress and Ideology: Fashioning Identity from Antiquity to the Present.* London: Bloomsbury Press, 2015.

McDannell, Colleen. *Material Christianity: Religion and Popular Culture in America.* New Haven, CT: Yale University Press, 1995.

Morgan, David. *The Thing About Religion: An Introduction to the Material Study of Religions.* Chapel Hill: University of North Carolina Press, 2021.

Neal, Lynn S. "The Ideal Democratic Apparel: T-Shirts, Religious Intolerance, and the Clothing of Democracy." *Material Religion* 10, no. 2 (2014): 182–207.

———. *Religion in Vogue: Christianity and Fashion in America.* New York: NYU Press, 2019.

Nielsen, Michael E., and Daryl White. "Men's Grooming in the Latter-day Saints Church: A Qualitative Study of Norm Violation." *Mental Health, Religion & Culture* 11, no. 8 (2008): 807–25.

Nolt, Steven M., and Thomas J. Meyers. *Plain Diversity: Amish Cultures and Identities.* Baltimore: Johns Hopkins University Press, 2007.

O'Neil, Mary Lou. "You Are What You Wear: Clothing/Appearance Laws and the Construction of the Public Citizen in Turkey." *Fashion Theory* 14, no. 1 (2010): 65–81.

Payne, Leah. "'Pants Don't Make Preachers': Fashion and Gender Construction in Late-Nineteenth- and Early-Twentieth-Century American Revivalism." *Fashion Theory* 19, no. 1 (2015): 83–113.

Piela, Anna. *Wearing the Niqab: Muslim Women in the UK and US*. London: Bloomsbury, 2021.

Pike, Sarah M. *Earthly Bodies, Magical Selves: Contemporary Pagans and the Search for Community*. Berkeley: University of California Press, 2001.

Powell, Adam J. "Covenant Cloaks: Mormon Temple Garments in the Light of Identity Theory." *Material Religion* 12, no. 4 (2016): 457–75.

Ribeiro, Aileen. *Dress and Morality*. Oxford: Berg, 2003.

Robson, Ruthann. *Dressing Constitutionally: Hierarchy, Sexuality, and Democracy from Our Hairstyles to Our Shoes*. Cambridge: Cambridge University Press, 2013.

Saracino, Michele. *Clothing*. Minneapolis, MN: Fortress, 2012.

Satter, Beryl. *Each Mind a Kingdom: American Women, Sexual Purity, and the New Thought Movement, 1875-1920*. Berkeley: University of California Press, 1999.

Schmidt, Leigh Eric. "'A Church-Going People Are a Dress-Loving People': Clothes, Communication, and Culture in Early America." *Church History* 58 (March 1989): 36–51.

———. "The Easter Parade: Piety, Fashion, and Display." *Religion and American Culture* 4 (1994): 135–64.

Scott, Stephen. *Why Do They Dress That Way?* Intercourse, PA: Good Books, 1997.

Silverman, Eric. *A Cultural History of Jewish Dress*. New York: Bloomsbury Academic, 2013.

Tarlo, Emma. *Clothing Matters: Dress and Identity in India*. Chicago: University of Chicago Press, 1996.

———. *Entanglement: The Secret Lives of Hair*. London: OneWorld, 2016.

———. *Visibly Muslim: Fashion, Politics, Faith*. New York: Berg, 2005.

Tarlo, Emma, and Annelies Moors, eds. *Islamic Fashion and Anti-fashion: New Perspectives from Europe and North America*. London: Bloomsbury, 2013.

Taylor, Ula Y. *The Promise of Patriarchy: Women and the Nation of Islam*. Chapel Hill: University of North Carolina Press, 2017.

Thompson, Beverly Yuen. *Covered in Ink: Tattoos, Women, and the Politics of the Body*. New York: NYU Press, 2015.

Von Busch, Otta, and Jeanine Viau, eds. *Silhouettes of the Soul: Meditations on Fashion, Religion, and Subjectivity*. London: Bloomsbury, 2022.

Westfield, Nancy Lynne. "The Foolish Woman Grows Angry Because They Teach Her." In *Black Religion and Aesthetics: Religious Thought and Life in Africa and the*

African Diaspora, edited by Anthony B. Pinn, 37–52. New York: Palgrave Macmillan, 2009.

Wheeler, Kayla Renee. "Clothes of Righteousness: The MGT Uniform in the Twentieth Century." In *Islam Through Objects*, edited by Anna Bigelow, 17–30. London: Bloomsbury Academic, 2021.

Wilson, Elizabeth. *Adorned in Dreams: Fashion and Modernity*. Berkeley: University of California Press, 1985. Revised edition, New Brunswick, NJ: Rutgers University Press, 2003.

CONTRIBUTORS

MARIE W. DALLAM, COEDITOR, holds a PhD in religion from Temple University. She is a professor of religious studies and associate dean of the Honors College at the University of Oklahoma, where she has taught since 2009. Her research interests focus on intersections of religion and culture within new and alternative religions in the United States. Her publications include *Daddy Grace* (NYU, 2007), *Cowboy Christians* (Oxford, 2018), and the coedited collection *Religion, Food, and Eating in North America* (Columbia, 2014). Since 2017 she has been co-general editor of the journal *Nova Religio*. She is also a cofounder of the AAR seminar that served as the initial basis for this book.

BENJAMIN E. ZELLER, COEDITOR, holds a PhD in religion from University of North Carolina, Chapel Hill. He is a professor of religious studies and department chair at Lake Forest College in Illinois. His research and publication interests focus on new and alternative religions, particularly aspects of material culture, as well as religion and science. His publications include *Prophets and Protons* (NYU, 2010), *Heaven's Gate* (NYU, 2014), and the coedited collection *Religion, Food, and Eating in North America* (Columbia, 2014). Since 2013 he has been co-general editor of the journal

Nova Religio. He is also a cofounder of the AAR seminar that served as the initial basis for this book.

ADRIENNE NOCK AMBROSE holds a PhD in the history of Christianity from the Graduate Theological Union. She is an associate professor of religious studies at the University of the Incarnate Word, San Antonio, Texas. Her research interests and publications focus on the history of Catholic visual and material culture. Her first book, *Holywood: Lights, Camera, and Catholics in the Age of American Spectacle*, is forthcoming from Fortress Press.

EMILY J. BAILEY holds a PhD in religion from the University of Pittsburgh. She is an associate professor of religious studies at Towson University in Maryland. As a historian of religion, her work explores the intersections of food and material culture with sectarian and innovative expressions of religion in nineteenth- and twentieth-century America.

KATE DAVIS holds an MA in women's studies in religion and is currently a PhD candidate at Claremont Graduate University. Her dissertation in progress is titled "The Aesthetics of Amiability: Performing Gender in Mormon and Evangelical Online Spaces." Her research looks at new religious spaces and communities through the lens of feminist theory, with a focus on new religious movements and religions of North America. She lives and teaches in Ohio.

JESSICA FINNIGAN holds an MA from King's College of London and an advanced diploma from the University of Cambridge, both in the study of religion. Her research focuses on contemporary Mormonism, particularly in relation to the Internet and gender dynamics. Several of her publications on these topics were written with her coauthor, NANCY ROSS. Ross holds a PhD in art history from the University of Cambridge. She is associate professor of interdisciplinary arts and sciences at Dixie State University in Utah. Her research interests and long list of publications focus primarily on Mormon feminism and digital culture.

ANDRÉ E. BROOKS-KEY holds a PhD from Temple University. He is associate professor of African and African American studies at Claflin University in South Carolina. He teaches courses in the areas of African American religions, Black social and political thought, and Black masculinity and sexuality. His research focuses on African American religious traditions in the twentieth century, and he has published several articles on Black Judaism and the Hebrew Israelite tradition.

JEROME R. KOCH holds a PhD in sociology from Purdue University, and he is a full professor at Texas Tech University in Lubbock. His coauthor, KEVIN D. DOUGHERTY, holds a PhD in sociology from Purdue University, and is a full professor at Baylor University. Both Koch and Dougherty are sociologists who specialize in the study of religion, and they are each the authors of an extensive list of publications. As a team, they have been conducting studies on religious tattoos since 2017.

MICHELLE MUELLER holds a PhD in religious studies from the Graduate Theological Union. Her research interests include new religious movements, gender and sexuality, and media studies. She is the author of *New Religions and the Mediation of Non-Monogamy: Polyamory, Polygamy, and Reality Television* (Routledge, 2021).

NAO NOMURA is a PhD candidate in area studies at the University of Tokyo and an associate professor on the Faculty of Liberal Arts at Saitama University in Saitama, Japan. Her research and publications focus on the material and visual culture of the Amish, which is based on her more than twelve years of ongoing fieldwork among the Amish in the United States.

LEAH PAYNE holds a PhD in history of religion from Vanderbilt University. She is associate professor of American religious history at Portland Seminary. Payne's first book, *Gender and Pentecostal Revivalism: Making a Female Ministry in the Early Twentieth Century* (Palgrave Macmillan 2015) won the Pneuma Book Award; her forthcoming monograph explores how popular music shapes the theological and political imagination of American evangelicals. Payne's coauthor, ANDREA SHAN JOHNSON, holds a PhD in history from the University of Missouri, Columbia. She is an associate professor of history at California State University, Dominguez Hills. Her research interests and publications focus on religion and activism in twentieth-century America. She is c-editor of a book on Oneness Pentecostal history forthcoming from Penn State University Press. Payne and Johnson are presently the cochairs of the unit on Pentecostal-Charismatic movements in the American Academy of Religion.

JEREMY RAPPORT holds a PhD in American religion from Indiana University. He is an associate professor of religious studies at the College of Wooster, Ohio. His research and publications center around the material culture of American metaphysical religions, with particular interests in the Unity School, Seventh-day Adventism, and Christian Science.

ELAINA TAZE SMITH holds master's degrees in theology from both Union Theological Seminary (New York City) and Boston University. She is currently a DMin candidate at Memphis Theological Seminary, where she studies pastoral counseling. Her interests focus on theology, psychology, and creativity as a mode, a balm, and a process.

KAYLA RENÉE WHEELER holds a PhD in religious studies from the University of Iowa. She is an assistant professor at Xavier University in Ohio. Her research and publications center on intersections of Black American Islam, gender, and performativity. Her first monograph, in preparation, is about Black Muslim women's dress practices.

INDEX

activist adornment, 9, 14; of African American Church women, 15, 271–90, 293n30; CoBM First Amendment jurisprudence, 15–16, 320–35, 335nn1–2, 336n5, 336n9, 337n13, 338n26, 338n30; of ISKCON adornment, 15, 295–316, *301*, *303*, *308*, 317n14, 318n22

Adhikari, Hayagriva das, 307

aesthetic action: A. Butler on dress intentionality, 283–84; Gilkes on, 282–84, 286–87; professionalism in Sanctified Church, 285; holiness and sanctification, 283–84, 293n28

aesthetic language: of Diaspora and religion, 281; Gilkes on historical tactics for, 280–81; image of power in, 282; Pinn on clothing choices and, 280; spiritual impact, 280

African Americans. *See* Black Americans

African-Edenic, 121, 131

African Hebrew Israelites of Jerusalem (AHIJ): Ammi as founder of, 133; divine garments of, 133–34, *137*; dress code of, 134; textile national and ethnic significance, 133–34

Afrocentric fashion: V. Lewis on, 131–32; NOI prohibition of hairstyles and, 200

AHIJ. *See* African Hebrew Israelites of Jerusalem

Alexandrian covens, 209; ritual nudity in initiation ceremonies, 217

Amish church: Amman leadership, 230; diversity of, 230–31; *Ordnung* guidelines for, 230–31, 234; Protestant Reformation and, 230; *Rumspringa* period in, 236–38, 249n44

Amish women's fashion, 14; age and, 232, 237–40, *240*; Amish-ification of store-bought clothes, 244–45; body contours concealed, 231–32; casual attire in, 236; fabrics, 216, 242–43, 250n55; fabric store shopping, 227, 242–43, *243*, 249n40; fundamental wardrobe of, 231; Hamilton and Hawley on, 228; head coverings, 234, *235*, 245–46, 249n36; Kraybill on flexibility in, 228; mainstream consumer culture negotiation, 242–45; Old Order Amish and, 229; public ethnic identity of, 228; social context through clothing, 234–37; uncut and covered hair, 232–34, *235*, 248n29; uniformity, 228; weddings and, 237–38, 249nn42–43

Apostolic Faith newspaper, 89–90

Arthur, Linda B., 7; on dress representation of culture, 121

Ashkenazi Jews: Black Israelites and, 128; cultural norms of, 122; IBOR dress of, 128

Assemblies of God, 89

Azusa Street Revival (1906): 87, 89

Back to Godhead magazine, of Hare Krishna, 296, 318n22; Adhikari on bodily adornment and sexuality, 307; adornment in, 305–7, 310–12; on antimaterialism, 306–19; on *bhakti* devotion of adornment, 310–12; Carana on, 308; fundraising by, 305; on gender and female sexuality danger, 312–14; on Hare Krishna look, 308; as ISKCON practice guide, 305; for religious proselytizing, 305

Bado, Nikki, 219, 225n19

Baht-Yah, Bayadwa, 138

Bakker, Tammy Faye, 96, 97

Battle Creek Sanitarium, 34, 39n44, 39n47

Baylor University. *See* Campus Tattoos Project

Beckford, Robert, 281–82, 283

Beckham, David, 169

Bell, E. N., 89, 90

Bender, Courtney, 334

Ben Hur (film), 73

ben Levy, Sholomo, 119–20; on Levi Israel, 132–33

Bernard, David K., 103–5

Beyond Birth and Death (Bhaktivedanta), 307

bhakti, 297–98, 310–12

Bhaktivedanta, A. C. "Swami," 300–301, 316n3; on adornment as political act, 303–4; Cox on, 297; Hare Krishna movement founded by, 297; culture of Krishna consciousness, 302; interview on adornment, 308–10; on material bodies, 307; on sensual pleasures, 314; Vivekananda and Yogananda predecessors to, 297; Western adornment norms criticism, 304

Bieber, Justin, 169

Black aesthetics: biblical, 136–38; E. Muhammad redefining of, 199–202
Black Americans: Black Israelites and culture of, 122–23; issues of identity and, 117, 124, 140n16, 199–203, 286–87; of Lost Tribe of Shabazz, 193; *Muhammad Speaks* for, 196–97
Black Israelites: African American culture and, 122–23; African and Indian styles of dress, 128–29; Bayadwa Bhat-Yah fashion for, 138; biblical modes of dress, 120; on Blackness as sacred symbol, 12, 121, 139; Black Power era influence on, 129; challah covers, 122; COGSOC Masonic influence, 126–27; cultural nationalism and ritual adherence conflicts, 12, 120; dashiki tunic, 117–18, 129–33, *130*; Harlem Renaissance influence on, 128–29; Jewish appearance of, 122–25; kente cloth, 122, *123*; Masonic influence on, 126–28; Orientalist odyssey of, 126–29, 132–33; orthodox Muslim dress of, 124–25; Rabbinic Judaism schism in Black Power era, 119, 131; sartorial evolution of, 120; *tallit* production, 122; *tzitzit* as fashion statement of, 118, 137; *tzitzit* ritual tassels on dashiki tunic, 118, 129–30, *130*, 138
Black Panther Party, 201
Black Power era: Black Israelites and Rabbinic Judaism schism, 119, 131; Black Israelites influenced by, 129
Black sartorial nationalism, 123–24, 139; Black biblical aesthetics, 136–38; social control and Black body, 120–22
Black women, 277–90; Deanar on dress of, 198; Hassain on natural beauty of, 199; MGT uniform and identity of, 13, 190; NOI on beauty and femininity of, 202; NOI on stereotypes of, 193; NOI protection of, 199; U. Taylor on NOI, 192
Blige, Mary J., 169
Bloomer, Amelia, 29, 30
body modification, religious, 320, 325–28
Body Modification Ezine (BME), 325, 327, 337n11
Bohn, Cornelia, 16, 143
Breen, Joseph, 64
Bricket Wood Coven, 212
bridal fashion choice: of Pentecostal women, 95–96; of White-Cain, 97
Brigham Young University (BYU), Wilkinson on student clothing at, 149–50, 162n22
British Traditional Witchcraft, 213; degrees of, 216, 219, 224n17
Bucar, Elizabeth, 6; on Islamic dress, 311; on veiling, 298
Buczynski, Eddie, 213
Buehner, Alice, 154–57
Butler, Anthea D., 283–84
Butler, Judith: on clothing rituals, 151; on gendered body, 145–46, 150, 153; on LDS women's public femininity, 143
BYU. *See* Brigham Young University

California Pacific International Exposition, 94
Callister, Tad, 153
Campus Tattoos Project, at Baylor University: affiliation tattoos, *178*, 178–80, *179*, 183; college student survey, 175; covert religious tattoos, 174; identity presentation tattoos, 175–78, *176*, *177*, 183; of Koch and Dougherty, 173–82; religious tattoos and religiosity, 181–82, *182*; religious tattoos data collection, 174; transformation tattoos, 180–81, *181*, 183
Cannon, Nick, 169
Carana Dasa, Caitanya, 308
Carter, Donald, 281, 283
Catholic Church: clerical dress, 45, 70; Eucharist understanding by, 68–70; nun habit, 3, 45; priest attire, 45, 70; Women's Day, 66, *67*. *See also* International Eucharistic Congress
Catholic vestments, in film and fashion, 61–80; Elliot on symbolism of, 69; *Heavenly Bodies* Met exhibition of 2018, 11, 76; Middle Ages affluence and, 70–71; Pope Pius XI on splendor of, 71; publications on, 64–68; rite of ordination and, 69; Second Vatican Council on, 71; vesting prayers and blessings, 71–72, 82n38. *See also* films
celebrities: Pentecostalism culture of, 93; tattoos of, 168, 169
chai jewelry, 122
Charge of the Goddess, The (Valiente), 207; as Wicca gospel, 209

Chicago: Middle Age reflection in landmarks of, 75. *See also* International Eucharistic Congress, Twenty-Eighth
Chicago Tribune, International Eucharistic Congress pamphlet, 64
Christian ascetic dress, Upson-Saia on, 5
Christian Science. *See* Church of Christ, Scientist
Christian Science Monitor, 40
Christian Temperance and Bible Hygiene (White), 28
Church of Body Modification (CoBM), 15, 320–24, 336n5, 336n9; Cloutier and, 329–33, 335, 338n26, 338n30; faith statement, 325; First Amendment jurisprudence on religious dress of, 16; Iacono and, 333–34; individual and private communication, 327; online communication of, 326–27, 328, 337n13; religious activism and, 329–34; religious organization legal status, 327; ritualized modification types, 325; virtual meeting sessions, 327. *See also* law, religious attire and
Church of Christ, Scientist (Christian Science): basic theology of, 41–44; Eddy clothing choices and, 11, 40–58; Eddy financial freedom from, 54; founding of, 51–52; on nature of world and humans, 43; on God as only reality, 42–43; on healing and human-divine relationship, 41; on human relationship with God, 43–44; New

Age movement and, 40; religious
dress, 10–11
Church of God and Saints of Christ
(COGSOC), 126–27
Church of God in Christ (COGIC), 284
Church of Jesus Christ of Latter-day
Saints (Mormonism): assimilation
push and pull, 147–49; comparison
to Seventh-day Adventists, 25; ERA
opposition, 162n16; femininity, 12;
Hinckley on peculiarity of, 147, 152;
lay leadership, 143, 160n3, 161n12;
Mauss on assimilation and
peculiarity of, 147–48; missionaries
of, 154, 162n19, 163n41; Nelson on
name references to, 160n2; Romney
and, 148; J. Smith and, 36n6, 251;
temple garments, 153–54, 163n40.
See also Latter-day Saint men;
Latter-day Saint women
Circle Sanctuary, of Fox, 213
Civil Rights Act (1964), religion as
federally protected category, 323
clerical dress: clergy collar
representation, 45; of da Graça, 70;
Fosdick on Protestant, 70; of
McPherson, 70
clothing: Amish women fashion social
context through, 234–37; Bohn on
language of, 16, 143; Buehner on
LDS missionary clothing, 154–57;
Catholic Church clergy and
monastics, 45; Eddy physical
appearance change and, 44;
Enninger on language of, 16; Joselit
on ready-made clothing
revolution, 46; law and religiously
defined, 321; LDS women religious
standards for, 144; as LDS women's
resistance, 149–51; O'Neil on
politics of, 303–4; social message
about identity, 46; as uniform,
44–46. *See also* dress; garments;
uniforms
Clothing Factory Store, MGT and,
195–96
Clothing Guidelines for Lady Missionaries,
155, *156*
Cloutier, Kimberly, 329–33, 335,
338n26, 338n30
Coakley, Sarah, 5
CoBM. *See* Church of Body
Modification
COGIC. *See* Church of God in Christ
COGSOC. *See* Church of God and Saints
of Christ
commercialization, of North
American Wicca, 211
communication: Bohn on textile
system of, 16, 143, 154; Enninger
on, 16; gendered bodies as form
of, 145
Comstock, J. L., 27–28
conforming men and Mormon
garments, 256; justifications of,
257–58; as LDS Church decision
makers, 257; on Mormon garment
covenant, 257–58, 270, 271;
Mormon health code and, 257
conforming women and Mormon
garments, 261; institution loyalty
and, 262; on modesty teachings,
262; on Mormon garment
covenant, 263–64, 270, 271; on
physical discomfort, 264; on
pregnancy and, 264–65

consent culture, North American Wicca and: Kraemer and Aburrow on, 210; values of, 220
Coolidge, Calvin, 80
cosmic stories, through Christian tattoos, 166
countercultural religion, Hare Krishna movement and, 296–98; stages of life in, 298–99
covenant: Mormon garments and ritual connection to, 251; Mormon garments and conforming men, 257–58, 270, 271; Mormon garments and conforming women, 263–64, 270, 271; Mormon garments and nonconforming men, 260, 271
covens: Alexandrian, 209, 217; feminist women-only and skyclad power, 215–16; Gardner Bricket Wood Coven, 212; Gardnerian, 209, 212, 217, 218; Gardner initiation into, 211
COVID-19 pandemic, face mask opposition, 1–3
Craft, The (film), Wicca growth from, 226
Crawford, Florence, 89
Crawford, Rheba, 96, 97
Crouch, Jan, 97
Crowdy, William Saunders, 127
Crowley, Aleister, 209
Cultural History of Jewish Dress, A (Silverman), 5, 118
cultural nationalism, Black Israelite ritual adherence conflicts with, 12, 120
Cunningham, Scott, 214

Curott, Phyllis, 213, 214
Curtis, Edward E., IV, 192

dashiki tunic: African American religious leaders wearing, 117; as African identity symbol, 117; J. Benning and M. Benning on, 130; Black Israelites and, 117–18, 129–33, *130*; Mtshali on, 130; *tzitzit* ritual tassels on, 118, 129–30, *130*, 138
Davis, Kim, 11; Esther comparison of, 106–7; on God as ultimate authority, 108; *Good Morning America* interview, 108–9; Huckabee and Cruz support of, 106; hypocrisy accusation for, 108–9; natural order preservation and, 106–9; Oneness Pentecostal attire and long hair, *104*, 107, *107*; Oneness Pentecostalism of, 88; as political figure, 109; Pope Francis meeting with, 106; same sex marriage license refusal, 86, 106–8
Deanar, Tynetta, 197; on Black women's dress, 198
degree system: of British Traditional Witchcraft, 216, 219, 224n17; of North American Wicca, 214, 224n17; for ritual nudity initiations, 209
DeMille, Cecil B., 72–73, 77
Devil's Playground (documentary film), 237, 249n44
dhotis, men in Hare Krishna movement, 302–3, 307, 308, *308*, 315
Dianic Wiccan traditions, 213
Diaspora, African: Beckford on role of suit in, 281–82, 283; Carter on, 281;

Pinn on aesthetic representation of religion in, 280–81, 290n1
Divine Messianic Dress Code (DMDC), of AHIJ, 134
domestic religion, of women, 29
Dorman, Jacob, 127
dress: Beckford on suit role in Diaspora, 281–82, 283; as both object and action, 16; clerical, 45, 70; domesticity and religion model in 1870s, 29; dress reform and nineteenth-century, 26–28; Hassain on Great Depression norm changes, 197–98; modesty in, 9, 32, 90; social and cultural meaning of, 7; White on frugality and modesty in, 32
"Dress and Grooming Guidelines for Sister Missionaries," 144
"Dressed for Spiritual Success" (Urmila), 315
dress reform: by Bloomer, 29, 30; by E. Miller, 29, 30; nineteenth century, 26–28; Seventh-day Adventist views of, 28–36; of White, 23, 30; White health-driven, 28, 30, 34
Dress Reform, The pamphlet, of Seventh-day Adventists, 31
Drutakarma dasa, 312
Duffy, John-Charles, 252
Dwyer-McNulty, Sally, 45

Eddy, Mary Baker, 11, *53*, *57*; appropriate dress of, 41; clothing and physical appearance change of, 44, 58; clothing as uniform, 44–46; early life of, 46–47; Gill on physical attractiveness of, 48; Glover marriage to, 48; Great Discovery of, 42, 51–52; health and illness attitude and practice, 47; health portrait of, 49–52; illness portrait of, 46–49; nature of God teachings, 40, 42; Patterson marriage to, 49; physical environment defining of, 54; prosperity portrait of, 54–58; as Quimby patient, 49, *50*, 51; socioeconomic status and appearance change, 42, 44; Weygandt memoir on clothing of, 55–56
EEOC. *See* Equal Employment Opportunity Commission
EEOC v. Abercrombie & Fitch (2015), 323
Elliot, Dyan, 69
Enninger, Werner, 16
Entwistle, Joanne, 192
Equal Employment Opportunity Commission (EEOC), Cloutier and, 329–33, 338n30
Equal Rights Amendment (ERA), LDS opposition to, 162n16
Esther: Bernard on biblical modesty example of, 104; Davis comparison to, 106–7; Harvey on biblical modesty with power example, 104–5; White-Cain and, 88, 99
Eucharist: Catholic understanding of, 68–70; Feast of Corpus Christi, 75; Protestant understanding of, 68–69. *See also* International Eucharistic Congress

fabrics: Amish, 216, 217, 242–43, *243*, 250n55; Black Israelite, 123, *130*,

134, 135; COGSOC, 126–27. *See also* garments; textiles
face mask, of COVID-19 pandemic, 1; bodily adornment link to opposition to, 2; religious identity link to opposition to, 2, 3
Faith and Opportunity Initiative (2019), of Trump, 99
Fall of America, The (E. Muhammad), 200
Fard Muhammad, W. D., 192–94
Farrakhan, Louis, 191, 192
fashion, 6–8; Afrocentric, 131–32, 200; of Amish women, 14, 227–46; Catholic vestments in film and, 11, 61–80; designers of, 76; film industry promotion of, 76–79; flapper culture of 1920s, 76–77, 93–94; interest in 1920s, 76–77; International Eucharistic Congress display of, 76–79; International Eucharistic Congress film, 72–75; R. Lewis on subcultural representation and, 7–8; *Muhammad Speaks* news journal on women, 196–99; Oneness Pentecostalism on holiness instead of, 102; *Photoplay Magazine* on, 78; of poor health and weakness, 47; shows in 1920s, 78; Tarlo on, 7–8; White on Satan's design of, 28, 32
Fashioning Jews, 5–6
Feldman, Stephen, 334
Fellini, Federico, 78
feminism: J. Butler on LDS women public, 143; in Mormonism, 12; NOI on Black women's beauty and, 202; North America Wicca and, 210, 213, 220; women-only covens and skyclad power, 215–16
Feri Witchcraft, 210
films: *Ben Hur*, 73; Catholic vestments in fashion and, 11, 61–80; *Don Juan*, 77; fashion and industry of, 76–79; *The Hunchback of Notre Dame*, 74; *La Bohème*, 77; *Life of Moses*, 72; medieval subjects in 1920s, 74, 75–76; *The Midnight Sun*, 77; *The Miracle* staged pantomime, 74; newspaper coverage of, 73; religious epic in 1920s, 72–73; *Robin Hood*, 74; *The Ten Commandments*, 72–73
First Amendment. *See* law, religious attire and
Five Acres nudist community, Gardner and, 212
Flake, Dallan F., 323
flapper culture of 1920s, 76–77, 93–94
Ford, Tanisha C., 129
Fosdick, Harry Emerson, 70, 93
Foursquare Church, McPherson founding of, 91–92
freedom, skyclad association with, 209
Freemasonry, 209; ritual discussion ban in, 252
Frueh, Rick, 325, 328

Gardner, Gerald, 207, 222n6; Bricket Wood Coven, 212; on clothing flow of magic blockage, 209; Five Acres nudist community and, 212; Hutton on, 211; naturist clubs interest of, 208, 221; on nudism and Wicca, 211–12; on skyclad power, 223n12; Wellbye and, 212

Gardnerian covens, 209, 212; ritual nudity in initiation ceremonies, 217, 218

garments: AHIJ divine, 133–34, *137*; Indian of Hare Krishna movement, 295–96, 302–3, *303*; LDS women wearing of, 14, *158*; Mormon temple, 153–54, 163n40; sacred, 14, 153–59, *158*, 251–72

garments, Latter-day Saint: agency and negotiation of, 253–54; of conforming men, 256–59, 270, 271; of conforming women, 261–65; covenants and ritual connection for, 251; description of, 252–53; design of, 255; Duffy on silence surrounding, 252; initiatory ceremony for receiving, 251; McDannell on, 252; of nonconforming men, 259–61, 271; of nonconforming women, 265–70; as sacred, 14, 251–72; J. Smith on, 251; study overview, 254–56

Gates of the Forest, The (Wiesel), 165–66

Gaudiya Vaishnavism, Hare Krishna movement and, 297, 298, 305

gender: J. Butler on clothing rituals, 151; J. Butler on gendered body, 145–46, 150, 153; daily clothing choice and, 145–46; ISKCON female sexuality and, 312–14, 317n14; LDS women's identity, 12, 145–46; NOI ideology, 190, 192, 193, 194; Oneness Pentecostalism dress, 102; status communicated through clothing, 146. *See also* men; women

Generation Z, religion and, 167, 173, 183, 184

ghost shirts, of Native Americans, 17

Gibson, Dawn-Marie, 191; on gender ideologies, 192, 194

Gilkes, Cheryl Townsend, 279; on African American Church therapeutic function, 283; on historical tactics for white uniforms, 280–81; on holiness visibility of white uniform, 284; on identity and culture of white uniforms, 282–83; on racialized, stereotype disruption from white uniforms, 286–87; on therapeutic functions of African American Church, 283; on white uniform role creation, 293n30

Gill, Gillian, 47; on Eddy confident self-presentation, 52; on Eddy physical attractiveness, 48, 59n20; on nineteenth century hysteria, 48; on suffering, 59n16

Glover, George, 48

God's Peculiar People (Lawless), 101

Goldman v. Weinberger (1986), 323–24, 336n9

Good Morning America, Davis interview on, 108–9

Gosling, Sam, 171

Graça, Marcelino Manuel da ("Daddy Grace"), 70

Gray, David F., 102, 103

Great Depression, Hassain on dress norm changes in, 197–98

Great Discovery, of Eddy, 42, 51–52

Gregory the Great *Pastoral Care*, 71

Griffith, Marie, 169

"Guidelines for Christian Dress" (Gray), 102
Guthrie, Arlo, 295–96

hair, 3; Amish women and, 232–33, 234, *235*, 248n29; Davis long uncut, *104*, 107, *107*; Gray on symbolic meaning of, 103; ISKCON *sikha* hairstyle, 295; Harvey on power of long uncut, 103–4; LDS women's hairstyles, 159; McPherson fashion of, 95; E. Muhammad on hairstyles, 201; NOI on prohibition of Afrocentric hairstyles, 200; Oneness Pentecostalism and, 101, 103–4, *104*, 107, *107*; Orthodox Jewish women, 3
Hare Krishnas. *See* International Society for Krishna Consciousness
Harlem Renaissance, 128–29
Harvey, Ruth Rieder, 103; on Esther biblical modesty with power example, 104–5
Hassain, Margary: on Black women's natural beauty, 199; on daily dress best clothes, 198–99; on Great Depression dress norm changes, 197–98
head coverings: of Amish women, 245–46, 249n36; Amish women adhesive spray use, 234, *235*; *Apostolic Faith* newspaper on, 90; law and religious, 321. *See also* veiling practices, among Muslim women
healing: Christian Science on human-divine relationship and, 41; power of suffering and, 47, 59n16

health reforms: of White, 34, 36n1; White health-driven dress, 28, 30, 34
Heavenly Bodies 2018 Metropolitan Museum of Art exhibition, 11, 76
Hinckley, Gordon B., 147, 152
holiness: Oneness Pentecostalism and, 102; Pentecostal women's power and, 11, 86; white uniform sanctification and, 283–84, 293n28
Holiness movement, Pentecostalism and, 87, 89, 95; McPherson original clothing, 91, 93; modesty codes in, 88; standards of, 100–101
Hunchback of Notre Dame, The (film), 74
hysteria, Gill on nineteenth century, 48, 59n17

Iacono, Ariana, 333–34
IBOR. *See* International Israelite Board of Rabbis
ICUPK. *See* Israeli Church of Universal Practical Knowledge
identity: Amish women public ethnic, 228; Amish young girls' social, 237–40, *240*; Apostolic, 105; Black Americans and, 117, 125, 140n16; Bucar on cultural, 6; clothing social message about, 46; COVID-19 face mask opposition and religious, 2, 3; MGT uniform and Black women, 13, 190; Mothers of Civilization NOI, 190–91; presentation tattoos, 175–78, *176*, *177*, 183; religious, 2, 3, 6, 170
identity adornment, 9, 11; of Black Israelites, 12, 117–33, *123*, *130*, 138–39; of LDS women's clothing,

12, 143–59, *156*, *158*; MGT uniform and, 13, 190–203; outwardly directed attire, 12; of religious tattoos, 12–13, 165–85

illness: Eddy and, 46–52; women's use for social interaction avoidance, 47–48

Indian garments, of ISKCON, 295–96, 302–3, *303*

initiation ceremonies: Alexandrian coven standards on, 217; Gardnerian coven standards on, 217, 218; ritual nudity in Wiccan, 217–20

interfaith coalitions, North American Wicca and, 214–15

International Eucharistic Congress: clergy public processions deterrence at, 61–62; Protestant 1908 resistance to, 62; scheduling of, 85n92

International Eucharistic Congress, Twenty-Eighth in Chicago 1926: Breen coverage of, 64; *Chicago Tribune* pamphlet on, 64; clergy procession in, 61, *65*; denominational difference and, 68–72; fashion, 76–79; Middle Ages interest and, 75–76; Moran on, 63; Mundelein and, 62–64; Passionist and Redemptorist religious orders in, *65*; publicity for, 64–68; Saint Mary of the Lake Seminary final procession, 66, *69*, 79; Stadium of Soldier's Field outdoor mass, *67*, 73–74; *Time* on Catholic liturgical wear, 66; traditional religion in changing times, 79–80

International Israelite Board of Rabbis (IBOR), 119, 137–38; Ashkenazi dress of, 128

International Society for Krishna Consciousness (ISKCON), 15, 317n14, 318n22; as activists, 314–16; Asian inspiration for, 299; Bhaktivedanta founding of, 297; chanting in, 305; countercultural religion and, 296–99; cultural activism of, 296; dress as political act, 303–4; early years of, 298–305; Gaudiya Vaishnavism and, 297, 298, 305; Ginsburg and Harrison in, 297; Indian garments of, 295–96, 302–3, *303*; Knott on, 314; Krishna god devotionalism emphasis, 197; Krishna god Vedic version, 209; member initiation, 300; men in *dhotis*, 302–3, 307, 308, *308*, 315; proselytizing in, 297; publications on, 296; Rochford on, 299–300; Seeger and Guthrie on, 295–96; *sikha* hairstyle, 295; stages of life and, 298–99; *tilaka* marks, 300–302, *301*; women in *saris*, 299, 302, *303*, 307, 315; women's status in, 312–14

internet, North American Wicca growth and, 214, 217

ISKCON. *See* International Society for Krishna Consciousness

Islam: Bucar on dress of, 311; Bucar on veiling in, 298; NOI dress practices and East, 198; religious dress traditions, 4. *See also* Muslim fashion; Nation of Islam

Israeli Church of Universal Practical Knowledge (ICUPK), 135–36; Bivens as founder of, 134; members of, *135*

jewelry, 3; *chai*, 122; Church of Body Modification, 324, 329–34; Cunningham on Wiccan ritual, 216, 223n15; law and religious, 321
Jewish culture, Ashkenazi norms in, 122
Jolie, Angelina, 169
Joselit, Jenna Weissman, 46
Judaism, 5–6. *See also* Black Israelites

kaffiyehs, Black Americans and Muslim identity, 124, 140n16
Karim, Jamillah, 192, 194
Karriem, Anna, 197, 200
Kellogg, John Harvey: Battle Creek Sanitarium of, 34, 39n44, 39n47
kente cloth, 122, *123*
Khabeer, Su'ad Abdul, 6, 124
Kimball, Spencer W., 148–50, 152, 153, 157
Knott, Kim, 312–14, 316
Kraybill, Donald B., 228
Krishna (god): Bhaktivedanta consciousness of culture of, 302; Hare Krishna movement devotionalism of, 297; ISKCON Vedic vision of, 298. *See also* International Society for Krishna Consciousness
Kuhlman, Kathryn, 96, 97

Latter-day Saint (LDS) men, 147–49, 152–53; garment wearing, 254–61, 270–71; missionary attire, 156–57

Latter-day Saint (LDS) women: Buehner on missionary clothing, 154–57; J. Butler on public femininity of, 143; Callister on modesty of, 153; clothing as resistance, 149–51; *Clothing Guidelines for Lady Missionaries*, 155, *156*; clothing standards, 144; "Dress and Grooming Guidelines for Sister Missionaries," 144, 157; garment wearing of, 14, *158*, 261–70; gender identity and, 12, 145–46; hairstyles for, 159; Kimball on modesty of, 148–50, 152, 153, 157; meaning of becoming, 159–60; Monson on modesty of, 144, 152–53; ritual of modesty, 151–53; sacred uniform of, 153–59, *158*; self-segregation of, 150
law, religious attire and, 321, 325, 335nn1–2; Civil Rights Act religion federal protection, 323; *EEOC v. Abercrombie & Fitch*, 323; Flake on religious dress and, 323; *Goldman v. Weinberger*, 323–24, 336n9; inconsistency in, 322; in prisons, 324; Protestantization of, 334; school settings, 322, 336n4; U.S. military and, 323–24, 336n9; workplace setting, 322–23, 336n5
Lawless, Elaine, 101–2
LDS. *See* Latter-day Saint
Levi Israel, Cohen, 132–33
Lewis, Reina, 7–8
Lewis, Van Dyk, 131–32
LGBTQ political culture, North America Wicca and, 210, 220
Life of Moses (film), 72
Lost Tribe of Shabazz, 193

Luhrmann, Tanya, 209
Lum, Clara, 89

Magickal Childe, 213
Masonic influence, on Black Israelites, 126–28
Massachusetts Metaphysical College seminary, 40
Mathuresa Dasa, 313
Mauss, Armand, 147–48
McDannell, Colleen, 44, 252
McPherson, Aimee Semple, 70, 82n33, 91–97
men: in Hare Krishna *dhotis*, 302–3, 307, 308, *308*, 315; Muslim fashion trends, 6; NOI leaders, 191; Oneness Pentecostalism and, 101, 102. *See also* conforming men; nonconforming men
Merry Circle tradition, of Bado, 219, 225n19
Meyer, Joyce, 96
MGT. *See* Muslim Girls Training
MGT-GCC. *See* Muslim Girls Training and General Civilization Class
Middle Ages: Catholic vestments and affluence of, 70–71; Chicago landmark reflection of, 75; Feast of Corpus Christi and, 75; *Heavenly Bodies* Met exhibition of 2018 and, 11, 76; International Eucharistic Congress 1926 and interest in, 75–76
Midnight Sun, The (film), 77
military, U.S., religious attire and law, 323–24, 336n9
millennials: religion and, 172–73; religious tattoos and, 173, 175, 180, 184; C. Smith and Snell on, 172

Miller, Elizabeth "Libby" Smith, 29, 30
Miller, William, 25
Millerism, 25
Minoan Wicca, 210, 213, 214
Miracle, The (staged pantomime), 74
modesty: *Apostolic Faith* newspaper on, 90; Catholic nun habit as symbol of, 45; in dress, 3, 32, 90; Esther biblical example of, 104–5; Holiness movement codes of, 88; of LDS women's dress, 144, 148–50, 152–53, 157; in MGT uniform, 191; Mormon garments conforming women on teachings on, 262; Mormon garments nonconforming women criticism of culture of, 265–66; Oneness Pentecostalism codes of, 87–88; Price on Pentecostalism code of, 95–96; UPCI standards for, 101; White on dress frugality and, 32
Monson, Thomas, 144, 152–53
Moran, Kate, 63
Morgan, David, 4, 5
Mormonism. *See* Church of Jesus Christ of Latter-day Saints
Mothers of Civilization, NOI identity of, 190–91
Moving Picture Magazine, 78
Muhammad, Clara, 194–95
Muhammad, Elijah, 191, 192; Black aesthetics redefined by, 199–202; *The Fall of America* by, 200; on hairstyles, 201; on MGT small businesses, 196; "Warning to M.G.T. and G.C. Class" speech, 199–200; white supremacy challenge by, 194
Muhammad, Ibtihaj, 202
Muhammad Sharrieff, Ethel, 195

Muhammad Speaks news journal: Gibson on women's use of, 191–92; "The Queen of the Earth" poem in, 190; "The Woman in Islam" editorials in, 190, 191, 197; women's fashion in, 196–99; writers in, 197
Mundelein, George (cardinal), 62–64
Muslim fashion, 6, 7, 124–25, 202–3, 298
Muslim Girls Training and General Civilization Class (MGT-GCC), 195
Muslim Girls Training (MGT) uniform, 203; Black aesthetics redefined by, 199–202; Black women's identity and, 13, 190; color coding of, 195; Curtis on self-making, 192; Gibson and Karim on gender ideologies and, 192, 194; modesty in, 191; C. Muhammad creation of, 194–95; purposes of, 191; small business for, 196; standardization of, 195; U. Taylor on Black women in NOI, 192; Temple No. 2 Clothing Factory and Clothing Factory Store, 195–96; white supremacy and, 13, 190

Nagaraja Dasa, 311
Nation of Islam (NOI): Afrocentric clothing or hairstyles prohibition, 200–201; all people of color connection, 201; beginnings of, 192–93; on Black women's beauty and femininity, 202; Black women's protection by, 199; on Black women stereotypes, 193–94; fashion legacy, 202–3; gender ideology in, 190, 192, 193, 194; Islamic East dress practices and, 198; male leaders of, 191; Mothers of Civilization identity, 190–91; U. Taylor on Black women joining of, 192; on white supremacy, 201–2; women as pioneer members of, 193. *See also* Muslim Girls Training
Native Americans, ghost shirts of, 17
naturism, 210, 222n10
naturist clubs, Gardner interest in, 208, 221
Neal, Lynn, 6; on Western adornment, 306
Nectar of Devotion, The (Bhaktivedanta), 301
negotiated adornment, 9; Amish women's fashion, 14, 227–46, *233*, *235*, *240*, *243*, 248n29, 249n36, 249nn42–43, 250n55; Mormon women's sacred garments, 14, 251–72; Wicca skyclad or ritual nudity, 13–14, 207–21, 222n10, 223n12, 223n15, 224n17, 226n38
Neo-Paganism. *See* North American Wicca
New Jew Cool, Silverman on, 5
New Negro movement, 128–29
nineteenth-century dress: Comstock on physical effect of, 27–28; corseting and heavy bell-shaped skirts, 25–26; physical harm of, 27; Walker emancipation suits, 27
NOI. *See* Nation of Islam
nonconforming men, Mormon garments of: conflicted feelings about, 261; on LDS church control, 261, 271; on Mormon garment covenant, 260; on Mormon restrictions, 259–60; sexuality and body shame, 260

nonconforming women, Mormon garments of, 270; on broken promises and, 267–68; on LDS church control, 271; on modesty culture criticism, 265–66; on physical problems and discomfort, 268–69; on shame of not wearing, 267; on symbol of doubt, 267
non-Wiccan Paganism, skyclad and naturism in, 222n10
North American Wicca: Alexandrian covens, 209, 217; California communities of, 213; *The Charge of the Goddess* gospel of, 209; *The Craft* film and growth of, 226n38; Cunningham on ritual jewelry of, 216, 223n15; degree system of, 214, 224n17; feminism and LGBTQ political culture, 210, 220; feminist traditions, 213; Gardner, nudism and origins of, 211–12; Gardnerian covens, 209, 212, 217, 218; interfaith coalitions and, 214–15; internet and growth of, 214, 217; Minoan, 210, 213–14; Oboler and Kraemer on changes in, 210; popularization and commercialization of, 211; popularization in 1960s-2000s, 213–15; ritual robes popularization and standardization, 216–17. *See also* skyclad or ritual nudity
nuns, Catholic, 3, 45
nursing uniform, McPherson visual association of, 91, *92*, 93

Old Order Amish, 229; on Amish attire, 236, 249n41
O'Neil, Mary Lou, 303–4

Oneness Pentecostalism, 11; Bernard on Apostolic identity of, 105; of Davis, 88; Davis and natural order preservation, 106–9; fashion abandoned for holiness, 102; gender-specific dress, 101–3; Holiness codes and, 109; Lawless on, 101–2; long uncut hair and, 101, 103–4, *104*, 107, *107*; modesty codes of, 87–88; public platforms of, 105–6; J. Urshan on gender-distinct dress in, 102; women's appearance standards, 100–106
Order of the Golden Dawn, 209
Ordnung guidelines, 230–31, 234
Ordo Templi Orientis, of Crowley, 209

Pagan Consent Culture (Kraemer and Aburrow), 210
Paganism. *See* North American Wicca
Pagan Polytheism, 22n10, 210
Pastoral Care, of Gregory the Great, 71
Pentecostalism: Azusa Street Revival of 1906 and, 87; celebrity culture and, 93; on clothing and inner sanctification, 89; early theology about accoutrements, 88–90; early twentieth-century influences on, 87; Holiness movement and, 87, 88–89, 95, 100–101; on modesty in dress, 90; Price on modesty code of, 95–96; prohibitions, 101; theological controversies within, 87. *See also* Oneness Pentecostalism; Trinitarian Pentecostalism

Pentecostal women: adornment and public life of, 86–110; bridal fashion choices, 95–96; Davis and, 11, 86; gender-specific dress, 101–3; holiness and power of, 11, 86; Sánchez-Walsh on dress of, 97; White-Cain and, 11, 86, 88, 97, *98*, 99–100, 109. *See also* McPherson, Aimee Semple

Piela, Anna, 6

Pinn, Anthony B., 280–81, 283, 290n1

Pius XI (pope), on Catholic vestment splendor, 71

popularization, of North American Wicca, 211, 213–17

power: African American Church white uniforms as image of, 282; on Esther biblical modesty with, 104–5; feminist women-only covens and skyclad, 215–16; Gardner on skyclad, 223n12; Harvey on long uncut hair and, 103–4; Pentecostal women holiness and, 11, 86; religious dress as expression of, 7; of suffering and healing, 47, 59n16; White-Cain message on prosperity and, 88, 96–100

Power Before the Throne (Harvey), 103

Practical Holiness (Bernard), 103–5

Price, Charles, 95–96

priests, Catholic, 45, 70

prisons, religious attire and law in, 324

prophecy: W. Miller Second Coming, 25; theological adornment through, 10; White prophetic visions, 25, 30–32, 33, 34

Protestantization, Bender and Snow on, 334

"Queen of the Earth, The" (Linda X), 190

Quimby, Phineas, 49, *50*, 51

Rabbinic Judaism, 5; Black Israelite schism in Black Power era, 119, 131; *tzitzit* tassels on prayer shawl of, 118

Rau, Kaumudi, 311–12

ready-made clothing revolution, Joselit on, 46

Reclaiming Witchcraft, 210

reforms: dress, 23, 26–36; health, 28, 30, 34, 36n1; Seventh-day Adventists and, 25

religious attire, law and. *See* law, religious attire and

religious tattoos. *See* tattoos, religious

Restored Church of Jesus Christ. *See* Church of Jesus Christ of Latter-day Saints

Retrospection and Introspection (Eddy), 51

Revelation (Book of), white attire and, 287–89

revivalists: early Pentecostal, 88; and McPherson, 91; Second-day Adventist foundation of, 24–25; on social and religious change, 24; White-Cain, 97

revival meetings, 36n2; of Seventh-day Adventists, 25

rite of ordination, Catholic vestments and, 69

ritual nudity. *See* skyclad or ritual nudity
rituals: adoration and adornment in, 170; Black Israelite conflicts with cultural nationalism and, 12; body modification and, 326–27; J. Butler on clothing, 151; Catholic Eucharist as sacrifice, 69–70; of LDS women's modesty, 151–53
robes: North American Wicca ritual, 216–17; orange, 3
Rochford, E. Burke, 299–300, 312
Roma (film), 78
Rumspringa period, in Amish church, 236, 237, 238, 249n44

sacred spaces, 166
sacred symbol, Black Israelites on Blackness as, 12, 121, 139
sacred texts, theological adornment through, 10
Saint Mary of the Lake Seminary, 66, 69, 79
Salomensen, Jone, 219
Salter, Roberta, 91
"Salute to Black Women, A" (Karriem), 200
salvation: Seventh-day Adventists on body as vehicle of, 26; Seventh-day Adventist women's attire and, 23
same sex marriage, Davis license refusal for, 86, 106–8
Sánchez-Walsh, Arlene, 97
sanctification: of body, 5; white uniform holiness and, 283–84, 293n28

Sanctified Church, 284–85, 291n4, 292n25
Sanders, Cheryl J., 285–86
saris, in Hare Krishna movement, 299, 302, *303*, 307, 315
schools, religious attire and law in, 322, 336n4
Science and Health with Key to the Scriptures (Eddy), 40, 44, 52
scriptural adornment, White on, 32–33, 35–36
Second Coming: church as bride and, 94; W. Miller prophecy of, 25; White on, 25, 33
Second Great Awakening, 24
Second Vatican Council, on Catholic vestments, 71
Seeger, Pete, 295–96
Seventh-day Adventist foundations: on body as salvation vehicle, 26; physical faith manifestations, 25; reform and revival meetings of, 25; revivalists, 24–25; social forms alignment of, 26; White on Israelites and, 35; White prophetic visions, 25, 30–32, 33, 34
Seventh-day Adventist women's attire, 24–25; dress modification for physical health, 10; dress reform implications, 35–36; *Dress Reform* pamphlet on, *31*; dress reform views, 28–34; nineteenth-century dress and reform, 26–28; salvation and, 23; scriptural adornment, 32–33, 35–36; White and, 10, 30–36; White health-driven dress reforms, 28, 30, 34
sikha hair style, 295–96

Silverman, Eric, 5
skyclad or ritual nudity, 222n10, 223n15, 224n17, 226n38; consent culture, 210, 220; for degree initiations only, 209; departing from, 218; freedom associated with, 209; Gardner, nudism and Wicca origins, 211–12; of Gardner, 208; Gardner on power of, 223n12; Luhrmann on, 209; of North American Wicca, 13–14, 207–21; religious negotiation of, 211; Salomensen on, 219; Starhawk on women and, 215–16; in Wicca initiation ceremonies, 217–20
Smith, Christian, 172, 173, 182, 184
Smith, Joseph, 36n6, 251
Snell, Patricia, 172, 173, 182, 184
social control, Black body and, 120–22
sociological imagination, 183
Starhawk, 213, 215–16
"States and Attributes of the Creation" (Adhikari), 307
Stevenson, Bryan P., 106
subcultural representation, R. Lewis on fashion and, 7–8
Supreme Court cases: *EEOC v. Abercrombie & Fitch*, 323; *Goldman v. Weinberger*, 323–24, 336n9

tallit prayer shawl, 118; Black Israelite production of, 122
Tarlo, Emma, 7–8
tattoos: of celebrities, 168, 169; Gosling on body orientation of, 171; Griffith on, 169; history of, 167–68; of Micronesian women, 167; of Polynesian and South Pacific cultures, 167, 186n10; religious bias against, 168–69; removal of, 169; U.S. military and crime, 167–68, 186n11
tattoos, religious, 165, 185; biblical reference to, 168–69; of Church of Body Modification, 16, 329; cosmic stories through, 166; covert meanings of, 12–13; Jensen, Flory, and D. Miller on, 169–70; Kang and Jones on, 166; law and, 321; millennials and, 172–73; research on college campus, 173–82; Sanders and Vail on adornment of, 170; C. Smith and Snell on traditionalists, 173, 182, 184; transition as motivation for, 171. *See also* Campus Tattoos Project
Taylor, Ula, 192
Temple No. 2 Clothing Factory, MGT and, 195–96
Ten Commandments, The (film), of DeMille, 72–73
textiles: AHIJ national and ethnic significance of, 133–34; Bohn on communication system of, 16, 143, 154. *See also* fabrics
theological adornment, 9; Catholic vestments, 11, 61–80, 82n38; Christian Science religious dress, 10–11, 36n6, 40–58; Oneness Pentecostalism, 11, 87–88, 100–107, *104*, *107*; through prophecy or visions, 10; Seventh-day Adventist women's attire, 10, 23–36, *31*; shifting cultural norms and, 10; Trinitarian Pentecostalism, 11, 87–89, 91–100

tilaka marks, 300–302, *301*
Time magazine: on Catholic liturgical wear, 66
traditionalists, C. Smith and Snell on, 173, 182, 184
Trinitarian Pentecostalism, 11; Assemblies of God, 89; fashion trends adoption by, 87, 88; McPherson glamour, 91–96; White-Cain power with prosperity, 88, 96–100; women's current fashion trends, 96–97
Trump, Donald: Faith and Opportunity Initiative in 2019, 99; White-Cain as pastor to, 86, 99–100
tzitzit ritual tassels: biblical reference to, 118; on dashiki, 118, 129–30, *130*, 138; Levy on Black Israelite, 119–20; Rabbinic Judaism prayer shawl and, 118

Under God's Authority (Davis), 109
uniforms: Amish plain dress, 228; Eddy on clothing as, 44–46; LDS women's sacred, 153–59, *158*; McPherson nursing, 91, *92*, 93; as religious dress, 3. *See also* Muslim Girls Training uniform; white uniforms, of African American Church
United Pentecostal Church International (UPCI): on gender-distinct dress lines, 102; modesty standards of, 101
Upson-Saia, Kristi, 5
Urmila Devi-Dasa, 315–16
Urshan, A.D., 103

Urshan, Jean, 102
Urshan, Nathaniel, 102, 106
ushers, African American Church white uniforms of, 278–79

Valiente, Doreen, 207, 209
Vanity Fair magazine, male and female fashion trends of 1920s and, 77
veiling practices, among Muslim women, 6, 191, 298
visions: ISKCON Vedic Krishna god, 298; theological adornment through, 10; White prophetic, 25, 30–32, 33, 34
Visnu-jana, 313

Walker, Mary, 27
weddings, Amish women's fashion and, 237–38, 249nn42–43
Wellbye, Reginald, 212
Western adornment: Bhaktivedanta criticism of, 304; Hare Krishna movement replacement of, 314–15; Neal on, 306
Weygandt, Minnie Bell, 55–56
White, Ellen Gould Harmon, 10; Battle Creek Sanitarium of, 34, 39n44, 39n47; dress reforms of, 23, 30; on frugality and modesty in dress, 32; on health-driven dress reforms, 28, 30, 34; on health reforms, 34, 36n1; prophetic visions of, 25, 30–32, 33, 34; on Satan's design of fashion, 28, 32; on scriptural adornment, 32–33, 35–36; on Second Coming, 25, 33

White-Cain, Paula, 11, *98*; bridal fashion choice of, 97; Esther and, 88, 99; as pastor to Trump, 86, 99–100; as political figure, 109; power with prosperity message, 96–100; Trinitarian Pentecostalism of, 88, 96–100

white supremacy: MGT uniform and, 13, 190; E. Muhammad challenge to, 194; NOI on, 201–2

white uniforms, of African American Church, 271–78; aesthetic action of, 282–87, 293n28; aesthetic language of, 280–82; belief in agency and tradition of, 278; Book of Revelation and, 287–89; Gilkes on practice of, 279–84, 286, 293n30; for leadership roles, 279; as political theology, 15, 287–90; ritual of theological statement, 278; on special occasions, 279; usher wearing of, 278–79; visual aesthetic of, 278; for Women's Day, 285–86

Wicca. *See* North American Wicca

Wiesel, Elie, 165–66

Wife Swap reality show, 105

Wilkinson, Ernest, 149–50, 162n22

Witchcraft Today (Gardner), 208, 212, 222n6

women: domestic religion of, 29; illness use for social interactions avoidance, 47–48; *Muhammad Speaks* used by, 191–92; as NOI pioneer members, 193; religious mainstay in 1870s, 29, 38n27; *saris*, 299, 302, *303*, 307, 315; white uniforms for denominational roles of, 279. *See also* conforming women; nonconforming women; *specific women's groups*

women-only covens, 225n35; skyclad or ritual nudity power, 215–16

Women's Day: African American Church all-white dress on, 279, 285–86; religious sisters and Catholic lay women at, 66, *67*

workplace setting, religious attire and law in, 322–23, 336n5

Wynia, Elly M., 126–27

X, Linda, 190

Zorine (Queen), 94

GPSR Authorized Representative: Easy Access System Europe, Mustamäe tee 50, 10621 Tallinn, Estonia, gpsr.requests@easproject.com